Mermaid in The Kitchen

Hope you enjoy the book :)

[signature]

Also by Sarah Delamere Hurding

StarScope

StarScope with Psychic to the Stars Sarah Delamere Hurding

Sarah correctly predicted the final line up of the pop band Six. Bono called her in when he was setting up his Kitchen nightclub at The Clarence, and according to Louis Walsh, she's "the woman who knows everything." Now Ireland's top psychic has decided to share her gift in probably the only horoscope guide you will ever need to buy. For the inside track on where your love, life, career and health are heading, keep this by your bedside. Which celebrity shares your birthday? What lies ahead for you this year? Are you in the right relationship or are you and your partner completely incompatible? Are you in the right career? Where should you go on holiday?

Get your life in balance with Sarah and *StarScope*
Published by *Poolbeg Ireland*.

Mermaid in The Kitchen

Chasing Rainbows
by
Sarah Delamere Hurding

Published by
Rainbow Wisdom
Ireland

Copyright © 2017 Sarah Delamere Hurding

All rights reserved.
No part of this publication may be reproduced, stored in a retrieval system, or transmitted, in any form or by any means, electronic, mechanical, photocopying, recording or otherwise without the prior permission of *Rainbow Wisdom*

This book is sold subject to the condition that it shall not, by way of trade or otherwise, be lent, re-sold, hired out, or otherwise circulated without the publisher's prior consent in any form of binding or cover other than that in which it is published and without a similar condition including this condition being imposed on the subsequent purchaser. Every attempt has been made to contact relevant copyright holders.

Names have been modified in the book to protect the identities of certain individuals. Others are included with full permission. While others are too strongly recognized by universal consciousness to be concealed.

ISBN: 978-0-692-98449-9

Cover artwork: *Mermaid Spirit* by Stefan Keller (pixabay/kellepics)

Mermaid in The Temple Bar

By Bono of U2 for ICROSS Charity, Oct 2002

To all those I have encountered along the way.
You are my Blessing and my Karma.
May God bless you all. X

CONTENTS

1	Chasing Rainbows...............................	25
2	Rite Of Passage....................................	41
3	Wolf In Sheep's Clothing.....................	57
4	Nine O' Clock Service.........................	84
5	Makes No Never Mind.........................	92
6	Leaving The City Of Ghosts................	107
7	Dublin Nights.......................................	124
8	The Reluctant Psychic.........................	133
9	Very A-Muse-ing.................................	146
10	Stuck In A Moment..............................	159
11	All That Jazz..	176
12	Superman..	185
13	Waiting For The Best...........................	201
14	Girl With Crimson Nails......................	215
15	Mermaid In The Kitchen......................	223
16	The Waiting Room...............................	231
17	Soul Mate Dilemma.............................	244
18	Mermaid Magic....................................	254
19	Seeing Stars...	268
20	The Circus..	276

CONTENTS

21	You're A Star.................................	287
22	Synchronicity..............................	296
23	Cracking The Code........................	304
24	Cold Cases...................................	312
25	The Twain Shall Meet....................	320
26	Mystical Madness.........................	326
27	Faustian Deal: No Deal..................	343
28	Taking A Chance...........................	359
29	Exmoor Knights............................	382
30	Dalkey Daze.................................	412
31	It's A Dog's Life............................	431
32	All That I left Behind.....................	441
33	Groundhog Day.............................	452
34	Coincidentally Yours.....................	458
35	Inner-Tuition...............................	465
36	The Law Of Neutrality...................	472
37	The X-Factor................................	481
38	It's A Gift.....................................	489
39	Nuts and Bolts..............................	509
40	Am I A Witch?...............................	521

The Mermaid's Song

I've watched you from a distance
for I live beneath the sea
calling from the rocky seashore
beckoning you to me.

The ocean, she has dressed me
in her finest pearls so fare
with golden treasure form sunken ships
and starfish in my hair.

Content until I saw you
for you, I'd give my all
there's nothing more lonely
than the Mermaid's song
when evening comes to call.

A thousand years I've waited
my tears have filled the sea
and a thousand more I'll call to you
beckoning you to me.

Sometimes, we only have to watch and listen to be inspired by those around us. Thanks for always speaking of Mermaids Sarah De La Mer.

Dianna Varga, author and poet.

TO BE OR NOT TO BE

PREFACE
A Melancholy Tale

It was nine years ago to the day that The Mermaid had walked out of the sea onto the sparkling sands of the bay. Welcomed by the fey spirits of the land; she was full of anticipation and expectant. Her new life beckoned. Leaving her fins and tail behind her on the beach, she was in search of a truth she knew was out there somewhere. Though why she had to come onto dry land to find it, was at this moment beyond her.

Mermaid left behind a wealth of love and riches beneath the ocean. But she had people to meet and places to go. Besides she knew that her Soul Mate was living in this land of warlocks, wizards and witches. This was the right time to hook up with him and come to some agreement. They had fallen out in their previous existence, and there was still unfinished business between them.

Dripping with seaweed, scaly from her years in the deep, Mermaid chose a private moment whilst she morphed into the proverbial archetypal goddess with long, flowing golden hair, cleavage, and legs. Legs were a strange phenomenon for this Mermaid. To date she had had no use for them, and certainly did not know how to use them. She could not get used to the different view when she looked downwards, and chuckled with glee at the prospect of where these legs might lead her.

Smiling to herself as she flowed towards a fresh new chapter in her life, she felt okay with her new image and identity. She had a date with destiny, and she knew it. Ready for the worst the Dublin scene would throw at her, Mermaid embarked on her journey with enthusiasm. She had a preordained pathway, and a sacred contract to fulfill, that much she knew. But she had mixed feelings as to how to go about it.

Mermaid dried herself off, the sea had been cold, and unforgiving, and her journey to the Fair Isle had not been easy. Choppy waters and gales in the heavens made her fear what was to come. But there was also a sense of excitement, and the ever present possibility of a bit of magic. Discarding her fins, scales, and life lines, she retained her waist, curves and a certain Mermaidish, *je ne sais quoi*.

Mermaid smiled to herself as she anticipated the adventures to come. But she was nervous too; for she knew that ultimately her date with destiny had a difficult price to bear. Mermaid knew that as the drama reached its conclusion, she was going to have to sacrifice her heart's desire on the rocks of the bay below. The irony was, it was the only reason she was here in the first place. She had to engage in the fray, and go through the motions. Sometimes fate required this. The bitter sweet ending, did not fill her with overwhelming joy. The first bits would be fun though.

Mermaid relished a challenge, and the prospect of what was to come filled her with a certain awe and anticipation. Magic was her friend, but in the land of the human, she knew she had to calm it somewhat. There had to be a level playing field for the correct outcomes, so that the karmic checks and balances, could be fulfilled.

The Mermaid loved magic. She did not need to practice it, for it came naturally to her.

Focus counts for a lot, she smiled to herself.

This is next bit will be interesting, she mused.

Mermaid had prepared herself for this Irish jaunt ever since the age of seventeen. She always had an inner knowing that her path led through the Celtic countries. Thus far, she had never been proven wrong.

There is always a first time, she pondered; and this made her nervous.

What if she had got it wrong? The messages that had revolved around her head since a tender age had never been wrong. She was anxious for the time when the magic faded. Perhaps that time would never come. But in the fantastical, mystical world, you had to be prepared for all eventualities.

Mermaid's arrival in Dublin heralded a new and significant chapter. She braced herself. Her saga to date had not been easy, that was for sure. Perhaps she was due a sea change, for it sometimes felt as if she had been dealt the short straw in her human related experiences. She had come ashore several times before, and each time was more arduous than the last. But this Mermaid was one of life's survivors, and had so far been a feisty match for most of what had been thrown at her. Even though she had frequently sought to escape and walk back into the sea, she always remained until the current contract was fulfilled

The soothing depths of the deep waters were her homeland. She often felt like a fish out of water traipsing the cobbles and pathways of ancient gothic cities. She found it difficult to breathe at times, especially when the pollution stuck in her chest. Her sensitive aqueous lungs felt like giving up in the smoke filled clubs and music halls, that had shaped a large chunk of her life. Mermaid enjoyed the buzz of the nightlife, but she often felt like Cinderella, who had to run home before midnight. So far, Prince Charming was nowhere in sight, and she had learned to make do.

Still, perhaps he lived in Dublin, or thereabouts.

Mm, who was she kidding? She already knew he did. The other encounters had only been rehearsals for what was to come now. This was the real deal, and she had to get it right, or else flounder defeated. Why?

Why was a question Mermaid had asked herself rather a lot lately, as her hopes, dreams and visions tumbled messily around her. Mermaid was in the process of realizing that she had fallen foul of some illusion. She realized that someone, or something, out there in the ethers had cast a spell. She had been seduced on several fronts, and now needed to take emergency action. Drastic measures were necessary to unravel, and sort out her situation. Always a past master at weaving her own magic, she had some important work to do.

Besides this horrific realization, which filled her with dread and fear, Mermaid also remembered that it was a case of, so far so good. Mermaid had always landed on her fishy feet. On dry land, things had a habit of coming right for her, however awful they seemed at the time. Mermaid tried to reassure herself in the midst of her blind panic. She was determined that nothing and nobody was going to succeed in alienating her from her chosen destiny.

She could certainly modify her plans. But she had to work out a "Plan B" to break free of the *Sliding Doors* syndrome, that had started to haunt her existence. Mermaid realized that she had a mission to fulfill that sometimes inspired jealousy. She found this extremely burdensome. For she could not understand why people did not always warm to her, or like her. She was possibly more human than she cared to admit. But Mermaid had learned to live with a path that had become increasingly irksome and troublesome. Often choosing a reclusive existence rather, than deal with the many issues she was sensitized to.

At times Mermaid found it very difficult to be in the company of the human psyche. She found it loaded and weighty, to the extent that she needed the sea to restore her light vibration.

Sometimes Mermaid could not cope with much at all. Other times though, her productivity and resilience shone like a beacon. She realized that lately, there had been few positive moments, and she was finding it increasingly difficult to recharge her batteries. She needed to take action.

Quick!

Mermaid frequently sat on the beach reflecting whether or not to walk back into her magical homeland beneath the waves. She was tempted on more than one occasion. Indeed, she had been tempted, tried, and tested beyond her endurance, she almost felt. She was at a loss. Many things had gone pear shaped in her life of late. Could she retrieve the situation? Should she even try? Now that was the question, and there was the rub.

How had it all come to this? She mused, as her four-legged companion, and friend Harley played amongst the dunes. Harley was mad, unlike his po-faced, seriously deep owner.

That Scorpio Moon has a lot to answer for, thought Harley, as he went about his doggish business on the beach. Harley was a wired to the moon Arian creature, darkly handsome with wickedly beady eyes. He answered to various names, "Pretty" being the most obvious. "Davor Sucker" being the most suitably obscure. Well, he *did* like football.

Permanently affectionate, and always licking things, Harley was a tonic, lovely to come home to, and amusing to look at.

A bit like my ideal man, thought Mermaid.

Sad, thought Harley.

Why doesn't she realize I'm just a fun loving dog?

Precisely Harley, responded Mermaid telepathically.

~ 14 ~

Mermaid's telepathic connection with her dog was a given. He would let her know when he needed water, and how much, and he hated being left alone. When Mermaid was out and about, he would tune in and let her know when he was cold. But he did love sleeping, so he did not usually mind too much.

Harley bore the marks of angel wings on his chest, so he thought he was pretty special. Mermaid agreed: he was. Besides his Grandpa was a supreme champion living in Japan, so he had good credentials for breeding. Harley was assured of both love and beauty. But he always felt a little bit uncomfortable; for he knew that Mermaid carried a sorrow in her heart regarding Freddie, his predecessor.

Freddie had left a gaping wound in Mermaid's heart that came at an emotive time, when things could not have got much worse. Until now. Mermaid remembered this, and contemplated whether that was indeed the most difficult time of her life. At this point she was not so sure. Freddie was at peace, resting in a secret location on the mystical hill above. Of course it broke her heart when she buried him. But the place he had in her heart and mind, was confirmed. When she dug down and found a Freddie-shaped nesting place, amongst the stubborn rock formations, she could not believe it.

This is too much of a coincidence, she thought.

Truly heart breaking, but obviously meant to be.

Mermaid had borrowed the spade of the Great Wizard, who had come to play such an important role in her heart and mind.

Destiny moments both, she mused as she remembered.

And maybe I could have done without them both too, she said out loud somewhat fatalistically..Mermaid could be quite the drama queen when she wanted to be.

Freddie Freagle had met with a nasty accident by Druid's Chair. He survived for a time thanks to a shepherd, vet and vicar, and the Mermaid's healing ability. The rotund vet said she did not think that Freddie would be able to move ever again. But the Mermaid and her dog had other ideas. They were not going to give up without a fight, and this healthy dose of optimism, amidst adverse circumstances, worked for some time.

On the third day, Freddie started moving his front legs, and embarked on the long road to some kind of recovery. But this was a cruel situation; an emotional roller coaster ride, which swung one way, one minute, and the other, the next. It took Mermaid quite a while to get her head around all this.

Things like this aren't meant to happen, she thought, as she reeled amidst the pain of unnatural suffering. Mermaid still had a lot to learn about the human condition. She knew was here to observe, assimilate and understand, and this, she surely did. She knew too, that she had signed up for this in all its complexity and glory. So she went about her fate, with as much grace as she could muster.

Mermaid needed more time with Freddie before his passing, and the next couple of months proved to be an enlightening stretch that revealed many secrets. She managed to do some miraculous healing against the odds. But Miracle Dog Freddie, knew that ultimately his time would come. He really had already overstayed his welcome, as part of his contract to his mistress. Enough was enough.

Mermaid came to realize that Freddie was a heavenly messenger, who had agreed to guide her onto the right path for the next stage of her human existence. Her evolution as a magical being was at stake, and she had to embrace the lessons, however difficult.

Faced with the option of giving her dog a set of wheels with which to gain mobility, Mermaid chose to preserve his dignity. She killed him. Undoing all her good work, she called the rotund vet to put Freddie out of his misery. For the skies had spoken.

One day, whilst meditating on what to do for the best, Freddie shaped clouds appeared in the heavens. The first travelled across the view from her window, as if on a movie screen. This was a fluffy clear picture of her sick dog lying down asleep. The second frame was a shot of him running freely across the heavens.

Well, I'm, still no clearer, thought Mermaid as she waited patiently. Eventually, after what seemed an eternity, the clear blue sky sent her a final heavenly vision. There before her, in clear cloud formation, was the distinctive shape of her beloved dog, leaping jubilantly *towards* the heavens. The Freddie cloud dog was jumping up into the heavens and away from terra firma.

Oh, great, thought Mermaid. But at least she had her answer.

The wise old soul, that was Freddie, did not deserve any more indignity imposed upon him. Freddie departed this earth, aided and abetted by The Mermaid; and he took a big part of her soul with him.

Harley knew it was his job to cheer The Mermaid up, but at times he found it an uphill task.

She can get awfully maudlin, he observed. But he certainly did his best. Mermaid found his company reassuring and comforting. Besides, she did not really care what people thought. Her dogs were not a substitute for some finer feeling. They were at this point the finer feeling. Mermaid knew only too well that the, "something else," that occupied her heart was another matter; nothing to do with her four-legged friends. She knew the difference between human passion and dog licks. She was not stupid. But to be honest, she sometimes found the later more straightforward.

At least dog love was uncomplicated and unconditional.

Mermaid was quite good at lying to herself too. Of course the "something else," was a completely different matter, that now needed some urgent attention.

My she does take herself awfully seriously at times, thought Harley in his simple doggy fashion. When he was on the beach Harley was much more concerned with what lay around the next band, than what lay in his mistress' heart. Mermaid understood her mad, funny dog, and knew he had better things to be thinking about, like where the next meal was coming from; and was it going to be fresh meat, or those awful tins of chum from the newsagent?

Until recently Mermaid had been full of magic and optimism. She could make things happen, and attract everything she needed. But increasingly her burden had become heavy. She had a definite cross to bear, and a karmic situation to work out. From the outside looking in, she was doing just fine. The world at large would have perceived someone making waves, as opposed to drowning in them.

One day, Mermaid conceded. She had covered every possible angle. She had given the Great Wizard every chance to come clean and sort things out. Despite her aching heart, she would have to get on with what she was meant to do. *Needs must.* Times had changed, and practical realities were pressing in on Mermaid, and threatening to take her out. Besides, there was a story to be told, and a stream of events to live out. Mermaid had stared the exit door squarely in the face. She was a fighter, and she wanted to survive. She refused to be a victim, and had looked at the many possible ways through her current circumstances. Some looked promising for a while. But ultimately everything turned into a temporary measure, and only worked for so long.

Mermaid kept listening to her inner guidance; and the recurrent message, was that she had to put pen to paper and tell her story. Mermaid had lost count of the many excuses she had thrown into the ethers. She had even explained the situation to the Great Wizard, and had asked for some assistance. But to no avail. He was a master at burying his head in the sand, clearly. He expressed genuine concern. But his hands were tied. Mermaid had been sorely bruised by his inability to act. But she knew he at least cared. She realized he had interests to protect, and it was more than easy to forgive the situation. Besides, she knew that from his point of view there was an inner need to deny that anything had happened at all. So never mind the Great Wizard's agenda. He *was* a big boy after all. Mermaid now had her own obligations to fulfill. Was selling her soul one of them?

It appeared so. In order to return to her beloved home beneath the waves, Mermaid had to settle up and clear the decks. She did not wish to leave under a cloud, and she could not justify any other obvious routes of exposure. Her connection with the Great Wizard had been sacred to her. A great love in fact, and it pained her now to even mention it to anyone else, let alone write about it. She apparently had no option, no choice, and no other way to go. The Universe had served up a *FATE accompli* moment.

Mermaid could not go quietly. Mermaid reasoned that an honest account would surely do no harm. But deep in her bones, she knew it could be different. At the same time though, she knew that it was too late to retrieve the heartfelt track she had been on. So what did she have to lose? She had already lost him. Mermaid's story could have played out before your eyes in reality, and not in a book. But as with all good fairy tales, the make believe aspect carries the story to its bitter end. Whether it is happy or not depends on the way you read it. Perhaps Mermaid's love for the Wizard was simply not meant to be in this life time at all. It certainly did not look good from the outset; and several years down the road, it looked even more complex. It did not feel completely unrequited. But it might as well have been, for all the issues it caused.

It never ceased to amaze Mermaid, the interest the Wizard inspired in people. She appreciated of course that he was compelling, and greatly loved by just about everybody. Mermaid started to feel, or was made to feel that she had no right to have these feelings. A lengthy struggle of pain and denial had begun, which was pretty isolating. She realized if she talked about it, people would think of her as delusional. The Great Wizard was unattainable, elevated on a pedestal by many. Disliked and misunderstood too, but that was not her problem. Appearances can be deceiving. The reality of the situation with the Great Wizard was oddly different. Many would assume one thing; the truth was something else. She did not even dare try to verbalize it.

Sometimes in a bid to detach, Mermaid pushed the Great Wizard away. Indeed, on occasion she played things so cool she could have re-frosted the Arctic Circle in a second. Her denial of what she felt to support the common good, now pained her immensely. She was haunted by regret. In many ways Mermaid had been taken in and led on by her own optimism and deep feelings. The White Witch down south, had assured her she would indeed be with the Great Wizard at the preordained time. She had felt bad even asking about this. But the conviction of the witch was so strong, that she was either right, or feeding a delusion. Her other prophesies had proven uncanny and accurate, so it really did look like she was onto something.

The words of the White Witch of Wicklow brought comfort intermittently. But the reality was, things with the Wizard were not progressing. She knew she was partly at fault. The situation had been magnetic, and had had a life of its own. Indeed it had consumed her for the best part of ten years. Ever since she first met the Great Wizard, she had felt a connection, and a longing, that really was from another time and place. It was difficult now realizing that her energies had possibly been expended on a complete fantasy. Of course it would all be so easily dismissed by all and sundry, not least the Wizard himself.

Mermaid did not want to risk bearing her soul. It was not really her style. Never happy with being an open book, Mermaid liked her privacy, and her secrets. There was no denying that her emotions had got the better of her. As things now stood, she had no choice but to stare the current state of affairs in the face, and speak her truth. Despite the karmic interference, henchmen, and diversions that surrounded her wished for Soul Mate, she had to soldier on regardless. The Great Wizard had the Midas touch, and his own protection anyhow. So she was not too uncomfortable about how he might react. Actually she had a weird feeling that he would not mind at all. That in fact he wanted an out, or escape route from his current state of affairs. He certainly seemed to be sailing close to the wind at times. The Great Wizard had always been publically demonstrative, and his affections had been on display and witnessed by a select few. Those people at least would know this was not all in Mermaid's head. But lately, the Great Wizard had been linked with someone younger and apparently more alluring. A friend of Mermaid's named the competition "Twiglet," for the sake of injecting a bit of humor into the proceedings.

Twiglet, really was stick thin, and looked like she might snap at any minute, so it was an appropriate tag. She was darkly gorgeous and childlike, very exotic and Irish, if that were a possible combination. Pictured with the Great Wizard, she always looked so smug, and annoyingly comfortable. Mermaid felt sickened to the core.

Mermaid was assured by the White Witch, that there was nothing significant between them. But she did not believe it. She could sense his distraction, and he was quite quick to disconnect and lose interest. This betrayal of her deepest feelings was difficult to stomach. In fact one night Mermaid was physically sick walking behind the Great Wizard, who was walking on ahead, arm in arm with Twiglet. She literally could not handle it. It used to be *her* he paid attention to.

The whole thing was becoming increasingly bizarre. Twiglet's resemblance to the Great Wizard's wife was uncanny. Was she a replacement for something he was not finding on the home front? To give his wife her dues, she never wavered, and was even photographed in sisterly pose with said Twiglet. The rumors were discounted, and the Great Wizard and his wife did a great job at dispelling any gossip. Perhaps the White Witch was correct after all.

All was well on the home front, and the Great Wizard had much support and solidarity. Indeed, the determined, gracious woman married to him, managed for a time to turn things around in her favor. This woman was very adept at guarding her own interests.

Of course, thought Mermaid,

it's her prerogative. But one day when Mermaid got a note from her, designed to wrap her on the knuckles, she felt dumbfounded.

Charming. And totally unnecessary. She thought, but at least she now sort of knew that the Great Wizard really did have some kind of emotional pull towards her. This made her feel a bit better, oddly. Perhaps the Wizard's wife was calling Mermaid out on her connection imagined, or otherwise, with her husband.

Twiglet was also sidelined by the Wizard, and had to move on. Supposedly she fell in love elsewhere. But Mermaid never bought it. She knew only too well the powerful feelings the Great Wizard could stir in a woman. He was clever, but he had not been smart. All the same Mermaid was happy to see him, apparently happy.

This is how it should be.

Words could not describe her upset, when she still continued to pick up the vibes and rumors-on-corners of the Great Wizard's dalliances with Twiglet. Mermaid knew these things she was overhearing and witnessing were legitimate. She was so connected to him that she could sense and feel his emotional direction. She could read him like a book. Still she tried to reason that the Great Wizard had his reasons, and that he knew what he was doing. She gave him the benefit of the doubt. Yet his lack of concern for her having been so caring in the past was eating her up inside.

At least now, Mermaid knew he had a pattern. And that she had possibly played into his hands as no more than a background distraction. This pained her greatly, since her best years as a mortal had seen her consumed by a love, loyalty and devotion to a Wizard admittedly powerful and well renowned.

But so what?

Mermaid had always known that she would have loved him, whatever his status. He had made her feel special, wanted, and loved in a land that had taken some adjusting to. So Mermaid ruminated, wondered, and pondered, for what must have seemed like an eternity to those waiting for her script.

What to do?

Well, there must have been some reason this whole thing happened in the first place. So, not wanting to spill the beans out of maliciousness, Mermaid proceeded to put pen to paper, in the hope that some good would come of it all. That there would be light at the end of the tunnel, and that her fishy tale might even help others, rather than instill suspicion, judgment, or pity.

She artfully drew a line in the sand...

WHERE THOUGHTS GO, ENERGY FLOWS.
MAKE SURE YOU FOCUS ON THE
RAINBOWS AND NOT THE RAIN.
ALWAYS LOOK FOR THE BLESSING!

CHAPTER ONE
Chasing Rainbows

My dear old Nan Mary once advised me to "not spend my life chasing rainbows." Her handwritten note was lovingly penned as I embarked on my university career north of the border. Did I listen? No, probably not. But I am assured that from her perspective in eternity, she would not now give me the same advice. Standing beside the Bannockburn monument at Stirling Castle gazing across at the University, Nan and I contemplated the scene which was to encapsulate my rite of passage, from introspective contemplative teenager, to independence, maturity and adulthood. Well, in theory.

As we pondered the valley, which had seen many a skirmish and bloody debacle in the bid for Scottish freedom and pre-eminence, a magnificent rainbow illuminated the landscape. From the rugged peak of Dymyat, western extremity of the Ochil Hills, the vibrant rainbow emanated encapsulating the most vivid colors I had ever seen. The rainbow encompassed the campus below and highlighted my new student accommodations in particular. There was something magical about its timing. So it gave me the courage to face the bleak reality confronting me, as well as confirming the promise of intriguing adventures to come. I definitely did not want to be so far away from home. But the fates had decreed that my exam results, combined with the prospect of a largely coursework assessed degree, would see me settling into room 333 of Murray Hall for the foreseeable future.

We had always loved Scotland as a family. Weather-beaten holidays with elemental walks down gullies, over ravines and sometimes nearly off cliffs, had long been a feature of my childhood. Isolated terrain was a life-long compulsion of my father's. He liked to push the boat out, and set survival challenges like existing on porridge for two weeks on remote Hebridean islands, with geese, gulls and canvas for company. Admittedly this recklessness was pre wife and babies, but something of the maverick rock climber remained with him. I remember my mother Joy having a serious meltdown moment looking up at my father and young brother scrambling on the rocks hundreds of feet above, without ropes.

Another time, we were all in situ in a typically elemental spot beside Loch Torridon, where my parents had honeymooned. I had a middle-ear infection and mounting temperature, our tent was about to be blown off its pegs, and my father had decided to scale the heights of nearby Beinn Alligin in the fog. Well, to be fair, it had been a fine summer's day when he set off. By six o' clock in the evening, there was a freak storm raging; winds threatening to blow him off the mountain, and rain turning to sleet. My father's blood sugar levels were doubtless low, regardless of Kendal mint cake, and my mother was getting increasingly frantic. The mountain rescue were called out.

These were difficult conditions for an experienced mountaineer, let alone a diabetic one.

Thankfully, they did not have far to go. The local farmers who had been sent out to find the intrepid Rog, met him sauntering back along the path, looking mighty relieved. By this time, his family had abandoned ship, and were sleeping and/or eating eggs in the nearby farm house. As our father recounted his tale, we started to pay a bit more attention. We learned that he had nearly walked off a precipice after taking a wrong compass reading. He had sheltered just below the summit and clambered down the cliff-face for a view of how to proceed. But the cloud was down to sea-level so he had to clamber back up the streaming cliff face. The compass was possibly waylaid by magnetic rock, yet he had to trust it to find the only safe way of the mountain, a narrow col between steep cliffs. An inner prompting, an earnest prayer and a pause for breath caused him to double check his bearings. Thank God he did. His previous course, arrived at by reading the small inadequate compass, would have sent him hurling to his death within minutes in the depths below. One wrong footing and he would have tumbled into oblivion.

My father's route off the mountain was thankfully not *that* dramatic. He had to get creative though, as he had lost contact with the correct ridge path. Also, he was up against the magnetic rocks of the area, which can play havoc with a delicate mountaineer's compass, let alone a basic one. Natural intelligence kicked in, and a strong survival instinct. With the help of a map and the dubious compass, he found a steep gully. Scrambling quickly downwards as the gradient was steep, and the ground slippery and treacherous, he finally stumbled upon a more trodden route home.

By God's grace my father was returned to us in one piece. This brush with mortality was sobering and affected everyone deeply. Obviously my father had used yet another of his nine lives. But the episode also showed us that we do not shake off this mortal coil, until it is our ordained time to do so. My father clearly had a lot more to do in this lifetime. It was also clear that, more haste less speed and a charmed prayer in precipitous situations pays off.

Clearly a love for the wilderness was inherent in the genes. My father Roger's first recourse on holidays was to head for the hills dragging us all, in various states of willingness, behind him. I certainly did not go reluctantly. My eternally patient mother struggled somewhat, home making in the series of damp, ancient and isolated cottages that came our way. She always did say, that the best part of a holiday was getting home. But us kids loved the adventures, and the rugged nooks and crannies of obscure parts of Scotland and Wales.

Holidays were a thing of fun and excitement. We all rather enjoyed trying to work out what off-beaten track our parents would lead us down next. Rog-Route roads to remote accommodation at the end of eight mile cul-de-sacs, were the norm. Walks in the freezing wind and rain, wearing florescent cagoules were the norm. Freeze-dried camping meals, to spare our mother the tedium of vegetable chopping were the norm. The love of isolation, in the midst of a loving family unit, was the intrinsic paradox of our communal life. Sarah, Simon, and Rachel, were the biblically named siblings who mucked in, with moss gliding, ice cold stream dipping, sheep chasing, building dams and sketching.

I apparently was so intrepid from an early age, that I had a temper tantrum, aged three and three quarters, insisting I be allowed to skinny dip in the arctic temperatures of Loch Sunart, on the South side of the Ardnamurchan peninsula. I did not let up until I was allowed to do this. I think eventually my parents conceded that turning blue and catching hypothermia would be a final comment on the matter, and a lesson learned. Not sure that worked. It was nearly as productive as telling me not to chase rainbows. I was probably feeling the pull towards Ireland already. But it was a long swim, and that impulse was premature, and not yet cooked.

On the same holiday, as we arrived in Scotland after an interminable drive north, our VW Camper Van came across the ruined Castle Tioram around six pm. So exhausted was I by the journey, that I was insistent there must be a room for the night ready and waiting. I must have been overly tired, lost in a haze between times, or sensing a familiarity that felt like home amongst the ruins. But my senses were so primed and alert to the mystery of the place, that I was sure I had a room there, and would not take "no" for an answer.

This young intuitive was clearly picking up impressions from the etheric energies, atmosphere of the castle, and its environs. It was a potent, otherworldly, out of time experience I can vividly recall, and feel even to this day. Magical as my parents are, there was not much they could do to rustle up a bustling hotel reception in the dank, dark ruins of an ancient castle sitting on Loch Moidart's tidally compromised island. Indeed it was imperative we got out of there as soon as possible, or a night on the island really *was* going to be a reality.

Clearly from a young age I was full of the intention and belief that nothing was impossible, even despite any real evidence to the contrary. I was a feisty, determined, if not stubborn creature, who knew what she wanted in any given moment, and was going to do her damnedest to make it happen. Perhaps I was entitled, and carried the energy of a princess who demanded that the world bent to her whims. I had the biblical name of Sarah after all. Bono, the lead singer of rock band U2, had waxed lyrical on the meaning and context of the name Sarah when I first met him, so who was I to argue?

There was inevitably drama as a toddler. At the age of two in a Romford shopping centre I required a frog instead of a doll: "immediately!" Several stores later, antagonizing increasingly frazzled grandparents, clearly this Essex born aspiring witch, was not going to get her frog any time soon. I had to settle a negotiation with my Nan, which involved making a cloth doll called a "gonk," from the *Family Album Craft Book*, as soon as we got home. Being allowed to play with

Nan's slippery, delightfully scented Camay soap in the bath before bed time, was also a suitable compensatory gesture.

The frog incident probably rooted the seeds of the historic "chasing rainbows" comment, conjured up by my ever patient Nan. Equally, I am sure there were many such instances which gave my guardians clues, that I was someone out of the norm, who was going to at least try to defy the odds at any given opportunity.

Doing things my way was an intrinsic part of my spirit from a young age. My soul was defiant that rules were meant to be bent if not broken; especially if they did not serve a true, authentic purpose.

I was obedient and helpful, but I did not like to be dictated to. Not much would put me off if my mind was set on something. I was a pioneer for universal law, and spirited intentions before I could even read or write. At the age of six I packed my little red suitcase, with only my pink dressing gown inside, and stomped out of the house. I was not sure why the pink dressing gown was so crucial, as opposed to warm clothes and camping equipment. But obviously it was a priority. I was leaving home. I had no idea where I was going; but leaving home, I was.

My mother panicked when she realized I was completely serious. I calmly stated: "I have two problems in my life, Mrs. Rees the headmistress, and YOU! Anyway, The Bible tells me to obey God not you." My mother's response was a stroke of genius. She quickly called on the faith she knew I had, and said, "God also says 'honor your parents for a long and blessed life'."

"Oh! Hmmm, yes. You're right. Okay then!" And I trundled back into the house. If I had been equally smart, I would have said, "But God does not say 'obey,' he says 'honor.'" Then again, that might have seen me homeless at a very young age, and there was time enough for all that. Annoyingly my mother had out played me this time. This was not by any means our last contretemps. But I generally was more compliant after that. At least it meant I finally left home at a more reasonable age.

My father quoted this incident in his book, *Understanding Adolescence*. I was six, not a teen, when this happened. But I always was advanced for my age, and I think the episode adequately made his point. I have no doubt I was a bit of a handful, for my mother especially. For some reason, she felt she could never teach me anything. I assured her that this was not the case. She was a wonderful homemaker, provider, and an exceptionally good cook. There really was no logical reason to doubt herself. I do think most of her inadequacy as a parent, was a deeper self esteem issue, which stemmed from the loss of her father in the war.

At the tender age of three my mother lost her father in The Battle Of Crete. Grandpa Harding was stationed on HMS *Warspite*, when the German raiders bombed the living daylights out of the fleet. Many lost their lives that day, and my grandfather, who was Master Boatswain, died in a direct hit on his gun turret, while manning the guns in defense.

Granny understandably shut down when news of her husband's passing reached home. Being personally acknowledged by His Majesty, King George VI would have normally gone down well. But in the current circumstances, the news was bitter rather than sweet.

The dreaded telegram was delivered from the war office by the Shamley Green post office lady:

"Is it bad news?"

"Yes! The very worst."

This formal message of condolence from The King was a mixed blessing. Granny's reaction to the vicar who then visited to console her was, "and how will being proud help me to provide for my three children?"

Granny, a practical Virgo, was left with the responsibility of providing the best possible outcomes for her children on a shoe string. She had the help and support of near and dear friends. Aunty

Frances, the lady whose piano was bequeathed to the household, was an ever steady presence. Uncle Pete visited frequently with his serious moustache, and even more serious pipe smoking. To this day, Uncle Pete's chair in the dining room, has the aura he imprinted upon it, and the wonderful smell of the rich flavored tobacco he smoked. Pete lived to the ripe old age of ninety something, so no harm done. No filter.

Manelhe, the Harding family home, is stuck in a time warp, a shrine to these times. The old navy sword, proudly worn by my Grandfather stands in pride of place. The antique brass, photographs, china, and fire place are static, and unmoved, except for polishing, dusting and sweeping purposes.

The old Grandfather clock I used to listen to as a child, still pervades the house every fifteen minutes with its magically graded succession of chimes. I would lie awake for long summer nights, listening to the cadences pace the house through the witching hours. If Gran's specialty roast lamb was on the menu for the next day, the night was particularly slow. Her silverware was always laid out correctly, with the prerequisite white napkins; and there was a little button bell to announce the fayre, be it breakfast, dinner, or high tea.

Manelhe had a lot of magic to offer a young child. The coal tar soap in the bathroom and its compelling scent, was not quite so infatuating when being used to try to scrub off my birth mark in the bath tub. Gran mistook this mark with the numbers 4, 11, and 26 at the top of my inside right thigh as mud. It took some persuading her, that it was not.

The Chinese pickup sticks kept at the top of the stairs in an antique china vase were fascinating, and it was a great treat when those were brought downstairs. We played snap, pickup sticks and a card game "Happy Families," which involved getting all the animal suits of one family as quickly as possible. I always aimed for the rabbits.

One summer I was unwell with a fever, and I remember Granny

nursing me with her unique perfume 4711. I hated the smell of it; still do, even though it is now obviously evocative. She dowsed me in it, believing it would bring my fever down. My pores were so clogged with this stuff, the virus was no doubt prolonged on a loop in my system. A twelve year old is liable to shake off most things. But, I was probably lucky to get through that in one piece. .

The apple trees in the garden were charming, the sweet peas in the allotment and the peas in their pods, all captivated a child's imagination. But best of all was the croquet on the lawn. Manelhe had a war time pantry, with a very distinctive smell. My Granny filled it with preserves, pickles, eggs, homegrown vegetables from the garden, and homemade purees from the windfall apples. It had a natural chill, and kept bread and milk fresh for days.

The kitchen remains the same as it was during the times of air raids and rations. The big old roasting range, the white cupboards housing all the specialist crockery. The old yellowing boiler above the sink for hot water. The green back door with glass windows leading out to the clothes hanging area, and across to the apple trees, and allotment; then on down and down the long, long path to the tucked away air raid shelter right at the foot of the garden. All still the same.

Michael, my godfather, and my mother's older brother keeps the memories alive. There is still a place set for Granny at the table, something which I find endearing and charming, but which bothers my mother and their younger brother Chris. To quote Michael, "no death goes down well. " He grieves in his unique way, and there is no magic recipe for dealing with such loss.

Michael remains a loyal and staunch defender of his mother; mindful of all she had to cope with. Michael is the retired Deputy Head, who will wear the same jumper for days, and keeps the old square box television sitting behind the flat screen, just in case. He will not throw things away or tamper with the layout of rooms. Michael was required to step up as the man of the house and protect his mother at the tender age of seven, when his father passed away. Very little has changed in the interim. Pretty much everything is just as my Granny left it. This is her space, and he honors that, and so preserves her name.

My mother is a staunch Royalist. This probably relates directly to the fact that her father died for King and Country. There is a definite pride that must be honored, despite the futility of Grandpa Harding's death. Us kids have been unashamedly irreverent about my mother's penchant for all things Royal. *God Save The Queen!* But underneath it all, we *do* understand. The establishment was inextricably linked with her father, and she has every right to be deeply proud.

When the bombshell of the passing landed, the drama of the shockwave tremor from a falling missile that had cracked the front porch doorstep, paled into insignificance. That air raid had brought the war close to home, but nothing could dissipate the sinister news that then entered and pervaded the house.

Joy was left coping with all sorts of issues, such as invasion of privacy, and having to be sure to "always do the right thing." She was provided for practically, and materially, but warmth of heart was somewhat missing. Gran had clearly died a little inside with the news of her husband's passing. Now, nothing was ever quite good enough, and there was a permanent underlying stress at home. With her brothers Michael and Chris away at boarding school much of the time, Joy was left to fend for herself. This must have been very isolating and painful for her. But she weathered it, and as time marched on, she got some light relief hanging out with Hilton, cycling the leafy lanes of Surrey, and watching the cricket on the quintessential Green of Shamley.

Once the war was over, Hilton's father Leonard Thorpe increasingly became an important father figure for her, as she blossomed into a beautiful teenager. Joy felt a guidance and reassurance from this man, which brought her inner stability and calm. A timely comment when she was younger from an elderly missionary also enabled her to maintain her equilibrium.

The missionary pointed out the magic of her name J.O.Y. Jesus, Others, Yourself. The words of this woman of God resonated with her. She took the message to heart. "Yes, it is indeed such a great shame that your earthly father has passed away. But there is a heavenly father up above, who loves you very much indeed."

Joy, thus connected to a way of life, which she adhered to religiously, exhibiting faith, hope, love, and impressive practicality. There was also some light relief in the village in the form of Sir Richard Branson.

No, he most definitely was not the village idiot. Quite the contrary, as you might expect. Richard was a character. As a youth, he came to have a bit of a reputation as a loose cannon. Somewhat notorious in his ways, he blossomed into a creative, infamous local. If they could bottle opportunism, enthusiasm, and making things count, Richard would have been feted. The Shamley Green gossips were never quite sure if Richard was going to be a millionaire, or end up in jail. I have it on good authority that he still owes someone seven pence in the village, and that the local deer population was often a bit depleted come hunting season. Say no more.

Sir Richard, was quite the trophy child, with his baby blues peering out from under his pristine white bonnet. My mother as a young teen frequently saw him being pushed around The Green in his pram. He was accident prone even then. On one occasion he was hurled unceremoniously to the ground, landing straight onto his head.

I am not sure if this close shave is amongst the seventy-five near misses Branson recounts in his autobiography *Finding My Virginity*, but obviously there were no adverse effects. Living on the edge is Richard's modus operandi, so he was merely setting a precedent with the pram tumble. Things subsequently panned out wonderfully well for this maverick personality with the Midas touch.

Richard clearly stayed more or less on the right track, choosing the high road in business, and in the stewardship of this wealth, and talents. I saw something of his enlightened approach when I needed funding for my M.Phil in Publishing. I had exhausted my government grants for education, and was having to resort to more imaginative means for paying the fees for my masters.

Thinking outside the box, my mother reached out to Richard, and he sent me two first class return tickets to sell in the German restaurant where I worked as a chef. I have to give him credit, this was an elegant and imaginative fob off. Richard expected me to find some stranded Americans, and sell them a flight home in order to fund my education. The catch was they had to *want* to go one way to Miami or LA. I guess he was envisaging that two people were likely to have mislaid their return tickets home to different destinations. Unlikely.

In the end I thankfully got funding for the M Phil from a postgraduate scholarship fund, The British Academy, on my third attempt. My mother, as always expressing the "J.O.Y thing" to the max, returned the tickets to Richard.

Oh! I was wondering if I might have done a couple of trips!
Oh well.

As my mother's horizons expanded, she left Sweetwater Lane to train as a nurse at Saint Bartholomew's Hospital in London. There, she promptly met my father, as he was carrying a bottle of urine across The Square. Awkward? Apparently not. They chatted and fell in love pretty quickly; locking eyes, minds, and hearts at the famous fountain. My father gave mother a small wooden mouse, and their fates were sealed. Joy's brother Michael queried the modest gesture of the mouse; but my mother clearly found it charming and endearing. If only the course of true love were always that simple, and romantic.

Despite their backgrounds of considerable hardship, and on-going challenges, my parents forged a lasting bond, which has seen them through some very testing times. My Father has written about their journey in his own autobiography, *As Trees Walking*. Much of their married life has been a quest to monitor and maintain my father's health. Diabetic since the age of seventeen, my father confirmed his intention to train as a doctor, during his first hospitalization. He had to totally revamp his A level schedule, and ended up with seven A levels, in both arts and sciences, having aborted his original decision to be a land surveyor.

The bottle of urine he carried at his first meeting with my mother, proved to be symbolic indeed. The backdrop of the trickling waters of the fountain also added irony and pathos. Diabetics obviously have to check their urine frequently for glucose intolerance; so really it could not have been a more fitting "meet cute."

My mother, a patient, facilitating nurse, was just the right partner to practically maintain the status quo, through two episodes of blindness, quadruple by-pass surgery and endless in-growing eyelashes. "Joy Birds" and Roger are a testimony to lasting love; and nothing is quite as charming as my father's proposal. This overlooking the fact that my mother was second on his handmade list of prospective wives. My mother's maiden name was Harding, and my father's surname, Hurding. So the proposal was a bit of a no brainer really. Ma readily agreed to "change her 'A' for a 'U'."

My parents have been through a lot together, but never failed to provide my siblings and I with a wonderful, safe, loving, and nurturing environment in which to blossom. They were open minded, never overly strict or unreasonable; and endlessly patient with their three unusual children. We all have huge gratitude for the way we were raised. Considering all my parents were contending with financially and health-wise, we were rich indeed.

Obviously as role models, my parents were pretty much perfect in my eyes. My brother had issues of our father being a bit controlling in moments. But I have no memory or recall of this. I actually think it was Simon's own internal pressure to live up to an expectation. A projection rather than a demand. Simon was talented creatively and artistically, and could have taken a more left field route through life like myself. But he went for the hard graft, and trained as a doctor. Even despite being taught the wrong course in Chemistry, Simon persisted, and eventually got all the results he needed to go and qualify as a doctor via Sheffield University. That, plus an elective position for a few months, in the snake infested wards of a North Indian Hospital in the middle of monsoon season, and he made the grade.

My father did not insist that Simon follow in his footsteps. But Simon certainly did a good job of achieving perhaps much of what my father might have wished for, had his own health been better. With a general medical practice in The Highlands of Scotland, and membership of The Mountain Rescue team for Glenelg, Simon had created an amazing life. The Hurding family traditions of splendid isolation and hard graft were wonderfully upheld by my brother.

I know I personally wanted to get results and achieve good things in life, but I did not feel it was ever demanded of us. The key was, we were loved and understood. It made leaving home quite a traumatic event. Although I wanted to spread my wings and be independent, I really felt bereft of the back ground support my parents had provided. Of course it was still there in theory. But there was definitely a sense of being pushed out of the nest to fly.

Stirling University was a mixed experience. The idea made sense on paper. Here was a modern innovative learning centre, set in beautiful and inspirational surroundings. Yet there was a melancholy about the place. One which did not go unnoticed, or unfelt, by a sensitive empath, such as myself.

Whether it was the ghosts of ancient struggles past; the imposing William Wallace Monument, the phallic majesty of which always commanded snickering whispers amongst the freshmen; or the lack of anything to do other than admire the scenery; I am not sure. But Stirling proved to be oddly disconcerting.

Here was a place which really should have provided much stimulation and opportunity. Indeed the courses, tutors, and curriculum were all exemplary. It was more the energy of the place. When my head was not buried in a book, or distracted by an essay topic, I was distractedly lonely there. It was impossible not to feel deeply the darkness and brooding backdrop, caused simultaneously by the geography and history. The fact that the campus accommodations were modeled on a Swedish prison, may also have had something to do with it.

There were rumors of the occasional suicide on campus. From my father's work as medical officer for the students of Bristol University, I knew this was part and parcel of what happened when people left home, and went to college. There were several recorded attempts a year, where troubled students contemplated the jump to certain death off The Clifton Suspension Bridge. This had not been the intention of genius Isambard Kingdom Brunel, when he designed this magnificent feat of engineering. But it was the obvious spot in the West Country, for those looking for a way out.

I was miles away up in Scotland, and not that way inclined. I was never about to travel home, and avail of this beauty spot for *that* reason. But clearly depression was potentially an issue for a sensitive creature cast adrift, a long way from home. This was all within a norm, I logically told myself. A natural part of the adjustment young people had to make leaving the nest to embark upon their adult lives. It was not so much about chasing rainbows, as getting bogged down in the quick sands of the swamp. I think it was safe to say, my feet were going to remain firmly planted on the ground with all that I had to contend with.

*THINK FOR YOURSELF. TRUST YOUR OWN INTUITION. ANOTHER'S MIND ISN'T WALKING YOUR JOURNEY:
YOU ARE!*

CHAPTER TWO
Rite Of Passage

There were a few enticements which made Stirling an appealing prospect. My summer camp, Scripture Union friend, aspiring actor Pete was there. His infectious humor, and cracking laugh, would always make me smile. But it was odd to arrive at Stirling and find him somewhat standoffish, sporting a fake Scottish accent, and definitely harboring no interest in helping me to settle in.

On reflection I can understand this. The Scottish were not madly accepting of the English, and I think the young males found their reception particularly frosty. I cannot say I had any problem with being English in a Scottish university, but I can understand why someone like Pete would want to go under the radar, and take on the mantle. Why, he even played Macbeth in a university production, so not much love lost there then.

Pete was already established, and had done his settling in. There really was no reason he would pay me much attention. Clearly he had moved on, and perceived me as out of context in this environment. The compartmentalizing brain of the male species can only cope with so much I think. I was Pete's summer camp girl, not his term time partner.

For me, Pete had been a dreamy summer romance, a wonderful kisser, charming, beguiling and lots of fun. All the girls at Great Wood Camp, in The Quantock Hills, had liked him. But my friend Sue won him over, first and foremost. Sue, a lithe, leggy brunette tended to take the lead, and got the first pick of the boys for some reason. For quite obvious reasons really.

Pete and Sue used to sit up talking until the camp fire burned to ashes; then did a sprightly sunrise walk up Will's Neck before everyone else got up. Somehow, after all that, there was Sue lively and full of energy at breakfast, as if she had just had a full night's sleep. High on Pete's company no doubt. I also later found out the kissing was pretty enlivening; so that explained it. .

Sue had first dibs on Pete, and Francis, the rugby playing team leader. She also had the run of the kitchen and the chores. To this day she is still running Great Wood Camp as part of her nurturing empire, and Christian ministry. Married to a minister, Sue took the correct route through life, remaining within the safe boundaries of church and family. I probably should have done much the same with boyfriend Phil. But there was more adventure and karmic adjustment to play out in my case. Clearly I had to walk the line, and chase those rainbows.

Pete was not hugely cool or buff, or jaw-crackingly handsome. But he was vibrant and mischievous, and had something about him. He told me that hazy summer that he had prayed to be sent a Christian girlfriend to Stirling University. His prayer was answered in the form of me. But by the time I arrived, he appeared to have retracted his desire for something seemingly wholesome. I say "seemingly" advisedly. Pete did not seem to find the option I presented pleasing enough to risk losing face in front of his compatriots. Clearly I embodied a, "be careful what you wish for" moment. Pete was friendly enough, but basically I was relegated to some "hi's and byes" on the lake bridge between lectures.

I harbored no hard feelings. Pete was eminently likeable. Looking him up on line many years later, I discovered that he had achieved his dream to be an actor, and had done very well for himself. Not exactly a house hold name, Pete had achieved major roles and accolades as a Shakespearian actor, treading the boards at Stratford-on-Avon, *The Globe*, and on Broadway. He had also had a movie role as a racing commentator, and had appeared on many prime time TV shows such as *Eastenders*, *Dr Who*, and *The Bill*.

I was delighted for Pete. He was an incredibly natural, funny and brilliant actor with spectacular timing. I am not sure life with a thespian would have been good for me. We will never know. It was not meant to be.

My father had liked Pete a lot, and once tried to steer things slightly saying "I think he really likes you." But that was about as proactive as he ever got in encouraging me to keep company with anyone of the male species. He was usually more protective, flickering lights when I sat outside too long in the car of my hunky welding boyfriend Gilly. I was fifteen, and David MacGillivray was twenty one, so I think that was pretty reasonable paternal behavior.

My parents both challenged me on this relationship after an article appeared in the local newspaper, reporting that Gilly had been caught up in a bust-up at the local gas station. I dismissed it saying, "I thought you taught us to forgive people?" My Parents anticipated I would say this, and used more logical and less biblical means to persuade me, that this might not be a great connection for me to maintain.

I have a feeling my mother performed some kind of back ground intervention, because the next thing I knew I was on the phone to Gilly trying to persuade him to remain my boyfriend. My mother over hearing this conversation told me to "let him go," and I realized I was victim of a fait accompli. Hmmm.

My father at a later point was concerned again at the level of my physical relationship with boyfriend Phil. But really he need not have been. I was eighteen, and Phil was twenty one. We were serious about each other, and not much was going on. I was brought up to be respectful and never to treat sexual intimacy lightly. I never did, and never will. I find sex for the sake of it as equally abhorrent as my father does. And I was a very trustworthy young girl.

Having said that, there was a near miss when Phil first arrived at Conifers our family home, for a visit. My sixth form boyfriend, was a boy named Lucy (not Sue). Easter time of my eighteenth year, Lucy had just left Conifers our family home after one of his regular visits. Zooming down Fircliff Park on his scooter, he would have been intrigued if he had noticed the broader, more chiseled frame of Phil Avery walking up Woodhill Road, the main route from Portishead High Street which aligned at right angles to the cul-de-sac Fircliff Park, which was home.

Dominated by a picturesque Georgian Terrace, Woodhill Road is a fine example of old Portishead. As school kids, we could be found sketching the various town landmarks for our local history lessons. Woodhill Road was a favorite, as was the old farm in the heart of the village run by Gertie Gayle. The Church of Saint Peter's beside this Elizabethan farm dates back to the thirteenth century, and has a number of coach houses, and historical cottages in its immediate vicinity.

The twenty one doors in a row of the fine sandstone sculpted terrace of the wooded hill road, told stories I am sure. The houses had spectacular views out across the Bristol Channel, which on a good day looked less like a muddy brown river, and more like the smooth luminous waters of the Rhine. (We were taught creative thinking also).

In Victorian times, Portishead had a healthy rivalry with the nearby town of Clevedon, for the affections of those who indulged the tradition of a promenade walk along the sea front. Clevedon boasted the iron clad moulded, wooden-slatted pier. While Portishead had Battery Point, and the ancient East Woods, which were prime spots for logging the movement of ships in and out of Bristol Port.

These days the shipping traffic is somewhat different, and the huge freight liners have to embark at Avonmouth, instead of navigating the tidal waters of the river Avon beneath The Clifton Suspension Bridge. With one of the highest tidal ranges in the world, The Bristol channel accommodates a huge amount of commercial carriers into Avonmouth harbor. The cruise sized ships sail close to the jutting promontory of Battery Point, and the view afforded is quite surreal.

Portishead, situated at the foot of the Gordano Valley on the west side, had a lot of appeal way before the Trip Hop band of the same name hit popular consciousness. Although, undeniably an impressive experimental keyboard fest, the dirge like predominantly depressing tones of Portishead, would give the impression that all the town's inhabitants were on the verge of suicide. Nothing could have been further from the truth. For growing teenagers Portishead was perhaps a bit dull and suburban, but it was also a place to grow, explore and flourish. It was somewhere we all knew we would leave. But it was undeniably a very good place to bring up a family. Offering a safe and secure environment for children especially, the schools were good, and the community spirit was conducive.

A modest sized dormitory town, Portishead served as a place of sleep, rest and recuperation for commuters at the end of a busy day, and at the weekends, it was conveniently placed for excursions further afield. The Mendip Hills, The Quantocks, Cheddar Gorge, or even The Brecon Beacons in Wales were all within easy reach, if feeling adventurous. And London was not much more than a couple of hours away on the train. My father chose this prime spot for his commute into work at Bristol University, and it served well to create a safe bubble for family life, at one remove from the bustle of a big city, and the working day.

In current times the development of a huge Marina where the old phosphorous factory used to be situated, has brought a huge influx of new blood, and has vastly swelled the real estate values and population of the town. Portishead is less personal these days, but it is still, a friendly and vibrant community.

Phil, from Bath, was I am sure pondering all of this as he climbed the hill to Conifers. He had taken it upon himself to come and meet his pen pal from summer camp: me. There had been a growing connection by post, but I had not given it much thought. I was "Lucy's Girl," or so I had overheard a group of Lucy's friends say as I sauntered by on a freezing night at The Victorian Christmas Evening in Portishead. "There's Lucy's girl," was the comment that had wafted across the crowded walkway. Psychics have spectacular hearing by the way. We do not need to lip sync, we just read the energy and thereby know what is being said. We also generally have amazing physical hearing too. I used to be able to make out most of what my parents were talking about up in the kitchen with the door closed, from my bedroom tucked away in the lower part of the house; and if I could not, sitting at the bottom of the stairs would more than suffice. Sorry mum.

I was dressed in my big brown bear coat, armed against the cold with woolen gloves and scarf. I would have had on the required eye liner and lip gloss; blonde hair, highlighted with "hint of a tint," was mildly wavy. I probably flatter myself, but there was a bit of the look of a young Princess Diana about me. I had the princess name, Sarah, but no aspirations to be royal. My mother would have been delighted of course. But overall, just as well I did not go too near Buckingham Palace in those days. I would have been even more of a rebellious disaster than Diana, in the midst of all those rules and regulations.

It is a shame that Lucy had not cleared this "being his girl" thing officially, as we might have made something of it. We got on, and were definitely seeing each other. But I do not think either of us assumed it was a long term thing, at what was still a fairly young age. Even though it was an innocent, kiss, cuddles and babysitting arrangement, I really liked Lucy. We used to be left to baby sit his younger sister. We would play Genesis, Marillion, and other magical other-worldly sounds to pass the time. Nothing much happened, though it had a very charming feel to it. I was not feeling a grand passion, but there were the stirrings of mild romance.

Suddenly there was a choice to make. Phil or Lucy. Do I choose the guy with the girl's name, or make a go of it with the Christian nice guy? My tendency to unwittingly overlap things clearly also had to be addressed; and not with a letter to Phil. Phil was the dark, thick haired handsome rugby player, with the finely shaped nose, and dancing eyes. Lucy was tall, dark, sensitive, and wore a burgundy jumper. He once made me lamb chops, peas and mash at his house. It was a bit of a no brainer really, especially as my family was largely vegetarian in inclination. Phil was more congruent with my background and romantic expectations for the long term. Sadly, I hurt Lucy with my decision. He told me he was, "all churned up." I felt bad. But needs must. My first serious relationship had arrived on my doorstep.

All's fair in love and lamb chops.

I had liked Phil a lot after he threw me in the swimming pool at Great Wood Camp. But that also jolted my system and gave me skipped heart beats for a while. It was a shock to be thrown into that cold water, after a struggle. But I guess it was a sign of the heart skipping in other ways too in time to come. At camp, Phil did not hang out with me. I was quite introverted socially, and insecure perhaps too; and he seemed diverted by a couple of the older girls. So I did not hold out much hope. I wore my red dress, black spurred riding boots and cream mohair jumper knitted by mum on the last night of camp. But to no avail. The last night of camp, was a bit like the prom, you generally tried to hook up with someone for a bit of a kiss and cuddle. In our dreams was more the reality. Expectations were high. But I do not think anyone but Sue got anywhere.

I was never madly successful at the last night of camp thing. There was a tradition of walking up through a natural tunnel in the dark as a group. The idea was this was a scary fun thing to do. In truth we all saw it as a way to get our wicked way with the guy or girl we had been eyeing up all week. This was a Christian camp, so nothing untoward went down. But as teenagers, we all still had our hormones surging through our systems, so certainly romantic possibilities were highly charged.

The previous Easter, before meeting Phil in the summer, I had received my first proper romantic kiss from Steven at a muddy Youth Focus camp. Steven lived in Rugby, so he was sort of prophetic in name at least. I am not sure the symbolism was assigning a groove for years to come. But it sure was a heavy universal blunder if you scroll forward some years to the dalliances with Irish Rugby.

Steven and I had walked around the mile long track which circuited Great Wood in the in the dark, in our Wellington boots. No doubt we chatted animatedly, I cannot remember about what. In retrospect, there was an unconscious agreement that we were each others' rite of passage moment. eventually, as we neared the gate to head back to the cabins, Steven zoomed in for the kiss.

So that was it!

It was the beginning of that strange fluttering feeling that I came to love when connecting with a guy. The romance of the first kiss was everything. I was still a teenager, so it was an understandable misconception. It was not until I grew up a bit, that I found out that not all guys even like to kiss. Shame. For me it is a great part of intimacy, and should not be glossed over. Leaving the possible exchange of germs aside, if you are exchanging bodily fluids with someone, you might as well go all in. Well that is my theory anyway.

That summer, Phil had no eyes for me that I was aware of, but I reached out with a letter, and he was apparently delighted I had done so. He told me he could not have been more pleased to hear from me, and that he had hoped the strange letter which popped through his door was from me. It just goes to show, it pays to follow through on those hunches. You will never know if you do not try.

In those days it took a bit more of an effort to connect. One text, in which you could be "left read" did not cut it. There was none of this swiping right or swiping left as a quick judgment of who is worthy of your time and attention. Apps like Tinder have replaced a lot of the romantic charm potential in our lives. And that green dot showing active on Facebook has been responsible for a many break-up and countless arguments. These on-line devices feed distrust and suspicion. Hardly useful. If only these "last seen" and "active" indicators were an accurate depiction of activity on line, they would be a stalkers delight. But they are not. Whatsapp, the martial affair facilitator is similarly misleading I gather. I mean, either trust the one you are with, or do not. Certainly do not rely on social media to relay your loved one's supposed whereabouts and interactions for you.

In the olden days, well several years ago, if someone took the time to reach out and write to you it actually *meant* something. One would at least be polite with a reply. The social etiquette was less sophisticated but also less devastating. You could reassure yourself that your letter might have got lost in the post. That ominous tick at the bottom of the "sent message," was not yet on the Richter scale of drama for one's love life.

Phil and I shared niceties, thoughts, and general chat by carrier pigeon. But there was not really any chemistry or frisson in the words we exchanged. This was a nice guy. who shared my faith, and who was at least a brother in Christ. I thought this way in those days. It was tricky to think outside the box of the evangelical smiley, happy, joyful Christian bubble I was in. My eyes were not yet open to the ways of the world. I was a good girl, if a bit stubborn. I was obedient, generally thoughtful, and hard working. But I struggled with anxieties and worries. What I did not consciously realize, was that in my sensitivity, I was picking up a lot of background stress from others.

Psychics, especially unconscious ones, not fully developed, tend to absorb energies like a sponge. That child or young teen you observe who is somewhat withdrawn, introspective, and creative, may not just be hormonal; they may also be gifted. For me, listening to the news with its commentary about nuclear weapons and their development, inspired great fear. I am not logically sure how much of a potential threat nuclear annihilation was in those days. But the reports of the cold war with Russia, and the analysis of the damage impact of these weapons, did not make for restful sleep. I used to lie in my bed at night, terrified of a huge atomic bomb going off over Bristol.

It was in those moments deep in the night that I wished I had not been born. I had not asked to be, and I was really quite terrified of death. It may have been that as children being aware in the detail of the implications of a long term disease like diabetes, was an ever present reminder of our mortality. But my naive rationale was that having *been* born, and now *being* alive, I should be allowed to *stay* so. Another example of my less than compliant nature railing at the way of things, I guess.

I used to tell my parents I was going to ascend not die, and I reassured them that this was in fact a very biblically correct possibility. Of course I had to make sure I was eligible for the rapture option, so I needed to tow the line.

At school there were the energies of twelve hundred fellow pupils to integrate, and at home there was endless worry and concern about my father's blood sugar levels and general health. The morning and just before supper ritual was quite the ceremony. I often asked to do the honors. Like all type one diabetics, my father had to frequently monitor his inner sweetness. It was always a great relief to me, when the tablet fizzing in a small sample of his urine turned blue. I got inwardly alarmed when I saw it go a hideous green or gunk orange. It used to mean he needed to eat immediately, or else go and lie down, depending on the read.

At church I would sometimes hear the rustling of the glucose tablets in his pocket when the blood sugars were plummeting. I knew we would likely not be held up with too much chat after the service on that particular occasion. Good. Lunch would be quicker today. My father's diabetes was like a thermostat for my well being. When Dad was okay, all was well in the world. If something was up with Dad, the security bubble was under threat. Dad's words were pretty much gospel to me. His voice was soothing, reassuring, and edifying. If a father were a demonstration of God's love for us, my father got the A grade. But his health concerns became mine, and much of the time I was concerned I too would develop diabetes. I used to get very worried if I had extra thirst or ran to the toilet once too often. I used to secretly check my own urine, and it was equally a great relief to see that fizzy tablet turn a deep dark blue, the color of my eyes.

On first arrival at Stirling, what sealed the deal for me was a random chance comment by the English professor doing a meet and greet for my father and I. This professor was eloquently selling the benefits and wonders of the English courses, and Dad was asking many pointed questions. The professor probably was sensing some of my own reticence and discomfort, and asked my father was he attending, or was I? This was a bit harsh and rude. But what he said next was one of those synchronous comments that make your hairs stand on end. On describing the stronger points of the semester system, the professor said it was all designed to facilitate visits for "Mr Wonderful from Canada," as the structure exactly correlated with the education system across the Atlantic. *OMG? How could this man have known?* I had literally earlier that year fallen for a Canadian artist at the L'Abri study centre in Hampshire.

At L'Abri I spent much of my gap year studying, cleaning, baking and communing with like minded people. I had quite an active row of suitors lining up. My Christian boyfriend, rugby playing Phil, was finally getting fed up with me after a year and a half. He had not wanted me to accept my place at Stirling University for the following year. It was so far away from Welwyn Garden City where he was a budding business IT type. I think he had marriage and family life in mind for the long term. We were informally engaged for a time. But really I knew my destiny involved a more elaborate path than anything quite so straightforward and sensible. Phil threw in the towel when I went to L'Abri, and started to get diverted by all sorts of interesting people.

L'Abri was an all embracing Christian community set up originally in Switzerland by Dr. Francis Schaeffer, a fundamentalist Christian theologian. The idea of his communities in Switzerland, Hampshire and USA is to 'shelter' those who need time out, and inspire those who are searching for life's deeper meaning. I was in my element, aside from the dubious daily tasks and chores. I enjoyed the study of cults, multiple religions, and Christian theology. It really set me up for my university career, and gave me independent study skills, as well as original angles on ancient questions.

I met some wonderful people from all over the world in this year out before university. It opened my eyes, and expanded my horizons. I also realized I was not emotionally fulfilled, nor was I in the right relationship. The time had come to spread my wings. Phil returned all my photos with a flourish, along with a statement, that he "did not want to now know the real me." He promptly took my cousin to the cinema instead. Oh well.

Before Mr Wonderful from Canada arrived, I had been romantically linked with a much older artist called John from Aberystwyth for a few weeks. There were discrete smooching sessions in the small lean to kitchenette upstairs and copious hand-holding moments, despite disapproving glances, frowns and whispers in corridors. I was eighteen, he was thirty one. John had a very long back, big warm hands, ice blue eyes, and a big nose. He wore baggy dark blue jumpers, and a rather maudlin expression on his face. I am not quite sure what need he fulfilled in me. It was one of those things where a guy needs solace and healing, because basically he is still in love with someone else. In this case, the someone else was called Pearl. All I got out of this fine romance, were some dreamy moments; a coach ride to Aberystwyth; a steamy movie viewing, during which John watched my reactions somewhat creepily; and an assurance that I had healing hands Not as bad as it sounds, I promise. I was able to lift his Pearl-induced headaches is all.

I was quite emotionally at sea on my arrival in Scotland for two reasons. One, I was about to be four hundred miles away from the safety and security of home; and two, I was really feeling the separation from my good friend Jim, with whom I had really bonded. This random comment of the professor's was enough to give me a slither of hope that Jim would return realizing the error of his ways.

In the end, Jim just sent some thought provoking poems, and his really annoying younger brother Phillip. The poems he sent showed an emotional connection, and one in particular, called, *What A Tragic Night It Turned Out To Be*, revealed that Jim had felt a surge of feeling, but too late. Typical. The too little, too late thing, began to set a precedent for much that was to come. At that point I was upset rather than jaded. Well at least he acknowledged the moment, was the thought I consoled myself with.

Phillip, Jim's brother, was over on a European jaunt for his rite of passage gap year. Jim had assured him I was a marvelous tour guide. Yes, I had shown Jim and his other brother Dave around Wales on a whirlwind notion, which had worked brilliantly well. It was invigorating, enlivening, and captivating for all, including the green VW Beetle which had been our trusty steed. The only embarrassing low points had been Jim stumbling upon me, white trousers down around my ankles, trying to have a discrete pee around the back of a church we were investigating. The night we all shared a tent was not much more conducive. Jim slept affectionately, with his finger placed on my head to stake a claim. But it really was quite pathetic in terms of permitted physical contact. With his larger, thicker set, snoring brother Dave alongside us, things were not about to get frisky any time soon.

I was overall annoyed and hurt by Jim, so I was not about to repeat such hospitality for yet another brother, when I was still pained by his lack of action. He had sent lame attempts to respond to my feelings in the poem. But that really did not cut the mustard. He was still engaged to his girlfriend, and about to be married. His younger brother Phillip could feel the full wrath of my anger instead. I was not going to play ball with Jim's inadequate, and somewhat insensitive fob offs.

The joke really was on me. There was no getting away from it. The universe had timed the tutor's pointed comment to perfection. In fact if not for this comment, I had been on the brink of asking my father to take me back to Somerset. If not for this uncanny professor, I would not have stayed in Stirling a moment longer. The Spirit world was clearly up to something, and exercising its right to spin a bit of dark humor at my expense.

Sometimes guidance like this can happen to ensure we stay in the right place, and fulfill the correct destiny path. It can be the smallest inconsequential moments which change the course of our choices. Or it can be a much more significant signal. The upshot is the same.

We need to keep our ear to the ground, respond, and listen.

Jim from Canada had been particularly captivating, and interesting to me. He had a similar energy to my father, and the same intelligent conversational ability, and artistic integrity. He was a professional artist over from Toronto, taking time out from his relationship. He needed to decide what to do with his life, including whether or not to make the huge decision to marry his girl friend. Clearly I helped him to do just that. Because, despite numerous twilight walks down flowery Hampshire laneways, and deep conversations into the night, Jim went ahead and fixed a date to marry on return to his home country.

One evening I had found him sketching two girls, a blonde and a brunette, as if he was trying to make up his mind, and the answer lay in his pencil. Seemingly it *did*. I lost out to a brunette, something which was to set a precedent for the times ahead. In a bid to explain himself, Jim told me he looked on me as a sister. One who helped him solidify his feelings for his girlfriend. He also was deeply grateful for my company, and the way I had helped him sort out many of his spiritual life dilemmas.

Glad to be of service Sir!

The whole Jim thing gave me a big demonstration of how things were going to roll for me. It showed me clearly, that however disappointed I turned out to be, I still had faith in life, the universe and God, to steer me in the right direction using signs, signals, and synchronicity. That a random comment from a professor was enough to commit me to a preordained course of action, should have made me wonder. Instead, it filled me with awe at how life works in uncertain moments; revealing how the smallest thread, can in fact be the most significant lead. It pays to be alert, willing and responsive, even when things are not going our way.

THE PATH TO FREEDOM IS ILLUMINATED
BY THE BRIDGES YOU HAVE BURNED,
ADORNED BY THE TIES YOU HAVE CUT,
AND CLEARED B Y THE DRAMA YOU HAVE
LEFT BEHIND. LET GO. BE FREE.
STEVE MARABOLI

CHAPTER THREE
Wolf In Sheep's Clothing

E ternity changes things. We can see beyond the veil, and time is all ONE. Space and time dissipate into a merged union of completion. All is present, and everything is correct.

Anything goes in this continuum, so you might as well live as if you have the perspective of eternity now. This was my life philosophy anyway, and the energy I encapsulated as a child certainly was a demonstration.

If being present, open and responsive to guidance, and clues in the moment equates to "chasing rainbows" in the consciousness of muggledom, then so be it. I am all in. All I know is that life is too short not to feel your way through it without second guessing every decision. If following the heart is chasing rainbows, then let the dance begin.

Ingrid was petite, blonde, German, germane, and a decade older than myself. But we instantly connected at Stirling University, and became great friends. She taught me how to stay trim by stir-frying carrots in lemon juice, with a touch of sugar. I must say I ate that rather a lot in the first term; along with the prerequisite student diet of pot noodle, and intermittent attempts at canteen food.

I once saw Pete coming out of Ingrid's room at a strangely unexpected hour. So that got me thinking. But there was an innocence about me at that stage, so I did not make any obvious enquiries, and parked any suspicion or retort. Usually I found a wry, curious, quizzical smile was enough in such circumstances. Perhaps I would have got further with the birds and the bees, if I had been more dramatic, feisty and determined in my dealings. But at that point, yes I was the well behaved Christian girl, who saw the best in everybody, and believed that every situation was redeemable, even when it was possibly dubious.

I probably fell between two stools with many things to be honest. For some reason, Old Testament lecturer John Drane had found me very atypical of someone who should be attending a University Christian Union meeting. When he targeted me as a very unlikely member I retorted, "there are two sorts of Christian: open and closed. And I'm the first sort!"

I guess he might have sensed a pagan, wiccan type nature connection, inherent in my energy field. But it just goes to show, you should not judge someone on appearances. He was right though, I did not particularly relish those meetings. Even so, I showed willing, and was very useful ferrying people to and fro the local Baptist church on Sundays in my beat-up white Morris 1100.

I had driven all the way up from Bristol in that car with Ingrid and Pete following the first mid-term break. It was bought from an old school mate Colin Leaker, who had attempted to romance me in the sixth form common room by playing *Stairway to Heaven* by Led Zeppelin on a loop. That did not work. But the car sort of did. The irony did not escape me when, as we approached Stirling, after four hundred miles of motorway, and eight hours of driving, the brakes failed. On another such journey, this time with my brother Simon, the clutch gave out at Carlisle. The car, the universe and Colin were probably trying to tell me something. In the first instance, I had to gingerly hand-brake my way back to campus. In the second, we arrived in style on a pick-up truck, car incapacitated in full rescue mode.

The back street garage Steering and Suspension rectified my issues, on both occasions. But when I finally had to scrap the car for ten pounds, I got the point. That vehicle was not fit for long journeys. It was a run-around to enable me locally, and I had killed it prematurely by demanding too much of it. Again, the symbolism: not lost.

Morrissey, the white Morris, not only failed me on a couple of occasions, it also rescued me in some serious moments too. I had been feeling left out and isolated in Stirling, most especially since the boyfriend John I had hooked up with in second semester, was proving challenging to say the least.

When I had first phoned my father about John, probably somewhat fretfully, Dad had said, "do choose not to fall in love with the guy. You do not have to go there."

Easier said than done, I thought.

Does one choose who to fall in love with? Is it really all that contrived and deliberate? I did not think so. But this pragmatic Aquarian approach of my father's raised all sorts of doubts in my mind.

My father's paternal instincts were clearly very good as I was soon reminded. Well, he was his mother's son after all. Regardless, I felt compelled to see where I got to with this darkly dangerous person who had crossed my path.

My father is a highly intelligent ex medical officer, writer and counselor, son of my intuitive Scorpio Nan, whom my grandpa affectionately called a white witch. My father has instincts, wisdom, and advice, which we all ignore at our peril. With the John situation, I thought it was time to take matters into my own hands and be a bit more independent. Even though I knew my father always tended to be right, I went ahead with John anyway; just to see what would happen. I was committed to chasing those rainbows, wherever they would lead. So in my loneliness, I was intrigued enough to give it a whirl.

John had caught my eye with the sexy scar over his lip, wry grin, beautiful but troubled green-brown eyes, a certain shyness and his uncanny resemblance to the lead singer of U2, on a good day. He was also Irish, crazy, and highly intelligent. A pretty lethal combination. A black belt karate expert, born and bred in Derry, John seemed to take the Northern Irish troubles out on me in ways I have not seen before, nor since.

We had meet in the smoky, den of iniquity on campus which went by the name of The Grange. It had one slot machine, on which I once won the jackpot of twenty-five pounds, a darts room, and some lucky students had their accommodations above the dance room. Not sure much work would have been done in *that* environment. I remember John being amused at some slim, red haired, pole-dancing type, who was touching herself dancing in front of him. God knows why, he gave the short blonde haired sweet Christian girl the option on his company instead.

Our first date had been to a U2 gig in Glasgow. I was captivated by the bright blue eyes, and energy of the singer Bono. His cocky confidence, Christian faith, and musicality, were a winning combination for me. But I had alongside me, what I thought was a handsome enough consolation prize, if not booby prize. John had a chance to prove he was *Even Better Than The Real Thing*. Besides I was not a groupie, I simply liked my music, and anyone who appeared to have the same world beliefs, and approach to life as me, was pretty compelling for reasons other than the obvious.

I had been given a U2 single for my eighteenth birthday, called *Fire*. I did not quite get what all the fuss was about. I knew they were a Christian Rock Band from Dublin, and that there was quite a buzz about them. My brother, a punk rock connoisseur actually played this band's music. So the fact that U2 wafted out of his bedroom, along with Magazine, Joy Division, The Stranglers and Killing Joke, said something about them.

Simon, my brother, was a cool, rebellious, handsome Christian lad. A Taurus like Bono, he looked vaguely like him too, with his pale blue eyes, and enigmatic middle distance stare. Bono actually said to me years later that my brother "sounded cool." Yes, he actually was. And. Still. Is.

A doctor in The Scottish Highlands for quite some time, Simon shaved his head, and did his rounds on his motor bike, sporting his carefully chosen tattoos. Currently, he drives around Edinburgh in a blue hot rod, and works in medical management of anti biotic prescriptions, for the Scottish Government. Back in the day, Simon spiked his red titian hair with sugar for maximum effect, and then headed off to church in holey green jumpers, and bondage trousers. He drove a blue pickup truck with souped-up engine, which on purchase he immediately took apart, so that he could understand how the engine worked. As far as I know, the Hot Rod has not yet met the same fate, but anything is possible.

Yes, Bono was right; Simon *is* cool!

Christian Rock back in the eighties, was usually bland, sickly sweet, and insipid without a beat. These live wires from Dublin, called U2, seemed to know how to channel something from the great beyond. They were magical and captivating. Their live show convinced me of that. Never mind the disc I had been given for my coming of age birthday, here was something I could really relate to.

John turned out to be nothing like Bono. He was a wolf in sheep's clothing. Paranoid, edgy, demanding, leaving me incredulous on more than one occasion with his actions and behavior. I think I was in shock if truth be told. I had left a loving home and family, and suddenly life in the cruel outside world had got very difficult. I needed stability and good friends, and the universe had connected with me the tumultuous whirlwind which was John. Great.

Probably those who met him, would not understand or compute my experience of him. He was on the surface funny, brilliant and good looking, and wrote a column for the local newspaper. What was not to like?

The John drama became was one of those scenarios, where what went on behind closed doors belied the appearance of the thing. We were two handsome people in the prime of life, yet emotionally I felt bewilderment and chaos churning up inside me. I was in essence being emotionally abused, and kept on my toes in a bid to keep his favor. God knows how a well-balanced Christian girl, with oodles of love and support even got into such a situation. But God knows I did; and I needed help. Fast.

My family were visiting the area for the Easter vacation of my first year at Stirling. They were of course tucked away in some obscure hidden spot down towards the borders, which we could not find.

John and I had driven out from Stirling in the white Morris 1100, and it was getting dark. Any psychic sense of direction I had was completely failing me. Clearly John had disempowered that too, amongst other things. I was beside myself. It was snowing, the roads were treacherous, and the windscreen wipers had just broken. John was having one of his psychotic meltdowns, and I began to actually be afraid of what might happen.

The battery of the car also failed. Completely inert. Dead. And it looked like we were going to have to spend the night in some verge, on an unfriendly, potentially dangerous, stretch of road.

How was I going to start the car?

John would not have had the patience to wait for motor rescue. I had not the patience to deal with his fear inducing temper tantrum. So I prayed. I prayed for what felt like the life of me. It was something I did many times in that relationship.

Divine and angelic assistance was mine that day. Not finding my family had rubbed in my depression and isolation. John's way of being compounded it further. But, it was confirmed that I had God on my side, when push came to shove, as it quite frequently did.

My prayer was literally a matter of life or death, or so it felt to me.

Please God. Please. You can see what is going on here. Please get me out of this in one piece. And I did not just mean the present scenario of being stranded on a verge on a dark, snowy night.

The prayer was answered on the third turn of the key in the ignition. The car started. I told John I had prayed. He was having none of it. But completely against the odds, like a bolt out of the blue, a spark of life revved things up, and the engine turned over. It was the required boost to get us moving and back to campus in one piece.

Gott Sei Dank!

The prayer, and my reaction to the situation might have sounded over the top dramatic. But earlier the same day, I had nearly been flattened by a huge double-decker bus doing an incredible speed, at a really busy junction in Glasgow. I had sat motionless in the middle of the cross roads, knowing that any movement could well have been fatal. The bus missed me on the driver's side with two inches to spare. So I was primed to be a bit sensitive. This, plus John's increasingly antagonistic disposition, and I think I was justified to call on divine intervention in that moment.

Things were looking increasingly dark and challenging for me. And although I was looked after in moments such as these, it was difficult not to also resent my situation a little. In all things I was doing my best. Even despite a descending depression, largely thanks to

John's incredible behavior. I still got good grades and performed well in all university activities; and as my mother said at the time. "If you can do all this without trying or thinking much, look at what you might achieve when fully engaged."

My parents did not really know what I was struggling with, or why things had all gone so peculiar. I kept it all very much to myself most of the time. I was biding my time, and waiting to find a suitable way out. I needed a way to strengthen inside, and gather my resources to leave John. He had unfortunately become a make shift family, along with his circle of friends. But things definitely had to change, or I probably would not come out of this alive.

On the upside, John was the person who introduced me to Edinburgh, a place I really came to love and enjoy on my own terms. John had moved there on graduation, and although I enjoyed the ambience and charm of the city, I also got a semblance of separation, still having room 333 to retreat to, and my university degree to complete.

Being locked in John's pokey bathroom on Albion Terrace, in full view of Arthur's Seat, on my twenty first birthday, was really the last straw. I built my escape plan. I needed to retrieve Archie the cockatiel, and get the hell out of there.

Archie liked to swoop into a pan of boiling potatoes as a kind of sport. God knows how he did not boil his feet in the process, but he managed to get his pieces of potato using his talons, and extended reach. John used to like teasing him with a broom handle, a game which probably amounted to stress for the bird, and amusement for John.

I packed all my belongings up and hid under the stairs in the main stairway, until I ascertained it was safe to leave there for good. I somehow managed to navigate the train platforms at Waverley Station, with a bird in a cage, several items of luggage, and a highly charged emotional state. I did not know it then, but John was clearly a sociopath. I actually think he had no clue that what he was doing was wrong. His behavior was totally justified in his own head. I was after all a live wire, totally uncontrollable and a liability, if not a complete danger to myself. How is *that* for gas-lighting? (Gas-lighting is a sinister manipulation utilized by narcissists to attempt to undermine their victims, inspiring them to question their own judgment and sanity).

One time I had arranged to meet my brother, and his girlfriend Caroline, in Princes Street Gardens, with John in tow. John had throughout that morning been typically abusive, and active in whatever the current torture was designed to make me cry. I am sure Simon must have noticed my distress, but apparently not. I could not give a damn clue to him about the danger I was in, whether real or imagined. I felt so relieved to see my lovely brother and his wonderful girlfriend. But I must have seemed stilted and guarded. Again apparently not. I was also a better actress than I had realized, clearly. It just goes to show how the scourge of domestic abuse can be so silent and deadly. There were times I felt in fear of my life. I was at this guy's mercy. Even amongst friends or family, I had no way out, or means to tell. I was totally under a cloud and controlled by this person.

Clearly, being in this situation, makes a woman or young girl vulnerable. One might think it is so easy to walk away. Trust me, it is not. Where you are economically or emotionally dependent, there is no easy way out. Real help can seem miles away, even if it is in the next room, or next door, or even the *same* room. Having been through this experience, I never plan to repeat it, and I never ever will. Any whiff of anything similar and I would walk, very, quickly, away. I urge all women suffering in this way to have the courage to reach out to someone. Even if feels like the world is going to end if you take action. *Do* so. *Tell* someone. Do not suffer in silence. There are safe houses. There are people who will take you in. Report the person, and get the hell away. Get help.

I brought Archie back to room 333, and shortly after, as if by magic, a Java Sparrow, flew in through my window to complete the unit. Arnold, my blue Budgie, had been decapitated in the triangular metallic spring door, of John's community flat on campus. But Archie was a survivor, and with Finch, he now comprised my family, who were feathered.

Finch, obtusely named in that he was a sparrow, was a character. He used to play dead if you held him extended in your hand. He would just lie there motionless for minutes at a time; only coming alive if you wrapped your hand around him. Simple pleasures. I am not sure who taught him this circus trick. But he performed it like a charm, right on cue.

This was probably the beginning of my use of animals to build a sense of belonging. I had been known when younger to breed frogs in a bucket in my bedroom, and bring home litters of kittens, because I could not decide on just one. I had had a rabbit named Flopsy, and a guinea pig named Patch. I was in the Animal Defenders, linked to the *Royal Society for the Prevention of Cruelty to Animals*, and loved all things feathered, furry and hairy.

As humans were proving increasingly problematic, and uncooperative, animals proved a valuable, rewarding connection for me. I had always loved them as a child, but as an adult, they began to have a role of support, and allowed me to express my nurturing side.

From the inside out, I understood what it was like to be a woman who loves too much. The experience with John, gave me an armory of resources. A depth of understanding to help me reach women in the same situation. This is such a difficult situation to relay, unless you have been embroiled in it yourself. Anyone who has experienced it, will not tolerate judgment or pontification from those who do not understand. You really have to have been through it to totally *get* the dynamics.

Through pacing myself, I strengthened and detached from what had become an incredibly dysfunctional, co-dependent relationship. In my own time, I extricated myself from the emotional web I was caught in. I would say, no harm done. But clearly this was not the case. My former best friend Eki, whose job I took as a chef at Lilligs the German restaurant on Victoria Street, had quickly noticed the tell-tale frightened rabbit look in my eyes, as we bonded over sauerkraut, bratwurst, and schnitzels.

Eki knew she had to step in, and help a girl who was presenting as vulnerable, scared, and at the mercy of a boyfriend, who probably did not even know consciously, that he was mistreating and terrorizing her. This she did, and a valuable sisterly bond was created between us, which ran through many years. I was family to her; and she, along with her daughter Emi, were support and family to me.

On graduation from Stirling University, I relocated permanently to Edinburgh. Stupidly, this involved sharing a dingy basement apartment with John, and two other Stirling graduates, Northern Irish Colin, and Ron. This was a much better domestic situation than the isolation I had felt in Albion Terrace. John was also initially better behaved. It was an odd arrangement though. I did not have a bedroom, and slept on the floor in John's room. My stuff was kept under the stairs in a damp, dusty, dingy cupboard. Needless to say this set up was completely ill-advised. But I did not have the means to get my own place. At least the presence of Ron and Colin made me feel a little safer. I recall Colin even banging on the door one night, when he heard the commotion of John threatening to pour water all over me as I slept. In fact, I guess he must have already drenched me, and woken me, since Colin responded to the noise of my protestations. The point is, I was minding my own business. I cannot even remember why John did these things half the time. Clearly something had fired his vivid imagination and paranoia again. We did not answer the door to Colin; but I noted someone had finally heard me. Finally, a male of the species, noting an injustice, had stepped up, and attempted an intervention. Something was not right here, and Colin was brave enough to call it. But still, I did not tell anyone, or talk about it, or report it.

There was no sex between John and I. In fact, the whole relationship had been devoid of it, with the exception of a real push on his part to steal my virginity on my return after a summer break. That did not work out well. He did not know what he was doing. He was probably a virgin himself, if truth be told. In fact he was a bit rough. There was an incident in my room, which drew blood. I phoned my father in distress and he reassured me. But hmm. Not much gentle romance was going on, that is for sure. My poor father. Having to deal with all this drama four hundred miles away, cannot have been easy.

John laughed cynically after the act. Hardly the stuff dreams were made of I thought. There were no hugs, no kissing, no affection, no nothing. Really thereafter, the whole thing descended into a power play. Even the minimal physical encounters were about control.

One time I had been doing John's laundry, and one of his disgusting brown towels with cream trim got mislaid. I was frantic, knowing that he would throw all kinds of accusatory bull shit at me. I kept going back down to the launderette to see if it had reappeared. This suspicious behavior was duly noted by John, and he immediately started to bully me for flirting with someone, whose existence I was not even aware of. Clearly he had noticed a guy called Paul looking at me. Clearly I had not. When John finally pointed him out to me, I was incredulous: "Not even my type. Duh!"

It just goes to show the measure to which I was intimidated. In anger and frustration at his behavior, I ran out of his apartment, and aggressively bashed in the fire alarm, breaking its glass all over the stairway.

Boy, that was loud and effective!

In super quick time, the Stirling Fire Brigade appeared, and I felt incredibly awkward at having caused such a commotion. I thought I had better reassure them there was actually no fire, for safety's sake. The whole building had been evacuated, and everyone was out there shivering in nightclothes.

Oops!

I dithered because of the possible consequences. But clearly I had been irresponsible, and needed to sort this. So I found the chief, and confessed my misdemeanor. Thankfully he had mercy. I apologized, explaining that I was being bullied, and to please not tell anyone why I had done this. He honored me in my desperation, and did not press charges or report me. He actually was incredulous, not that I had done the deed, but that I had told him about it. He observed that it was, "most unusual that I would confess such a thing." Ironically I seemed to impress him, and he clearly had sympathy for my plight.

Eki obviously felt the same concern. John's intimidations had taken a darker turn by this time. He would threaten to rip my nicest things. My books, clothes, photographs, valuables, indeed anything that I *liked*, were all under threat and at the mercy of John's volatile temper. I think he sensed my attraction to Harry Horse, the front man of Swamptrash, which I do confess was real. All the same, it was none of his business really. We were not together by this point, and still he was trying to dictate to me with his bullying. I am not even sure what prompted all this. I was hardly a difficult person to get along with. In fact I was most obliging, amenable, and a good support to my friends and those that loved me.

Clearly there was some kind of abuse in John's past, which was triggered by the slightest flicker of independence in me. I am not sure the psychological reason for this. But it was horribly real, and intimidating to the extreme. John made mention once of an uncle who used to beat him on his lower back. Beyond this, I could not hazard a guess about what prompted his behavior. I certainly did nothing at all to warrant it or provoke it.

Harry was dark, gothic, and intriguing. Real name Richard Horne, He had a posh English accent in reality. But at any given opportunity Harry faked an Southern American drawl, as if he had stepped straight out of the swamp. He was something of a genius. A very talented artist, who did pen and ink political satire cartoons for the main Scottish newspapers. I commissioned him to do a *City of Ghosts* pictorial map for my brother's first wedding. The result was stunning. It was supposed to be a first edition exclusive. Harry being Harry printed copies and sold them on the streets of Edinburgh. The passing tourists were pleased, I was not. But I understood his entrepreneurial streak had to take advantage where it could.

Being a commercial artist was not an easy way to pay the bills. Harry did well to get the gig at *The Scotsman*, and his cartoons of Margaret Thatcher were merciless. Harry called using his pen and ink quill to vilify politicians the "last freedom" he had in the midst of the corruption of Margaret Thatcher's Britain. His delight was to be able to use artistic expression as a weapon against the tyrant in charge: "it is my pinprick in her backside, if you like," said Harry on the television show about his work called *Halfway To Paradise*.

In the end I was pleased to have given him the idea of a pictorial pen and ink map of Edinburgh. It was a good money spinner for him. One of Harry's gripes was that, despite his many talents, he was not making the money he potentially could. In reality, Harry was the son of quite a wealthy English family who lived in the Midlands, somewhere near Rugby. But we will not dwell on that as it compromises his persona. The demeanor of struggling artist wore well on him. He could tread the boards of the next offered stage, earn a crust performing for gratuities at The Mound, or sell his "pen and inks," rolled in scrolls, down in The Grassmarket. Edinburgh needed characters like Harry. He suited the bohemian, haunted, brooding energy of the city. So did I, but in a different way.

Harry was exotic with long wavy hair, tall and melting brown eyes.

I was sold. He totally captivated me. I am not quite sure why in retrospect. But at the time he was very alluring. Dangerous, mysterious, fairly psychic and intuitive, and very musical too. He took Edinburgh by storm with his Cajun band Swamptrash. Their gigs were a complete hoe down. A maelstrom of whirling dervish energy. The magic was palpable. The music scene in Edinburgh at this time was just what I needed. I felt as if I had come alive once again. The music had started to save me. It was a trend that was surely set to develop further, as the musicians and their notes, lit the way ahead.

Needless to say the thing with Harry was somewhat unrequited. It was sort of awkward whenever we were in each others' company. Nothing was going to happen. I think we were both a bit too reserved and English, ironically. I liked him a lot and he knew it. There was only one time I felt he let his guard down, and that was when he walked by the public launderette on the main cobbled street of Stockbridge.

Stockbridge was the trendy, bohemian down town part of Edinburgh, between Princes Street and Leith. All the artists and musicians congregated in various apartments. It was a magical and vibrant community. Not as historic as the haunted old town up by The Castle. But certainly atmospheric and compelling in its own way.

Harry's eyes met mine.

Woah! Okaaaay.

But *no*, we were not in business. Nor were we ever going to be. Harry's very Scottish girl friends were always in the way. Kimberley, a gothic brunette, was a bit of a nightmare. She was openly jealous, and sometimes deliberately vindictive towards me. She turned down a conciliatory kitten I bought her to compensate for her dead cat, who just got run over. I was being kind, and obviously naive, considering her behavior towards me. Not surprisingly I was left "holding the baby," as Harry so aptly put it.

Travesty the cat, astutely named by my mother, then had to travel to Bristol with me on the train, to be homed unceremoniously with friends of my parents in Portishead. I could not really manage two cats. Mellish, my black and white cat, who actually thought he was a dog, was profoundly jealous. So Travesty was not destined to live with me in Scotland. I had clearly been somewhat stupid to think I could replace one dead cat with another random live one.

On reflection, I was well protected regarding Harry. He was under the skin quite prickly and odd. I often used to wonder if he was concealing that he was gay, but there was never any rumor, let alone proof or admission that he was. He was just "British," which in itself lends itself to some ambiguity; especially in the artistic communities, where eyeliner, tight pants, and feminine gestures were pretty much the norm amongst glam rock devotees.

Harry's genius left him open to much torment. He was complex and brooding, and never really seemed that happy. Years later in a looking back over my shoulder moment, I looked him up on line, and found that he had relocated to Shetland with the beautiful Mandy. Mandy was the softly spoken Shetlander who had artfully captured Harry's heart after Kimberley slopped off into the shadows. Mandy was luminous and ethereal, and quite frankly I was no competition. Harry clearly preferred the dark, sultry brunette look. So I needed to find someone who liked blondes as this was becoming a bit of a habit.

In my next life, I have decided to definitely come back as a brunette. I may actually have a more straightforward time of it. Being blonde was obviously proving to be challenging. I think people expected me not to have an opinion or a brain. I was blonde; so what else did I do? Time and again, it really seemed like I was victim to my blondeness. I am exaggerating of course. But the men I was attracted to, definitely all settled for, or were already with, women of a more dusky hue. I was the danger zone. Blonde and carefree, and a whole lot of trouble.

I obviously need to make better use of that brunette wig.

On trying out said wig, one time in Dublin, Bono had looked visibly shaken and panicked, that I might have dyed my blonde hair a rich brown red. While his wife graciously said it suited me, Bono looked relieved when I reassured him it was a wig I donned from time to time. "You little minx," he said, doubtless ironically. But that experiment was interesting, and showed me that at least one person in my circle liked the blonde hair.

Graham, the dish washing kitchen assistant who took ballet classes, also seemed to like blondes. He enticed susceptible girlies with his cheese sandwiches. Of course, the red leg warmers, and dance lessons should have sent alarm bells ringing. But for some reason I missed this red flag which surely was as bright as his dancing gear.

Graham probably hated women. He was troubled, smoked pot, slept with his sister's friends, and put his fist through windows. My hunch was that he had a background of abuse, for he was certainly pretty abusive. Bob, the chef had warned me in his Christmas card to "watch out Graham, and his beguiling cheese sandwiches."

Of course I did not listen, and chased this tarnished rainbow for a wasted few months. No, I did not join in the smoking. Everyone around me smoked, I did not. However, I did stupidly spend way too much time trying to help and settle this guy. Graham, was potentially good company. An off-beat handsome chap. But there was an intrinsic sense of humor failure, a screw loose, and a tangible darkness within his energy field. He was a foppish private school type, with a permanent frown, restless pale blue eyes, and his mouth in repose resembled, for want of a better way to put it, a cat's bottom.

Eventually, Graham announced himself to be gay, which explained everything. A couple of years down the road, and we saw him setting up home with some guy, sporting a defiant grin, and sneering glare from those menacing baby blues. Problem solved.

Thankfully, I had not got too involved with Graham. He seemed to think he stole my virginity, or my "cherry" as he called it. He did not. But I let him think that he had. Psycho John had had that dubious privilege. But really what was new? Here was just another kind of emotional abuse I had stumbled upon. Not as intimidating as John's manipulations, but still somewhat disturbing. The signs were all there in retrospect, but much more subtle this time; easily missed in other words. As with all things we meet along the way, it is easy to be wise after the event. We do what we do, and although our life experiences shape us. They are not who we are.

As the few months of the Graham interlude had progressed, it was easy to see that he was indeed as f*cked up, as he said he was. He also enjoyed getting f*cked up, even more than talking about it.

Graham's most annoying trait was to say that something was "important" when he thought he was making a valid point. Us "girlies" were supposed to ponder what was "important," and make sure we understood it. Whatever "it" was I was never quite sure. But that was my inherent failing apparently. I remember literally wracking my brains lying awake at night trying to understand this guy. It really was a pointless exercise.

On the few occasions we had sex, I was paranoid about getting pregnant. I enjoyed the intimacy. But really that would have been the worst mistake of my life, and I knew it. After a session, in which he experimented on me, rather than connected with me, I would jump into the tub, and purge all trace of him from my being. This Mermaid was not about to be caught off guard by this crazy fellow. On the up side, Graham had a wickedly appealing laugh, and was compelling enough in his perversity. He stirred up controversy and provided much food for thought. But overall the experience was very uncomfortable, and nothing whatsoever to do with love.

Of course we were all falling foul of a basic gas-lighting attempt. Graham was a novice at manipulation, except with those who fell for his surface charm. It was difficult to pinpoint exactly what his appeal was. He was not classically good looking. He was a spotty youth really if you objectified him. An angry young man, who was trying to process his karma and his bull shit, whilst dragging others along with him. He did have something alluring in his energy, and intensity, but his contrived grip then fed on those who had complied. Some kind of vampire, he fed on people's distress and confusion, because of his own need for attention. He was probably reeling from mother issues, and not being truly understood. I have no doubt he was a bit of a magician too, a necromancer from another life time, who we all would have done well not to meet in this one. He was a challenge; but then all narcissists are.

Graham probably needed a course of medication, counseling, and a spell in the army. Instead he prayed on the vulnerable, and projected his issues onto whoever would listen. His sister Kathy was fun and cool. But she had her work cut out dealing with him. I do not think he did her any favors regarding her own equilibrium either. He tried to be everyone's psychologist, priding himself on being some kind of Charles Manson figure. He claimed to be able to plummet your psychological depths and inadequacies. But really, he was trying to work out his own.

I was ironically named "Dolly." Eki and Colin from Lilligs, had christened me "Dolly" when they rescued me. Graham and his harem then proceeded to twist what had been meant as a term of endearment, into a term of torture. Graham's ex girlfriend, an intermittent double-breasted comfort cushion for him, had the nerve to write a poem about Dolly Daydream and her cat.

"Dolly" was apparently lost, lonely, pathetic, weak, broken etc. I actually was *not*. But this group of young upstarts projected all of their drama and pretention onto me, to the point when it began to be undermining. I allowed it; more fool me. It was a very negative situation. I was privy to what was going on, could still objectify it and distance myself. But it is amazing what boredom and loneliness will do to a person. The Graham saga also shows that groups of people tapping into the same warped energy field, are just as detrimental as the individuals who endeavor to control things. There is not always safety in numbers.

The whole thing was a regressive nightmare, which never should have happened. I was better than all of this. It was also impossible not to wonder what I had done to deserve it. I began to think everyone in Scotland was less than *compos mentis*. It was hugely detrimental, and a complete waste of time, to hope for anything sensible from a group of immature kids, who were actually many years younger than myself. I was late twenties, going on thirty six, and Graham was twenty three. The girls were younger still. Instead of going for older guys, I was starting to choose the toy boy route. But really, I was still too young for that. So I made a quick exit left, when I realized the depths of Graham's depravity, and the extent of his experimentation with people's emotions. I hope him and his boyfriend are very happy in their pokey flat down in Leith. I am really not sure what dish his karma latterly served up. But I bet it was juicy and well deserved.

My brother and sister stumbled across their own lessons in abuse down in Sheffield at around the same time. Simon, Rache, and their circle of friends all became heavily involved in NOS, aka, the *Nine O' Clock Service*. They acted in predictable Hurding left-field fashion, and chose to attend this church service; which was to all intents and purposes a nightclub, hosted by a wannabe rock star.

The worship in NOS communion services was generally quite awe-inspiring. Here was a vibrant young Christian community led by an inspiring charismatic leader. The energy and spirit of the project was fresh and innovative, and the air was thick with excitement and expectation. When I visited a service in Sheffield, I certainly experienced the tangible and magical feeling first hand. It was not a typical church service, that is for sure. Here was something different for young people who wanted to make a difference.

The emerging social consciousness of this group was applied in practical ways to benefit the broader community; and the church's ethos was to actively reach out evangelically, as well as to help those in need. The intentions were all good.

What then unfolded over time was nothing short of tragic. It all became a bit of a mess. Some years later, a horrible truth emerged that a number of people, mainly young women, had been abused and taken advantage of by the ordained vicar Chris Brain, who my brother came to call Voldemort. This was painful to many, and many are still hurting to this day because of this man's actions. Yes, it was all a long time ago now. But abuse of any kind does not always get processed easily; particularly not when exercised by someone you are supposed to be able to trust. Are some things unforgiveable? If so these acts of treachery may have come close. They certainly did nothing to instill confidence in people spouting the word of God in hypocritical fashion. In a similar way to the scandals inherent, and subsequently exposed, in the heart of the Catholic Church, this sad reality damaged many people.

My sister Rachel, who had studied History of Art at Manchester University, had moved to Sheffield to be near Simon and his young family. Rache in her teens was "Rache H, famous fashion designer of the future," to quote her art teacher. Rache H, was prone to bringing out the natural colors in her hair using various dramatic hair dyes. A natural brunette, her coloring ranged from bright red, through purple, sometimes black, other times blonde streaked. Rache was artistic like her siblings, and liked alternative music, also like her siblings. She chose to do her High School years some distance away in Bristol, because she did not want to hang out with the "false nail brigade" in Portishead.

My brother and I cannot have minded the "townie" Kardashians of Portishead quite so much, as we both finished up our designated terms at Gordano, the local comprehensive school. Thanks to the more elite Cotham Grammar School, Rache was able to get the correct grades she needed to further her studies at University.

Gordano, named after the "arrow-shaped" valley in which it could be found, was actually a pretty good school, with an impressive array of open minded teachers. It was big for local standards, and it was easy to get lost amongst twelve hundred people, and the warren of corridors. Built in the sixties, Gordano was designed to serve the local community, and the surrounding villages in the valley. The layout of the school was complex. At the top of the ramp were the science blocks on the right, and on the left, the arts buildings housing music, art and drama. Math tended to be in the oldest part of the school, along with home economics, and languages. The sixth form was more informal than the rest of the school, which was appropriate for those preparing to graduate and go to college, or university. Found by the library, the sixth form was also near the exam rooms, computer rooms, and the staff room at the top of the vertiginous wooden slatted stairs.

I enjoyed my arts teachers Mr Hallam, Mr Porter and Mr MacDonald in particular; and Miss Plimmer, the English teacher was a sight for sore eyes, with her long red nails, peroxide blonde hair, skinny jeans, and little lap dog. But, I was somewhat of a loner at school, and often chose to take my lunch break reading up in a classroom on the first floor. Obviously a natural introvert, I hated team sports, and group activities. I only came into my own when on familiar ground up in the mountains, or playing pool with all the handsome guys in sixth form common room.

I was much more of a "boys girl", though had some good close girlfriends in the form of Ginny, Jan, Bev, and Australian Vanessa. We were the cool girls who were in it for laughs, as opposed to the bitchy girls who were in it to persecute and find fault. Vanessa and Ginny were the girls with the long blonde hair I envied as I was never allowed to grow mine long; because I had a nice neck "like Granny" apparently.

I've heard better excuses.

Jan was spectacular with her blue eye-shadow, and long nails, invariably black or blue. I was good with the lipstick, I am reliably reminded. But the darkest shade I was allowed to go with my nails was a rich chocolate brown, which made them look positively edible, or disgusting, depending on your mind-set.

I was not very forthcoming or extravert at school, though Ginny remembers my laugh. I felt very uncomfortable in morning assembly, and generally did not like crowds of school kids, or activities involving big groups. I was too sensitive, and the bombardment of the senses in these situations I did not always know how to process. This young psychic preferred to skip gym, school trips, and any hectic participation activity. I would much rather have my head in a book, or be doing my art homework, or perfecting the essay assignment. I was fine if I had something creative to engage in. But I did not like socializing except with close friends. I have always been better one-to-one. Even now I prefer a quality interaction with one person, to an overwhelming over stimulating group event. As a mutable Virgo I was variable though, and sometimes I would shine and perform well on the days my confidence peaked.

Mr Ackland our House Head Teacher had been glowingly impressed and proud, when I led a small school camp along the ridge heights of *Crib Goch*, on Mount Snowdon in Wales. There are a couple of ways up Mount Snowdon. Most of the party had chosen the slow, methodical route, *The Miner's Track*. Being my father's daughter, I chose the precarious, precipitous ridge route that is *Crib Goch*. With sheer drops on either side, this is a tricky climb, and not for the faint hearted. I am not actually sure why a school party were even attempting it. But there we were in the fog and rain, with dusk descending rapidly, without ropes or a compass.

Understandably, we were a little edgy, nervous and panicked, and feeling various degrees of discomfort. I had already done this route before, so I confidently kept my cool and took over. In respectably quick time, I guided everyone across the ridge safely. I would have been great as an extra in *The Lord of The Rings* clearly, and Bear Grylls, survival expert, would have also been proud. Thankfully no one had to drink their urine or eat rats for protein. But we did well, and I was perceived in a new light after that. It just goes to show, a kid needs just one chance to come good, and everything can change. My confidence increased, and somehow I had made the connection between home and school life. Yep, I truly *was* my father's daughter, and thereafter recognized that my private and public self, were one and the same. Life needs an integration point like this. In that moment I grew up, and became independent. Well, in theory.

All three of us Hurding kids had a penchant for risk taking, and choosing more alternative approaches to life. Brought up in the punk era, we all had spiky hair, and at one point all pretty much had the same prerequisite mullet. Mine was blonde, my brother's ginger, sorry titian; and my sister's varying degrees of brunette, red, purple, or black. We were victims to the trends just like anyone else.

We all loved our music, shared similar tastes in fashion, and painted on our walls at home. My sister splashed hers with abstract flicks of red, green, yellow and blue; my brother painted a spectacularly OCD Hot Rod with not a blurred line insight; and I painted mine bright orange, which did not quite work, so promptly pasted it over with a magazine friendly collage. Obviously my glamorous, media friendly sensibilities began in my teens. This collage was full of painted lips, high fashion, musicians, and beautiful scenes.

The music which floated out of these downstairs split level bedrooms was assorted. My mother upstairs in her kitchen could hear a curious blend of Fleetwood Mac, Elvis Costello, and The Stranglers.

When teatime came, a loud bell placed strategically at the top of the stairs, was required to drown out the music, and imprint upon our eardrums that food was served.

Sarah, Simon and Rache were all artistic, creative, smart, and generally cool. We found out retrospectively that certain family members were prone to dyslexia. My mother, brother and some of Simon's offspring were diagnosed. I most definitely was not. My wordiness, and colorful language thankfully did not have that restriction. My mathematical sensibilities however most certainly did. My dyscalculia was marginal, I think the truth is we studied some difficult mathematics subjects. I have not had a need for algebra since I marched out of those exams with a C grade.

At school I was in the top stream for all subjects, but there was a definite mismatch with the math. I managed the course work, but needed three attempts at the GSE to pass for university. Finally, I managed to make the grade, as I simultaneously studied for S level English to help boost my application for Cambridge. My father had done his medical training at Cambridge University, and I fell in love with it when he showed Phil and I around. Our school was not primed to prepare students for Oxbridge, but I was guided to see how well I could do in the entrance exams.

My friend Jan recalled being horrified that I had chosen a question *not* taught in our English class for the A level English exam. I assured her it was fine, as I had been independently studying for the Cambridge entrance exams. I had not liked the questions on the books and subjects we had covered in class, so I intuitively chose a general Shakespeare question. It worked out, and I got a B1 for English, which was a score, as Gordano did not teach the S level either.

What it showed me, was that I was a natural student, who could self teach on subjects that were of interest to me. This independence set me up nicely for the three academic degrees that were to come. I did not manage to get into Cambridge for undergraduate work, but was offered a place for postgraduate teacher training on graduation from Stirling University. I turned it down. By then, I was too deeply embroiled with all the prerequisite karma of the Celtic Countries. The Rainbow Road was leading me in a completely different direction.

My entry in the Publishing Studies year book published on graduation, stated that my ambitious life intention was to "live in Dublin to work at The Kitchen, U2's new night club; and to possibly take up PhD study at Trinity College Dublin or University College Dublin." This statement shows where my energies and ambitions were leaning. I was on a mission to call in my Irish karma, and make some soulful connections.

*BEWARE THE FALSE PROPHETS WHO COME
TO YOU IN SHEEP'S CLOTHES AND
INWARDLY ARE RAVENING WOLVES.
MATTHEW 17 V.15*

CHAPTER FOUR
Nine O' Clock Service

T he *Nine O' Clock Service* had all the hall marks of being an exciting experiment when it first began. Chris Brain, a young apparently brilliant, funky, open-minded vicar had been given charge of the young people in the congregation of St. Thomas' Church, Crookes. This innovative measure inspired many people, and NOS gained recognition for its innovative worship nationally, if not internationally, in Christian circles.

Bono told me personally that U2's *Zoo TV* light show had been inspired by NOS's use of projectors, words, and flashing images in worship. This confession of Bono's surprised me. But I could see what he meant. NOS was essentially a nightclub come to church. The ethos was designed to accommodate youngsters who loved music, who would not usually hang out in a church.

The creationist theology of NOS was also a bit more all-embracing and forgiving than narrow fundamentalism. It had a broad appeal, for those who found traditional services staid and lacking in joy. In short, NOS caught imaginations everywhere.

Bono and Edge of U2, had been members of a similarly innovative Bible class in Dublin, and they were always on the lookout for refreshing worship ideas, and non stifling ways to express a love of God. Bono talks freely about his love for the Glide Memorial Church in San Francisco, where the rubber meets the road merging musicality, message and soul. "Radically inclusive, just, and loving," is the consciousness of this innovative church. Bono equates it to a voice of freedom, for the people. When a church is authentic and works from a place of honesty, integrity and commitment, it is a political, social, and personal weapon of strength.

To observers and participants alike, it seemed that the *Nine O' Clock Service* was onto something. An energy was generated at these services, not unlike that of a U2 gig if truth be told. Chris was the first mystical vicar of modern times, who could whip up a frenzied energy in a communion service. While Bono was a master on stage, who channeled God, even singing in tongues for his devoted fans. It was easy to see how U2 may have tapped into some of the presentation tricks of innovative worship. Indeed, Bono basically told me they had done so. I am not sure I would have noticed the connection otherwise. One would have assumed it was more likely the other way around; that Chris had gotten inspired by U2, instead of visa versa.

If truth be told, Chris's energy was probably more that of a druid, than a rock god. The Church of England would have been truly alarmed if they had worked that one out more quickly. Chris was open and tapping into some universal energy that is for sure. But was it purely pagan and overtly all embracing with no boundaries? This might sound ideal to those who choose to believe all is equal under the heavens. But to those who are aware that being open to a fault is actually dangerous, this was indeed a potentially alarming approach.

Being a channel for spiritual energy is an admirable pursuit, when discernment is employed. Ditch wisdom, healthy boundaries and a holy reference point, and all hell can break loose. Literally.

The *Nine O' Clock Service* was a family concern for many. Those who were twenty-something, met and married at this Godly nightclub; my brother and sister included. My parents had understandably been concerned about my Edinburgh shenanigans, and urged me to consider a move to Sheffield. I suppose it could not have been worse than some of the things I was encountering. But I did not completely warm to Chris when I met him. He had all the right accoutrements. A thick head of dark wavy hair, piercing eyes, and a lanky tallish demeanor. In theory I would have normally found him appealing. But he could not look me in the eye. I saw a hidden, secret element within him that I did not warm to. It was as if I saw through him. I gazed into his soul for a moment, and did not like what I found. I do not judge people, but if I get such a warning sign, I do keep distance and steer clear. I did not feel the pull to move to Sheffield, that is for sure.

My perception of Chris is of course is a bit ironic with all I apparently missed up in Edinburgh. But if truth be told, I did not miss things, I simply walked into tricky situations eyes wide open. It was a choice really. I own it. The Edinburgh scenarios felt karmic, and I was emotionally engaged in order to learn and grow. I do not actually think any of it was a waste of time really. It gave me an armory of experience, which I now use to help people. So it was not such a raw deal. Sheffield was not my learning curve, Edinburgh was.

Things ran smoothly in NOS for quite some time. Long enough for the newlyweds to start families, and commit to a community vision for the church. An ethos, practices and approach was agreed. But the overall point of concern was that Chris was given free reign. He answered to no one in the church hierarchy, and was left to do his own thing.

The congregation NOS was initially an observed experiment, performed advisedly by The Church of England. But, somewhere along the line, the truth got distorted, power went to someone's head, and megalomania set in. If the gossip is to be believed, a small select group of women started to tend to Chris's needs beyond the call of Christian duty. Chris had a set of darkly clad handmaidens who gave him massages; or so the rumors went. If the tabloids were right in their conclusions these massages invariably had a happy ending too. Girls started to feel used and emotionally toyed with, and one day someone blew the whistle.

Of course the fragmentation of NOS was excellent tabloid fodder. Probably much that was printed in newspapers was an excuse for badness. Yes, things had gone horribly wrong. Many felt hugely betrayed once Chris's antics were uncovered; and many then fell away from faith in God, because Chris had let them down. This was a classic guru scenario, where the people had become over reliant on one human being rather than God himself.

It was not strictly right or fair to blame everything on Chris. But clearly he did take advantage of his God given position. No one really knows the extent of any abuse or manipulation that went on, except Chris himself. Winnie, his wife at the time, claims to have known nothing about it. What apparently went on under her nose, was well hidden, and subsequently covered up. No one knew quite what to believe, and the testimonies of the abused, obviously had to be proven and substantiated. Needless to say the rumors and stories were damaging enough.

Just as people were originally united through NOS, they then became torn apart through the same channel. This was all so devastating and ironic. What had started as a wonderfully refreshing movement inside the church, became abusive and misleading. NOS had started to serve Chris Brain. He had lapped up the attention apparently, and had started to take advantage, feeding a lavish lifestyle of travel, designer clothes, and those handmaidens to alleviate exhaustion. God was nowhere in sight by the time he was uncovered.

When it all fell apart, Chris had nowhere to go. Technically he could have been arrested on charges of embezzlement, abuse, and fraud. But I think the Church wanted him to lie down quietly and disappear. This whole thing had become a huge liability and embarrassment. True to his innate loyalty as a Taurus, my brother Simon, protected Chris, and gave him shelter in The Highlands. Simon was the one member of the congregation who stood by Chris, Winnie, and their daughter. Despite the fact that Anita, Simon's first wife, had actually been very close to Chris, Simon decided to remain true and supportive to a guy who now had no friends, and no future. Until the dust settled on the whole sorry mess, Simon gave Chris the benefit of the doubt. He was godfather to two of Simon's children, and things were by no means clear in the immediate after math. I think Simon's saint hood is probably lined up in the heavens, to be bestowed at some point, as God sees fit.

My sister and her husband Graham did not have any such tolerance for Chris. They knew more than Simon did in the initial stages of the scandal, as some of their closer friends had been directly involved. They wanted nothing to do with Chris, and saw the devastation first hand, of how Chris had manipulated and taken advantage of his position.

Simon de Montfort, as we called him, clearly had some sort of Knights Templar brotherly karmic contract to up hold with Chris. He did his best in a messy situation. Anita his first wife departed, to spread her wings and explore her independence, leaving Simon custody with mutually agreed custody of their three kids. Two divorces and a wedding later, and Simon is now happily married to the wayward vicar's wife. Result!

The NOS debacle kept the tabloids busy for quite some time.

Journalists were actually camped outside my brother's house by The Isle of Skye for many weeks. This scandal was not going to go away in a hurry. That London journalists would hike up to obscure parts of Scotland to flush Chris out, demonstrated the wide reach of this drama. The tabloids were hoping to get a photo of Chris, Winnie or Simon, and so all three had to camp inside until they left.

The Daily Mail in Dublin contacted me also. They wanted photographs of Simon's first wedding to Anita, where the bride wore black instead of white. I said "no." There was nothing insidious about my brother's first wedding. It was not a black satanic mass. It was a group of cool young people celebrating the love of Simon and Anita. The bridesmaids were dressed as green wood fairies. All very Irish in fact. I used the chance to explain to the journalists what had actually gone on, and that they would do well to let the whole thing go.

When the NOS scandal blew up, I cannot say I was completely surprised. Suddenly the way Chris had looked at me, made perfect sense. I had also noticed he was somewhat patronizing with my father which I did not like one bit. I was glad I had not got overly involved in NOS. My reservations made complete sense, when these revelations came to the fore. I never would have been one of Chris's handmaidens, and I think he knew it. I did not find him attractive, and I am sure he did not find me appealing also. I was blonde after all. He looked creepy and fishy to my way of thinking. My instinctual reaction to him, proved to be very correct indeed.

In Dublin I gave Bono a book on the NOS story so he could better understand what had happened. He read it pretty quickly, and told me that he identified with Chris, and understood him rather well. I was surprised at his response initially. Then I realized Bono is not one to judge, and he would likely always understand the guy in the pulpit preaching to the masses. I told him in more detail what had happened on a personal level to my family; and still he admitted that he really related to Chris, and the temptations of his position. Bono was concerned and somewhat humbled by the story. It seemed to be a bit of a "there but for the grace of God go I" moment for him. Clearly he understood my brother's patience and tolerance of Chris. Bono is nothing if not loyal to his lifelong friends. Understanding the NOS debacle with a more open mind, and Bono's wise perspective, was certainly useful.

In such situations, people's reactions can get dramatic and out of hand. Babies are thrown out with copious amounts of water, and extreme judgments sweep away all the good that ever was in a situation. It always pays to take a breath and see the other side, if only for a revealing empathetic moment. There but for the grace of God go we.

MUSIC GIVES A SOUL TO THE UNIVERSE,
WINGS TO THE MIND, FLIGHT TO THE
IMAGINATION, CHARM TO SADNESS,
GAIETY AND LIFE TO EVERYTHING.
PLATO

CHAPTER FIVE
Makes No Never Mind

Harry, had been my background daydream and fantasy, throughout the Graham saga, and indeed during the last throes of the John nonsense. He was an emotional thread and reference point during my time in Edinburgh. Darkly alluring, brooding and mysterious, as he was, I also loved that he was doing his own thing, and was a highly creative artist and musician. Essentially he was a story teller, who led a magical existence fired by his imagination and natural intelligence. His life was certainly not an open book, and he was far from clearly readable. But he was compelling.

A misfit, who was somewhat out of place in our modern times, Harry looked like he was from another century, and I am sure his karma was playing out from another time and place. He dressed like a dandy from the Renaissance, with ruffled billowing white shirts tucked into black cloth breeches, which were in turn tucked into black riding boots. He really looked like he had stepped off the set of *Dangerous Liaisons*.

That scene where John Malkovich uses pen and ink to write on the back of a prostitute? *That* was Harry.

I would see Harry and Mandy walking arm in arm around Stockbridge. He was much more receptive to me than he had been when he was watched like a hawk by Kimberly. But he definitely was all about Mandy. She did not live with him permanently. They had a to and fro arrangement which involved him going up to The Shetlands for part of the time. I lived on the corner of the main street in Stockbridge, and Harry lived in his garret a few doors up on the right. My building was somewhat bulbous, jutting out into the thoroughfare, which accommodated traffic running from Cramond up into the New Town, the steep cobbled streets which connected with Princes Street.

The cracked window of my wooden-floored, wood-lined, and wood-paneled room had a view right up the streets to the left and right. Mellish the cat used to sit on my pine desk surveying the landscape, before opting to brave the communal stairs to go outside for a reconnaissance expedition. He was lucky not to have been run over in this bustling corner, at the intersection of five roads. But he had a way of disappearing out the back, over the walls, and down the path which led to the Water of Leith. In the evenings, Mellish would trot along the street beside me to get our groceries from the store. He was allowed to accompany me around the aisles also. Basically he was a dog that purred.

I visited Harry in his garret once to drop off a pen and ink picture I had found for him in an antique shop on Dundas Street. He liked the picture. But did not like me. Not in *that* way anyway. He had ample chance to take advantage of me as I sat uncomfortably on a wicker chair in his tiny attic flat; and did nothing. It clearly was not happening.

I lost contact with Harry for years after that. But on searching for updates at one point, I found that he had published several illustrated cartoon books, and had a documentary made about himself, Mandy his wife, and their dog Roo. I was delighted to see that Harry had achieved this level of success with his work. He had cut his hair, put on weight and in his domestic bliss, was much less attractive. He actually looked of this time now, so had obviously worked through his Renaissance karma efficiently. At least he was happy, I mused.

The next articles I found about Harry and Mandy were much more worrisome. A few years on, in some dark, full moon moment, Harry had murdered Mandy, who suffered from multiple sclerosis, and all their pets, before then mutilating himself fatally. What was initially presented by local papers as a suicide pact, born out of frustration with Mandy's condition, and their isolated circumstances; was in actual fact a brutal murder. *Omg*!

In that moment I realized, I had been protected from another John type scenario, which could have turned out even more violently.

What a tragedy and a shock. What a horrendous story, and such a grizzly end, for two talented, handsome people with so much potential. Reading these pieces gave me my own, there but for the grace of God went I, moment. Hardly an appropriate time to voice "it should have been me." But thank God it was not. It just goes to show that we are protected sometimes when the things we really want do not happen. God protects us from what we think we want, and blesses us with what we do not know we need.

I still feel Harry's presence occasionally to this day, as if he is trying to get some message through. But I do not give him too much attention. I simply observe, sense him, and telepathically say "hello." Brian, an American colleague, and a talented medium, has also felt his energy. He assuredly told me that Harry was: "sorry for everything that did not happen; and that I fully deserve a happiness which he never could have given."

Okay. I will take that.

With his weight of experience, and an accuracy that precedes him, I had no reason to doubt Brian's account of Harry, and the messages he wished to convey. Subsequent circumstances certainly illustrated that Harry could have been a disaster waiting to happen.

Harry must have been high on a hallucinogen that fatal night. His impotence in the situation with Mandy dying of multiple sclerosis before his eyes, got a ruthless grip of him. He actually became possessed by a dark force. This would make sense of all the energy he stirred, and conjured during his life time. Harry was wont to walk on the dark side, and I think a fleet of entities piggy-backed his existence if truth be told. Sometimes such energies can take over, or build to a crescendo point, and *BAM*! The outlet is not pretty.

Thankfully, latterly, I chose to hang around with Pierre Le Rue instead of Harry. Harry had turned me down, and was never going to make a move. I certainly was not going to inflict myself on someone not interested, so I moved on. Pierre Le Rue, or Pete The Street, was much more wholesome energetically, and a more talented, authentic musician also. Harry was a showman and travelling salesman. Pierre was the real deal, straight from the Bayou. Well. Albuquerque, and the deserts of New Mexico.

Pierre actually *was* American, and a skilled Cajun fiddle player. He had a similar tall and lanky vibe to Harry, but even deeper meltingly chocolate eyes, revealing a depth of soul. Harry had clearly modeled himself and his Swamptrash story on Pierre, or at least taken huge inspiration from his ilk. I came to much prefer the kosher version, as opposed to the fake. Harry had to act and compensate for quite a bit. He was immensely talented and driven, but also thwarted and ultimately doomed. Pierre was apple pie in comparison.

Pierre was a true gentleman, and an intelligent, humorous companion. Harry was apparently the type who would have locked me away in a tower; and then murdered me. Pierre took me on the road. playing his fiddle joyously. Magically night after night my soul and vibration were lifted. After all the drama it was a gift from the heavens. My eyes were opening. There were other interesting men out there. I was never an easy option, for a guy and was always somewhat "proper" and well behaved; boring you might even say. Except I was *not*. I was the girl who would stand in the bar and not drink. But who would dance, and socialize, and have lots of fun. I did not need recreational drugs, nor drink, nor meaningless sex. I was into music, and people, and soulful connections.

Before the days of Harry and Pierre, I warmed to Kenny, one of the managers of the German restaurant, Lilligs. The Edinburgh Lilligs family opened me up to some company, love and support, and John did not like it. I was a prolific chef. My dishes filled the fridges to overflowing, and I was well liked. I enjoyed the camaraderie the restaurant afforded. It was hard work; but it was also social and intriguing.

Kenny was fun, but he had a connection and fixation on someone else. That somewhat unrequited affection was not dissipating any time soon. Kenny was on his own journey with his personal situation, and clearly not about to be diverted. He had a formidable live-in partner, the very Germanic Claudia, who was fielded by her even more formidable and Germanic mother, both lovingly labeled "Schatzi." This duality of Germans were the hub of the restaurant. They did not crack the whip, or rule with the iron rod, but it was all pretty efficient. It was strudel for breakfast, soup for lunch, schnitzels for dinner, and stuffed savory croissants at any time of your choosing.

Kenny was tall, lanky with piercing blue eyes, and deep auburn wavy hair. Not really my type if truth be told. But his voice was wonderfully soothing and resonant. He was playful and entertaining, and liked his food. I greatly enjoyed his company, but of course wished for something more. In my head the Kenny thing was important for a number of months. An energy link to muse and dream about, even while knowing it was not ever going to be a reality. Sometimes I indulged my Piscean ascendant in these ways. Such reveries were a means to get through boring or demanding times. After all there is nothing wrong with a bit of fantasy. It can play a valid role in our lives, if we know the difference between someone we are dreaming about, and someone who is actually *there* for us. My feelings for Kenny were nothing overwhelming or overtly powerful. But they were important. I do not want to diminish the connection; but basically it was an attempt to move on cleanly from John, and innocently enjoy someone else's company.

It was Kenny who first discovered The Proclaimers. I have to confess I am also indirectly and partly responsible for the bespectacled Scottish twins, who were then launched onto the world stage. Sorry. Not Sorry. Craig and Charlie were actually very compelling and brilliant live. They offered something intense, and refreshing, which was very appealing on the back of all of the eighties nonsense.

One evening, Kenny, whilst doing the dishes, played me their demo tape, as I banged out the next schnitzel. "What did I think?" he asked. I told him in no uncertain terms to, "Go for it."

Kenny was dithering about the Reid twins. They were clearly very talented and dynamic; but they were also very unique and unusual. He was not sure if they were commercially viable. To my mind there was no doubt. They absolutely *were*. My psychic powers kicked in, and I gave definitive advice, which Kenny listened to.

The Gift, in combination with my musical instinct and interests, was starting to be recognized as a viable tool. Anything that I have ever done, combining psychic intuition with music, has been incredibly productive and powerful. My connection with musicians and their music, was important and a life saver in many ways. I sometimes think I would not have lived through the traumas without it. Well, I would have done. But the journey would not have been such fun. That *is* for sure.

Between them Kenny, Colin and Eki hatched a rescue plan to deliver me from John's clutches for good. Colin was a talented ginger artist in his own right, and yet another Lilligs partner to boot. There really were too many chiefs, and not enough Indians running Lilligs. It was a vibrant place to work, and visit. But eventually it inevitably went out of business, simply because too many couples were draining its resources. It was hard work for them all, without much return. I learned first-hand that running even a successful restaurant is no guarantee of a financial return, let alone profit.

Scottish Colin pronounced me a "delicate flower" that needed careful feeding, nurturing, and rescue. I was allowed to sleep on the floor of Eki's flat, which she shared with Colin. Strangely this was just around the corner from John. Small steps. I was really only yards away from the boys, but it felt cataclysmically important. Finally I had some personal space, but of course only through invading the space of the generous Colin and Eki. Clearly, I would not be able to sleep on the floor of their small sitting room permanently. But with John? It. Was. Finally. Over. I never went back into that dingy basement apartment inhabited by John, Colin, and Ron. But ended up instead in the attic flat of the same building.

Minter, a social worker, single mum, who had just given birth to a gorgeous half Chilean baby, needed a roommate. I jumped at the offer. Of course I ended up being a surrogate mother, and helping a lot with the lovely five month old Lucy. But I did not mind. I had a healthy degree of separation from John, and life was picking up. I really enjoyed the nurturing experience of bonding with a young baby too. It was therapeutic, and obviously helpful to my roommate. Lucy was the most beautiful baby I think I had ever seen. Her half Chilean genes gave her a wonderful depth of caramel complexion. Her hair was dark, silky and smelled delicious, and her eyes were big orbs of soulful deliciousness. I have always been good with both animals and children. They tend to fall asleep on me. My healing energies make them feel safe and secure, and I can quickly calm them with the use of my hot hands.

The time with Minter and Lucy worked well until such a time as Minter accused me of not having the rent. There was a check lost somewhere in the works, and she doubted my explanation about what had happened to the funds. She was incorrect and overly distrusting and accusatory. So she totally blew it with me, and lost her live-in babysitter. I made immediate plans to move across to Stockbridge, to my own apartment on Saint Stephen's Street, before she realized the error of her ways.

John was still attempting to monitor my movements in and out of the attic flat. So on two counts, I needed to wean myself away from the claustrophobic situation in Gayfield Square. Several times I had managed to sneak out unnoticed, and go spread my wings at some gig or other. I was living dangerously, and doing my own thing. Those that would control me did not like it. Everything John had tried to squash or stop within me was coming back to the fore. I had the music in me.

Hanging out with musicians, and enjoying their talents was fast becoming my *raison d'etre*. All this without resorting to being any kind of groupie. So, I guess I *was* somewhat unusual. I had the long-haired Extreme bass player, Nuno Bettencourt staring at me post gig in The Edinburgh Playhouse, and I gave him nothing in return; even though he was undeniably cute. Stupid perhaps. He really was very attractive.

Then the cute glamorous one in The Dogs D'Amour, commented on, and was transfixed by my "wasp waist," pointing out, "how rare that look is these days. Like something out of the forties." I guess that was a compliment. But I was not quite sure what he meant by the wasp waist thing. Again he got nothing for his troubles. I was simply there for the music. I did enjoy being "seen" by these men though. I would be lying if I said I did not like the attention and appreciation. After being so, or allowing myself to be so abused, I was starting to discover who I was as a woman. I probably had no idea up until that point really.

John had panicked and cried like a baby when he saw that I finally had the means to leave. I even felt sorry for him, and there was a flicker or remorse. He finally looked vulnerable after years of bullying, and I felt some defense within him was down. Perhaps he would even get help. I think he was finally forced to at least contemplate his behavior. Or not. John hated Eki, and all the Lilligs crowd. He had baited me mercilessly about them. Essentially, he tried to put the doubt in my mind about every good thing that would threaten to take me away from him, and diminish his control over my life. Even to this day, I do not think he really would understand how his treatment of me was unacceptable. I honestly believe he thought me to be the one at fault. My mere existence was a problem that needed to be knocked into shape somehow. I was I guess a female he could not contain or over power. So he became a bully, probably because of some complex psychological projection issues.

What may have completely defeated some people, became a source of strength and depth for me ultimately. I still do not fully understand it. But it is a long time ago now, and the memories stir only in the writing. Certainly it is not something I give a second thought to otherwise. Irritating though it is to recap such events. It does go to show that there is light at the end of the tunnel with many of life's challenges. We all have the ability, if we tap into our own power, to turn things around, and make the dark times, light times once again. Nothing is beyond our capability as human beings. And it is so true, God does not throw challenges at us which we cannot handle.
The enjoyment of study and solid friendship with my deutsche freundin Ingrid had got me through the first year of my time at Stir-

ling. John then commandeered the final three years, and beyond. Still my experience with the academic side of life was invaluable throughout this time of personal difficulty. Modeled on the same structure as American Universities, Stirling had long term times, and long holidays in which to recover. Even though Mr Wonderful from Canada most certainly did not show up, I loved the structure of the two semesters, as well as the study of Philosophy, English Literature and Religious Studies. I did well in all these subjects. The predominantly coursework assessment helped, as I did not enjoy the pressure of exams. Having the memory of a gold fish did not suit the need to perform to the ticking of a clock.

I used to write essays psychically. I would sleep with the books under the pillow, and skim read some notes and a few chapters, and so be able to write quite definitively on the essays as required. It is not that I did not want to read all books from cover to cover. But I found that I could short cut the subjects by observing comments in tutorials, and psychically dipping into the important bits. I did not really know I was doing this at the time. I found myself knowing things about books I had not actually read, and being able to answer questions quite deeply on subjects I had never studied. One thing I learned at university was that I could write comprehensively on any subject you care to mention, and that I was able to research quickly and efficiently.

They do say you learn how to study at University. I certainly found this to be the case. More than what I was studying, the methods and techniques I was starting to use became of interest. I could write much which made sense from the top of my head. I could actually channel information on subjects I knew nothing about, as if from nowhere. I began to experience in a very concrete way the practical application of skills I had come to realize I had.

Post Stirling I enrolled at Edinburgh University to study for an M. Sc.

in Modernism and Post modernism. This saw me through the recovery time needed post John, and the Lillig's days supported me financially and familiarly. The pattern of me working in restaurants, cafes and bars, as I studied, was established. I became an eternal student deliberately. I enjoyed study and writing and research. I did not really want a proper job, and I had no idea what my career path was meant to be. I wanted to study, to learn, and to grow, and I actually liked the social aspects of the jobs I took. Besides, after the John debacle, it really was much more important that I stabilized my life and emotions.

Agoraphobia had become something of an issue as I sought to expand my horizons, and spread my wings after the John trauma. I had been in some kind of energetic funk, and confinement in the unnaturally stifling situation. I was contained in chrysalis form, and my hatching was a real stop and start affair. I had to take a few months out from the studies at Edinburgh as I was not able to successfully get up into the heart of the city without having a panic attack. Taxis became my safe mode of transport. Whenever I had to get somewhere which felt in any way awkward, I would manage it as long as I could, "wrap a taxi around me," to quote my father. That tendency has not changed much over the years. I still much prefer to get somewhere independently than brave the hordes of commercial travelers on planes, trains, and automobiles. I seek the smooth, easy, hassle free way. It is a legacy of the John days. A legacy which has had an effect on quite a lot. But thankfully the psychological damage was not as lasting as it might have been. The gift in the situation is that I can now understand and help people with post traumatic stress disorders, anxiety, depression and agoraphobia.

I am perfectly fine now, and the trauma feels like another life time at this stage. But having been there myself, and emerged through the tunnel, I am able to help others shift those tricky energies, and get their healings much more quickly than I was able to.

I really had to manage much of this aspect of my journey independently. I refused to approach a doctor for medications I did not need. And wanted to confront, process, and experience all I was going through without dampening it down in any way. I cannot imagine what it would be like to go through something like this in a medicated fog. I felt I needed my wits about me, and it was imperative that I was fully engaged in my life, even though it was difficult.

I attempted spasmodic counseling at one point. But it was pretty useless. I was open, honest, and not in the least bit defensive or evasive. But I was able to run rings around the counselors with my answers for everything. Something my mother had always said about me, proved very pertinent in this situation. I really did have an answer, an excuse, or at least an intelligent explanation, for everything. I could easily justify my decisions, reactions and behaviors, as I was fully conscious throughout of why I was doing what I was doing. My inner stability required that I back off slowly and deliberately from John and his obsessive monitoring. Going cold turkey and disappearing would not have completed the karmic loop on this relationship. For some reason, I needed to see it through, and come out the other side through a choice which ultimately led to my empowerment not my diminishment.

Like any addiction weaning, people have to realize something and take action in their own time. Interventions are all very well. But ultimately only the person embroiled in the energy can extricate themselves on the deeper levels. Knowing what I knew did not always help. I did not actually need insights. I am able to verbalize insights and analysis until the cows come home. What I needed to find, was how to change things. I really needed energy work, and energy shifts, to finally sort the trauma. The emergent path I took to master healing, and my psychic abilities, became a means to cope. It proved to be an education, and a way of transmuting all the negativity.

I began researching readers, and went regularly for readings at The

College of Parapsychology in Edinburgh, and started to visit commercial psychics. My phone bills were rather scary from all the phone calls to psychic lines at this time. I began to look outside of myself for perspective and answers. I hoped I was not looking away from God for those insights, but my journey spiritually certainly had become much more complex.

Celia was an amazing grassroots Scottish psychic that Eki and I visited quite regularly. I asked her about marriage at one point. Her response? "You don't need a man!" I guess that was one of the most pertinent things she said, because I sure as hell have had to manage without a partner for much of the time.

In the name of research, I was taught first hand to understand the "when, when, when," which then pervaded most of my client's questions subsequently. I had asked that question myself on more than one occasion. And it was some time before I learned to stop asking for the "when," in order to find out the "why."

As I searched for the healing I needed, I essentially became an apprentice in the healing and psychic arts. My understanding of psychology amplified, and my life skills grew. It was initially very much a case of, "do as I say, not as I do." But as I developed, my road became increasingly congruent and authentic, and I began to walk my talk, understanding just what that meant.

My suffering had become the means to help people. Through not giving up, I began to turn my story into a tool for guidance and healing. I obviously needed to learn to apply my skills, gifts and insights for other people's benefit. I needed to know I could speak accurately and with authority, and not be wrong. I had listened to a lot of nonsense during my research quest. I wanted to provide people with a service that was actually relevant and helpful.

A path of spiritual responsibility was unfolding. I had not planned it. But it was the upshot of not taking the suicide options, which had presented rather frequently if truth be told. I was never ever going to take that route. Times were surely dark, but the flicker of the flame of hope was never extinguished.

Whatever happened to me, the love of God never left me; nor did an implicit faith in his/her ability to deliver me. The dark night of the soul was an ever present reality. I did not baulk. I knew the night was darkest before the dawn, and I was not going to waiver in my faith. Nor was I going to run away from my calling. The road less travelled had certainly taken a hold of me, and there was no turning back.

*STILL ROUND THE CORNER THERE MAY WAIT, A NEW ROAD OR A SECRET GATE.
J. R. R. TOLKIEN*

CHAPTER SIX
Leaving City Of Ghosts

I first arrived in Dublin, disheveled, despondent and more than a little knackered. The drive down from Belfast had been interminable. So tedious in fact that we had to halt the journey before reaching our destination. At the Castle Hotel we stopped off for a night's rest to gather our thoughts, energies and intentions before driving into Dublin's Fair City the following day.

Over a sleep inducing pint of Guinness in the down stairs bar, we contemplated our big decision to up sticks and head for the Republic of Ireland. After a curious and intermittently disturbing chapter in Scotland, I was more than ready for a change of scene. But it was as if I sensed the enormity of what was about to happen, and I did not fully like what I saw. Obviously it was a big step to pack up and leave Edinburgh, a city I loved, relished and adored. Moving to what was essentially another country took courage, and it was much more disarming than I thought it was going to be.

Although it is so close to the United Kingdom, Southern Ireland has a totally different energy. Coming in through the North also stirred up many anxieties in the days before peace talks and uneasy resolution. Many impressions bombarded a psychic on arrival in Northern Ireland. The all pervasive heaviness was tangible. This sensation, combined with the observation that anyone I had ever met from the north was always slightly crazy, did not help. My psychotically disturbed, and paranoid ex boyfriend John, had been a case in point. Enough said.

Was it safe at the cross border check? Would they wonder who we were in a laden white van heading south? Was there a crackpot border raid, or ambush about to take place. Certainly the feel of the air at the meeting of the borders had all this potential swirling. Northern Ireland did not strike me as safe, not then, and I am not sure it is even now. There is something in the ethers inducing a fiery, twitchy, heightened sensibility, which would surely drive you over the edge given enough time. I had panicked at the ferry terminal, and this discombobulating energy that greeted us probably did not help. I had a compelling wish to turnabout. Never a good sign.

Although the overall decision to move felt compelling, it also felt very uncomfortable. I felt a destiny calling linked to the south, and I could not turn back. This move was a leap into the unknown, especially as it was done holding hands with someone I did not even know I had a future with. In retrospect Billy was delivering me to where I needed to be. I would not have done such a big upheaval alone; and even in the company of a good friend, which Billy was at this stage, it still felt very challenging.

I had had the notion about Dublin for some time. But it was just an intriguing thought, which floated through my consciousness intermittently. I just as quickly squashed it and parked it for later perusal. In truth this move had in fact been precipitated by a restless boy friend. One who could not face life in Edinburgh with me in a small, potentially floodable, cottage apartment by the waters of Leith. Fair enough. I was clearly a ticket to a bit more excitement than that; and said boyfriend also needed a change of scenery.

I had been cautious and in two minds about the whole thing. It did not seem practical or doable. It was back to that not chasing rainbows thing; the very definition of which is not to embark on anything impossible or impractical. I still had my Masters of Philosophy in Publishing Studies at Stirling to complete, and was not looking forward to commuting all the way from Dublin for exams. Plus, I had the small matter of a thesis to wrap up. *Making an Impression* no less.

The restless boyfriend syndrome, in the form of Billy, was inconvenient to say the least. What was most odd about the whole thing, was that my tutor at Stirling supported the requested upheaval to my schedule. In what you might call an unprecedented agreement, the media expert instinctively realized that I was about to step into an environment that would afford me opportunities to apply the instructions of the Publishing Studies course. Scroll forward a few months to me working in the cloak room of The Kitchen night club, and I was less sure. But there was no turning back by that point.

The tutor at Stirling, had felt that I should just roll with the opportunity resenting itself. That the time was now. Billy had spoken, the tutor had spoken, and destiny it seemed had everything in hand. Billy had issued one of his ultimatums. Nothing too heavy. Just a threat to scarper if this "life change" did not happen. Spain or Dublin it was. Him to Spain, or both of us to Dublin. He had recently come back to Scotland from an extended trip to Spain. He had not wanted to return, and probably would not have done, only the summer season was done, and he was at a loose end financially.

At the time of Billy's departure to Spain, we had only just moved into Warriston Terrace, out of a much loved communal flat shared with several of Edinburgh's finest Goths. I had loved the shared life with this gathering of dark musicians, who ate scrambled egg rolls for breakfast, and who raided the bakery across the road at two in the morning for as many freshly baked goods as possible. Two pounds passed into the hand of the on-duty baker would see us all carrying bags of warm yummy goodies back to the apartment.

Tongue of Alba, as these Scottish rogues were called, produced an intense wall of sound. I would say "noise," but that would be unkind. Suffice to say, I do not know how the long-haired, dark red-headed, lead singer Colin maintained his throat health. But his raw, primal guttural growls certainly charged up some serious gothic energy. I once did a Siouxsie And The Banshee's type backing track vocal for them in studio which was fun. But I am not sure my future as a singer would have recommended following that lead too religiously.

Not much sleep happened in that huge high ceilinged, corniced second floor apartment. The toilet was cracked, the bath was slippery and dirty, and the kitchen was a health hazard. But we all muddled along with a mutual understanding of the conditions, and some slap stick camaraderie. I had painted my room cream, lime green and pink in a bid to be creative, and add to the flavor of what was essentially a dump.

Some time before, I had visited my drummer lover Greg for a few hot and sweaty months in this apartment. Not much sleep was had then either. I had had to agree terms that Greg would be allowed to see his ex on Sundays for a cozy roast and time with her mother. But like most cool, aka stupid, girls I had a bit of the #whatever about me, and I accepted the conditions.

My best friend at the time, Alexandra aka Eki, remembers seeing me fleetingly for afternoon cake and chocolates in the back room of her sweet shop. I stopped by briefly on the way to my evening job which involved baking and waitressing, at the Spanish Tapas restaurant Boxers. I was as prolific a baker as I was a chef, and a wordsmith. I do not seem to be able to do half measures in anything really. All forms of my self-expression creatively, professionally and personally are overly generous. I was taught to go the second mile, and that is just what I do. Ask me to bake a cake, and I will bake you four. Just as well Jacqui the boss had a large freezer.

Sadly, and quite bafflingly to me, it all ended oddly with Eki. For some inexplicable reason, many years after our timely meeting in Lilligs, Eki got prickly and defensive when I found a measure of success in Dublin. She was proud of her own Irish ties, and I think I put her nose out of joint by digging in and making something of myself in Ireland with the media work, writing and broadcasting. Not only did she make the flippant comment, "Oh Sarah is finally making money out of her madness," to a mutual friend. But she actually *told* me she had done so. #whatever. #goodbye.

It was such a shame and so hurtful to be phased out by Eki after everything we had shared down the years. But it was one of those examples of a friendship having a life span. I guess, not everyone is supposed to be in our lives for the duration. Sometimes people change, or a specific connection has a shelf life. It can be a shock and difficult to accept. But I found it was healthiest not to take too much umbrage, and to get on with what life was delivering.

I actually had begun to have questions about the friendship myself a few years before. Eki had seemed to take a shine to Pierre Le Rue, and oddly she did herself slightly resemble Pierre's wife. When Eki went out of her way to come to a Glasgow Le Rue gig, dressed to the nines, and proceeded to deliberately eyeball Pierre, I knew I had a problem. Eki, had designs on the man she knew I was in love with. "Mrs Gummy Bear," as Pierre called her, in honor of the copious amounts of confectionary, which made their way to the tour bus via me, was on a mission to catch his attention. I was not best pleased, as she knew how deeply I felt for him. Here was a potential betrayal. I am absolutely sure Eki would have happily gone ahead with a fling with Pierre had he been interested. Eki was already intermittently having an affair with a married man, a major music promoter in the area, and possible father of her child Emi. So she was more than capable of playing the role of mistress. I, on the other hand was not.

They say women have intuition. Well psychic women have it in spades; probably times ten on the Richter scale. It is not the most comfortable ability, when it is automatically applied to your personal life; which of course it inevitably is. Greg was sneakily and artfully won back by Dee, a spasmodic friend with benefits, who did not like that he had been diverted by me. We all eventually ended up working at Boxers, the Spanish Tapas Bar, which sat just above the beginning of Saint Stephen Street, the cobbled road, which descended into Stockbridge. I looked down on Greg and Dee one night as they locked up the restaurant after work. From my top floor shared apartment across the street, I chanced upon them as I gazed out of the living room window. Often I was in charge of managing the evenings, cashing up and making everything secure. But on this occasion, the night after Greg had called up to unceremoniously dump me, Dee was in charge. She looked in charge in more ways than one too, as she headed off down the street home with my boyfriend. I mean my ex.

The two of them seemingly resumed relations for about five minutes, while I moved on quickly. Had they ever stopped? Well , who knows. But clearly Dee had been annoyed by my connection with Greg, and she made it her mission to re-stake her claim; despite having a steady dreadlocked boyfriend, whose main ability was losing himself in a haze of smoke. Dee had been aware of my friendship with Pierre Le Rue, and I am convinced she used the inside information to poison Greg against me. Later on, after I had conceded to have Dee as a roommate, I spied Greg sneaking out of her room very sheepishly when I unexpectedly returned home from tour to Victoria

Street. They were still at it, even then. Cannot keep a good boy down, I guess. Then again, Dee and Greg just did not seem to be able to quit each other. I am sure Greg's next girlfriend, would have had something to say about all this. She was certainly feisty enough when she drowned me with a bucket of water, whilst I was sitting beside an electric fire.

I remember knowing exactly what was up, when I went to call in a debt of twenty five pounds from Greg. There was an awkward silence in the communal Goth sitting room. To break the ice I was persuaded to jump in Dee's red mini with them both, and do a round of Edinburgh's cobbled roads for fun. Exhaust falling off, and body work clunking, it was not much fun for the psychic chick who was both jangled and exhausted, and could see through their ploy in an instant.

The days of Billy the bass player were different. There was a good friendship connection, as well as physical satisfaction initially. I had not had an orgasm with Greg, even though he was a very good lover and kisser, but I immediately did with Billy. Probably I held that part of myself back from Greg, because he was still seeing his ex once a week. But aside from that, I had no complaints. We appreciated each other for a time, and the connection was intense; probably too intense to go the distance. Billy was also interesting. Whereas Greg had been the groovy drummer of Tongue of Alba, a gothic affair; Billy was the bass player of semi-successful rock band, The Crows. He was hot, slim, and leather clad; with long layered black hair, off set with green eyes, and a cheeky grin.

Ben, the good looking Shooglenifty fiddle player had derided The Crows, formerly known as First Priority, as "cock rock." I had asked Ben's band to support The Crows at a gig at the infamous Venue in Edinburgh. He refused in no uncertain terms. *Jealous much?* Not sure. But I know a can got kicked across the floor when Ben first clocked that I had got it together with Billy. Shame I had not recognized the attraction from his side. I in fact had liked Ben a lot also. But he was set to marry the fair Iona, and had a baby on the way. Much as I liked Ben, his spiky disheveled hair, and his ripped at the knee jeans, it was really not the thing to do. One of Ben's friends had suggested that I give him a night of abandon before his wedding day. We were all socializing in the Stockbridge watering hole The Antiquary, when this went down. I was intrigued, mortified and embarrassed in equal measure. Of course I declined, and did not facilitate this last fling option. But it made me wonder if Ben had been concealing a soft spot for me all along.

I had found Ben, and the group he was associated with, a little standoffish at times. But the kicked can, when I got it together with Billy, seemed to indicate that there may have been a reciprocated frisson after all. Damn, why does one always realize these things too late? With the benefit of hindsight there are things we would do over; and Ben was one of these for me. Judging by my track record, such an encounter would not have led to a different destiny. But it might have done. I will never know. I do know that anyone I have been with finds my company somewhat addictive. So there is never really an "only once" option with me. They always come back for more. A case in point being Billy. He had intended only one night. He got several years instead.

Never mind the good sex, the developing emotional link with Billy was fraught. He was in resistance much of the time. and totally preoccupied with an ex girlfriend called Julie. Billy was initially a torturous nightmare to relate to. There was all the emotional turmoil of his lingering infatuation with Julie, which hardly enhanced our growing relationship. Then out of the blue one night, he announced that suddenly he just "tends to go off sex." I laughed, and thought it odd seeing as we had been having *no* complaints in that department. I actually did not believe him, so incredulous and unexpected an announcement was it. But sure enough, off it he did go.

On reflection, Billy was probably the type who liked to have sex with strangers. Girlfriends tended to become sisters to Billy. He got emotionally bonded, and then some block occurred within him, and he found that his situation was not sexy any more. Over our time together, he always had an internal conflict about being attracted to women he did not know very well but worked with. Every time he got a new job, I would wonder who the new flirtation was this time; and more often than not I guessed correctly. I would find the relevant phone numbers in pockets, and Billy would have made some connection that ended up making him confused and upset. Not to mention that it always pissed me off greatly.

A particularly annoying phase came a couple of years later, once we had arrived in Dublin. Billy was helping Sara with her singing demos. All of a sudden Billy was a dance keyboard pro, and Sara was the next best dance act. I have to say I did support him and went out of my way to hand the demo tape they made to Louis Walsh. Louis was curious and he felt Billy Bowie was a name with star quality. What was even more interesting was that a backing loop on the next Westlife single sounded uncannily like a riff Billy had pegged down on his demo. Probably one of those universal synchronous coincidences. But even so, a bit curious.

Billy spent long hours up at Strawberry Hill, a magnificent white Italianesque mansion on Vico Road, situated between Dalkey and Killiney. The views from this vantage point are spectacular across the bay. The sweeping flow of the green-blue water, and the soft lilt of the land culminating in the distinctive peaks of Great Sugar Loaf in the distance, created a breathtaking vista. This landscape is my heaven on earth, my home from home. It really is the ultimate place to live, and Strawberry Hill is the ultimate roof over one's head. I am hoping my track record of address manifestation does not fail me on this one. We will see.

Sara had the right to stay in her marital home for the duration of her divorce proceedings from Rick, the bass player with Def Leppard. She obviously had a thing about bass players, as Billy was one too. I was not allowed up to the house with Billy, and he made a point to gloat about it. The Great irony was, within a few months, my friend Paige was living in Strawberry Hill, as Rick's partner. Rick's divorce had finally gone through, and he had got his house back. I was warmly invited for tea, whenever Paige wished it. I also got to spend Christmas Day there with them all, and after yummy crisp well cooked turkey, we all sat through *Titanic* on the big screen. In your face Billy. (Just kidding).

Every time Billy got diverted by one of his work colleagues, a little piece of me died inside. And every time it happened, I distanced myself further from him. He was not a bad person, and would end up getting quite distressed and upset about his latest encounter. He felt stuck, emotionally involved with the person, and unable to do anything about it. I wound up being his therapist, healer and counselor, as he processed whatever current emotion he was dealing with.

One time I found a phone number of a girl he had spent the night with down the road from Dartmouth Square in Dublin, in a hotel. Dartmouth Square was the red bricked Victorian apartment we shared with our sausage dog Freddie. It was a spooky eerie location, and Freddie used to anxiously await my return from the night club, gazing out the window steaming up the glass from the inside with the warm breath from his huge snout. Billy worked at The Pod nightclub and generally got home much later than I did. On this particular night, he did not get home until the morning. This Spanish girl had apparently bashed her head off the head board until it bled, which sounds kind of interesting. All the same, I was mortified. I found her phone number in his pocket, when I was assembling the next day's laundry. I was mortified, and then did something really out of character. I phoned her, reprimanded her, and then dumped him. I did not get intimate with him much at all after that; once or twice, if that. The years passed. I seemed to be good at picking guys that I ended up not having sex with.

I became more and more fraught and upset, by the apparent nonchalance that Billy had for our relationship. He did not seem to be able to put the brakes on when a new flirtation came his way. Billy was a typical astrological Cancer type. He did not know what he wanted until it was gone. He used to constantly cast his mind back to the past, and dragged around a bucket load of pity and regret. It really was at times quite exhausting and exasperating.

Billy could never quite engage fully with what was under his nose. With every passing minute he was stacking up the future regrets of tomorrow. I used to say to him repeatedly "one day you will be lamenting the loss of me also." Sure enough this happened. He randomly texted me once during a drinking session while he was listening to that song *Let Her Go* by Passenger. Those vodka induced wedding proposals came way too late, and spectacularly out of time.

Scotland was a learning experience. I certainly was beginning to understand men. Or should I say musicians. Or should I say, messed up Scottish musicians with commitment issues? Dick was another one. I worked for Dick in an Edinburgh nightclub every so often as a hostess. He eventually got engaged to the luminous, lovely, leggy, blonde Karen, and I babysat their daughter as an infant. There was an easy jovial connection between Dick and I. He was Billy's old school mate, and someone Billy aspired to emulate in terms of worldly success. I guess there was a kind of rivalry between the two of them, though Billy did not have much to be jealous of in terms of personality or looks. What was going on under his nose might have caught his attention however. If only he had *paid* more attention.

Dick was fast becoming a millionaire with his band nights, nightclubs and promotions. I was not overly impressed, but his attentions were warm, friendly and amusing, and often cheered me up if truth be told. Dick was always pressing me for smooches, intimacy and any kind of bodily contact he could get. If I had not liked him it would have bordered on sexual harassment at times. But I liked him. I valued him as a friend, and I was attracted to him, most of the time. I loved Billy, and it conflicted me that I got more in the way of physical attention and appreciation from Dick. Surely, the guy I was actually *with*, should be the one all over me? It was irksome, upsetting, and sometimes tempting.

One day though, it suddenly became distinctly unfunny. I had been helping Dick and Karen decorate their bedroom and hallway in their ground floor apartment. For some reason I had agreed to help out. I liked to decorate, and I thought I might as well help, seeing as they were both busy. One particular evening Dick called by to assess my progress, and something happened. There was a physical connection, on the floor in the front room, windows open, curtains not drawn. I had said "no" in the moment. He did it anyway.

I did not know what just happened. It was a typical grey area type scenario, where the guy could so easily have said, "she was gagging for it," and that, "no meant yes." But this was *not* the case. I had an emotional pang for Billy, as I rightly should have, and I wanted him to STOP.

I have never been the type to engage in an affair, so this was strange territory to me. Technically it was not an affair, Dick was not married, but it was crossing a line I was not comfortable with. Suddenly I came to my senses and realized this. The encounter should have stopped before anything major happened. In that moment I said "no." *Tha*t would have been the time to do a rain check.

At what point does the woman's right to say "no" get overridden by the commitment of seeing through a hormonally driven encounter? I do not know. But the next time I saw Dick he said it had been "like a dream," and that he hoped I was not pregnant. Charming.

Dick, obviously thought something significant had happened, and wanted to make it clear that he could not take the whole thing further. I in turn shrugged the whole thing off. Being kind of shell-shocked I was not sure if it classed as rape, or was something I had wanted regardless. I had said "no" because of Billy. But it still happened.

I cannot fairly isolate this incident as a unique one however. Sometime after that, we were together again; and then again. The next time, was with my *full* permission. We had sex in the front seat of his car on the way home from a night's work at the nightclub. Our encounters then became a bit of a habit. Dick smooched me all the way home after that aforementioned Dog's D'Amour gig at The Venue; and then made more definite moves in my own apartment before work another time. I did not put up any resistance, verbal or otherwise on those occasions.

The connection was strong enough with Dick. But it did have a take it or leave it element. Not least because of Billy and Karen. It could have been a choice, or a wife swap scenario, I guess. But once Dick made his full commitment to Karen I took myself out of the running. So really, what can I say? I was not physical with Billy at all by then, and Dick paid me way more attention as a woman than Billy ever did. But really, it was all kinds of wrong. Dick told me to "deny, deny, deny," if we were ever questioned about our fling. I just looked at him and made no comment. We liked each other and were compatible as buddies. But he was not being fair to Billy his long term friend, nor his partner Karen, nor to me.

Dick and Karen finally got married, after the longest engagement in history, and Billy and I attended. It was odd for me to go, but not too much to cope with. Nothing ever happened between us after that. Billy and I had already moved to Dublin by that point, so the distancing was not exactly painful. One of the reasons I had to move away myself, was that this liaison could not continue. There was a mutual assumption that we remained good friends, who might occasionally flirt. I certainly would have said "no" and completely meant it, if he had even dared make a move. Dick had chosen Karen, and even though I was not full on with Billy, I definitely still had an emotional, familiar connection with him.

I refuse to fool around with a married man. That has been my *modus operandi* from day one. I have spent my life trying to avoid the single parent thing, and thankfully I have succeeded. Not that there is any judgment on those who take this path. In fact, sometimes I reflect back, and wish I had weakened on this decision. But overall, I am glad that I did not. My pack of dogs fill my nurturing requirements, and they bring with them only unconditional love, copious licks, and *Pasteurella* apparently. Don't ask.

Someone once said I tended to walk on the dark side with my love life. I am not sure this is literally true. It certainly was not intentional. But I sure have processed some karmic lessons, and an intense learning curve along the way. Much of the knowledge I acquired now enables me to help people come to grips with their emotional struggles. I am able to help focus clients on what they need to do to stay with their partners and make it work. Equally, I am able to help them leave with their head held high, if needs be. This is the upside and reward of my colorful experience. I get to apply it in productive ways to help others.

With the disintegration of the gothic nightmare, Edinburgh started to wear thin, and the time had come to take serious action. The left field community of black-clothed, eye-lined, hair plaited Goths had been ordered to leave their sanctuary; and so ended an era. In real language, the kip rented to us by one of Edinburgh's finest doctors, was long overdue a refurbishment. The days of that cracked toilet, and bug infested kitchen, were most definitely numbered.

For all of us, the notice to quit was the bottom falling out of our world. Despite its disheveled presentation, number eight Brandon Terrace, top buzzer, was home. It had most definitely been a comfort through unsettled times. True, I had nearly died there when one of Greg's unhinged jealous girlfriend's came in and dowsed me liberally with that bucket of water, whilst I was sitting beside an electric heater. Greg got her to apologize to me several weeks or months later in a night club. She offered to let me throw a pint over her for some retaliation. I declined. Not really my style.

Overall, times were pleasant enough on the terrace. In the previous couple of years, I had liked being able to just turn up and sleep on the sofa. Sometimes things got a bit lonely and intense in my ancient haunted apartment on Victoria Street. So when I was able to move in with Billy and all my friends, I thought I had finally found a safe haven and family in the north.

They say change is good. This false, somewhat otherworldly, comfort zone had to come to an end just like they all do. With ultimatums flying around, I found myself and Billy the lovely ground floor apartment with a cottage feel, by the flowing waters of the River Leith. It was just across the road from our gothic haunt, so there was not too much to deal with in the way of lumbering luggage. Though according to Billy, I possessed more books than it was humanly reasonable to possess. An issue that surfaced with every move thereafter.

Billy lasted about five minutes in this somewhat claustrophobic damp lower level apartment. The Warriston Terrrace accommodation was small with a wicked damp problem. Very quickly Billy announced he had to do something different. He did not like anything which smacked of commitment and would not be persuaded to stay. No wonder I was vulnerable to the attentions of Dick, who actually seemed to *like* me and enjoy my company.

Before you could say "Jack Rabbit," Billy was off to his brother's time share in Benalmadena to work in Spanish nightclubs for the summer. Banal was the word, and it was certainly not my scene. But Billy loved to drink, he loved the sun, and he loved the night life. For him this was a no brainer. As for me, I finally admitted I had hooked up with a guy who was happy to drift along, to not settle down or have family, nor commit in any way, shape, or form.

Clearly it was time to start letting go of the notion of finding a soul mate for life. Celtic guys just did not seem to be wired for domesticity. I had lived and breathed in Scotland for some time. Here the men were footless fancy free, and had a thing about their mothers. Even once they were married with five kids, the dynamic tended to stay the same. There was no competing with that really, though a move to another Celtic country was worth a shot.

I LIKE MEN HOW I LIKE MY COFFEE: HOT, STRONG AND IRISH!

CHAPTER SEVEN
Dubλin Nights

What I knew about Dublin, I could recall in a sentence or two. I knew I was drawn there energetically, and James Joyce's *Dubliners* had given me a taste of what to expect.

Apart from that, I knew that the River Liffey flowed through the town centre and that Bono lived there, along with Van Morrison, and Enya. I did not know what any of it would mean for me. But one thing was for sure; I was going to find out, thanks to Billy's restless nature and consequent ultimatum.

I have always found that certain places of significance stick in my consciousness, and when they really stick, I usually end up living there. Dublin was just such a place. I had no active plan to move there, since I was quite content with my lifestyle amongst the artists, musicians and rockers of Edinburgh. But I always knew on one level that Dublin's fair city would offer some important and fateful experience. Boy, did I turn out to be right. In ways that not even my strong intuition could have anticipated, Dublin was about to hit me squarely between the eyes.

By invitation, Billy and I attended the wedding of one time Virgin Prune, Gavin Friday to the lovely unassuming brunette Rene, his childhood sweetheart. Gavin, now a dear friend, was part of Lypton Village, a group of Dublin artists and musicians who gathered together, much as we all had in Scotland, to rail against the dying of the night.

Lypton Village were a motley crew. The lineup included Bono, Guggi, David, Strong Man and Gavin, to name but a few. They were brothers in arms, who had each other's backs. Their art was experimental, and in 70s Dublin somewhat risqué, if not offensive to those who did not understand it. Gavin and Guggi dressed as women, pushing the boat out, and people's boundaries with their performance, politics and antics. Bono, formerly known as Paul Hewson, was named after a hearing aid store Bono Vox; Guggi, aka Derek, had an uncanny resemblance to a "Guggi egg;" Edge was just The Edge, whom no one was cooler than; while the whole synergy of Gavin was greater than the sum of his parts.

I found it very charming that half of Dublin, and the whole of Cork, seemed to hook up with their first love, and stay with them for the duration of a lifetime. This was the way it should be. The way it was in the good old days, and the way I had been brought up to expect it to be. Although very unadventurous, such simplicity and normality, was also refreshing and inspiring. I was used to seeing my contemporaries drift in and out of meaningful monogamous, and not so monogamous, connections.

No dour messed up Scots on the prowl here then was my thought, as I looked around the wedding guests in attendance.

Oh, except the one I had brought with me. Hmmm...

Gavin looked handsome and glamorous in a crisp white suit with a huge sunflower tucked into his lapel. He seemed a bit tense and hassled though, anxious to get the drinks in for his select corner. With Naomi Campbell draped on one arm looking eminently feline, and his new wife obligingly demure on the other, Gavin looked dapper, and quite the dandy.

The sharpest dresser, and probably the coolest guy in town, I concluded. Gavin was the guy you wanted in your corner. He seemed to have a radar for bullshit, and minimal tolerance for wannabes.

Things started to heat up as the drinks flowed in The Kitchen. Little did she know it but The Mermaid had entered what was to be her primary habitat for the coming years. The Kitchen Nightclub was so called because it was renovated from the old cavernous kitchens of the boutique hotel above.

The main reception for the wedding had been upstairs in The Tea Rooms of The Clarence Hotel. The Charles Rennie Mackintosh inspired wooden and white decor of the tearoom, gave an elegant backdrop to the wedding reception, where the elite of Dublin and the big wide world, gathered to celebrate Gavin's nuptials.

Just before the party settled into its groove, there had been some kind of crisis. Christy Turlington, the beautiful doe-eyed super model, with the smiley mouth full of immaculate teeth, had been inconsolably distressed. I thought it rather weird that a woman of Christy's usual class and poise should have freaked out whilst tumbling out of her limo onto the pavement. I guess those heels were too high after all. The drama which threatened to over shadow a joyous event, was averted by the limo driving a couple of times around the block, so that its glamorous contents could reset and re-present.

Spirits were soon lifted by the mounting energy in the room, rather than by any white powder that may or may not have been consumed. I found myself playing the role of hostess, and was charged with the responsibility of ensuring a healthy flow of white wine to Bono's table, and to Bono in particular. Bono was disconcerted that someone kept walking off with his wine, and commissioned me to keep him fully replete throughout the night.

Billy was in seventh heaven at the wedding. Long time buddy AK was in tow, along with a wiry, silver-haired character called Diarmuid. Between them, this old boys club eyed up every super model that passed by their drinking corner. These old die-hard Dubliners, used to letting it all hang out at The Pink Elephant, had never had it so good. Their years of trawling for talent had finally reached its fulcrum point; and Billy seemed more than slightly bemused that he had landed in Dublin and was sharing his first Irish shindig with the likes of Christie Turlington, Naomi Campbell, and Kate Moss.

Surely he had died and gone to heaven?

I was matter of fact as usual. I had work to do, and I never had been particularly fazed by celebrity. Nodd, the Scottish manager of The Kitchen Nightclub, was checking me out for an assistant manager position in the night club once it opened. Originally I had been in line to be interviewed to manage the club itself. But I had not been well enough to attend the interview in Manchester with Mr O' Driscoll. So Nodd, was given the nod. With his vast experience of nightlife and running clubs, Nodd was the natural choice. Rather annoyingly he brought his side kick Ralph from my home town of Portishead to fill the position I thought I might get.

Small world, I thought.

Ironic, I thought.

Regardless, the wedding was a joyous occasion. So I engaged in the energy of the event and offered to help with sustenance and fluids. I was generally happy enough to flit around making sure people were fed and watered. I never did really drink myself, despite long hours and nights at gigs and nightclubs. I was content enough to get a feel of the place and enjoy the ambience. By this time the centre stage karaoke machine had been switched on and the weirdest duets and ensembles began to pervade the night air and massacre our best-loved songs.

How bizarre. Here I am in Dublin listening to Bono singing karaoke with a drag queen called Mr Pussy, and he is not sounding much better than your favorite uncle, if truth be told.

I remembered all the white wine I had plied him with, and immediately gave him an excuse. But it was indeed amusing to watch the supermodels sing, along with Bono's wife Ali, who seemed particularly gracious, in a studied way.

Probably an ingrained response and practiced demeanor, designed to see her through all eventualities, I reflected. Luminous and vibrant she surely was. Never a truer word was thought or said, as subsequent events began to unravel to prove me very right indeed.

The second time I met Bono, was the following February on Valentine's Day; the day of the official opening of the nightclub. After Gavin's wedding I had returned to Scotland to keep attending the Publishing course at Stirling University. Ali was gracious enough to take the hand bound book I had made for him in the mean time. It was a creatively complied version of *The Song of Songs*. I had even managed to work out how to build a hard back cover; something no student had managed to do before on such a thin book. Bono was very touched and appreciative of the gift. He graciously declared the next day when I met him upstairs in the hotel, that he would "treasure it forever."

This was a wonderful introduction to the unofficial king and queen of *Dublin's Fair City*. U2 had definitely been my musical landscape during my tricky time in Scotland. I had a strong sense of Bono's energy as being very familiar somehow. When we met at Gavin's wedding, and then again at the opening of The Kitchen, there was an immediate comfort and recognition. Something I am sure his fans worldwide would understand, and identify with. I was not trying to factor myself in or conjure anything up. But I did feel it if truth be told; and the way he looked at me with warmth and curiosity, showed he acknowledged something of the same energy.

At this stage my musings were fairly innocent and not in the least bit contrived. Of course they were never about to be contrived, since I do not do superficiality in any guise. But, one thing was for sure, I did not fully appreciate that Gavin's wedding was going to be as much of a watershed moment in my life, as it was for Gavin.

Obliviously floating around in my Sarah bubble, I was always one for observing, watching and connecting with people I did not know from Adam. But all this felt a bit different. Something more was engaging my underlying attention. This was deep interesting stuff that I had not fully bargained for. Quite honestly things were stirring that I did not want to deal with. Something was evoked like a distant memory and my heart was unwittingly involved. There was a quality of soul in the air that I had not experienced before. This was the real deal, never mind all those Scotsmen.

As usual Billy managed to piss me off by chatting up the nearest model. Not Naomi, Christy or Kate thankfully. No, Billy had grabbed the interest of an attractive red head, over from London with her mother especially for the wedding.

Safe enough, I thought.

But duly observed and noted too. Besides I had other fish to fry. For the first time I was consciously aware that Billy had serious competition. Even though I was only just waking up to the fact, I amused myself with the notion that Bono had apparently taken quite a shine to me.

It was all Billy's fault. We should not have even been there. I had a degree unfinished in Scotland, and somehow here I was in a Dublin nightclub dishing out wine and sorting out coats in a cloakroom. I had been quite happy with the prospect of settling down and enjoying Billy's congenial, for the most part, company back in Edinburgh. I loved and missed the old historical town which had inspired my senses and stirred my soul. But here I was serving drinks at a party in "dirty old town" Dublin, with a special request from Bono to keep him plied with wine, as someone kept marching off with his bottle. You could not work that out or plan it if you tried. A most bizarre subterranean triangle with echoes of another time, another place was beginning to play out; and I was not really ready for this karmic destiny moment.

No wonder I freaked out on the ferry from Stranraer six months later, when the time had come to face the music. I had fallen under a spell or into some kind of other worldly dalliance at the wedding and was loath to come over to Dublin to see what it was all about. It was compelling, but also dark and inexplicably dangerous. The whole scenario felt uncomfortable, panic inducing, and beguiling in equal measure. Little did I know it, but I was experiencing one of those multiple-choice scenarios you sometime get in life.

Depending on how I reacted, one of several things could happen. I could get seduced by the glamour of the fashion jet set lifestyle in Dublin; which was not really my thing; I could return to Scotland with, or without Billy, and then split up with him as he scarpered off abroad again; or I could sit with the new connections I was making and see what happened.

It is clear that sometimes you walk into something that is the exact opposite of what you really want or intend. You get embroiled in an emotion from which it is difficult to retreat. A masterful web is spun and you wait for an answer, but none is forthcoming. It is the magic of a compelling and powerful alluring moment that causes you to hang on for dear life; and such is the charisma of a good man on a good day that you are happy to oblige, or at least wait and see what it is all about.

I found Gavin's magnificent Sunflower later on, on his wedding night. It was discarded and crushed on the night-club floor, muddied and lifeless. I retrieved it for Gavin and Renee, hoping it was not a bad omen for their union, and resolved to put it in water, and then dry it out when I got home.

The nightclub in this form only saw one night of entertainment. After Gavin's wedding, Edge, Bono, and Harry Crosbie, deemed it too dangerous with its tiled staggered steps and copper trimmings. Having taken months to renovate and create a wonderful eclectic space, the owners decided to unceremoniously rip it apart after only one event. The Kitchen reopened on Valentine's Day five months later as a mysterious winding cavern complete with nooks, crannies, water features and moat. The moat was a new design flaw which was impossible to keep clean for any length of time. But enough energy had been wasted getting the club in order. It was now down to business.

The Kitchen was re-launched officially amidst a flurry of fuss, and the prerequisite supermodels were in attendance all over again. This time drama was kept to a minimum. Bono was sober and on his best behavior. With the press present, this was a "Zoo," to use his words. U2 were on display, and their night club had come of age. Edge wore his Sergeant Pepper type purple suit, while Bono looked cool, drink in one hand, cigar in the other. Ali his wife, glamorous as ever wore a big furry off-white jacket which off-set her raven black bobbed hair.

I was simply confused and bedazzled. I had not exactly chased this rainbow. But it had certainly been sprung upon me. The creeping sense of wonder and connection was only just beginning, in my head and heart. I was not star struck, but my heart sure was enlivened.

*WE ARE WHAT WE PRETEND TO BE,
SO WE MUST BE CAREFUL WHAT
WE PRETEND TO BE.
KURT VONNEGUT*

CHAPTER EIGHT

The Reluctant Psychic

Generally speaking we all have a measure of intuition which enables us to have a sense of what will happen. Being hypersensitive can definitely be a mixed blessing. Firstly, it is tiring if you do not know how to protect yourself. There is a temptation to walk around in a heightened state of awareness, which can lead to exhaustion. It is not really necessary to scrutinize everything, but it is an easy trap to fall into. The perks of the trade are the fun part.

Thinking symbolically is stimulating and gives life another dimension. Inside information is handy, and the ability to read situations is invaluable. But, it is easy enough to forget to put up your boundaries and sensitive psychics often learn the hard way. Being bombarded with energetic frequencies from people and the environment in general is not a very peaceful way to live. So, time to walk in nature and to still the mind is imperative when one reaches a high level of psychic ability.

When I was younger I thought it was normal to know who was on the end of a ringing phone, or who my sister's next boyfriend would be. My sister Rache used to get cross that I knew her own mind better that she did when it came to her love life. Come to think of it I did find myself saying, "see I told you so," rather a lot.

It was during my twenties that a fuller awareness of my Gift developed. I would find strange things happening, like when I looked at a picture of The Crows in the local paper. I thought they were all rather cute, got a flash of a wedding ring in my mind's eye, and promptly went up to the gig. Sure enough, Donald the guitarist's engagement was announced, and shortly after that I started dating the bass player Billy Bowie.

Nah, I did not believe him either. Cool name; cool guy? Time would tell. What was a possible one night stand for Billy, I gather that was his intention, actually turned into a lengthy relationship. Even though I did pick him up at two thirty in the morning in the nightclub next to my apartment, I knew it was a safe thing to do. What were the chances of that working out? It really went against all logic. Sometimes a deep knowing can cut corners, and be very useful indeed. Okay, it did not ultimately last with Billy. But we had some adventures, a good bond, and got along very well. We were essentially great friends.

Psychic messages can be complex, and frequently they need to be unraveled. Equally they can be as clear as day, and when this happens, there is a moment of conviction that no one can assuage.

When I know, I *know*. This can be annoying for people. Family, friends and clients alike love to test out my insights, and challenge my suggestions. More fool them, for it does not get them very far; even though it may amuse them to try. I do know this is not easy for those on the receiving end. But in urgent situations for example, I would urge implicit trust. Test me by all means in other situations. But if you call me in when in a tight-spot, it pays to follow the advice. I mean it comes from God not me anyway, so what is the deal?

My sister was once outraged when I told her she would marry someone other than her current boyfriend. When they both visited me in Edinburgh with another couple, I teased her that she would marry the other guy. She said "you're definitely wrong there; he's married to *her*." I told her to wait and see, as I knew I was right.

Sure enough in two years or so, without contrivance from anyone, the situation changed, and she married the guy I predicted she would. My sister was not in the business of doing something so profound, just to make me look good. The whole thing had a natural organic flow. It just turns out I was correct against all the logical indications.

On another occasion when working for my soon to become good friend Carrie, I predicted for her the man she would marry. We were hanging out on the set of the Tyrone television production of *Celebrity Farm* in Ireland. This was the first time we had met, but we had an instantly good connection. I was jokingly able to tell her that the psychologist Ian, whom she had also only just met, was going to be her future husband.

Celebrity Farm was a farmyard version of *Big Brother*, operating with the same principles of psychological analysis, fly on the wall observations, and public evictions. I was on the show to predict the weather for the week. Based on an astrological survey of current planetary activity, I provided a weather report with a difference, and a psychic prediction about the contestants. Ian was on the show to profile the contestants, and get the measure of Carrie it seemed. A few years down the road, and I predicted the timing of both her pregnancies too, with the second one being the most impressive. She was giving Harley the dog and I a lift to the beach for a walk, and I said "you're not pregnant again are you?" She was. But only by a week or so. I knew before she did.

An accurate psychic can blow your mind like this. But you usually will not actually believe it until you see it, and experience it in the context of your own life. This kind of thing happens a lot. It is part and parcel of what being a psychic is all about. Probably most of the time it would be best for me to keep my mouth shut. But I also have to live, breathe, react with people, and be normal. So yes, predictions fly out of my mouth from time to time, before I have time to think about their implications. Strange things occur, as a norm. It is abnormal in fact, when I am not picking up on something leftfield. At those times I wonder if the Gift has left me. But of course it has not; nor will it. Reluctantly I have had to develop and master it. There is no point having such a Gift and then not using it to the maximum to help people.

Why reluctantly, you might ask? Well, being a commercially viable psychic out in the world was really not in the game plan of my life. You can see from my upbringing I was academic, bright, with Christian faith and boundless optimism in the midst of challenges. I also had great sensitivity, perception and randomly knew things that others did not. It was always controversial when I picked up something against the odds or unasked for. I duly noted the mixed reception this phenomenon got. It is all very well helping people when you are asked to do so. But sometimes you are required to intervene so that people do not make mistakes or harm themselves. Try implementing that that when your message is not well received. Thankfully there are ways of intervening on the ethers, and through the hidden dimensions, by tuning into a person's higher understanding. So it is not always necessary to actively explain things to the nth degree.

This whole psychic thing is challenging in the extreme. It has to be responsibly mastered, understood ethically, and applied effectively. You have to be able to deliver. Plus you are expected to be accurate to a fault, and have the confidence to know you are correct. Done in the wrong way, this can come across as egocentric. Who likes someone who claims to be able to heal, and who apparently knows it all? Yeah. Now you get it. Wink.

Thankfully, I know that people understand me on that point most of the time. I have noticed that spirit guides, most significantly the Holy Spirit, bring the correct people to me. I do not ever go looking for work. It comes to me. I have my columns out there and my web site up, but I do not push or advertise myself unless guided to. When I do, I usually quickly understand why. Spirit uses the information to reach someone who needs my skills. I have noticed that people seek me out also. Whether by word of mouth, because of my reputation, or because of a prompt within themselves, they find me. And they know I can help them. For reasons I have not quite worked out, I instil trust in people. People have an underlying knowing that I can help them, whether it be for information, healing, or energy work. This is absolutely correct, for I *am i*ntrinsically trustworthy.

Human I am, God I am not. But I *do* deliver to the best of my abilities, with God's grace and help. I find that when I am in a relationship with someone, that I am highly connected psychically. Those to whom I am telepathically linked do not get away with much. Or rather they *do*, because I am tactful, and keep any misdemeanors discretely under wraps. Let us just say that not much goes unnoticed. But a whole lot probably goes unmentioned.

When personally engaged with a client, friend, or family member, I always know if something untoward has happened. This freaks people out, fascinates them, and invariably scares them off pretty much in equal measure. Generally male friends have a healthy cynicism towards my profession, and trust their own judgement. But their pragmatic side actually gives me more of a head start than they appreciate. I understand pragmatism, because despite all appearances, I am more systematic and grounded than people perceive. They usually see a funny, bright, blonde girl, who is perhaps a little "woo-hoo," rather than a weird witch who should be burned at the stake. The reality is, I implement my magical side as guided, but I am also quite hardcore, focused and practical.

With girlfriends I can be a useful ally. I habitually turned up on Eki's doorstep when she was pregnant with the relevant craving of the day; and on the occasions when she phoned asking for something, more often than not it was already in my bag and I was on my way. If I am close to someone, I can often tune into what is on their mind, even if they are miles away. Mum has often commented that I get home at just the right time. Dad's health has been challenged at points over the years, and we have found that the timing of my visits home has always been perfect, for one reason or another. This is not down to contrivance on my part, I just follow my instincts, and move when the time is right.

During the mid noughties, there was a huge road block which prevented me leaving Ireland and getting home at all. It was as if I was meant to hold the faith, and belief that all was safe and well, even as the family worried. It was not an ideal situation. But it was unavoidable, and it was tricky weighing up if to stay or go. Destiny had brought me to Ireland. Was it appropriate to even leave? At times it seemed most definitely not.

Healing can be very mysterious and I do not understand all aspects of the challenges I went through. At times it felt like a fight for survival; at other times a battle for my very soul. I was cornered by circumstances, or so I thought. But as always an elegant exit presented itself exactly at the right moment. For a long time, and for complex reasons, largely linked with my work in Ireland, I seemed to be thwarted every time I tried to make an arrangement to get home. I think a deep part of me knew that if I actually *got* home, I would not be able to return. So it was easier not to leave for a while. I carried on in faith, knowing and perhaps assuming that the way ahead would clear itself at the opportune moment; which of course it did.

Psychic gifts have a very practical application, and I find that I can utilize this knowing in just about any situation you care to mention. One really amusing incident was when my own car did not *feel* right. I was convinced the clutch was not performing properly. Obviously a mechanic or sales man would have thought me most odd. However the red Ford KA I was leasing at the time made me uncomfortable for no apparent reason. I enquired if the model was available with power steering in the same colour. The salesman said they did not make the KA 2 in the radiant red that I desired. Again I was absolutely sure he could find what I was looking for, so I asked him to humor me, and phone around. Sure enough by four-thirty in the afternoon, on the same day, he had found the car I knew was out there. A couple in Cork had ordered the model specifically but did not want it. So, much to the garage's bafflement, I got the same deal on exactly the car I had visualized.

Not even holidays are safe for the psychic on the loose. One summer, I went for the first, and last, time to my Uncle's sixteenth-century house Hill Hay Farm in Cornwall. I was looking forward to relaxing, and enjoying my holiday in Fowey. Apparently this was not to be allowed by the powers-that-be. My sister and her husband were there for the first two days, so I did not particularly notice the unease creeping up on me.

As usual an innocent joke proved to be my downfall. An "is it haunted?" tripped off my tongue as soon as I stepped into the house, and once the others had gone the fun began. It was not only myself experiencing the discomfort of the haunting. Both Freddie my little dog and Billy were also greatly perturbed and unsettled. There was a perpetual feeling of being watched from the upstairs landing, when in the galley kitchen below. I nearly choked on my vitamin pill one evening, and once my sister left, we all ended up sleeping down by the front door. I almost contemplated sleeping outside as it felt a little safer. There were doors banging, the piano strings were brushed, rather than played, which was somehow even more unnerving; and I actually felt under severe attack. I awoke pretty much every hour during the night; and at several points had to pray for protection. There was an overwhelming sense of something trying to possess me. This was at this point my one and only experience of such menace, and I never wished to experience it again. Not pleasant. But of course it was not the last time.

Being from an evangelical home, I am not the sort of psychic to be madly interested in haunting or séances. You could call me a reluctant psychic in this respect also. I actually dislike and recoil at a great deal of the things normally linked with my profession. I would not actively look for such entertainment even out of curiosity, and I do not particularly feel comfortable with the sensationalistic approach of programmes like *Most Haunted*. I appreciate their public appeal, but would not be tempted to go on as the resident psychic. Apart from anything else, you never know what you are going to meet on a dank, dark night in some obscure haunted property. No thank you.

Even though I do have mediumistic ability, I try not to use it except when I am really called upon to do so. I wondered why my father was taking me so seriously on the phone when I described what was happening in Cornwall. But it was not until I got back to Bristol that he told me a practicing medium used to live in the house. She apparently used to hold séances, and must have therefore stirred up a whole lot of tricky energies. Even though the house had been blessed by a priest, it had probably not been done effectively. There were obviously still plenty of energies in residence that were keen to come out and play with a psychic on holiday.

Psychic people are admittedly much more susceptible to these experiences, but what added to the feeling of unease was that Freddie my dog could not sleep either, and kept growling and fidgeting throughout the night. Even more indicative was that Billy, a matter of fact, pragmatic, no nonsense Scot, was also terrified. It turns out that we all chose to sleep precisely where a child girl ghost had been seen. This amused my Uncle Chris, who owned the house. But I can only conclude that the innocent spirit must have been protecting us. Everything else in that ancient cottage was having quite some party once the lights went out. My brother jokingly renamed it Hell Hay Farm, which is perhaps a bit extreme. But it gets the point across.

When I lived in Edinburgh there were other such happenings, to which I sat loose, and simply observed. I lived in the heart of The Old Town on Victoria Street, the steep cobbled road which links The Royal Mile to The Grassmarket. Victoria Street is an ambient laneway lined with restaurants and colorful shop fronts. It is a world set apart, and its environment is steeped in the energy of historical muggings, hangings, haunting, and murders. The gradient of this quaint ancient slip road, is steep. It is mounted on either side with high buildings which tower over unsuspecting pedestrians, threatening to intimidate them with daunting intensity. On one side of the street stands Victoria Terrace, which disconcertingly allows passers- by to gaze into the top floor window of the flats opposite. Walking along this precipitous path, even the most unobservant tourist is confronted with the majestic height and impressive curve of the West Bow. It is impossible to climb Victoria Street musing at the shop windows laden with antiques, second hand books or the latest ethnic outfit, without the accompanying sense that a loose slate might career from the precipitous buildings above. This is rendered more than a paranoid imagining by the wind tunnel effect, notorious amidst the Wynds and closes of Old Town Edinburgh.

Victoria Street, is found just below George IV Bridge, a busy road which crosses the Royal Mile, and connects The Mound leading up from Princes Street with the University Buildings, and various training hospitals. This unique street offers an instant impression of depth and serenity. Despite its noisy cobblestones, busy Aztec Indian craft shops, cafes, and night club venues, it possesses the peace which commonly emanates from an ancient monument.

If walls could talk?

Many spooky experiences have been reported throughout Edinburgh's history, but I did not expect my own flat in Victoria Street to be troubled. In the middle of a Highlands and Islands tour I had booked for the American Cajun fiddle band Le Rue, we were all lazing the morning away in my flat before an Edinburgh Festival performance the next day. I was talking to the banjo player, Martin at about noon, when suddenly this hideous demonic voice spoke over us. It was clearly audible, as loud as you like. We both heard it, looked kind of incredulously at each other, simultaneously said, "no way!"and resumed our conversation. Early the next morning the older members of the band, who had not believed the account of our experience, were themselves freaked out when the heavy solid door of the front room opened all by itself.

My bedroom in Victoria Street overlooked the famous Greyfriars Bobby graveyard, and there is of course a history of devastation by the plague in this particular area of Edinburgh. I did not think much of it at the time, but there was always the intermittent smell of rotten vegetation in my bedroom, which I would effectively get rid of by saying "F*ck Off Ghost!" Weird, but it worked. What seemed to confirm its effectiveness, was that from time to time I would remember that I had not smelled the smell for a while, and it would come back simultaneously and telepathically with the thought. I would then have to use my simple banishment, and there you go: gone, once again.

Of course we got all the drains checked, but there was no logical explanation for it. Perhaps the atmosphere of the flat was not helped by my roommate, Paul, who had started up the famous *Ghost Tours of The Old Town* with his brother. On a nightly basis, these two lads from the Orkney Islands dressed up as ghouls to spook and entertain tourists. All good clean fun, but there was an innate risk of conjuring something undesirable nonetheless. People do not realize the dangers of messing with the supernatural. Entities, demons, and negative energies are very real. Psychics know this. Thankfully I was away on the road most of the time.

Being psychic is useful when you need clues about the way ahead. I was always able to find gigs in strange towns without knowing the precise address; a very handy skill when there was a bunch of tired moaning rockers in the back of a van. Similarly I have always had a strong sense of where I would live next. On the way home from the family holidays of my youth we would pass through Stirling. I knew it was going to be a significant place for me. sure enough it is where I saw that rainbow with my Nan, and where I studied for a BA (hons) in English, Philosophy, and Religious Studies, as well as the pre Dublin Publishing Studies M.Phil. I was also aware that I would live in both Edinburgh and Dublin well in advance of the time I spent there. I was in Edinburgh for several years, and then in Dublin for several more.

This pre-knowledge of important places also applied to specific addresses. The German restaurant Lilligs was directly opposite the aforementioned haunted Victoria Street flat. For several months when I still lived down in Stockbridge, I would look up at the flat, while chopping vegetables and bashing schnitzels, thinking,

I sure would like to live up there one day.

The flat was very high off the ground, and one of only three properties available to rent in the street. Eventually my future flat mate came into the restaurant looking for a place to pin his Ad. for a roommate, and I staked my claim. I did not even let him put up his advertisement. I gather he subsequently fell in love with me; which was something I did miss at the time, or perhaps chose to ignore. He never told me, but he did tell Eki, who only told me years later in Dublin. Hmm. Sorry Paul.

Similarly, the first time I got off the train in Dalkey, a year after I first moved to Dublin, I mused that I would like to live on Railway Road, the road which leads straight down into village. At the time this was not an area of domestic rented property, but there I was, a couple of years later, living just where I had wished for. They had built and converted apartments as if by magic in the interim.

As soon as I saw the Dalkey apartment I knew it was the right place for me to work as a healer. The energies in the Dalkey and Killiney area are absolutely unique and powerful. They really lend themselves to psychic and healing work. Both the apartment and the layout of the village itself, proved crucial to the success of my subsequent work and practice. Healing work, requires a conducive energetic environment. It is not really ideal to work just anywhere. The beauty of living out of town was that I could clear my head on the beach after appointments. This simultaneously kept me sane, and enabled me to effectively do the work. I would not have been able to function so easily as a healer in the heart of Dublin City. Dalkey proved to be just perfect.

It is unquestionable that if you follow your inner guidance, things happen. I have never been one to do the obvious or conventional thing. I completed my publishing degree and came to work in a Dublin nightclub. Against the odds I got permission from the department to study under my own steam, and to finish the studies from a distance. I managed to convince the powers that be, that the move to Dublin was too good an opportunity to miss. You can imagine that I did then question my judgement when I was initially put on cloakroom duty in The Kitchen, when I had originally been in line to manage the club. But ultimately the decision to move to Dublin was validated. I am sure my parents thought I was mad moving on spec like that with a restless partner. But over time the opportunities to write and publish myself began to surface, and it all started to make some kind of sense. Just about.

*BUT THE FACT IS SHE, (THE MUSE)
WON'T BE SUMMONED. SHE ALIGHTS
WHEN IT DAMN WELL PLEASES HER.
SHE FALLS IN LOVE WITH ONE ARTIST,
THEN DESERTS HIM FOR ANOTHER.
SHE IS A REAL BITCH!*
ERICA JONG

CHAPTER NINE
Very A-muse-ing

It is probably abundantly clear from some of these stories that the spiritual, intuitive route through life is not the most logical. But it does have an uncanny way of being the most interesting. It is certainly useful to have some idea of what lies ahead, but ultimately best if the details look after themselves. Otherwise life would have no mystery at all; and I do like surprises. God laughs at our best laid plans. But I still have that post-it note my father wrote for me before I went to Stirling University: "For I know the plans I have for you," declares the Lord, "plans to prosper you and not to harm you, plans to give you hope and a future." Jeremiah chapter 29, verse 11.

Sometimes psychic insights can be a bit sad. For instance I do not feel that it is inevitable I will marry. I mean, look at the chequered history, and catalogue of karma which has played out thus far. I must be romping through the list of checks and balances. Perhaps this is not sad but sensible at this stage. Perhaps too, someone cool will want to prove me wrong on that point. Men do love to prove me wrong after all. Perhaps the situation is more promising than I know.

The pattern of my relationships has had many spooky twists and turns. The upshot is that I have learned to be amused rather than disappointed a lot of the time. I fell heavily for Jim the wonderful Canadian when I was eighteen. He was only over "on a break" from his girlfriend; so I gave him and his brother the whirlwind tour of Wales instead. Then there was the sexy American Pierre Le Rue, who was married a week before I met him. So, I went on tour and became his Scottish agent, rather than bust up a marriage. And so it goes.

I was sitting in Pierre's company in a bar in The Grassmarket, when a band member rather pointedly asked him what he would do "if a Mermaid fell in love with him out of the blue, now he was married." Rather aptly and wittily he replied: "why, I would take her on tour." And so it was. Pierre fiddled his way around much of the United Kingdom, and parts of Ireland and Europe with me in tow. Nothing untoward happened. Something nearly did a couple of times. But, vague opportunities were only half heartedly noted, and were duly intercepted by people on the lookout for Pierre's wife. Fair enough.

One time in the middle of nowhere at The Aultnamain Inn in the Highlands, there was a crackling chemistry building between us. There was literally a luminous ring around the moon that night. The Highland's other worldly, and mystically evocative atmosphere hung heavy in the air. Pierre in gallant fashion was attentive, and pointedly knelt before me, lifting the glove I had accidentally dropped to the ground. He literally handed me his "favour" on bended knee, just as a knight would propose to his lady.

It was very moving and romantic I thought. A special moment. I gathered later that it was symbolically bad luck. But it felt pretty magical at the time. I guess it cannot have been much worse luck than meeting him and falling in love a week after he married. I felt feted for sure in my love life. That night Pierre, who was prone to sleepwalking, walked right into my room naked. I pretended to be asleep and nothing happened. I will never know if he was literally sleep walking or pretending to. My suspicion is that it was a genuine sleep walking incident that I could have taken advantage of had I been that way inclined. Instead I kept my eyes firmly shut, and remained studiously asleep.

Another time I was in the top bunk above Pierre on the Dutch Island of Terschelling. We all had to wake early to catch the ferry back to the mainland. I awoke in the early hours to find him standing gazing at my face, and I asked for the time. His reply? "Time enough." That comment sort of held a resonance for me, and I relaxed deep inside.

Of course yes, if something is meant to be, there is always time enough, and no rush whatsoever.

I was something of an innocent, and certainly a well behaved girl. So I kept my mystique, and urges went unfulfilled as the tension grew. I gather my presence in the van on tours was a bit of a puzzle to the other band members. I picked up that I was sometimes resented, and certainly not always understood. One particularly annoying time was when Alfred, Pierre's brother in arms from America, was travelling with us. Alfred was a lovely man, but he was looking for a wife, and in the back of the van Pierre pledged to play at the wedding should I consent to marry him. This was much further down the road, but it did get me wondering.

How did it go from people in Bruges, Belgium asking me if Pierre was good in bed, to Pierre offering to play at my wedding to Alfred. He was obviously annoyed with me after a while, and looking to offload me onto one of his band mates. Either that, or Alfred's studied verbal devotion to me gave Pierre the perfect excuse to hide any residue of feeling he might have. When we got to Belfast, thankfully the pressure eased, and Alfred met his match at a gig in a bar in some dark dingy corner of a grey area in the city. I was not sure how safe we were hidden in this staunch protestant enclave, with our flamboyant, republican mandolin player Fergus in full flow. But, we weathered it and got out of there alive. Alfred realized the love of his life, had morphed from a mermaid into a buxom blonde barmaid who warmed to his friendly advances.

Okay, good, Pierre could play at that wedding instead!

After Belfast we had headed across to The Netherlands. Arriving back into Dover on the ferry, we were hauled in for a thorough search by customs. Alfred had been drumming with Le Rue for some months, and had clearly overstayed his visa option in the united kingdom. He should have had a work visa. He did not. So in an incident which was very distressing to all of us, my ex future "husband" was exported off to Paris, and then unceremoniously across to the States. Obviously the universe had other ideas about who I was going to marry, or not marry. It was not going to be a random drummer looking for a visa extension anyway.

All on board the tour bus were friendly to me, and I had a good friendship with most of them. But, Mark, a former bass player with The Psychedelic Furs, was a bit of a problem. Mark directly confronted me about my presence on the tour in Ireland, and upset me immensely. Nothing was going on. I just enjoyed the company of the lads and the music. He annoyed Pierre intensely anyway, and Pierre told me personally that he was about to get his marching orders. This event gave Pierre the perfect excuse to ditch Mark, rather than the Mermaid.

Yes, I was in love with Pierre, but I meant well, and certainly was not going to break up his marriage or disrespect his wife. As usual, I turned a situation which was disappointing romantically for me, into something fairly constructive for everyone. I booked gigs for the band in Scotland, and I designed a T-shirt for them, and sold it at gigs. All very wholesome. There were moments of frustration and temptation, but nothing got out of hand. Neither Pierre or I were into causing any problems for anyone. Pierre had a job to do, and I was enjoying the camaraderie, and dancing the night away as they played their intoxicating music.

Pierre was immensely talented. He had worked originally with Queen Ida in America, and is a real deal, grassroots Cajun player. I loved the music and energy conjured up by Le Rue. It made me happy, and gave me a purpose for quite some time. I had a lot to get out of my system, and being able to keep company with these musicians enabled me immensely. I know my presence was resented and challenged by some of the team. But #whatever. Pierre himself, did not seem to mind, and that is all that mattered to me. I even overheard him turning down his wife's request to "get rid of Sarah," one night when we were sleeping in adjacent rooms after a New Year's gig at Hebden Bridge in Yorkshire. Pierre was an all inclusive gentleman, and really there was no need to be mean or bitchy to The Mermaid.

At the beginning of this Christmas and New Year Tour, I had booked a gig for Le Rue at The Preservation Hall in Edinburgh on Boxing Day. I prepared a huge Christmas feast for everyone, on the off chance they would accept it. Tina, Pierre's wife looked like an alarmed rabbit in the head lights, when she met me at this seasonal time. I felt jolted emotionally too, and surprised at Pierre's taste and choice of wife on first glance. She need not have worried. But sadly, it looks like I did cause some stress to her marriage. I guess she should have trusted her husband more. She certainly could, so it was a shame she did not. In typical Taurus fashion, Pierre weathered the accusations and drama, without compromising his friendship with me. That was good of him, and is a testament to his character.

Of course, Tina declined the Christmas feast, and I was left with a lot of turkey to consume alone. Mellish, the cat was very pleased indeed, and I was left upset, feeling something like a loser. I had chosen Christmas alone to be on hand for the gig, and the band were then blocked from accepting my hospitality by a jealous wife. I was not best pleased. But I had no intention of giving Tina a real problem to deal with.

The gig on the day after Boxing Day in Shotts, saw Pierre changing some song lyrics as he was singing about *Billy The Kid*. He sang of a wrong road taken, and I knew when I heard the lyric switch that he felt the same way as I did. I am sure being wrongly accused would have been a big part of his frustration. It just goes to show that we as women do not always do right by our men when we assume they are being unfaithful, or are guilty of a wandering eye. Trust is everything in relationships. It can be a self-fulfilling prophecy to accuse someone of something they are not doing, let alone contemplating. Steer clear of such behaviour would be my strong advice. We should not expect men to have to bolster us in the face of our insecurities and inadequacies; nor have to placate our unreasonable accusations.

Keeping company with all these men, as a friend most of the time, has taught me much about their ways. In essence, men are simple creatures, and they want a simple, stable life. Just like us women they get thrown off track. But overall, I do believe that not half as much goes on behind our backs as we think. Trust your man ladies, in order to prevent issues that are actually nonexistent before your anxieties, insecurities, and worries kick in.

Of course women's intuition can be correct. Tina was not wrong to pick up the connection between Pierre and me, and being pregnant, she was understandably hormonal and concerned. She could trust Pierre. What she did not know, was could she trust me? She could. I have a fairly strong sense of sisterhood, and I am also a person who was brought up to, "do as you would be done by." Women friends have betrayed me a few times by going after boyfriends or men that they knew I loved. But I have never returned the favour and gone in for the kill with any man that I wanted. All things considered, I really was not mistress material.

Steven, my roommate in Stockbridge, had shocked me once, by saying that he thought I was mistress material, not wife material. He could not believe that actually I *wanted* to get married and have a family. Son of a Scottish mason, Steven was ultimately mean and bullying to me. He judged me by appearance I guess, projected his desires onto me, assuming I was a potential liaison, not likely to inspire commitment in a man. Charming. But hmm. Perhaps he had a point?

I think Pierre liked my calm energy, presence and support. We were friends and kept a respectable distance from each other. He never told me to leave. But I am sure if I were ever not welcomed by him, he would have said something immediately. That was approval enough for me. I also got signals of the connection whenever he played *Jolie Blon*. Pierre played his own version of this Cajun anthem adlibbing with phrases like: *Jolie blon, my little darlin' you are the flower of the bayou and my sweetheart.* At the time I did not even register that it might have been sung partly for my benefit. It probably was not. But, a girl can dream. In retrospect, it *did* feel like it could have been pointedly sung as a nod to our connection. I certainly did not assume it at the time. In fact it was Eki that pointed it out to me and said "Duh."

I was never really sure what Pierre felt for me. Taurus men can be incredibly passive, and generally do not make the moves. They are also incredibly loyal. What I did note was that when I took Billy to a London Lawyers' Shindig, hosted by Le Rue, Pierre ignored me totally. The gig was fun. I had started to see Billy, as there seemed to be no chance of anything ever happening with Pierre. Billy was intermittently moaning about and grieving Julie, so it was not totally dead in the water for me with Pierre. He only had to say the word really at this point. But clearly he was jolted to see me *apparently* happy with someone else. I did not turn up with Billy to be mean or rub his nose in it. I genuinely had concluded that he was not interested by that point. It was a bit of a shock to note *his* shock, and as we all stood in a circle parting ways after the gig, Pierre was pointedly polite to Billy, but totally ignored me.

Oh... Duh! Ooops....

I guess I enjoyed being some kind of musician's muse, in my own head at least. I loved music, and its players. Music, the company of musicians, and the energy they conjured made my heart soar, and my soul sing. I needed this diversion after all the traumas and dramas, which were in sequence, John, Graham, and Harry. It was my way of processing a whole load of nonsense without actually having to think too deeply about it.

I was musical myself, but never tried to be in a band at this stage of life. I was happy enough watching everyone else express themselves. I was along for the dance. I could sing and played the piano, cello, guitar and recorders. But, I never really pursued any of this beyond Grade Six Cello at School, and strumming folk songs on the guitar. My claim to fame is that I can tune a guitar by ear. Aside from that, and having a respectably good singing voice, I did not do much with it. Perhaps I could have been a backing singer and percussionist. I just never had that opportunity. Nor did I look for it.

The whole muse thing came further unstuck when Mike Scott of The Waterboys seemed to take a dislike to me. He was much less amused by me than anyone had ever been. I seemed to get under his skin somehow. Eki and I had been following along with *The Highlands and Islands Tour* in a big white van. I ended up sleeping alone in the van when Eki left the proceedings at Ullapool. We had shared hotels with the entourage on the previous nights. But Eki was somewhat upset at the situation, as she had been having an affair intermittently with the CEO of the company organising the tour. She could not handle aspects of our tagging-along scenario, and decided to return home by coach to Edinburgh. I was left alone to continue the journey I was committed to. They wanted only work people present, so they found me a job on the door helping with tickets for two elemental gigs in a big tent.

I had creatively extended the borrow time on the white van from the social center next to my house. Obviously I had permission to use their vehicle. But I artfully extended the lease with tales of bogs, intrigue and scattered sheep up north in the wilds of Scotland. It was very naughty, but it was my only way to tag along with the ride I was enjoying. I never thought Mike Scott was any kind of soul mate, and the Brussels sprout shaped hat on his head really was quite ridiculous. But his music, and lyrics in particular, moved me.

Mark, the promoter of Regular Music, eventually ordered me to go home after the final Ullapool gig. They were all concerned for my safety sleeping in the van. I had gone into the tour hotel to use the bathroom once the convoy arrived in Perth. I overheard Mike talking to the tour manager about me, calling me Stevie Nicks. It was not the first time this tag had been bestowed upon me, and it amused and flattered me to hear them use it.

I guess I looked a bit like Stevie Nicks on a good day. At some point I had morphed into a modest version of her as I grew up. I had been transfixed by the back cover of the *Rumours* album as a developing young teen, and really decided she was everything I wanted to be. Perhaps it was my first organic experience of cosmic ordering. It sure did work. It was not a conscious modelling, it just seemed to unfold to the point that people noticed it. When Stevie put out her track *Sara*, I felt even more of a connection. Her muse and inspiration was revealed to be someone called *Sara*. I liked that. I had to once prepare a tape for a backing vocal demo, and Eki observed that when I sang her songs my voice had a better more resonant quality. It was kind of spooky actually. I probably could have done a Stevie Nicks *Stars in their Eyes* if required, or perhaps a Fleetwood Mac cover band.

Mike's vaguely apologetic dismissal of me via Mark took the amusing form of, "Mike says he likes to party as much as anyone; but really he is here to just work at the moment." I thought:

What the f*ck? What exactly did he think I was there for, or hoped for? Whatever it was: he was horribly wrong.

I did not party either. Never have really. I just *liked the music.*

It was one of those do not get close to your idol moments. Either that or Mark was just passing the buck, and Mike was in fact a neutral bystander. Mike was never my idol actually, but I very much resonated with his music. I decided in that moment, I was not sure I liked what was going on around him. But yes his music was wonderfully evocative, elemental and eminently spiritual. It made my soul sore, even as the situation made my heart soar.

I dutifully trundled home in the white van and returned it to the social center under cover of night. There were some flickering lights inside. But I was quickly gone, the keys were posted back with a note, van unharmed, before anyone could say "peekaboo!" I'm kidding; but I guess it could have looked like that. The reality is, that is the time I made it home; late at night when everyone was asleep.

Not to be defeated, I returned to The Waterboys Tour in Glasgow the following week, with a different hat on. I was never someone who would be told what to do. The way I had been unceremoniously been exiled from joining in with something I loved, had hurt. They were probably correct, it was a bit of a liability for their tour insurance to have a young woman connected to the tour, sleeping in a car park in a van. But at the same time, I was more steely and intrepid than they realised. I do not like to be told "no" when it is something I want to do, or feel guided to do. Sometimes I have to stick my neck out when guided to do controversial things. I do try not to offend in the process. Obviously I do not always succeed.

In my Edinburgh Days I was a makeshift promoter and driver of bands. I helped book gigs, and I even put on a few highly successful gigs. I generally made myself useful to musicians through my aspiring business Quantum Leap. At that time, wannabe business executives could get a payment from the government, akin to getting a state benefit, as they established and developed their entrepreneurship. Through this means, and by virtue of the fact that I had actually booked Le Rue to be Mike's support in Glasgow, I felt justified in showing up for the next leg of the tour. I was the makeshift driver of The Wee Free Kings, who were the third support slot for this Glasgow gig, and indeed the rest of the tour.

Mike had always supported the Edinburgh band The Wee Free Kings, and I artfully travelled alongside them as their tour manager for the final stages of this tour. There was not much the powers that be could do. When they saw I was back, they unceremoniously turned Le Rue around. Pierre and co had made it up the motorway as far as Liverpool, and were not best pleased at having their journey aborted.

Hopefully the two events were not connected, and there was no need for anyone to slip into paranoia. But It felt like they *could* be. I had probably been expected me to show up with Le Rue, seeing as I had booked them for the gig. Instead, I rocked up working with the band who were already booked to complete the whole tour, as their driver. Do not mess with The Mermaid. She is innocent enough, but *likes* to be included.

Annoyed as I was that Pierre had been turned away from this pre-arranged gig, I was highly amused when Mike sang *Be My Enemy* with a less than subtle lyric change. The resounding climax of that track had extra resonance that day for some reason. As Mike changed his somewhat paranoid lyrics to *from the top of your hat,* I knew I had possibly irritated him somewhat. I wore a hat, and was never without it. It was my trademark, so the change of these lyrics seemed to be a bit pointed. It may of course have been a complete coincidence, but I assumed he was being personal. It certainly felt like it. I had not heard that lyric modified in this way ever before. Apparently he was pissed I had outwitted him. Funny. Okay, the guy was newly married. Yes, *another one*! But I was not trying to disrupt his focus.

Unless the "hat" reference in the lyric change was a complete coincidence, clearly Mike felt bothered, if not distracted by me, so I guess I will take that as an inverted compliment. All I know is, he did not then turn up for his curry night the following day in Newcastle, with the Wee Free Kings, and their annoying blonde van driver. Stalemate. #nothingdoing.

These shenanigans were all a long time ago now, and I may not have been such an issue as I thought. But this was how it felt and looked at the time. Hindsight can be interesting as we garner more wisdom and perspective further down the road. But just in case I had offended Mike in anyway, on the final night of the tour in London, I tried to sweeten him with an ironic gift of a (better) hat, and some chocolates. To be fair he *did* thank me for these. All good. #oops.

HERE WE ARE TRAPPED IN THE AMBER OF THE MOMENT. THERE IS NO WHY...
KURT VONNEGUT

CHAPTER TEN
Stuck In A Moment

For some reason marriage and children have eluded me. But as I get older I think I want such responsibility less. Well not really, but I have to kid myself it is the case at this stage. I do know psychically that I have the potential to have a boy if I so choose. He is a choice, and will come along at the right time, not a moment sooner. Strangely, I started to get the sense of a boy for Bono "after a gap." He and Ali already had two beautiful girls, Jordan and Eve. There was certainly a gap of some years if Ali were to then have any more kids with Bono.

Anke, the spooky psychic from Wicklow, had predicted that I would have his child. Clearly a dangerously off-whack prediction. Perhaps there had been potential for this, at the point she said it. But I remember clearly her later reading, where she had to tell me that Bono's wife was pregnant again. She looked genuinely shocked when she saw this. She literally could see the foetus in her crystal ball. Aw. I was pleased for them. But it made me wonder what on earth Anke had been meaning previously. Anke had been merrily telling me that Bono and I would be together in the "future," and obviously this news was going to be upsetting to me. It was. To give her credit, she did not baulk at the task of telling me, taking the tack of "imagine how I feel having to tell you this." She could have easily glossed over the truth, though I would have found out soon enough. I had been questioning Anke's prediction for some time, asking if she was *sure* it was a child for me, and not Ali. She had assured me, it was for me. I was really less and less sure. In actual fact my own strong intuition about a boy gave the timing of Ali's next pregnancy "after a gap." Not long after this misleading kerfuffle, Ali had her first boy Elijah with Bono. Clearly I was a more accurate psychic in this moment. I had my emotional component and attachment to Bono in the mix, but at least I sensed the reality. It was still very upsetting. I remember seeing Ali being asked in an interview if she was having any more kids after her four. She said adamantly not, and that if Bono was having five the last one would not be one of hers. At that time I did sense five kids for Bono, so that was a curious comment to see. Yet it still did not validate Anke's prediction. Things were as they were meant to be, and it feels awkward even recounting this part of the saga. Embarrassing in fact. I know what I would have liked way back then. But quite a different tale unfolded.

This was obviously a huge crossroads moment for me. It energetically felt like I had moved on and not chosen the Bono path some months previously. I consciously did this. Ali in the mean time sensed her opening for another child and duly delivered. Sometimes destiny forces choices upon us, which for various reasons we decline. Others simultaneously operate their own karma and life opportunities, and we are denied. Dithering can be costly. But some things are just not meant to be. Anke may have been correct, there had been a potential for Bono and I. But he was married, so I kept my distance, and did not pursue or respond to something "more." It was clear what the reality was. Ali was blocking my way. Not deliberately. She was married to Bono, I was not.

Anke finally conceded this also. The drama when I was scheduled to go onto *The Late Late Show* in Ireland, and it got cancelled at the last moment was conclusively symbolic. My replacement? Ali Hewson. I was all booked in. The details, time of arrival, taxis to and fro, were all arranged. I got the cancellation call very close to show time. Ali had not been listed as one of the names I was appearing with when the researcher originally called me. But, I guess it could have been that we were both booked, and she did not wish to appear alongside me. I do not think there is an ounce of the diva in down-to-earth Ali, so I doubt that. Anke's comment was that it was the universe showing me what was in my way. "Duh."

I had met Michael Hutchence of Australian rock band INXS several times whilst hanging out with Bono, and it seems all the rumours were true. This sexy guy loved his women. One hilarious moment occurred at a small party held in Simon's rather pokey bleak red brick flat. The ex The Golden Horde singer, Simon, lived amongst the back streets of dilapidated urban Dublin, in the midst of a large warren of apartment blocks. It was a curious place for a seasonal gathering. Fairy lights softened the atmosphere, and a cheery warm coal fire burning in the grate soon raised temperatures. Bad Dog Reggie kept urging me to warm my freezing hands, and seemed quite concerned at my body temperature. He was right, I probably was running a metaphoric fever inside, for reasons unbeknownst to him.

Michael was off to the side doing his thing, flailing all over a model type called Antoinette. He had been playing with her, now substantially holey, tights all the way from The Kitchen nightclub to Simon's house; and by the time they got there, she looked pretty dishevelled. All sorts went on at the party; mostly in the rest room I suspect. But then again I am not privy to all that so I would not know for sure. Bono stomped in late, in a strange mood, and went straight up to the elevated platform bed, to be quickly joined by Antoinette, Simon, and Michael. I overheard a somewhat sycophantic, attempt by Antoinette to fish for compliments and reassurance from the men all around her. I dared not climb the wooden ladder to join in. I was not inclined to do so, and certainly was not invited. I could not quite work out the dynamic of Bono on a bed with Simon, Michael and this opportunistic girl, who had tagged along for the ride. I am sure it was totally innocent having said that. I think Bono was tired if truth be told, and simply wanted a lie-down.

After a while Michael came down to join Guggi, Reggie and Siobhan, myself, and a couple of others. He chatted to me about his attempts to record in Dublin. Heavily pregnant Paula Yates was apparently being very supportive of his times away from home.

Quite.

Michael was a nice guy. But he struck me as a little insecure, and he did not seem to be able to cope with a woman who was not fawning all over him. He was cute alright; but clearly felt more comfortable just flirting and fooling around, than talking philosophically. I did not fancy him enough for the rolling on the floor part, and besides Antoinette was doing all the running on that score. I was also totally straight, not being a drinker or a substance user, so again, not much energy connection there.

Whether or not you believe in reincarnation, I do believe that Michael did not really want to leave the earth plane at the time he did. From what he was saying to me, he was looking forward to family life, making more records, and generally embracing the future. He seemed possibly a little scattered and ungrounded in his energies. But nothing untoward for someone in the music business. I had seen worse cases of ego confusion. Here was a very attractive man with a lot to live for. But depression can be a scourge, and is no respecter of persons whatever their background or situation. The use of toxic substances, and an ultimate refusal to commit, would have also been underlying issues for Michael.

Michael must have got himself into a strange mind-set that fateful night in 1997. It feels similar to the energy which consumed Harry Horse ten years later in 2007. Both were drug users, prone to depression and random bouts of anger. Something took over Michael, and he was no longer at the wheel of his destiny vehicle. His spirit gave out within him, before he could rectify the situation. He was out of it, and not in control. But had he realized a split second sooner, he might have pulled himself back from the brink. It was not quite the same thing as giving up completely.

Some conspiracy theorists may well have found the circumstances of his death highly suspicious. As with all these high profile untimely passings, there is an element of intrigue, if not subterfuge. It certainly had all the hallmarks of a strange and unexpected ending. I tend not to give the "illuminati sacrifice" accounts too much attention. But there was certainly something tragic, shocking, and out-of-time about Michael's demise. Having seen his behaviour socially, I was not totally surprised he would meet an untimely end. He had more than a suggestion of Jim Morrison's energy about him; and his lifestyle was certainly an indicator of a possible premature exit.

Souls which depart this life prematurely, have been known to attach themselves to fellow humans, or animals, as they choose to remain earth bound. Such souls do not pass smoothly to the light, and they linger until they are ready to accept their fate. Sometimes they need help. Other times, they bide their time, and move on when they are ready. Michael was a bright spark who went out like a light. He did not want his life to be extinguished, and it is my belief he came straight back into the mix at his first opportunity. I have my theories about where he landed but I will keep those to myself as I do not want to offend anyone.

Instead of clucking around Michael and Bono, I used my time constructively at the party, and re-established my ability to call in the lucky numbers. An incredulous Guggi kept testing me on a mini roulette wheel, and I kept the hits coming, getting three red sixes in a row. Guggi was gobsmacked. I did not really understand what had just happened, as such things were fairly normal for me. He proceeded to explain that I would now be a very rich woman if we had only backed those three red sixes in a casino.

I was not a gambler. But here was some food for thought. My only experience of anything with numbers previously had been when I was eleven years old at the school fete. I just *knew* the number five was going to hit on the spinning wheel. I must have a penchant for tuning into the energy of a wheel, as sure enough five came up, and I proudly took the bottle of Champagne I won home to my parents.

I remember mum and dad rather downplaying my enthusiasm when I told them that I *knew* the number five was going to hit. Perhaps they already were aware that they had a psychic daughter on their hands, and were not sure quite how to handle it. They certainly would not have wanted to actively encourage too much spinning of the wheel. I did not understand at the time why they did not believe me about the number five thing. So it may well have been sceptical pragmatism speaking rather than overt concern. Quite possibly, it was simply disbelief that such predicting is even possible. I have proven the doubters wrong on that count many times since. Numbers are my forte.

I liked Bono's friend Guggi. He was always friendly to me, and we used to have lots of good, deep and connected chats. He shared my faith, sense of cool, and artistic temperament. I visited Guggi and his German wife Sybille with my young puppy dog, Freddie the dachshund. All went swimmingly well until Freddie had an untimely "accident" on the floor of Sybille's fantastic elegant, wooden-floored dining room. Oops. Both were gracious about it, and I was then privileged to be shown around a lot of their artistic and creative endeavours on the walls and in the studios of their home. It might have been a quicker way to get us out of the door to be fair. Freddie still a young pup, was obviously not yet completely housetrained. #oops

Guggi's studio was outside in a separate building converted for his exclusive use. It was a fascinating, a riot of colour, with splashes of blobby paint everywhere, and tubes of acrylic and oil bursting open onto mixing boards. The life of an artist is summed up in such places. The delicious opportunity to create and play with paint on various shapes of canvas is compelling, and absorbing. You can get lost in there, channeling the next concept. With Guggi it was usually a jug.

Both the Germanic Sybille, and the Guggi, formerly known as Derek, have wondrously long, blonde hair, and share a mutual talent for painting. They spawned five children all with amazing biblical names, who also all grew their hair long and blonde, never mind their gender. The family portraits were fabulous.

Guggi has appropriately exhibited at The Guggenheim in New York City, and his painting of jugs and bowls still adorn the walls of The Clarence Hotel in Dublin. I remember giving Bad Dog Reggie an elaborate explanation of the Freudian elements indicated in Guggi's work. It was a definitive analysis of his tendency to paint receptacles, rather than phallic protuberances. Clearly in touch with his feminine side, Guggi honored the goddess within, in his work. One could call his back catalogue a monumental tribute to The Holy Grail in fact. I wish I could remember it all now, but I am assured by Reggie, it was a genius interpretation.

Guggi had done an amazing painting onto the wall of The Kitchen nightclub too, in preparation for its reopening. Unfortunately with the smoke, damp and sweat, it got quickly damaged. I took it on myself to repair it for him, using my own painting skills. It was seriously chipped and peeling off the wall, so after the repair, I also sealed it so the same thing did not happen again. Guggi approved the job I did thankfully. I did not want to assume to tamper with an artist's work, but I knew I could do the repair required. I rightly assumed that he would have found the task tedious. Having inherited artistic skills of drawing and painting from my father, I love to be creative. To repair a painting was much more my preference than serving drinks at the bar, or selling the tickets on the door. Of course that did not last long, and I had it fixed within a few days. It was a good feeling while it lasted.

Guggi and Simon were definitely a bit like Bono's body guards at points, and policed him to an extent. Certainly this is true if you were new to the circle, or hovering around its periphery. There was an understandable wariness mixed in with a fairly accepting friendliness. These old school mates were still hanging out years down the road. They were open to new blood, but also closed to being made to feel uncomfortable by those with agendas. Sounds reasonable to me. This group of lifelong friends had each other's backs. Some of them were better known; but under the Lypton Village umbrella they were all equal. It was a privilege to see, know and experience the camaraderie, and witness their brotherly bond. These lads loved a laugh, and had a wicked irreverent sense of humor, as well as considerable intelligence exhibiting strong opinions on politics, religion, music and art. I feel honored to have been made welcome as a modest add-on, for the times they graced the nightclub with their presence.

It is true that Bono had a touch of the "innocent abroad" about him. A generous hearted and warm man, he was always keenly interested in people who interested him. Perhaps he really *did* need his mates looking out for him, lest he get into trouble. But I know from what he said to me about being too heavily policed and guarded, that he did not really like too many obvious security measures around him. It is essential in some situations for an A list celebrity to have a several sets of eyes monitoring the environment. But some seem to need it more than others.

Prince came into The Kitchen heavily flanked by huge burly minders. Whereas Bono tries to be more low key, when he can get away with it. The reason he loves to return home to Ireland, is that he can largely go about his business untroubled. Even the modest level of security we provided at The Kitchen irritated him sometimes. He wanted to just be left alone, and did not like to cause a fuss. Bono really is a down to earth dude from the north side of Dublin, who happens to have a big mouth that sometimes gets him into trouble. On the up side, he can sing like an angel, has wonderfully warm hands, and is a spokesman for many worthy causes.

Obviously his need for security has had to be stepped up since he got more heavily involved with politics. But even so, in Dalkey, you can randomly happen upon him and his wife, or him and an offspring walking around unguarded. Sometimes, security measures really are a big fuss about nothing. A celebrity can be as incognito as they choose to be in reality. It was interesting to see the range of protection each person chose in the nightclub. Prince was the equivalent of Fort Knox, flanked by four burly minders about three times his size. Bjork sauntered in alone carrying a ghetto blaster blaring at full volume, then fell unceremoniously down the stairs. While Jack Nicholson and Michael Douglas were two old men out for a brandy night cap before bedtime upstairs in the Penthouse.

One time we had all been drinking late night tea at Mr Pussy's Cafe, a colourful, bohemian, extravaganza den of iniquity, with cubby holes, velvet lined walls, and lounge sofas. Bono offered to give me a lift home in his yellow Ford Cortina, equally decadent and lined with leopard print, furry dice et al. Simon very promptly clocked this, and interceded. He invited me to cram into an already packed car instead.

Mm...Wonder if my luck would have been in had I taken the furry dice option! If not for the somewhat tactless intervention of the "Simon

Community," the Irish gossip media's moniker for Simon, I certainly would have had a serious opportunity to connect properly with Bono, the man I loved.

I did wonder about Simon. He was always inexplicably by Bono's side. Sometimes friendly, other times standoffish. I wondered what his role was. The word was that he helped with music, lyrics, and provided general companionship. That was the theory anyway. I remember Gavin curiously implying he had an issue with him at one point. So the situation was somewhat loaded. Simon had somehow put Gavin's nose out of joint, and they seemed to be in competition for Bono's time, attention and input.

There was a general distrust of new people on the scene, since the hub of the Lypton Village squad had been together since their teens. Simon was right at the heart of the inner circle, yet he had been a late arrival. Bono must have had his own good reasons for this, and Gavin probably felt he had to earn his stripes. In later years, Simon and Gavin ironed out their differences. But, up until that point, social nights usually had one or other of them present. Gavin and Simon tended not to grace the same room during the 90s. The " have you ever seen Simon and Gavin in the same room" thing had a slightly different meaning, because of course they looked nothing alike. It was only once bygones were bygones that they would sit around a large table gathering for a birthday celebrations, or Christmas dinners.

Gavin always comes to the fore in the U2 machine, to grease the wheels during the preparation phase of the next major tour. He works with Willie, set designer extraordinaire, to ensure that all aspects of the stage show run smoothly. He is heavily involved in prepping the band as they depict their conceptual story, and he works particularly closely with Bono on his presentation of the songs. Gavin travels alongside at the beginning of tours to make sure all is ticking over correctly. U2 used to call their first manager Paul Mc Guinness, the fifth member of the band. In truth, the fifth member is Gavin

Friday.

During tours, Simon tends to get left at home, except for the occasional gig, like other family members that cannot go along for the ride. Simon fills the recreational space between tours. He is the off-duty guardian and companion. Nights out, and holidays, generally have the Carmody influence for added zest and fun. During the traditional August South of France sojourn, he is found *en famille* once the work is done. Not exactly Bono's accoutrement, there was a time when Simon flanked him pretty much all of the time.

On the night of Simon's party, only a few days after a momentous intimate slow dance with Bono in the night club, I finally got my lift home. Two years too late? Perhaps. Flood, the producer, had asked Bono if he and I could get a ride home at about seven in the morning. As dawn was breaking, I was driven through the hazy, lazy streets of Dublin by Hugh, Bono's driver and permanent body guard. Hugh is a personable, handsome, ex army martial artist type, who also must have had the patience of a saint. Night after night he had to wait on the whims of his social and fun-loving master. Hugh never knew what time he would get home. But he could be pretty sure it would be in the small hours of the morning.

I thought it was hilarious that as we left the party, Bono said "well, phew, nothing too much went amiss there then!" I looked back over my shoulder at the sight of Michael flailing all over the floor with Antoinette, and mused, "well not so sure you are correct. Perhaps we can and should turn a blind eye to *that* at least." I did not like to think that trouble was going to go down once we had gone, as I did not really think it was madly fair on pregnant Paula who had retired early to her hotel room. Anyhow, as Bono took my arm as we walked down the dark stairway to the car, and then stroked my back affectionately as I got into the car with a "come along, Sarah darling," You can imagine that I thought I might be getting into a bit of trouble myself.

Bono helped me into the car, all the while rubbing the back of my soft, long, furry, brown coat. Sensual Taurus. He then sat in the front seat of the brown Bristol car beside Hugh his driver, and Flood sat in the back beside me. What amused Flood greatly was that Bono somehow twisted and contorted his hand behind him to stroke my knee, and hold my hand throughout the entire journey. Flood was intermittently chuckling under his breath as he witnessed this.

Shut up please! I thought, but cast him a perfunctory ,glare and confused smile now and again. Bono seemed to need physical contact, and the intimacy of that kind of reassurance and connection. He really should have sat in the back of the car, it would have been much more cosy. Flood could have giggled to himself on the front seat then; no harm done.

On the way home, Bono asked Hugh to take a particular route, and gave me a guided tour of St Patrick's area of Dublin where he had gone to school. Psychically I could pick up a loss in his energy field from so many years ago. He was speaking with warmth and regret, as if explaining himself somehow. It was shortly after this, that I gathered Bono had been working on a song about his mother Iris around this time. He must have been feeling nostalgic and reflective still at the echoes stirred from times past.

Bono had showed up in the night club late one night, having seeped in the energies of his Iris tribute piece all day. He was visibly shaken and introspective. Clearly it had stirred a very primordial and raw emotion within him. Years later, *Iris* is now out there for the fans to hear on the *Songs of Innocence* album. But it clearly took Bono a long, long time to be able to play it publically, let alone talk about it. His father still being alive may also have had something to do with the time lag on the release date. All very understandable.

As fans will know, Iris collapsed at the graveside of her beloved father, suffering from a cerebral aneurism as she grieved and mourned him. Bono thus lost his mother and grandfather in a very bleak month, at the very tender age of fourteen. This he admits is a primary reason why he has cleaved so hard and fast to his dear wife Ali, and lifelong friends. After this tragic loss, he needed family, consistency, a female companion, and stability. By the age of sixteen he had found it all in the form of Larry, Adam, Edge and Ali.

Aside from being a typical loyal Taurus, Bono is someone who thrives in the bosom of an established family, and trusted network of support. He had lost his lifeline Iris at an early age; did not particularly resonate with his father at that stage; and lived in a predominately male environment, with an older brother who could be a bit testy. Nothing has been the same for him since the passing of Iris. It was a rite of passage which felt particularly cruel to him; and is his main vulnerability in life even now.

Despite the brushes with his own mortality, which sober him up every time they occur, this loss of his mother has shaped Bono. At the core of his being, he is all about Iris. Everything he has done is inspired by her, is for her; while everything he has rebelled against is a testament to his father, with whom he had a more complex relationship. Like all of us, Bono is the alchemical expression and integration point of the affect his parents had upon his psyche; the fusion of his deoxyribonucleic quotient.

His musical outlet is thus infused with passion, heart and honesty. It is his therapy and his catharsis. Edge's guitar creates the emotional landscape and context, Adam's bass, the throbbing heartbeat, and Larry's drums the driven force and energy. It is no wonder U2 reach so many, and speak to the souls, hearts and emotions of their fans.

U2 are admittedly an acquired taste, which not everyone "gets." I remember being puzzled myself when I first heard them. That first single *Fire* took quite a few plays to resonate. But once savoured and experienced, U2 definitely grow on you. I won't say "like a fungus." The truth is, I have lost count of how many times they have put out a song which I do not immediately like; but which gets under the skin after a few listens. Really this is a testament to the subtlety of their work, and depicts the energy they build in layers, with words and music. It is also true, they have had some disasters. But they recognize and outgrow these pretty quickly; and simply omit such tracks from their shows or frame of reference going forward. Not all their work stands the test of time, and not everything they put out is a classic.

U2's occasional experimental indulgences can be irritating even to hard core fans. But this is a band which is constantly in flux, and seeking to grow. They want the next record they release, to be the best thing they have ever done. They want the next gig to be the best one ever. It is this dedication and commitment, which keeps them relevant thirty years on. U2 will go out all guns blazing. They are the epitome of Rock and Roll, with a unique twist. No one else sounds like them. No one else would want to. They are magicians in the best sense of the word. You will not really understand this outfit unless you see them perform live. Your senses have to feel into their passion and drive. The alchemy does not always translate to vinyl. Or Spotify.

Bono is a patient, kind and tolerant man, loved by many. I think he is also misunderstood by many too. When I first arrived in Dublin, he talked to me about how he felt misunderstood, even mocked in his own country; and I could tell it weighed heavy on his heart. I loved the ease between us with these early conversations. To be honest Bono helped me settle into Dublin. He energetically felt like my home from home. He was the one very warm and welcoming person, who actively supported me at a deeper level. If not for his grace and kindness I would not have stayed. Truth is I was away from home in a foreign land, even if family were only a quick jaunt back across the Irish Sea.

There is a social gaucheness about Bono which is somewhat surprising. He wears his heart on his sleeve, and responds instinctively to what is kicking off around him. He lives through his senses, and smells what to steer clear of and what to embrace. Clearly he is also intelligent, interested, and loves to meet and understand a broad spectrum of people.

Those reading about our connection will probably assume much of it was going on in my head, and that I have a vivid imagination. This is probably correct. Only Bono knows what if anything I meant to him. I can only describe and account for what he meant to me. I hope I have been self-depreciating enough in my description. I am not assuming I meant anything to him at all. But all I know is I followed my heart where he was concerned. Up until the point I did not.

My connection with Bono was not a case of chasing rainbows really. It was more about following the organic flow of the feeling. Was it not allowed simply because of who he is? He is a human being, and it was the human being I connected with. I found him grounded, kind, warm, affectionate and funny. Not enough was acted upon it is true, and the opportunities were fleeting if frequent. All of this was witnessed and watched by people. There was nothing hidden or underhand. Did I make more of it than I should have? No, I did not.

If I were making "more of it," I would have actively tried to seduce him, and *make* something happen. I never did this. I was somewhat passive, polite and responsive when *he* expressed a feeling. I cannot help the way I felt. Did I make it all up? No, I don't think so. Was it meant to be? Clearly. No.

My mother said years ago that I would catch someone on their second time-around, and she felt that I would marry secretly, on the quiet. What she is picking up on I do not know. She is not even psychic, though she is my mother, and does have her moments. One thing was clear, I needed to seriously rethink my hopes and expectations. If one is walking the talk and following the recommended principles of cosmic ordering, one must be careful what to put out for. I knew there was a charming connection with Bono, but he was an adorable married man with a wonderful wife and family. I was not about to do anything to compromise that even if I thought I could. Although I do energy work for clients and loved ones, I am scrupulous about not using it to give myself an unfair advantage. So I did nothing to try to affect a result in this situation. Some will say I should have. Others will judge me as delusional regardless. I assure you I am *not* delusional, but that will not change what people say or think. My work lends itself to the same criticisms. So, never mind, being misunderstood is not a new thing for me. I live with it.

As I tried to emerge from the depth of feeling I had for Bono, it really was an uphill task. I began to apply some logic to the situation, and began to ponder what I thought might work. How about manifesting a hunky rugby player, who was gorgeous, intelligent and a little bit dangerous to know? I had noticed that rugby players tend to be health conscious, attractive, sober and hot-to-trot, but also inclined to commit and actually *marry* their partners. So yes I found me one such player. Was he anything like the prerequisite list? No, of course he was not. But I had to try to get over Bono.

I had to try to forget the electricity that surged when he kissed me on the lips, or hugged me, or held my hand in the corner of the nightclub. Somehow I had to move beyond the man who had shown me the most romance and soul depth I had yet experienced. I could not afford to get *Stuck in a Moment* for very much longer if I was going to have any kind of successful life myself.

THE DEVIL DOESN'T COME IN A RED CAPE
AND POINTY HORNS. HE COMES AS
EVERYTHING YOU'VE EVER WISHED FOR.

CHAPTER ELEVEN
All That Jazz

I am pretty fussy when it comes to men and if the chemistry is not there, I will not bother. This might sounds highly ironic considering my history. But I would rather be celibate than with the wrong guy. I really do have to feel passionate someone, or it is just not going to happen. I give one hundred percent to even the more dubious candidates I have stumbled across.

I am an all or nothing girl. By that I do not mean that I am difficult to please. A simple cup of tea does the trick for me. I am not one of those girls who will go with a guy for status, money or a fleeting good time. I am open to the potential of what presents itself. I guess you could say I have had a lot of karma to clear, as opposed to a run of bad luck. Whatever happens, I take the positive, once I have processed any disappointment I might feel.

I have learned to be quick to objectify emotional challenges, and generally I have the view that nothing is wasted. Obviously the results are not that amazing in terms of a family situation, which I do long for. But, I have had some amazing adventures. I just try not to feel hard done by. None of this was intentional. It is what happened.

I went through a lot of trauma in exiting the relationship with Billy. Billy had begun to have a drink problem, and it affected our friendship, as well as our ability to stay on an even keel even as roommates. There were a few incidents where I started to get afraid when he drank. He would never remember any of the things he said or did when drinking. The next day it was all a blur to him. It certainly gave him an excuse for some very bad behavior. Billy seemed to get taken over when he drank, and I became very concerned for him. Certainly my heart sunk whenever he announced he would be having a drink that night. Anyone who has lived with someone who abuses drink will understand this. In Billy's case it was once a fortnight when he had a job, three or four times a week when he did not.

Our sex life had been pretty much nonexistent for years, but we had remained close emotionally. We were essentially friends who had moved to Ireland together; who then lived in a kind of limbo, sharing quarters, thoughts, humor, and food. Neither of us knew if we should stay or go; so we just blundered on.

Bono kept me sane and interested when I saw him, and recharged me somehow. I loved that he was always so warm, affectionate, and kind. I think he sensed my loneliness, and he was good enough to support me as best he could. He helped me greatly, and gave me the emotional boosts and courage I needed to keep going. He probably did not know he was doing this, and was just being his usual friendly self.

Things with Billy were very dicey. He was never violent, but he was intimidating, and upset me greatly, with what he said while under the influence. It is true what they say about the demon drink. It does not help anyone. Those who have had life with a drinker will know what I am talking about. Literally, you are communicating with the bottle, and not the person. You get to a point where you are living off the memory of what was once good; just hoping that the self abuser will see the error of their ways. You cannot point it out for them. Well you can, but they will not listen.

It is true what they say. Someone will only stop the abuse of substances, when they feel it is *their* time to do so. They have to *want* to do so. Very often these outlets are justified as thoroughly deserved after a tricky week, a terrible day, etc. A disconnect is needed, and the abuser feels fully justified. If the drinking has an emotional trigger, the self saboteur will wallow in their misfortune, stating that they "need something to look forward to." It can be drinking out of boredom, anger, upset, or "just because I *want* to." Nothing changes unless the person decides to reform.

Billy did not drink daily or nightly. But when he did, he did it in style. To the point where in my mind his nickname became "Bottle of Vodka." The tendency Billy had to drink himself into oblivion really was the last straw for me. I do not mind people who drink at all. In fact they say do not trust anyone who does not drink. What I cannot abide now is the abuse of drink. Having lived through this, it is such a turn off when someone drinks to excess. It does them no favours, and it really is not in the least bit attractive or constructive.

There were a few domestic events that triggered alarm bells, for which Billy would be full of remorse for, once he was reminded of them the next day. The last time I conceded to be around him when he was drinking he leapt across the room grabbing me by the neck and pushed the couch across the floor. That was the only flicker of physical violence from him ever. But that was enough for me. Having gone through the John saga, I was not going to fall into a pattern of forgiving and forgetting, only to have something else happen further down the road.

I could no longer justify sharing an apartment with Billy, and I asked him to leave. He went to the house of the girl he had been seeing in Bray. A connection which was of course much more established than he had declared. Being psychic I knew this. Being psychic though, did not protect me from all the effects and upset and emotions I then had to deal with. Billy got his marching orders as a flatmate when I found a girl's planted underwear in his suitcase on return from a Spanish holiday he had supposedly gone on with his brother. I was doing laundry and found the offending garment strategically placed, and charged with intent.

Although I was only Billy's flatmate, I had made it very clear I did not want to be his flat mate if he was off seeing other people. The emotional triggers when he drank were too much to deal with. I asked him very specifically to leave if he were still seeing this woman Caroline. Of course it was Caroline he had been seeing all along, and she planted this offering for my benefit. To give her credit, the ploy worked. Billy left. I asked him to.

As a direct reaction to Billy's destructive behaviour, I began to wish for and put out for a hunky rugby player, who was "gorgeous, intelligent and a little bit dangerous to know." Billy was the fitness instructor who smoked, and drank intermittently himself into oblivion. He was super fit, and able to keep up with his spinning classes at the gym. But he then totally unravelled all his efforts when he drank and smoked. I needed someone whose health care regime was a little more wholesome and consistent. And yes I did find him. Or rather he found me. Room 102, the disabled toilet, and the computer room at The Fitzpatrick's Hotel have a few tales to tell.

The Irish Rugby Team opened my eyes to what a crap time I had been having. They provided me with a bit of healthy male attention, which apart from my daily companionship with Billy, I had been sorely lacking. Bono was a married man, and there was only so much he could do; even if he were inclined to do more, which of course he probably was *not*. Without sounding too dramatic, my link with these forces of nature gave me the incentive to move on, and fight another day. The adopted Irish Rugby motto at that time, *Carpe Diem*, rang true for me, and I began to see other options for my life than the paths I had been treading. I felt I had exhausted my fair share of musicians. Now Irish Rugby had better be ready for The Mermaid.

The last thing I ever thought I would be, was a rugby fan. I have never actually attended a match, so I guess I am not strictly a rugby fan, even now. But there was something intriguing about the way the destiny of the team started to tie into my daily routine.

The Bono and Billy dynamic had turned out to be very debilitating. Well debilitating except for the profoundly felt gestures from Bono. I could have convinced myself I did not need any more than this. Indeed I did for quite some time. But the truth is, I was looking for more. For something to "be enough."

The Irish Rugby Team appeared to be a way out of the tunnel which had held me in emotional stasis for so long. After the Bono shenanigans, I had begun to have this intuition about a Mr Rugby. But, I really had no idea what it meant as none of the current line up caught my eye, let alone my imagination. I was obviously looking for an emotional diversion. The connection with Bono had been so real to me for so long, that this really was an exercise in suspending judgement and feeling.

John Mayer's sentiment of forcing yourself to like someone new comes to mind. In his moving song, *Never on the Day You Leave,* which I gather he can hardly bear to sing, Mayer describes the untimely end of his relationship with Katy Perry. He sings of the mess, and emotional entanglement we all feel when we try to move on, and find the "disconnect" difficult to achieve. The lyric describes a girl who fights for someone with all her might, then concedes defeat, forcing herself to like "some other man." Although the song is much more current than the times I am recounting, the sentiment is totally appropriate.

That was me, in this moment. I was forcing a change in my emotional landscape. The turbulence and stress of the route I was taking had become too much to bear. In the end, after so many years, the "forcing" part was not ultimately too difficult.

On a personal level, the reason for my uncertainty and puzzlement regarding the Irish Rugby Team became clear soon enough. Before I knew it, I was being hotly pursued by an Ulster rugby team member, with the best name. I could preserve his identity nicely since there were three guys by the same name in the Ulster team at this point. Those in the Ulster camp who are curious to know, which Player was the best Player in my opinion, will probably be able to solve the riddle fairly quickly. I need say no more. He is just going to be called "Player" for our purposes.

Player had not been in the Irish team when I first met Paul O'Connell and Donncha O'Callaghan. He had attended the summer camp in Killiney, and was duly summonsed for the Autumn Internationals following the Six Nations, in which I had helped Paul with his shoulder. Certainly this Player was primed to cause a stir in more ways than one. For some time I had been picking up that I was destined to hook up with one of The Irish Rugby Team. I just did not know which one. I know who I *wanted* it to be, but said player already had a long term girlfriend. As you know, I am not in the habit of going after someone who is already spoken for. And even though they are all pretty cute in person, it was certainly not a case of any of them would do. I just had to wait and see what it all meant.

I had obviously been meant to help Paul O'Connell with his shoulder injury, which enabled him to get into shape for a very important rugby match. Plus I had started to make endless predictions in the papers about how it was Munster's destiny to win the Heineken cup, and the Irish Team's destiny to win the Championship in 2009. Both of these predictions were recorded and correct predictions. But it was the liaison with Player that trumped it all, and caused yet another oil spill in my chequered romantic history.

I sure knew how to pick 'em...

I had been innocently sitting in the computer room of The Fitzpatrick's Hotel, when I noticed this bundle of mischief bounding by with the most gorgeous blue eyes. I went frequently to the hotel just up the road from my apartment to escape Billy's antics. It provided a comfortable mixture of anonymity and friendliness which I loved. Lunch by the pool, email and word doc file sorting in the Business Center, or an evening by the fire, were just what the doctor ordered when things got stressful at home.

Player had obviously noticed me sitting there doing my work over time. I had been bemused to notice the rugby team moving around their team hotel. But to be honest I did not take much interest before the time I offered to help Paul. The banter started full on after that. Rugby players are nothing if not irreverent. Donncha wrote about the mysterious lady who came to sort Paul armed with "crystals and stuff," in his newspaper column. And there was much interest and amusement in any predictions I might throw their way as they passed me having my lunch by the swimming pool.

The Player who had smiled at me with intent during the summer camp, stepped up his moves pretty quickly come the autumn. Those few weeks later, I was more responsive, and less quizzical. A flirtation started to shape up. Munching on an apple, Player stomped into the business centre, chucked his offering into the bin, gave me the cheekiest grin and I was sold. Way. Too. Easily. Halloween was an emotive time. My Nan had wooed my grandpa by giving him an apple many moons ago, and this was Halloween, the eve of her birthday, All Saints Day.

More spookily, I had just asked my deceased Grandpa Fred for some clarity in my love life. You might say I got a quick answer when the Best boy barged into the room. Or did I? At the very least I now knew who Mr Rugby was, and why I had been picking up energetically on the rugby shenanigans to come. I can personally vouch for the fact that these lads do have time between kicks offs to get some action of a different kind. Having been on the receiving end of some delicious attention from Player, I do feel qualified to pass comment. I guess there always is time if you care to make it.

Yes, I did my duty for the country and cheered up the teams hard hitter, before, during and after International games. Was I distracting the lad from his work? Yes, probably. But not to his detriment. He played like a dream, and got man of the match against Australia, so I do not feel too guilty. I gather he was a wrecking ball in that match, and it is cited as the highlight of his career. He single-handedly picked off the formidable opponents of this top elite professional team. Again, don not feel guilty. I honestly think he *benefited* from the energy we had conjured.

The connection with me strengthened his reputation at this time rather than damaged it. This guy was on a roll, so I must have been a fairly positive influence. I will not bore you with the details. But suffice to say what this guy did so well on the pitch clearly has a knock on effect into his personal life. Paid to flatten the opposition, he was as effective off the pitch as on. A blindside flanker of the highest order, he came up on the inside and knocked me for six.

It just goes to show that not even psychics see everything coming. This was obviously a disaster waiting to happen. The guy had a girl friend, and wanted to keep it all off side. It was an impasse right from the off. I held hope for the situation for way longer than I should have. It really was a non starter. But this force of nature, had given me some reconnection, and a swirl of energy which revved up my engines again. Not bad seeing as I was technically just about old enough to be his mother. So I will take it.

I DIDN'T BELIEVE IN REINCARNATION IN MY PAST LIFE, AND I STILL DON'T.
WOODY ALLEN

CHAPTER TWELVE
Superman

I am not sure where the intuition about the rugby team came from. But it was not in the least bit contrived. Over the years I would occasionally catch sight of a team photo and get a sense of something. It was just a vague impression and I did not even study the faces. The feeling was very fleeting and intangible. Something and nothing. I started to take a bit more notice when Anke, the White Witch of Wicklow read for me. She saw a rugby ball in her crystal ball, for which I had no explanation. I did not watch rugby, nor was I interested in any of the players. It did not make any sense to me that a rugby ball would suddenly appear in my energy field.

I had been going to readings with Anke for some time for support about the Bono and Billy situation. But when she mentioned the rugby ball, I really did think she had lost her marbles. I was not a rugby fan, and I have still never been to a live professional match in my life. But, as always, Anke's readings had a habit of being uncanny; and before I knew it, I was linked to the rugby lads in many and various ways.

I used to like the rugby physique when I was younger, and my first "proper" boyfriend Phil used to play a bit. But when I moved up to study at the Scottish universities, Stirling and Edinburgh, I developed a taste for the bohemian groove. Musicians, writers, and artists hit the spot, not macho, alpha rugby players.

Even though I got on really well with Paul O'Connell, Donncha O' Callaghan, and Ronan O'Gara in particular, none of them seemed to be drawn to me in *that* way. Intuitively, though they are all undoubtedly attractive, I did not feel my link with them was meant to be of *that* nature. Equally, having been celibate for a good few years, I am sure I would not have said "no" had any of them made a move.

I felt linked to Paul for a time. But that is because he is such a lovely upstanding guy. Donncha's humour always made me giggle, as did the twinkle in Ronan's eye. Paul was a little too close to my ginger brother in colouring and appearance for that connection to have clicked in any major way. Anke had confirmed it was a "just mates" scenario when I asked her about Paul and Donncha. I had helped Paul speed heal his shoulder injury. It was not going to count for any more than that. I knew this. Just checking.

The healing for Paul was a profound experience. Without sounding too dramatic Paul gave me an awakening with his own talismanic healing energy. When I was healing Paul, the first place I put my hand was on the back behind his heart. His energy was really grounding and powerful. I could really feel the life force of the man. Healers will understand this. I admit it does sound odd if you do not understand energy very well. But those of you who do, will get my point.

After I had experienced such psychic bombardment on the ethers, Paul's energy rescued me. There was certainly a fair exchange of mutual help, though perhaps he was not aware of this. Paul is pure of heart, bravery, and focus as many Irish rugby fans will tell you. This simple fact really helped me in a very unanticipated way. I wondered if I was going to fall in love with him at one point. But Anke put me off that path saying he was not husband material; well not for me anyway. One thing I did know is that I felt safe with him, and that his energy grounded and connected me to a vital male life force. Paul's strong presence allowed me to feel protected and affirmed once again. This had definitely not been the plan from my point of view. I did not know this was going to be the upshot of my first meeting with him. I was simply offering to help him in his predicament. I did not anticipate he would help me equally in return.

Not ever having even watched a game of rugby from start to finish, I had been originally bemused to encounter the odd member of the Irish Rugby Team in the corridors of their team hotel. The Fitzpatrick's Hotel in Killiney. I had been getting those psychic flashes about "Mr Rugby" on and off for months; and here they all were in the hotel where I had lunch and did my on line work.

As I described earlier, the impressions were not anything I could strongly pin down. I had never even met any of them formally, and from what I could see I did not actually fancy any of them either. When I saw them intermittently on their rounds at the hotel, I just assumed I had been simply picking up that The Irish Rugby Team would be staying and training nearby. A visually pleasing backdrop to my daily life. Something persistently niggled me though, and I got increasing impressions I was going to have something more to do with the team.

I had first made a prediction on RTE's *TTV* for Aidan Power re The Six Nations in advance of the French game. I felt that Ireland should not be written off, and that they could indeed go onto win *The Triple Crown*. Rugby fans will remember that this was at a time when the team and Eddie O' Sullivan were subject to major flack in the media and from the Irish Nation in general. I felt strongly that the tables were going to turn very rapidly, and that The Golden Age of Irish Rugby would dawn. What can I say? I was right. Such predictions come easy to me, and I was able to say with confidence that everyone would be celebrating in grand style before too long.

One Tuesday during this particular Six Nations campaign, I was watching the news. Paul O'Connell, who I personally had not heard of before, was on television, saying that he was only fifty percent likely to be able to play the important game against Scotland on Saturday. I picked up that he had an acromioclavicular joint injury, and that he was troubled with residue pain that would affect his chances of playing. I had one of my "ding" moments, and knew I was meant to help.

I knew from my days of running the healing practice that I have the ability to lift pain. These AC shoulder joint injuries can heal if minor in two to three weeks, but sometimes if more serious they need surgery. Paul's issue was clearly not going to go away quickly. I felt strongly that I should at least offer my services. Of course it would have been a bit odd to go up to the hotel and make a song and dance about it. So I figured if I was meant to help I would meet the right people when I went up on spec.

I always listen to my guidance and intuition with this kind of thing, even at the risk of looking crazy. It is my calling to respond when so prompted, and I still listen to those promptings and whispers when they happen. I always will. I could not ignore what I was being guided to do, and I had to go up to the hotel for a work reason that evening anyway. So I thought I would make myself available simply by being there, and that the spirit would move if the rest was meant to be.

Believe it or not. The only people I saw that night were Paul, the team doctor, and the physiotherapist. The hotel was totally quiet, but these three characters were in situ. How is that for a meaningful coincidence?

The first guy I bumped into in the computer room was the physiotherapist, who did not seem too impressed at my suggestion and self introduction. I thought that was going to be as far as I got. But suspending judgement, he conceded and went to get the team doctor, Gary O' Driscoll, who asked if I knew how important Paul was to the team. I responded, "honestly? No. But I was guided to offer and see if I could help him." Gary then went to get Paul who was up for "giving it a go," as all other the options for getting him match fit had failed.

I had explained to Gary who I was, and that both my brother and father were doctors, so I fully understood medical pragmatism regarding such things. For what it was worth, I told Gary that my father had to attend the Bristol student rugby sessions as part of his work remit for Bristol University. He seemed to like this story, and interestingly he was refreshingly open to an alternative approach, so long as I was not going to stick any needles in Paul. I had not realised that Paul O'Connell was indeed such a key player, and I think at that point, they were so keen for him to play Saturday that they would have tried anything. They did. What is more it *worked*.

Manchester United is a football club very open to all sort of alternative therapies for their sports stars. Leaving the infamous Spala treatments in Poland aside, I am not sure the IRFU have been *that* dynamic with their imposed regime to date. Sometimes a little taste of something different is all it takes to shift persistent problems. It does not have to always involve deep freezing players to within an inch of their lives. I am sure the macho traditionalist and regimented regime of Irish Rugby would not usually make room for the likes of me. But then again perhaps it would benefit from doing so? Pain can be lifted very quickly with what I do. I am not sure what happens exactly. But I know it does work.

Of course Glen Hoddle made ample use of faith healer Eileen Drury, and stirred up a bit of controversy with his left field approach. I am sure Glen and Eileen did a lot of good between them, and Glen gets a prize for being open minded that is for sure. It is unfortunate that Hoddle then put his foot in it by waffling about aspects of karma that he clearly did not fully understand; or should I say that the recipients of his comments would not fully understand. Intrinsically, Glen was working in a fairly enlightened way, so it is a great shame that he came unstuck through what you might call a lack of wisdom. He was doubtless the victim of a media witch hunt, which jumped on his ignorant comment about our karmic choices. I am sure most people in wheel chairs, do not feel that they actively chose to be there. I am not excusing what he ill-advisedly said, but Glen was trying to convey the truth that we agree to life's challenges in quite specific ways before we incarnate. These imprints remain in our unconscious, and our reality takes the shape that we have signed up for, whether we know it consciously or not. I do believe though that God's grace gives a get out clause to all of life's arduous circumstances, freeing us up inside and out for whatever our true destiny may be. Anyway, that was Glen. This is now.

Personally, I am very matter of fact about hands-on healing and figure that if it works do not knock it. I know many sceptics find it impossible to believe in the power of healing. But I have found through many experiences that it is very effective, and not simply a matter of auto suggestion. The results are tangible and surprisingly quick with animals and humans alike. When guided to reach out and help people, I do not question it. One wonderful story about a woman, who was not officially a client, took place in deepest darkest Somerset. I was in the local Porlock library, and overheard an elderly lady complain about her knee. She was asking the assistant to phone for a taxi as she could not walk home. I offered her a lift, and then once we got to her house, offered to try a quick healing on her knee.

The hospital had not been able to find relief for the intermittent excruciating pain, and mechanical issues, she suffered from. But literally five minutes of hands-on healing and she could walk freely and move around unimpeded. She was blown away. I said "my pleasure." I saw her some weeks later and she was still fine. The booked surgery had been cancelled, and no one had an explanation. I love stories like this, and I have many of them. But at the risk overload, I will just recount this one, along with that of Paul. Suffice to say, I do not just help rugby stars and rock stars. I help those I am *guided t*o help, no questions asked. God heals through me. I am just a vessel to connect with the chosen person who needs the blessing.

I was delighted to read on the day after the match in question, that the lads had had a laugh about Paul's determination to play. So determined was Paul that he called in a strange blonde psychic to help him get match fit. As Donncha said in his Ireland on Sunday column, "Paul will do anything within his means to get ready for work, and if that means forty minutes with a new age hippy so be it." Fair play to Paul for taking a chance, and being so open. Needs must. It says a lot about him as a guy that he would be open to trying such a thing. To set himself up for merry ridicule from his team mates, shows the metal of the man. Perhaps Superman really does exist in the fine form of Paul O'Connell.

It is a validation of the link we made that Paul's performance in the Scottish game proved to be so crucial. I had told Paul with certainty on the Tuesday night that he would play. It turned out he was even named man of the match against all the odds. I am only sorry for Donncha that Paul's recovery put him back on the benches and out of a job for the night. Still I am very glad to have helped in some way. I had been touched that Donncha, The Gentle Giant, had really grasped what my work was about. True, he wrote up quite a jokey account of Paul's healing, and my subsequent apology to him. But I thought that took a rare humility from such a hunky macho guy.

Donncha has such a strong work ethic himself, that I am sure he was miffed that I put him back on the benches by helping Paul. But I did apologise, and he was gracious enough to say that the "more able bodies there are in the team the better." Donncha did get his karmic reward shortly afterwards, when Malcolm O'Kelly's injury problems paved the way for him to get some match time. I left this one well enough alone , and did not offer help to another member of the team at this point. I seemed to have had a very specific contract to help Paul only, at that time. I learned some lessons too with this incident. I was meant to watch carefully and only offer healing when it was absolutely right to do so. In Paul's case it was right. But Donncha took the impact. Then again he was paid to do just that.

The healing interchange is mysterious. I know Paul probably helped me as much as I helped him. The spirit world moves in weird and wonderful ways. Little does Paul know that the lung difficulty he complained of after the Ireland v Scotland match was possibly linked with the healing, as opposed to him not being match fit. He took on the residue of darkness I had been grappling with, and freed me up to love and live again. I had no idea this was going to happen. But because I am so hyper sensitive to shifts of energy and the reasons for them, I knew this is what had happened. Sometimes we do have strange, mysterious life contracts with each other, which may stem from other times. Equally, we may be just meant to help each other in the here and now. I think both are probably true.

Renowned healer and numerologist, Lila Beck had told me previously, that I was just about to enter a phase in my life, where I would sort out karmas with many of the guys I had been married to, or otherwise linked up with, in other life times. Clearly I have mixed with many troubadours, poets, artists, and musicians, in the past, judging by the men I have attracted, and been attracted to, in this lifetime. I sit loose to the theory of past lives. I am not sure whether to fully believe it, or how much importance to give it. But, there certainly seems to be a precedent for meeting up with people, we knew in other times. A magnetic pull and resonance, which means that the same energies hone in on each other every time we incarnate.

On a soul level, past lives have a resonance. We can all relate to those meetings where we connect with someone, and there is so much familiarity about them, even though technically they are just strangers. These meetings have happened many times in my life. But over all I sit on the fence with the past lives debacle. I believe we are meant to be present in the here and now. I think the theories can sound a bit odd, and I do understand that some people cannot get their heads around the concept. As with all things keeping an open mind is what works best. Of course you would go mad if you over analysed such things. But when you develop psychically, you certainly do become much more aware of the energy echoes which haunt and influence us from other times.

When we pass on, I strongly believe that life goes on, and that energy cannot be extinguished. Everything is energy, so clearly, the energy is transmuted into another form. People who are deceased leave a residue energy for quite some time, and of course they live on in the heart's of loved ones. It would make complete sense that we would find the energies which resonate best with us, each time we incarnate. Whether we come back again for another round is apparently up to us. What I do keep hearing is that there are many people working through very loaded karmas in a bid not to have to return to the earth plane again. "No thank you," is the general consensus of opinion.

I personally do not think there has to be a contradiction between Christian faith and a belief in reincarnation. I am sure Christian and Buddhist philosophers have yet to reconcile the two. I believe it can be done. The disciples asked Christ if he was Elijah reincarnated, so they obviously thought it was possible.

Edward S. Casey, "the sleeping prophet," did much research on the validity of past lives, and their coherent connection with faith in Christ. Born in 1939, Casey, channeled a great many spiritual books, and worked on complex case studies, particularly medical and those involving children. He was an incredible medical intuitive, and knew the exact day he was going to pass and how. He could have a patient sit down in front of him, and just know the correct diagnosis and treatment. Psychic healers like Edward Casey, give people like me validation and a historical context. Not enough is known about such healers, aside from what they write about themselves, or channel for their patients and clients. There really is a case for much more open minded research to be done on these comprehensive Gifts, and their application. The potential is immense.

Casey did not find belief in reincarnation to be in conflict with his personal faith. He felt past life theories provided a context and setting for the current life being experienced. Similarly to me, he did not feel it was advisable to overly focus on who an individual had once been. This philosophical view is not out there so that we can brag or speculate about who we once were. It is there to provide a framework enabling us to understand the consequences of patterns and choices. It really is all about personal responsibility in the here and now.

Only in this way, does past life theory have any relevance or valid application. We have the free will to choose how we apply the lessons. Past lives provide an indicator and framework of our potential and possibilities, should we wish to understand awareness of our psyche on these levels. What we experience in this life time is not dictated by inevitability. We are not obliged to repeat patterns, replay, or balance all the karma. We are best advised to be personally savvy, wise, and responsible. It is more a case of "know thyself," than a provided reason to panic or over analyze.

I was told by someone quite respected in this field that my name has always been Sarah down through all my lifetimes; and that I was something to do with the Holy Grail bloodline. This was forwarded as a way of explaining the pressure I was under regarding my public work, personal life, and all its accompanying challenges. To me it sounded like potentially loopy talk, but you never know.

Someone else, said that I had always been a woman, and had floated and wafted through all my lifetimes, like some kind of ethereal, otherworldly goddess. I will just stay mildly amused at that theory also. Again, it could well be the case; but "how does it help me *now*," would be the main question.

A former colleague in The Psychic Society, Brian Hunter, noticed on our travels in Europe, that ethereal muses in my likeness were depicted on many of the ceilings, wall hangings, and portraits of stately homes, palaces and castles. It became an on-going joke. where would I be found next? I personally resonate with Botticelli paintings, and have always loved *The Birth of Venus* in particular. So, I will admit to *that* much.

I sit loose to all of this, as I think it could give you inflated airs and graces if you gave it too much thought. The study of past lives undoubtedly has curiosity value. Energy echoes and patterns through history make for fascinating speculation. But I believe in living in the present time, and think it is important that we focus on *now*. Giving the past too much thought can be distracting and detrimental. Leaping further back into past lives, without pointed direction can be even more seductive.

Having said that, there is an opening for healing through correct recognition of the source of our pain, as it plays out in this lifetime. Past lives can be invaluable to ascertain the trigger points, and deep causes of what is playing out before us.

A friend of mine, who is an expert in karmic astrology, has pinpointed links in my natal chart to Botticelli, the Pre Raphaelites, Nostradamus, Biblical times, Tudor times, and The Cathars. I resonate with all of these, as I had psychically picked up the connections myself. It is interesting that they were then confirmed without me saying anything through a study of my natal chart. Again at this superficial level it is observational, and curious rather than profoundly important.

I can certainly take on board the Tudor life time, as I was fascinated by the Tudors at school. I used to stare at a family tree history of the kings and queens of England on my bedroom wall, and was particularly obsessed with the Tudors. This was a teenage girl's compulsion, which took on a new meaning when I had a hideous and inexplicable panic attack in Hampton Court aged eleven. I do not know what overwhelmed me, but I just knew I had to get out of there as quickly as possible. My parents were not amused, but my intuitive Nan understood, and came to sit with me on the banks of The Thames, while the rest of the party traipsed around that "hell hole," in unnatural heat.

When I returned to Hampton Court with Brian on our pilgrimage trail, he tuned into the situation using his mediumistic abilities. He felt psychically that my energy was linked to Jane Seymour, the only wife King Henry VIII had really loved. She was the only one of Henry's wives who had a Queen's funeral, and is buried beside him in Saint George's Cathedral at Windsor Castle.

Jane Seymour had died prematurely of complications giving birth to her son Edward. She went through a very uncomfortable time struggling to hold onto life in Hampton Court, expiring defeated and deflated as she left behind her beloved husband and son. Brian himself felt he connected energetically to Jane's son Edward VI. So apparently I had an energetic imprint operating as Brian's mother. Makes sense.

Such theories pertaining to past lives are complex. There are many who feel connected to John of Arc, or Mozart for example. These could be explained through a theory of soul fragments, or it could mean we are all crazy trying to pin our identities on historical figures.

We will have to reserve judgement on that all this as it is not definitively provable.

There are many recorded case studies and lifetimes recounted under hypnosis. Arthur Guirdham did some comprehensive research on *The Cathars and Reincarnation*. He established through research and hypnosis that there was a substantial link between former Cathar incarnates and the West Country in the United Kingdom. He found through many recorded regression accounts that there was a pattern of those who had been around during the Cathar persecutions, reincarnating in the Bristol in particular. Such observations are anecdotal. They are indicative, but do not stand as substantiated proof. Guirdham was criticized by colleagues for his sweeping general comments, which defied science and elevated the supernatural. Does it mean he was wrong? No. Is it verifiable? Also "no."

Psychically, energetically, and spiritually this is a fascinating topic. Moira Lumberg, a respected medium in Ireland, pinpointed the Cathar lifetime as crucial to me. It is certainly interesting that I was raised in the West Country, and Bristol area in particular. So according to Guirdham, she was onto something. In the middle of my tests and trials, I went to see her for guidance. She told me the overriding lifetime I needed to heal was the one where I had committed suicide in Paris out of loneliness. The Cathar life time. I have to say something resonated deep within when she said this. It was kind of shocking and I was also somewhat indignant when she said it. It also felt unreal, and not what I had signed up for. I had certainly been through stretches of extreme loneliness, not to mention disappointment. Did this automatically link me back to a Cathar lifetime which I needed to heal? I was not sure.

In the lifetime Moira identified, I had been a well respected healer. I had escaped the horrors of the Chateau de Montsegur, and the Cathar persecutions; only to self destruct later in Paris from grief, desolation, and a broken heart.

The Siege of Montsegur was a nine month siege on the Cathars, perpetrated by the French Royal Forces. The Castle eventually surrendered in March1244, and all the remaining Cathars, who refused to renounced their Gnosticism, were burned and murdered in a mass grave bonfire. Many perished during these persecutions, well over two hundred souls lost their lives. I was allegedly one of only four people who escaped, carrying with them the secrets of the Holy Grail. I left behind my father, husband and son to die in the flames. The man I loved, who also loved me, was in an arranged marriage, living locally. He was a prominent Prince, famous in the region, who could do nothing to break free from convention, and his material circumstances, despite the passion between us. I was commissioned by the Cathar community to carry and rescue *The Book Of Secrets*.

The heretics of the Languedoc, the Cathars, possessed the book of love, and etheric writings which expanded the consciousness, and contained the hidden knowledge, which only the alchemical elite could handle. These secrets could not fall into the hands of the enemy who would decimate them without mercy. I fled to Paris, and set up as a healer for a couple of years, before succumbing to incredible loneliness. Apparently I hung myself out of sadness; despite being a herbalist of some repute.

Past life expert Andrew Brewer did not agree with the part about hanging myself when I ran this by him. I would like to say he is correct on that. But you never know. Again no proofs either way. Overall, I have to say there was deep familiarity, and a resonance sparked in my soul, when Moira was recounting this life time.

The account had some uncanny echoes in my life since arriving in Dublin. The PhD I was signed up for in the Department of Philosophy was on Gnosticism; I was fast becoming a "healer of some repute;" and I was excruciatingly lonely, and in love with an unavailable, local married man, akin to Irish royalty. Also, it always puzzled me that, despite struggling with A level French at school. I came back fluent in French after a five day trip to Paris, just in time to get a reasonable grade in the summer. Maybe something unblocked within me. All I know is, my French teacher was incredulous.

This reading on the Cathar lifetime was incredibly powerful, and has haunting echoes for me in this lifetime. I think we know the truth when we hear it. When such a crucial lifetime is pinpointed, healing is essential. Really, such information is a gift, and indicates where breakthrough opportunities might be. There is no denying that a pattern is playing out. What the outcome and resolution will be is anyone's guess. This provides the ultimate transformative opportunity.

Labyrinth by Kate Mosse, *The Da Vinci Code* by Dan Brown, and *Daughters of The Grail* by Elizabeth Chadwick, are books which speak to my soul. These books demonstrate the truth of The Holy Grail. It is not a cup, but a process. In pursuit of the Holy Grail, we are perfected. The alchemy hones our consciousness, and our souls, so that we step out of the purging fire, ascended and radiant.

I have seen much evidence that past lives are relevant to what happens to us in this lifetime. It is a concept very difficult to prove, and yet energetically it makes so much sense. I find in client readings that past life impressions filter through, and that these are often responsible for the dynamics which make people feel stuck. The deepest healing takes place, when these lifetimes are exposed, and transformed. A person can be fundamentally redeemed, if not totally transmogrified.

BE AS PICKY WITH YOUR MEN
AS YOU ARE WITH YOUR SELFIES!

CHAPTER THIRTEEN
Waiting For The Best

P aul O' Connell was a link in the chain which would eventually solve the riddle about Mr Rugby. Anke, the white witch, had talked about, "a man who would step out of the shadows," to declare himself. What then followed were the dramas that pertained to "Player." I am not sure really on analysing events if he really was *the* "man in the shadows." But he was certainly lurking with intent. After I helped Paul, we proceeded to have a good old banter in the media about whether or not it was Munster's Destiny to win the Heineken Cup. Paul would speak in riddles and maintain his humility, saying he would not assume that the victory was "set in stone." In response, I did numerous small pieces on Munster in particular, assuring them all that their coming victory was indeed "set in stone," at least from this psychic's point of view.

The sports pages themselves covered the story about *The Psychic And The Rugby Star*. It was very amusing to me to have mention of my work included in serious sport pages. I regularly had pragmatic sports journalists ringing me up for quotes and commentary. To be taken seriously on that level, in such a male orientated environment was quite something for an apparently flaky blonde female psychic. Except that is not what I was, and they knew it.

I was regularly consulted for match predictions, and even asked to give an assessment about how a match would play out. I became the predictor of outcomes. I was consulted by journalists about politics, elections, celebrities and sports stars. I was the Sarah who had *Stars In Her Eyes*. But one thing is for sure. I was taken seriously.

My healing of Paul O' Connell made the papers quickly, and against the odds Paul played the Scottish match on Saturday. He was not fit to play this only a few days before. Seemingly in an odd twist of fate, I was the factor that made this possible. Or, I should say God using me as a channel made it possible. I had nothing to do with it. I listened, and followed the command. There may have been a lot of amusing locker room talk about the strange psychic lady. But in the hotel, I even had the coaches of the Irish Rugby Team walking up to me for predictions, insights and tips. I was obviously a source of amusement for them all, as well as delivering food for thought intermittently. At one point, I was wondering if the IRFU would even employ me for insights on strategy and help with healing. I am kidding. There was no chance of that.

I did wonder about Donncha O' Callaghan romantically. He is a real dreamboat, and I am sure many of the women, and some men, who watch rugby find him super attractive. We got on well, and he is a really polite and well mannered man. But there seemed to be some kind of mismatch, and screw loose in the attraction. Probably it was one sided. It did not quite compute. I would have; I am not the sentiment was returned. He never really gave any sign that it was.

At one point I was climbing the walls about him and did not quite understand why; beyond the obvious. I liked him a lot and knew he was kind, sweet, hunky, honourable and humble. But the reason for the energy I felt was not fully revealed to me until Munster's book *The Road to Glory*, celebrating The Heineken Cup victory was published. It seemed that the reason I had been so tuned in to Donncha, apart from the obvious, was that his father had passed when he was such a young age. I felt there was a strong message of pride and joy for Donncha from his dad. But I did not really get the chance to relay this to him at the right time. There was more to it, but that is private. Some things *are* after all.

The moment passed with Donncha and I let it all go. Player winged in and seemed more risky, vibrant and forbidden. Of course that all went wrong very quickly, and six months later, just as Paul had done, Donncha unwittingly saved my bacon.

During the Six Nations, Player had come to find me in the computer room specifically to drop a bombshell in my lap. Right at the beginning of The Six Nations campaign, he obviously had to be on his best behaviour. He had been involved in a hushed up training flare-up with John Hayes. He was on disciplinary watch, so his backtracking made some sense professionally, in theory. I say in theory because the energy between us had actually helped peak his career in the autumn. He subsequently messed up on all fronts. Everything started to deteriorate for him once he was obnoxious to me. I can quite understand why Player was being overly cautious. He was a loose cannon at the best of times, and there were some serious career opportunities at stake.

It does not really help people when they are mean to me or exclude me. Something happens to their energy, and things turn challenging for them. There is nothing I do, and I certainly never fire any bad energy at them. I am very forgiving and understanding, and I would never ever hex someone with bad feeling, however horrible they have been to me.

Player was intelligent and lively with a seriously sexy northern Irish accent. But there was also a streak of insanity in the mix. Discipline was obviously not his strong point. He was frequently red carded and sin binned during matches. But his skill was flattening people, and blocking out their progress down the pitch. A number five or six on his shirt, he was always in the thick of things. He was fearless, and brought passion to the team. On one hand he was taken very seriously. On the other, he was perceived by some as a bit of a chump. He was a hot mess, and somewhat of a liability. But he certainly delivered, creating some unexpected surprises, both on and off the pitch.

I liked Player, and it was cool that a handsome, *seriously* well endowed twenty seven year old found me sexy and attractive. He had no idea of my age, since I have always looked more youthful than my years. I persist in my intention to remain "eternally twenty-seven" forever. But in actual fact, for eight-hundred and six years old, I am not doing too badly. There is such a thing as using energy to age backwards. I am all about this, and love to keep clear and maintain a youthful attitude. You would not know I am centuries old from my voice either. I have not yet had to resort to plastic surgery, and do not verbalize my age as a form of energy maintenance. Player never even asked my age, so I thought it was not an issue. Clearly he was attracted and I looked passably okay to him.

Player will probably never quite know how much he disrupted my world at that time; and for sure he would not particularly care. I had blindsided him just as much as he blindsided me. So it really was a case of just calling it quits. He was clearly an opportunistic player who took advantage and followed a feeling. Nothing wrong with that. No judgement. But it was not what I really needed. I was looking for a partner to enjoy life with. Player definitely was not the right person. He was attracted and attractive, but not open.

With all the drama of these years, I had lost sight of myself in many ways. I really had no clue if I was in any way appealing as a woman anymore. My life was basically there to facilitate clients, and to solve problems and issues for other people. I remembered overhearing Declan, a hot security guard at The Kitchen, call me, "one of the best looking woman he had ever seen." It was one of the nicest compliments I had ever heard. Music to my ears. I never really get many nice compliments, so when I do hear them, I absorb them like a sponge. They do not go to my head. I simply appreciate them. People are inclined to be a bit mean or bitchy to me, especially women. The friends I have are amazing. But not everyone warms to me. I guess I am like marmite (yeast extract); you either love me or hate me. I understand this. But I do get greatly misunderstood and misrepresented. People project a lot onto me sometimes because I make them feel uncomfortable. It matters not. Yes, it can be challenging. But I deal with it, and I always try to understand the person with compassion.

Perhaps Declan was one that got away. He was certainly as cute as any Irish rugby player. A bit like Ben in Edinburgh. I enjoyed working with Declan at the nightclub and he hovered for a while. I enjoyed flirting with him a lot too, and did not like it when he eventually got fed up and went off with an ex of his. One night, Declan had followed me out of the VIP room to invite me to a party. I stupidly declined because of Billy, and Bono. Even though I knew Billy had recently been unfaithful, and Declan was super attractive, I did not go for it. Around this time he had tried to advise me about Billy too, and I should have listened. The bouncers in the night club saw things. Clearly Declan got fed up with me blowing hot and cold, and understandably moved on.

Being a Scorpio, Declan was probably ideal for me in many ways. He never declared himself. But I did not give him much chance. Much of this is speculation really. But I told Anke, about this attraction, and she warned me off him because of Bono. She was still selling me her line about Bono. I explained I really liked Declan, but obviously I was in love with Bono. I asked her how was it all even possible with Bono. "Should I not move on?" She advised me not to respond to Declan. She said Bono would not be best pleased if I was gallivanting around with one of his nightclub security guys. Anke was so sure I would be with Bono, she did not want me to mess up that chance. She was probably right, but we will never know.

Right after I first met Player, I asked Billy to leave the apartment we had been sharing. We had been living as flat mates since he got back from his year or so in Glasgow, where he supported the passing of his father from cancer. I thought that asking him to leave would help us both finally move on with our lives. I figured if we were to ever to get back together, a separation would be a good idea anyway. This was a huge adjustment for us to make after so many years. We were like family to each other. But I had engaged with the drug that was Player, however misguidedly. Billy's acquired habit of drinking himself into a stupor at least once a week, still grated on my nerves, and stressed me profoundly. I was really worried about this self sabotage streak within him, and thought I would be doing him a favour if I asked him to finally leave. It was not working as flatmates for me, let alone as exes or even friends.

Player temporarily put a smile on my face after years of difficulty it is true. I thought that all the changes were playing out for the best. He was at the very least a catalyst of change in my life. He will have no idea how much he stirred me up, and would not now give it a second thought. I gather he is, or was, married with children, and this would all feel like a very long time ago to him; as it does to me.

Straight after he dropped his bombshell, I was shaken and in shock. I could not speak and I just let him go saying I had work to finish. Perhaps I should have kicked up and been a drama queen. He might have liked that better. But I kept my cool seemingly, and just sat in silence trying to get on with my work. Besides, I had a knowing

I had not seen the last of him. What was really distressing was that it all happened exactly the same night as Billy left for good, for the first time. Billy and I made a couple of attempts at parting ways over a couple of years. Player set the ball rolling, and the discarded underwear in the suitcase saw the final demise of the whole thing with Billy. Billy knew something was up. He was, in his own way quite psychic. But after all his own infidelities, it really was none of his business. I wondered if it was all a big sign I was making the wrong decisions. I just did not know. I knew though, how I felt about Player in that moment. The universe was daring me to call Billy back home. I did not do so. I took the thing with Mr Rugby as a sign that I really had to sort my independence and equilibrium. All these men were getting quite overwhelming and confusing.

Donncha's own timing the night of the "bombshell" was just brilliant. I had not had much to do with Donncha since he wrote up the account of how I had helped Paul with his injury. But just seconds after Player coldly sauntered off, Donncha bounded in like a breath of fresh air. Mr O' Callaghan was discussing his schedule with a coach, and just the sound of his Cork accent was a wonderful change from the harsh northern Irish tones of Player. I bathed in that energy to ground and centre myself. Weirdly I felt immediately comforted and safe. His voice struck me as absolutely gorgeous, and I thought I would just sit back and enjoy it until I had gathered enough equilibrium to get myself home. I was still in shock, but I thought the synchronicity of it was pretty amazing. It seemed so precisely timed to cheer me up after such a hideous encounter with Player. No, of course I did not get over him that quick. But I am sure I should have done. I did not want to start passing myself around the rugby team any time soon. Enough was enough. I had clearly made the wrong choice is all. Yes, this psychic *did* see it all coming. But there was not much I could do about it. I had picked up over Christmas that this was going to happen. But it did not prevent the immense hurt that came over me when it actually did. Because I had just met Player, I did not think it was appropriate to go home to Scotland with Billy as planned. So I faced yet another Christmas on my own because of a guy I hardly knew. Well that, plus Billy's wayward ways and the protracted end of *that* connection.

I got very sick by New Year's Eve with a nasty bug and could not go to the Ulster v Leinster match as planned. I lamely sent a fax to Player at The Radisson to say "hello." But something did not quite feel right. I did feel he was still with the girl friend he had made light of, and that perhaps the link with me had ironically brought them closer. Brilliant. It was becoming clear that Player had assumed I was some kind of groupie for the rugby team. How ironic. He had duped me in the fashion of a player by stating that he was not "really" with anyone when he made his first moves.

Sometimes psychics can be stupid yes, and they are as susceptible as anyone to following their emotions, even ill-advisedly. I was caught in a catch-22. I knew that this hot stud probably was not the most reliable person on the planet for a female. But I had the urge to follow through and see what unfolded. I needed to shake up my life and inject some new energy; so that goal was certainly achieved.

Player made out it was not serious with his girlfriend, and assured me they had not been together long. I did repeatedly say "what about your girlfriend?" to him just before it all took off. And he dismissed her entirely. I could pick up that he really liked me; and everything did seem to be so intense and right between us in terms of passionate attraction. Unless I made a severe error of judgement, I did not think he was merely chancing his arm. He was also temporarily taken over by the vibes between us and I certainly was not complaining. Having been celibate for a long time, this was interesting. Who would say "no" to an intelligent handsome rugby Adonis? I imagine members of both sexes agreeing with me that I was right to go for it.

In somewhat contradictory fashion, Anke encouraged this connection. She felt Player really *did* like me, and saw that the connection had potential. Clearly, she had parked her Bono theory for the moment. I was not sure if she parked it for good. I did not ask. She had not approved Declan, but she *did* approve Mr Rugby. In retrospect I think she might have got it the wrong way around. Never mind. I needed to stop asking her every little thing, clearly.

Player and I had originally ended up in Room 102 in The Fitzpatrick's Hotel, because of an amazing synchronicity. I was just checking into the hotel, because Billy had not yet found anywhere else to stay, when two of the Ulster boys walked in. "My" Player had just been named man of the match against Australia, and joked that he was knackered. Having destroyed the whole team single-handedly I guess he must have been. But he clearly got a second wind, as I had a visitation that night, and he seemed very able bodied to me. Unless I was imagining it of course.

On the fateful night before the England v Ireland match at Croke Park, I checked into the hotel again. Player knew I wanted to see him. He came down to me in the computer room and apologised for not having called by. Room 102 had been waiting; but he had not managed to pay a visit. He then said that he thought his girlfriend might be pregnant. I knew immediately that is was not true, and I found myself saying very adamantly that I did not think she was. I also said that I had picked up over Christmas that I *knew* I would be hearing this news. It must be quite frustrating trying to lie to a psychic I think. But I did not really care at that point. Who likes to be messed with after all? Usually I am more careful to give someone personal leeway, but I could tell he was trying to fob me off. On reflection I should probably have pretended that I did not know the score, as it could have been his girlfriend trying to fob *him* off. But sometimes when you are psychic, things just trip out of your mouth before you can stop them.

I think Player was thrown off balance. I hoped he was not just making it up, so I acted as if I thought she had sprung it on him. What really hurt was that he then said he would be *pleased* if she were pregnant. I knew then he had lied, about the whole thing. He said they would need to do tests though to know for sure. "Yes, one test which takes a couple of minutes. How long does it take to wee on a stick?"

This bullshit was obviously his way of ending our connection. For now. After what happened between us in Room 102 it was like a dagger to the heart. Though on reflection, he did spend rather a lot of time admiring himself in the mirror fishing for compliments, so that in itself begs a question or two.

I know that he had panicked. Things had moved very quickly between us. I knew too that he needed to be concentrating on his work. But the irony is after he hurt me like that he never seemed to get *any* match time at all. He also went onto have two serious injuries, a dead leg and a freak accident in Rome which damaged his Achilles Heel. Oops. Player's career then embarked on a steady decline thereafter. He was certainly never called to be in the Irish Rugby Team again. I gather he settled on some time at Worcester Rugby Club, and then London Scottish, finally winding up off the radar in Singapore as an engineer, coaching local rugby sessions.

I guess it does not pay to be mean to me. Though I have to say I never abuse this power. I bore him no ill will. It was probably just his karma to be fair. I kept in touch with him occasionally, even after that bombshell moment. I had a feeling he would not be staying with that girlfriend, so thought I would just bide my time.

Just before The Irish Team left for the Paddy's Day showdown, I picked up that something was going to happen to him. I left him an amethyst for protection advising him to be careful. Yep, more of those weird crystals Donncha. It was then no surprise to hear later that he had had a freakish accident in Rome on the Saturday after the Ireland v Italy match. He did not even play that time, but the injury put him further out of the running for a few more weeks. Clearly larking around in Italian fountains has its pitfalls.

Overall I had felt that one of his team mates had been influencing him adversely. He had probably just advised him to stick with "the devil he knew," ie) the girlfriend. Anke confirmed this hunch. The friend would have known about our liaison for sure, even though we were supposed to be keeping it secret, as I had to phone his room once instead of texting, or leaving a note . Also said friend had passed the computer room with a wry smile on his face just before Player came down to deliver his "nappy" news. It seemed transparently obvious that he had told him I was there. It was all rather juvenile I thought; especially when the following week they both bounded by, totally ignoring me.

I was sick to the core to be honest. This was something that might have happened to an innocent teenage star struck girl. I was a grown woman who had been momentarily blindsided. I had wanted to explore the connection. But realised, this guy was way too immature in many ways. He was also seemingly a player who had been caught in a hotel scandal with a couple of team mates which had been covered by the *Sunday World* not so long ago. Old habits die hard I guess. On discovering his likely track record I was highly relieved the level of intimacy had not been too full blown between us. Thankfully there was not a condom in sight, and I did not take up his suggestion of ringing down to reception to get one sent up. The *Sunday World* article did not name names, but I knew from the energy of what I was reading, and from the person I had encountered, that he was more than likely one of the guys involved.

When I saw this, I anonymously emailed his girlfriend to tip her off. She replied to me and claimed to be in the know, and that this was "old news". But they split shortly afterwards. Serves him right. I am not a vengeful person, but when push comes to shove you do not mess in this way with someone who has a Scorpio moon. Oddly he phoned me in tears after all of this wanting to know more about me. But no. Too late. It was all too late. I had been waiting for that phone call knowing it would come, and it did. He then hung up on me when he did not like something I said about not telling him my age. I explained my belief about not speaking my age to anyone. If an authority figure, or booking agent asks me my age, I give my year of birth and ask them to do the math.

Player did not see the funny side of my response. So clearly he had an issue that I was apparently older than him. He could not process either my beliefs or way of being either. I gather he was a pragmatic bio chemist type. He was not going to entertain a psychic energy worker in a serious way any time soon; except to get his rocks off apparently.

When he phoned, Player's ego was still interested that I had feelings for him, and had I said the right thing in that moment I do believe he would have wanted to see me again. But by that time it was clear to me he could not handle who I was in any shape or form. He had already told me he thought my work was a "bunch of bullshit," so, we were not going to appreciate or understand each other any time soon.

Being a glutton for punishment, I sent a birthday card after that. He had told me not to be in touch. But I felt sending a birthday greeting was fair enough. He then reported me to the police, and got them to caution me for harassment. Oh my!

I thought this was hilarious, sad, and annoying all at the same time. He was apparently in a new live-in relationship, and did not want niceties and notes from me arriving at the house. The irony is, I had no intention of keeping in touch with him. He had really shown his true colours, and I was done. I had been waiting for that phone call for closure, and I sent a birthday card. End of.

Player had liked my intermittent attempts to stay in touch, and had thanked me for them. Now he did not want any contact. Fair enough.

But it was below the belt to report someone sending a card, and quite frankly totally ridiculous to go to the police. What. A. Joke. Seriously. When I got the letter, notifying me of the complaint, I immediately phoned them to tell them what had actually *happened* between us, and they amended their notes. Clearly that was a narrow escape for so many reasons. Player and the blonde psychic were from different worlds. Square peg: round hole. A combustible mix for sure.

The Mr Rugby thing had turned into a complete disaster for me. It was yet another disappointment, though it was also a colourful adventure. It was emotionally traumatic and devastating. But also enlivening. I had not even pursued Player in the first place. I was in a good space after previous difficulties. I was happy to have fallen in lust again. But it all felt very thwarted. It was like some entity or energy just did not want me to find a happy equilibrium emotionally.

Was Player used to further rock my boat? Quite possibly. He had made a huge play for me and I had succumbed. Things moved very quick and I could handle it, but perhaps he could not. I was momentarily swept off my feet. I acted out of character and just went for it without thinking.

I had sensed such an encounter was on its way. I had made the decision several months previously to follow the lead of my hormones for once. It is something I had never really done before. Billy had been a one night stand in his own head. Several years later, clearly he had been a safe bet, bar the drinking issue. Mr Rugby, on the other hand was a player and an opportunist. To be honest it was refreshing in that moment. But it is something I will never do again. At least I can say I did it once.

HOW FAR AWAY THE STARS SEEM, AND HOW FAR US OUR FIRST KISS, AND AH, HOW OLD MY HEART.
WILLIAM BUTLER YEATS

CHAPTER FOURTEEN
Girl With Crimson Nails

On the back of a lot of heartache concerning Bono and my ex Billy, the rugby lads reawakened my interest in life, love, and everything else pertaining to a good time. I had been isolated and working hard and solidly since the closure of The Kitchen nightclub. The Clarence Hotel had been a home from home for me on arrival in Dublin, and the team at The Kitchen, and Bono in particular had been like my extended family.

The real inner magic kicked in way before the rugby interludes when I first fell completely for Bono. At five o'clock in the morning, the night before Clinton's first trip to Dublin, Bono asked me to slow dance to a strange Howie B mix of Elvis's *Silver Bells*, and Madonna's *Like a Virgin*. You could not make it up if you tried. A strange combination, but somehow the genius that is Howie B made it work. This was my first and only slow dance with a guy ever. I have not experienced anything so powerful either before or since. It was truly magical.

Earlier, I had seen Bono watching me sway to the music somewhat transfixed, and I thought to myself *surely not*. I had previously caught him eyeing me across the room on an interlude visit home during a long gruelling tour also. That time I was wearing a black velvet dress with gold shimmery cosmic motifs. I had declared my feelings to him before he had left, and he still seemed to be engaged, if a little distantly.

Bono had always been affectionate and warm whenever we crossed paths. But his attentions were apparently stepping up, and had a different deeper quality. Obviously these were my perceived responses, I have no idea what he was really thinking and feeling. Suffice to say, the night of the slow dance, I fell hook, line and sinker for him. I was wearing a red Chinese top brought in George's Arcade - the bustling bohemian enclave between South Great George's Street and Drury Street - and my mermaid tail, black velvet skirt. I guess I hoped the magic of this red brick gothic area of Dublin, situated in the back streets behind the famous Grafton Street, would work like a charm.

The bottle green warren of an Arcade housed sweet smelling incense shops, a wicked cafe, full of bakery goodies and the most ridiculously good fry up materials, a stall of obscure luscious olives, numerous colourful stalls over-loaded with odd clothing, and a gypsy tent, which housed in coordinated sequence, a family of seven psychic sisters. Needless to say I checked them out, and found them curious and beguiling. They supplied relevant insights and entertainment more than gut wrenching details, or accurate predictions. I am not sure anything they said regarding the future actually happened; but they did give pertinent advice.

Anke, the visionary Aquarian, was the winner hands down when it came to picking up glimpses of the future. She was uncanny. Noel the tree surgeon in Phoenix Park, with no lines on his palm, was a close second, if not an equal. He got upset at my reading, because he picked up Bono in my energy field and identified our connection. It triggered the memory of a personal situation for him, and he found it too traumatic to go into. Tell me about it.

Bono smelled gorgeous, and was so sensual and inviting. People were pairing off for the slow dance, amongst the small select crowd in the nightclub. Bono crossed my path, beside the moat and gestured to the dance floor. He chose me, and very gentlemanly led me to the dance floor, for what might had been the highlight of my life up until that point. It might sound a bit pathetic, but I had not had much experience of romance in my dealings with Scotsmen. There was always something coarse and rudimentary about their approach. I guess they were refreshingly real, and without affectation. But they really would not win prizes for romancing a woman. Bono, on the other hand, would get the trophy.

It was a very rude awakening when Saoirse, the nanny of Bono's children, butted in and broke up our dance. She had obviously been commissioned to be on guard duty, and intercepted us at her first opportunity. Either that or she rather liked him herself. I just knew I felt bereft to be thus separated. There was a tangible quality to the sensuality of our closeness that I did not want to end. I did not know whether to be moved, delighted or embarrassed. In truth I was all three, in probably equal measure. I knew there was a chemistry between us already as every time I saw Bono my heart leaped. Whenever he planted a smooch fair and square on the lips in greeting, the warmth and feeling was electric. For me anyway. I loved that he had no shame in expressing his affections. I watched to see if he kissed other women on the lips, and he did not seem to. Though Bono is undoubtedly a very warm and sensuous Taurus, he did seem to save me some special attention. One time quite early on he gave me a lingering hug as he was leaving the nightclub. Ali his wife was waiting for him, and moved to get into the car. But he would not let me go. I was embarrassed, and moved, but again confused. Perhaps Ali saw things like this a lot and had endless patience. She may have put it down to a rock star embracing a fan. I did not know at that point. I still do not know really.

The energy charge when we connected, was electric. I had noticed a really strange frisson when he had stroked the inside of my wrist on arrival at Gavin Friday's private gig in The Pod. Bono walked up to me at the door, where I was attending to the guest list, and intimately stroked the inside of my wrist with his forefinger. I did not know a touch on the wrist with a mere finger could be so sensuous and sexy.

Taurus, though. What do you expect?

I did not understand what was happening. I just knew it was a chemical romance of sorts. Bono's wife was with him. She walked in ahead, and he managed to artfully do this without anyone noticing. It was intimate and highly charged. Bono sure did have a way of making a girl feel like she was the only one getting his special attention.

I cannot remember at what point I had declared my feelings to him in a note. It was certainly after all of this. Indeed all of this probably *prompted* the declaration. There was certainly some serious reciprocity going on by this time. These encounters spanned a number of years. He was nothing if not consistent, and for me the feeling grew steadily. There were interactions too numerous to recount; and overall I was floating and slightly bedazzled by the quality of the feeling. This was a Scorpio feeling stirred by the interaction of our two Scorpio moons. The Mermaid in The Kitchen was coming alive, and feeling deeply charged from the inside.

Others noticed the obvious affection between us, and there were whispers in corners. The slow dance had been unceremoniously intercepted. But Bono still found me later, and held my hand affectionately and unashamedly for quite some time in a corner of the nightclub. I did not know what to think. I only know I liked it. My heart was his for sure.

Emotionally, I had not been having an easy ride. Billy my long term partner had been unfaithful the odd time since we moved to Dublin. Even in Edinburgh, my love life had worked its way through a catalogue of betrayal and confusion. Not through any lack of clarity on my part. I just did not seem to make the most intelligent choices. But I always did follow my feelings, wherever they would lead.

To be honest, I made a direct link with Bono as soon as I met him. Our eyes locked, and there was definitely a sense of having known this person before. There was a sense of familiarity and comfort as well as highly charged energy. As he got increasingly touchy feely, I found it difficult to keep my emotions on an even keel. I became susceptible to his attentions for quite a while; many years in fact. He would always greet me with a lingering kiss full on the lips. I remember being quite embarrassed when he once smooched me well beyond the time limit of a socially acceptable peck, whilst his wife was in the same room. He was about to go off on tour, and obviously found the thought a bit emotional. As did I.

Bono wears his heart on his sleeve as those who love him know. He is a gutsy guy unafraid to show his feelings. Even fans get a flavour of this when he pulls the requisite girl on stage during gigs. One could say he collects hearts, perhaps energy too. But all in all he is a genuine well meaning person.

Bono's major smooch was a direct response to the declaration I had made to him a few weeks before. I had been finding it impossible to cope with my own feelings, and had to tell him. Not in the hope of busting up his marriage. But simply to try and make things easier and more fluid. Somehow. It was probably a naive thing to have done. But he was gracious and warm in his reaction. For a while he had kept a polite distance. But the smooch I took as a direct more unguarded response. A signal that his emotions were also engaged.

I was never deliberately divisive or destructive of his relationship with his wife. Quite the opposite. I always remained quite cool and measured. But I could feel Ali being jolted emotionally from across the room when she noticed what was happening. She very smartly came right over and embraced me too. That is what it takes to be the wife of a rock star, and she had it well under control.

It is quite clear how Bono's wife has kept hold of her man for so long. She is beautiful, intelligent, hardworking, and wonderfully socially savvy. There is also a natural easy affection between them, and she knows just how much rope to give him. One thing is for sure, Bono will never hang himself on that rope. He is too devoted to his wife and wonderful family for that. Ali is his rock, and she has played such an important emotional role for him; especially following the death of his mother Iris at such a young age.

Bono and Ali have mutual friends with my parents in Bristol, and my cousin Dave is married to one of Ali's Chernobyl colleagues. Philippa, Dave's wife was on the BBC crew for the filming of Ali's Chernobyl documentary *Black Wind, White Land*.

Like Bono and Ali, my parents were close friends to Charlie Chaplin lookalike, Steve Fairnie and his wife Bev Sage. Writz, Steve's post punk rock band connected U2 with their expert stage designer Willie Williams. While Steve and Bev then became the Techno Twins, who charted with a cover of the hit *Falling In Love Again*. Steve sadly died of an asthma attack on a field trip with Western-Super-Mare College, where he was a lecturer. Bono and Ali attended the funeral in Bristol at our family church Christ Church Clifton. When I met Bono in Dublin, we chatted about Steve's funeral, and Bono commented on the blonde pall bearers in particular. He was aiming to have the same treatment for his own send off. Steve Fairnie had a small but significant influence on the U2's Zoo TV Tour. The phrase Bono greatly used during this tour "I have a vision, television," is a direct tribute to Steve's lyric from a Writz track, *Muscle Culture*. I later gave Bono an impressionistic poem by Steve called *New York, New York*. Presumably, this was direct inspiration for the subsequent U2 track of the same name which followed within a few of years on *All That You Can't Leave Behind*. Aside from these initial loose links, and common ground with my parents, Bono's friendliness and ready affection made me feel welcome and stable for much of my time in Dublin. Bono explained himself as a "friend of my father's" in some meeting or other, according to the hotel manager at the time Mr O' Driscoll. I thought that was cute; especially as they have never met. But Bono is right, they do have a lot in common, and should they ever meet, they would doubtless talk for hours. They have a similar soul filled energy, and generosity of spirit too.

For quite some time, Bono and his chums were my main mates in town. When I first arrived in Dublin, it took me quite a while to assimilate the culture and ways of the Irish. Even though my mum's great grandfather was the customs officer at Wexford harbour, I did not really feel very settled or connected when I first arrived.

Really my emotional exile began with that big panic at Stranraer on the way over. I was all for turning around and going back to Edinburgh, where I had actually been quite content. But Billy calmed me down and persuaded me to continue with the adventure, to follow through with what we had signed up for. Having made a good connection with Bono at Gavin Friday's wedding , and with Billy urging me to follow through, I ignored my intuitive wobble, and decided to give Dublin a whirl. If I had listened to that profound wobble, my life would have taken quite a different path, and I would not have had many important adventures and learning curves. It does not always pay to override your intuition. In fact it rarely does. But in this instance, a lot of formative stuff happened. Perhaps it would have been better to avoid it all. But then again, that would have been taking the path of least resistance, which essentially leads nowhere.

*THE PRICE OF ANYTHING IS THE AMOUNT
OF LIFE YOU EXCHANGE FOR IT.
DAVID THOREAU*

CHAPTER FIFTEEN
Mermaid In The Kitchen

Once I arrived in Dublin, my "stuff" sat for two weeks in what is now the resident's lounge of The Clarence Hotel. Nodd Mc Donagh, the Scottish manager of The Kitchen nightclub, kindly allowed me to camp in the hotel until I found a flat in Dublin. I quickly became more established in Dublin. But it was a huge adjustment. It was mainly Bono's friendship that settled me down and cheered me up. It was he who placated me, and made me feel emotionally safe and secure. He was actively concerned that I was okay and not feeling too isolated. What a Gent.

I used to work in Edinburgh at The Cathouse for my friend Donald, so I felt quite at home in nightclub land. Weirdly though, I do not smoke or drink and I have never been drunk in my life really. I love music, being sociable and dancing. But I think my lack of curiosity regarding drink, drugs, and general debauchery made complete sense when my path as a psychic healer took off. To be effective in these vocations, you have to be a clear, accurate channel. Substance abuse, though I am not in the least bit judgemental about it, never interested me. I am strange enough already, you might say.

From the off in Dublin, Bono was kind, friendly and interesting, which is more that can be said for some of the security guys and a couple of the female managers at the night club. I guess I came across as a bit of an outsider at first. I was kind of keeping an eye on things, and reporting back for Bono through his assistant Marc Coleman. One time Bono had been dining, and had been really perturbed at the quality of the music playing in The Tea Rooms. I was commissioned to go out and source a broad range of traditional jazz music to spice up the dining experience upstairs. My brief was, to make The Tea Rooms more ambient, and a whole lot more classy.

Some people seemed to be wary of my link with Bono, and at one point I was made to feel so unwelcome, that I penned a farewell note to him. I had been deliberately barred from socialising with Bono, Guggi, Gavin et al, because under a new staff rule, we were not allowed in the VIP bar. I was the only one who used to avail of this anyway, so it seemed to be deliberately targeted to cut me out. I finished on the door in my tickets and hostess role, sooner than anyone else, so this was a deliberate ploy to keep me separate from my friends, and was clearly the manipulation of someone jealous. I know who.

Perhaps I really should have left The Kitchen whilst the bad vibes were going on. But I was already totally in love with Bono by then, and felt I should stay around. After a while, he was really the only reason I stayed put. Ultimately I got on really well with the door men, and the unfriendly phase only lasted for six months or so; the duration of a particular manager's reign in fact.

At the time of the persecution I was so upset, and it was Bono himself who stepped in and enabled me to stay put. It was a strange synchronicity moment which kept me at The Kitchen for some time longer. I had penned my farewell to Bono, and was carrying it around with me, with no idea how to get it to him discretely. Weirdly, or not, I happened upon Adam Clayton, U2's bass player, stuck in a traffic jam on Camden Street; looking cool and approachable in his soft top on a brilliantly sunny day. The universe thus provided me with the means to get my message through, and it was this strange postal delivery that ensured I was able to stay on at the nightclub for several more years. Poor Adam, stopped innocently in the traffic at Portobello, had no idea he was helping perpetuate my feelings and links with Bono for quite some time to come. He knew who I was though, and happily took the letter straight to Bono himself, since he was on the way to the studio to meet him.

Within two weeks, in a quite unprecedented move, Bono intervened, and sorted my little problem out. He understandably does not like to interfere with the running of his businesses, and told me so. But he made an exception in this case, which was really kind of him. So I was able to float around the nightclub unimpeded by bouncers acting on strange orders. Bono clearly wanted me to stay put. And why not? I had been very useful to him thus far. Besides, I really did not deserve such shoddy treatment. After Bono's divine intervention, I was understandably curious as to what shape my future links with him were meant to take. I was very grateful he had sorted out the situation. It would have been a very unfortunate way to have left The Kitchen, and all that it had come to represent. It really was my anchor and home reference for quite some time when I first came to Dublin. I would surely have returned to the United Kingdom if I had left under a cloud at that point. It was my destiny to stay. Some part of Bono must have known this. I had some unusual public work to do, the scope of which I had not even imagined at this point.

The Kitchen was overall a really fun time. All the staff bonded well, and we have all made lifelong friends through the nightclub.

Many of us still stay in touch, and there is talk of annual reunions, now we have re-bonded and reconnected after a few years. It was a great place to work. The music was always loud and good, the craic and jokes were mighty. And there was a sense of us all being in it together. The crazy humor and merciless teasing was the best bit. I was slaughtered one night when I took a call from a rough Northern Irish voice announcing that there was a bomb in the night club. I told the bouncers on the door, climbed out of my ticket box, and scarpered up the street. I was not hanging around for the immanent explosion. This was funny I guess. But the security guys had not heard the voice on the end of the line. It was sinister enough. It was resolved pretty quickly, the club searched, the Garda called, and I sheepishly returned to the wooden box, where I spent hours of time doodling, reading and chatting up security to keep myself amused. The cold nights on the door were not always comfortable, but at least I finished earlier than everyone else. I would not actually have managed staying up nightly until 4 am as many of the staff did. I generally left work as soon as I could, to go see my dog and climb into bed. The years of late nights were not easy, but I did get used to it. The advantage was that it was possible to sleep late, and have personal time during the day for developing projects and my own business. Really it was not many hours work for a week's salary. It was just the late hours that were the bugbear.

The Kitchen was a fun house, with lots of amazing people in and out of the doors. The DJ's were top class, the security guys were amusing and friendly, and there was a sense of family amongst those who worked there. I would tend to the aches and pains of bouncers who had over done it in the gym, either on arrival for work, or once the work was done. I was beginning to develop my skills as a healer, and I certainly could lift and sort such strains pretty quickly. Whoever was in trouble on that particular night would come and chat to me as I sat in my wooden box for final last half hour countdown to when I could get out of there. So the quiet last half hour from one o' clock in the morning to one thirty in the morning, saw me tending to various limbs and backs. Strange but true.

Those ailing, or wanting a philosophical chat would come and visit with me once the club was full, and so we passed time until the curtain call. I managed to shift some very persistent injuries for a couple of them also. Obviously these were the training sessions for my work which later helped The Irish Rugby Team. I was able to offer those services in confidence as I had already seen what I could do with my healing hands; and quickly. My client list was expanding as I did more and more work in the papers and for the Irish media on television and radio. But I liked to still work at the nightclub when I could to touch base with my family unit in Dublin. Doing my own thing was sometimes a bit isolating, and I still enjoyed the buzz of the nightclub and all the gossip.

The kitchen spawned a magician and a psychic. Keith Barry, the famous Irish magician has done very well for himself. This psychic has achieved some things too. I did not usually attend the stay late events, as I needed to get home to Freddie the dachshund who was sitting waiting patiently for me staring out the window. But Keith would regularly entertain the staff on stay-backs, and he was brought in to impress the celebrities too. His party trick was sticking cards to the roof of the nightclub, and we would often come in for work the next evening, and find playing cards littering the vault bar ceiling, with names written on them in black marker pen.

Keith has become one of the world's go-to magicians; and in theory, I have become one of the world's go-to psychics. We have never had much to do with each other, as our paths only vaguely crossed in the night. I was usually on the way out the door as he was on his way in. It is possible that we would be a bit wary of each other. Many magicians do not rate psychics, and feel they are con artists. The irony is, it is the magicians that do the deception tricks, not the psychics. I have my suspicions that Keith is more than a little bit psychic himself. He would never admit this of course, as those who ply his trade often take it on themselves to challenge and criticize the psychic brigade. It is curious and odd that The Kitchen would be a launch pad, and platform for a magician and a psychic. But it fits with the eclectic nature of all things Bono. Once, again back to his classic statement: "being in the middle of a paradox, is the best place to be."

It needs to be said that nothing untoward ever happened between Bono and me. Nothing of a sexual nature occurred. I never tried to break up his marriage; nor would I ever do such a thing. I have the utmost respect for him, his work and his family. Okay at times the expressions of affection were intense; for me anyway. But Bono is a perfect gentleman and such a kind guy. This was an emotional and spiritual link, which left me reeling for quite some time. It was tangible and real, and not in my imagination, as some will be tempted to conclude. Bono is a friend to this day.

I might have married and had my own family if not for this situation. But that was my decision, and was nothing to do with any requests or implications made by him. I remember Billy interrupting an evening session in The Kitchen. I was sitting beside Bono, and Billy showed up. Bono made a quick exit, grabbed my hand meaningfully in farewell, and scarpered. I was annoyed as I was feeling particularly bonded with him in that moment. Billy turning up was most inconvenient. Perhaps for both of us. It showed me he was awkward in the company of my assumed boyfriend; so again indications were, there was some level of involvement.

I guess our chaste but intense connection was meant to be for a time, or it would not have happened. To the onlooker I was in a long term relationship with Billy, the Scottish guy I moved over with. Throughout this time, we were companionable and good friends. More like brother and sister if truth be told. I did not understand what was happening with Bono; but loved Billy as family, and also was still fairly devastated whenever he was unfaithful. It became less and less of an issue though, as time proceeded. I should have ended it completely much sooner than I did. Probably I held myself in stasis by not being brave enough. Essentially I was vulnerable, living abroad, and needed that sense of belonging. I would have been more independent in retrospect. But easy to say after the event.

Billy was my family in Ireland: Bono was my spiritual dalliance. Bono was my grounding rod, security and reference point. The quality of emotional connection between us was everything. There is no doubt I would have been long gone from Ireland, if Bono was not in my life, however tenuously.

*WE ARE ALL IN THE GUTTER, BUT SOME OF US ARE LOOKING AT THE STARS.
OSCAR WILDE*

CHAPTER SIXTEEN
The Waiting Room

One of the perks of hanging out with Bono and co, were the amazing experiences socially. I probably, over the years, met most of the significant Hollywood players, and many famous musicians. Not many people can say they sat at a table with Bono and Dennis Hopper and his wife, with her magnificent pearl necklace; or that they sat chatting to Mathew Modine until the early hours about Tijuana, constructing a road trip down to Mexico in his soft top sports car. Or that Michael Stipe of R. E. M. demanded their huge lemon shaped candle for his hotel room. Or that Robbie Williams bounded across the night club to sit beside them, and that he was duly dismissed in their head as a "chump." Probably a mistake ladies, Yes? Or that Michael Douglas, and his absolutely huge aura, made a beeline for them tripping over feet in the process, and then followed them to the rest rooms deliberately bumping into them to garner attention. Pre Zeta Jones, and yes, probably another mistake. I could go on.

Kevin Spacey played a mean game of Snakes on his Nokia phone, for example. He would sit in the corner and keep himself amused, on the occasions he was not surrounded by a coterie of handsome young men. As we all know, name dropping is annoying and tedious. Any VIP nightclub hostess would be able to regale such tales. Security personnel would be even more of a liability without their contract agreements. I am not contractually bound by anyone or anything; but I do want to keep a modicum of respect to the proceedings. These snippets will at least show you, that these were fun times.

Even though I did not drink or party myself, I kept elite company, and met some very interesting people. I am very grateful for these memories and good times. And yes I occasionally wonder what would have happened if I had responded more favourably to Michael Douglas and/or Robbie Williams. My attentions were obviously focused elsewhere. I am not the smartest when it comes to gold-digging, simply because I do not do it. It is not my style. I have to authentically feel a connection, or I am not interested. The man can be rich or poor, his status matters not. For me, it has to be a soul thing, or emotional link, for whatever reason, or I am gone. I do not even give it the time of day if I am not feeling it.

I spent a particularly memorable evening in the company of Prince, his young belly dancing wife Mayte, and Bono. I was commissioned to light Bono's cigars and keep Prince plied with his drink of choice. I ended up sitting with the trio as if I were Bono's date. This little dream was somewhat squashed when Prince's minders pushed notes into my hand as a generous tip once the party broke up.

Prince's performance to a small crowd at *The Pod* later that night, was nothing short of incredible. His performance of *The Cross* with Bono was absolutely off the scale in its brilliance. From what I saw that night, Prince was a very short, but perfectly formed shy, humble, funny man, who was an absolute musical genius. And he liked Stoli and Kahlua with a straw. RIP Prince.

Bono was surprisingly lacking in confidence both before and after his performance with the master, "formerly known as" After he had done his bit with Prince, Bono sought out my opinion of how he had done, and I genuinely reassured him of his brilliance. I had been left holding his cap and gloves, so he returned to me immediately.

Bono asked my opinion on musical things a number of times over the years. Another momentous moment was when he wanted to get feedback on "The Band's" new single *Hold Me, Kiss Me, Thrill Me*. U2 were working on this for the coming *Batman Movie*, starring Nicole Kidman. I pointed out that it was evocative of T-Rex in parts, and a funky departure. A good rocking forerunner to the experimental days of *Pop*. It was a critique he rather liked I think. Bono valued my opinion on things, and I really liked and valued that he did. I felt important in his eyes, or at least mildly significant. All the affections expressed between us were more than an added bonus; they engaged my emotions fully.

When I first met Bono, it was at Gavin Friday's 1993 autumn wedding. His special request that night was for me to keep him plied with wine as someone kept running off with his bottle. I thought it was an ingenious, novel suggestion, and I duly kept him topped out throughout the night. Bono's dear old dad Bob did not look too impressed with our arrangement. But I felt an attraction growing as we shared humorous asides. Throughout the night, he seemed to warm to me too. It could have been the wine of course, but I like to think it was a familial soul connection. It certainly felt that way to me.

I did not really know what a fateful meeting this would turn out to be. I knew something of U2's music. I was given that record *Fire* for my coming of age party; had attended a gig in Glasgow with John; and *The Joshua Tree* had resonated deeply with me, during a very bleak phase. But from the time I first met him, I was not in the least fazed by Bono's rock star status. I seemed to connect direct to the man himself. The flow was easy between us, and when I finally moved over the following spring, the chats and vibes were greatly inspiring whenever our paths crossed. (For me anyway).

I personally predicted for Bono that divorce laws would be established eventually in Ireland. He was concerned about Edge's situation, and I assured him that divorce would be available shortly after the coming referendum. Our chat was on the eve of the big Dublin march protesting the lack of social liberty on this matter. The images of Bono and Ali, heading up the march I found rather incongruous. I hoped they would not prove to be in anyway ironic. Bono looked very pleased with himself the next time I saw him. He scuttled into the club with a big mischievous grin on his face. Condition normal.

Once the feelings began to get more complex, it was never awkward; but we tended to just greet each other with a kiss and then moved on. It was as if deep chats could not be risked, indulged, or entertained. It seemed very odd to greet each other so intimately, and then walk on by without any social niceties at all. Perhaps it was just his way of keeping me sweet. It worked.

Many a time I tried to handle a slightly different approach to the situation that was very difficult for me. I even attempted to ignore him once or twice. A bit juvenile perhaps, but sometimes I really did want to try to move on with my life. I felt sometimes held in place by it all. I could not be with anyone else, as I loved him. Bono knew this after a time and he held me in check, perhaps not consciously though.

At the Meteor Awards, in what is now the O2 arena, I ignored him studiously. He was having none of it, and seductively stroked my belly through my semi see-through dress, to get my attention. I melted of course. I was a bit lost by it all to be honest. I knew nothing could happen. I was not going to be the pushy girl, and would never have tried to seduce him. Again in retrospect I probably would have had more confidence and done so. But we do what we do in the moment; and this moment was an impasse.

I was extremely miffed when Bono started to hang out with Andrea Corr. I felt displaced, and could feel the emotional shift and separation. It was just as tangible as the connection had been. I felt he was being friendly with her in the same way he had been with me, possibly more so. You could hardly blame him. Ms Corr was a young slightly more vampy, exotic version of his wife. Her energy and presence were different, but she certainly must have felt very familiar to him. That plus their shared musical talent, and their union, even as friends, was pretty inevitable.

The first years after I met Bono were tricky for me emotionally. I tried to do the right thing. I deeply fell for this man, though I tried to stay cool about it because of his, and my own, situation. Ironically his song *When You Look At The World* describes the scenario and depth of emotion to a tee. Bono will doubtless say it is about something completely different; and of course, it would be daft to assume it was about the situation. But equally it could have been, even if unconsciously.

Some of the songs written by Bono from this time are very apt descriptions of all the elements that were at play throughout this time. In fact a highly psychic colleague on an *Aura Soma Training Course* had asked me out of the blue, if I felt in any way drained when the *How to Dismantle An Atomic Bomb,* and *All That You Can't Leave Behind* albums were being put together. She said my energy was "all over" the music from this time. This was a random, highly intelligent person's comment, which I had not sought out. I thought it was odd, then went back to listen to the work. What struck me was the theme of emotional pain and disconnect throughout. Bono's searching for healing, acceptance, and recognition was tangible. People think U2 lyrics are largely political and provide a world stage commentary.

They undoubtedly do this. But look a little closer, and you will see a raw emotion and longing as an underlying theme. Draw your own conclusions I guess.

At the risk of sounding crazy, I could forward some theories on all this. Yes of course musicians use what is going on around them as their inspiration. The unconscious mind of anyone is a complex beast. Amplify that ten-fold for the creative mavericks that walk among us, and you start to get the picture. Now I am *not* claiming to be any kind of muse for Bono. His wife Ali is the obvious port of call for all that. But how I disliked the song *The Sweetest Thing* which winged in from nowhere on the back of all these older songs. I am officially allergic to that song. Sorry. It felt so compensatory to me. I know it was said to be an apology to Ali for missing her birthday one time. But it felt to me so much deeper than that. It was fitting, more so than she realised perhaps, and served a multi-faceted purpose.

I noticed that U2 have never called much attention to the song *When You Look At The World*. As far as I am aware they did not play it live much, if ever. The video for the official track depicts the world and its suffering. It is about the human condition. But the under tones of the song, feel so personal to me. They really capture how I was feeling throughout this experience, and I cannot listen to it without being deeply moved. The same applies to *Electrical Storm*, the video of which shows Larry rescuing The Mermaid but placing her in a bath tub on the beach. That sentiment of being in someone's mind all of the time, and it not being enough? To me that sums up my experience of the Bono ride.

Whether intentional or not, *When You Look At The World* seems to be about someone who "sees" things the writer cannot see. I have no doubt that Bono will claim that this is also about his wife, and perhaps it is. But I cannot get passed the words in the song which put the lie to that. There is clear mention of the night belonging to someone else. So it is *not* about the writer's current partner. It is about an unrequited longing, and the pain of feeling disconnected. There is a phrase which mentions not being able to see through the smoke. This obviously evokes the atmosphere of a night club. The writer talks about feeling they are stuck in a waiting room; which totally describes that feeling of stasis I lived with for years. Was Bono living it too? And there is clear reference of the protagonist's Bible, or Holy Book, in a line which implies the formidability of this person's faith, as all those around them flail and suffer. This could well allude to Ali, as her serenity is undeniably impressive in the midst of a storm. But it also evokes a similar line in another song which mentions a girl "with crimson nails, " and Jesus around her neck. This girl is in that night club again dancing to the music.

I used to wear a distinctive turquoise cross around my neck to work in The Kitchen, painted my nails red, and certainly swayed to the music in my fish tale skirt. I know I should not flatter myself, and I will doubtless be vilified for pointing this out. But, all the same, the lines definitely have resonance to what happened, if not a direct reference to an emotional landscape.

Anke, the infamous psychic from County Wicklow, who had by this time become a very good friend, jokingly called me a "cruel woman," when she read the lyrics of this song. She felt the pain of it. I was not sure what to think. I was a bit horrified and upset when I saw it, and realised if this was about me, I had actually been spectacularly standoffish, and it had pained Bono. I felt awful, and needed a rewind. Anke's comment made my reaction and perception of events even more complex. I had not meant to be in any way aloof or cruel. But what more could I have done?

There was one time where I had driven down to the studio down on Hanover Quay to find Bono late at night. He was there, his Bristol Car parked outside. I waited only a couple of minutes, and then baulked, driving off around the block. It was a big block and one way system, but I came back around to try once more, and he was already gone. I had the intention to finally try and sort it all out. For some reason this particular night stuck in my head as the night something might have happened. It felt significant, and psychically I was meant to resolve things, now or never. I would have at least got the closure I really needed. Or something might finally have gelled. Clarity would have been had. This was the energy of life's cross roads; and I chose the wrong road. I dithered and hesitated. I bet something happened within him that night too, but there is no knowing as I do not even remember the date. Only the feeling.

Thereafter I distanced myself from Bono quite considerably; and his Ms Corr saga followed shortly afterward. I just know I was severely jolted when I heard their version of Summer Wine. I was on the way down the N11 to Anke when it came on the radio. I froze, went into shock, panicked, and had to call an ambulance to escort me home. They took my oxygen and announced me "okay but fragile," and accompanied me back up the N11 to the hospital on the roundabout. When I left Anke a message about my no-show, she seemed more concerned about the money she had not earned that day, than my trauma caused by the connection I sensed, between Andrea and Bono, which had hit me right between the eyes through the music. Psychics are sensitive creatures. Sometimes, infrequently and out of the blue, something registers and it is simply overwhelming. Anke said quite adamantly that Bono and Andrea Corr were simply friends, and that Andrea wanted a relationship all to herself. She was not the type to share a man. Well you know what? Neither was I.

I was pretty interested to see the lyrics of the track *Elevation* when it came out. Bono spoke of a mole digging up his soul. This was a lyric with a unique ring to it, an unusual lyric, and very specific. I had given Bono a little brown mole for his birthday; a soft toy, not a real one. So I was very surprised to see this mention in a song which talks about his head, heart and soul being in a spin. I could certainly relate to what he was saying, even if was not intentional. This whole time was riddled with "meaningful coincidences" like this. All I know is I felt hideously divided for a very long time. The dynamic with Billy and Bono really stressed me for years. I fell between stools emotionally. I would have responded whole heartedly to Bono if he had made a concerted move. But he did not, and it robbed me of a chance to be with someone who wanted to be with me completely. There were a few times I tried to ignore Bono, or play it more cool in a bid to play down the link. But Bono always pulled me back in to his heart with a well timed intimate gesture. I guess he could have been messing, or indeed just being kind. But it really did feel like he meant it. From my point of view, the connection dominated much of my adult life. It felt significant indeed. I did not feel he was a rock star doing his "thing."

Bono is in no way a player. He is a man loyal to his wife, family and friends. He is a sensitive, deeply feeling man who makes soulful connections. His affection was intense and genuine, and I do not feel he led me on for a second. More likely he was being generous hearted trying to support me, knowing how I felt.

Ali's own behaviour also indicated that she sensed something between us. She possibly had to deal with this with other women too, I just do not know. I saw no sign of it, but I guess that is possible. Ali had very adeptly intercepted the intense farewell smooch Bono gave me, with a kiss on the cheek. Ali is a lovely woman, and I do not think Bono should have left her for me for a second.

But Ms Hewson is a clever woman who is not quite as cool about her husband as he thinks she is. I am sure he would actually be quite pleased to hear that. On one occasion she wrote a curt note to me about a bottle of Tequila I had left at The Clarence Hotel reception, addressed to "Bono and co" for Christmas. It had ended up at the house and she perhaps was not best pleased.

"Whether it was meant to or not - that bottle ended up back at the house...from the both of us. Many Many thanks." Ali then even went to the trouble of calling by The Kitchen in the New Year to make sure I had received her response. She did not have my address, so she sent it to The Clarence Hotel, hoping I would receive it. I did. But only after she had told me it was there. I went up to get it from reception later that night. I was quite surprised at her reactions, as the Tequila gift and card certainly did *not* exclude her. It was addressed to "Bono and co," but it was supposed to be taken up to his staff Christmas event. I was off home for Christmas, and I left it in reception for the works event upstairs the following night. Clearly it went astray and ended up at their home instead. But, no big deal, I would have thought.

A specific day in March still haunts me. Bono was standing expectantly in front of me in Finnegan's Pub in Dalkey with no one else around. I was already so hurt by the situation that after an intimate embrace I pushed him away with a flippant comment. I just did not know how to behave in this situation. I knew what I wanted to do. But was it acceptable? No.

Well, they do say in Ireland that "everyone has a Bono story," so I guess I can say, "this is mine." But that feels very unsatisfactory. I am sure if he had not been who he was, something more could have happened between us. But that is like saying night should be day, and day should be night. He was who he was. I did not particularly wish for or look for a connection. It was what it was. Let us just say, if he still has not found what he is looking for, then he never will. As for me, it is clear that sometimes you walk into something that is the exact opposite of what you want or need. You get embroiled in an emotion from which it is difficult to retreat. A masterful web is spun, and you wait for an answer. But none is forthcoming. It is the magic of a compelling and powerful love thing that causes you to hang on for dear life. And such is the charisma of the man on a good day that you are happy to oblige.

Shortly after I arrived in Dublin, in alignment with our growing friendship, I got especially commissioned by Bono to keep an eye on things at The Kitchen. It was completely unofficial, and I was certainly not a spy. Bono would get his assistant Marc to see or phone me for the latest updates; and I would let Marc know if anything untoward was going down. Not that there ever was. I wrote up regular reports on club nights for him and generally tried to be helpful. I had lots of ideas about club nights etc, but became a hostess at The Kitchen rather than a manager or promoter. Generally outside promoters ran the club nights, which is probably the main reason why the club eventually closed. There was perhaps not enough in house effort towards the end. That and the fact that Tuesday nights were a messy accident waiting to happen.

The five star hotel above clearly objected to the incongruous riff raff tumbling out of the basement in the early hours of the morning. Many young people used to come along off their heads, and even though the club never condoned drug taking in any form, there were some near misses regarding safety. The last thing U2 needed was a scandal or drug related death on their door step. It is also perfectly understandable that the hotel did not like having such a noisy riot to cope with every night. The boom of the bass notes certainly did vibrate up into the floors of the posh hotel above.

Towards the end, I hardly worked at the nightclub. My own work as a professional healer and psychic had taken off, and I only worked as a hostess or on the box office occasionally. The energies at The Kitchen nightclub had changed and it had become very run down and dowdy. I liked the club best when it was quiet and empty. It was tranquil and could even be quite crypt-like with its underground stream, nooks and crannies. I knew something was really wrong when it was not even pleasant to be in when empty. Energetically it needed a big clearing. It really was time to close down a chapter.

Things were reaching a crescendo, and new pastures for all were beckoning. I sensed this, and gave Bono a letter on Paddy's Day. The club closed very quickly after that in April. He was in Finnegans sitting all by himself. I had just penned my dilemmas for him to read. No, it was not another declaration. But I did need to make some practical moves. I wanted to leave Ireland. Even though my work had taken off, I was finding it very stressful and hurtful to be stuck in Dalkey without the means to leave.

For very complex reasons I was stuck. I sounded Bono out about sponsorship for my work; explaining again how difficult the whole emotional journey had been. Largely in my head I am sure. I left the note with him, and he agreed to read it. Shortly afterwards there was a buzz at my door, 8 Railway Road, which was literally just around the corner from Finnegans. In my embarrassment I ignored it. Probably yet another chance missed. This was becoming a habit.

I gather there had been plans to run the club right through that summer, even though we all knew it was going to close down at some point. I felt perhaps Bono wanted to put some distance between us and quite rightly so. I was ready for that. There were obviously business reasons for the closure of the club, and I do not want to assume that he took that decision because I wrote to him in that way. But the timing was pretty significant. Perhaps I just sensed the closure was more immanent than we all thought. I was not really working there much anyway since my healing and psychic work had taken off.

I messed up on reflection. I perhaps should have been more forthcoming about the whole thing. Where would that have got me? Who knows? I tried to do the right thing, respect his marriage and wonderful family. I simply loved him. It may well have been an echo of another time and another place. But love him I did.

*IMPORTANT ENCOUNTERS ARE PLANNED
BY THE SOULS LONG BEFORE THE BODIES
SEE EACH OTHER.
PAUL COELHO*

CHAPTER SEVENTEEN
Soul Mate Dilemma

Many people get so confused about soul mates and twin flames. I have clients consult me about these different relationships. They speak to me, so eager for confirmation of all the wonderful things they wish to happen. Often I have to give them a bit of a reality check. They are flying on the energy of a new connection, convinced that they have found the "one, "mainly because of the intensity they are feeling. Of course, they may indeed have done so. But one thing I will not do is mislead a client. Deep breath.

There are many types of connection we humans make. We may be feeling an emotion from other times and other places. There are soul families, soul mates, shadow souls, karmic ties, twin flames and many more sub texts and variables. How on earth do we unravel all of this, Especially in the real context of our own lives.

Soul Families are the soul groups and communities we connect with, who feel supportive, comfortable and give a sense of well being. Connected groups of friends, relations, networking contacts on line, those we meet randomly and feel instant rapport. There are many signals identifying those in our soul family group.

Soul mates are more easily identified. They are those specific, defining relationships in our lives, where we have a solid shared knowing, which does not need to be put into words. There is natural empathy, sympathy and caring in these connections. A strong telepathy also. Our best friends, a parent, a mentor or teacher, a twin, a brother or sister, could even be the postman.

Soul mates are potentially everywhere, though they are also rare, and should be valued highly. In many ways they are the connections that make life worth living. These links nurture us, help us grow, and within we know we are loved and accepted as completely as it is possible for humanoids to be. Soul mates are deliciously uncomplicated and reassuring. There is an unconditional acceptance, where we know we do not have to explain ourselves. There is a quiet understanding, and a loving supportive energy goes without saying.

As many of us know, karmic ties are something else entirely. These are without a doubt challenging. They can be complex, and infringe upon many of the categories mentioned here. The only exception is the Twin Flame. There is actually *no* karma involved with the Twin Flame connection. It is a clear, meeting of souls and minds without the funk.

Our karmic ties are the contracts we have signed up for in this life time. They generally precede the Twin Flame connection. Karmic Ties can be compelling, alluring, seductive, but they often have a twist or a sting. They are rarely fulfilling and straightforward ultimately. A big clue, if you find yourself asking questions on repeat, you can be fairly sure the connection is karmic, and therefore a mind Fu*k. Sorry. The truth hurts.

"When is my ex coming back?"

"When will I finally connect with so and so?"

"Is it going to work out with me and X?"

Obviously, this is all the everyday stuff which bothers us minute to minute. It is all perfectly normal and life can be about a succession of these connections. They are the people we have agreed to connect with to balance karma and to work through our stuff. They usually come as a preliminary to the tricky shadow connections; which precede the magical connection of the Twin Flame.

The shadow soul connection is very confusing for people, and it has a very strong link to deeper karmic ties. This connection is frequently mistaken for the "one." This is a compelling, confusing and intense link; and it often leaves us questioning our sanity. It is guaranteed to put us through the ringer, even though initially it looks as if it might save us.

This shadow soul link is why some people are walking around with the belief there may even be more than one Twin Flame for them. This is not the case. The shadow souls are like a reflection of our shadow side, our unconscious, our alter ego. There feels like a strong resonance with our soul in these connections. Yet they are much more about lessons, karma and playing out a specific chapter. Usually a chapter which precedes the connection with your genuine Twin Flame, who in fact is a part of *you*.

The potential for misguidance and confusion and deception is often heightened in these unions. The shadow soul link throw up some deep issues. They represent a need for purging, clearing, and cleansing. Anyone wading through this experience, is made ready for the real thing on the other side. The shadow soul acts like a mirror. They help us deal with our issues, our shadow side, and in fact they probably help us grow up also.

The time before the pure connection of the Twin Flame comes into being is often turbulent. The likelihood is you will not cruise or sail into the reunion with your Twin Flame. Much work and experience has to be achieved before you are wise, discerning and smart enough to work with what is.

Meeting your Twin Flame is not an easy journey. There are many forces at play which try to stop this powerful energy and connection. Drama will often manifest at the off set to try to stop it. The past often comes out to play and old stuff may need to be finally resolved. But the beauty of the Twin Flame is that there is a serenity, peace and knowingness to it. Despite everything, you both know the bullshit will eventually wash over you, and you can get on with some really cool stuff together. The Twin Flame is what it is. It is a pure connection with not intrinsic drama. This person is you, and you are this person. It does not equate to a loss of independence. Quite the opposite. The merging of this union gives you the greatest independence possible; because there is a natural nurturing, acceptance, love and freedom inherent within it all.

You do not actually fall in love with your Twin flame; for in combination the two of you are love personified. You are drawn together to work in the world in a union of service. You are them and they are you. There are complications as this reunion occurs. The past has to be cleared and released for the union to come fully into its power.

Many of us know who our Soul Mates are. But do we recognize our other half? Our Twin Flame? Your Twin Flame awaits. But be warned it is not necessarily going to be an easy ride.

Each of us has between six to twelve Soul Mates ranging from siblings to spouses to teachers to lovers to friends. Our soul mates in this life are the people who support us and whom we are closely connected with. They probably have a lot in common with us and are always there for us, understanding, encouraging and sharing every step of the way.

Our soul mates feel familiar to us and this is because more often than not we have had several life times together. In each life time we meet up again and replay our connections, sometimes more successfully than others. We cannot avoid our soul mates. Indeed our lives would be pretty empty and meaningless without them. These deep friendships and bonds are what makes life worthwhile. Together we always have the opportunity to transform ourselves and clear the karmas and controversies of previous times.

We all adore our soul mates. They give us that warm fuzzy feeling full of love and support. These are the relationships where we can say and think pretty much anything and be confident that we will be forgiven. The purpose of connecting with Soul Mates is to learn, share and grow together. We would find it hard to manage without them. Yet as our spirit develops and changes sometimes we are tested with a letting go process which can be quite difficult and painful. The good news is, these trials and difficulties often pave the way for the real humdinger of a connection, our reconciliation with our Twin Flame.

So if you have been having a hard time of tests and challenges, take heart that a very worthwhile relationship is more than likely just around the corner. All roads lead to this magical point. It is where we should all aspire to get to and this is now what many of us will be lucky enough to experience. Of course many people are already in established and happy relationships with their soul mates and young families and they do not need to be reading this with a hint of panic. Sometimes the Twin Flame thing is too much for some. This is okay. If it is meant to happen it will do so, and if it is not then life rolls on, no harm done. What will be will be.

The reality is that the times ahead will accelerate our lives in ways we have not yet anticipated. There will be unpredictable and unanticipated changes as the energies change. The planet does need more and more spiritually conscious people to get busy on its behalf. This why the Twin Flame thing really could stir the pot and take you by surprise.

Just remember you have free will and you have choice. Even when confronted with your other half, you can just say "no" if you are happy in your current situation. Just be very self aware if this happens to you and double check that you are not in some kind of unhealthy denial about who you are and whom you should be with. Whichever way you look at it your Twin Flame will stir you up to look deep within. Can you handle it?

Our Twin Flame unions have the potential to be a whole world apart from what we have experienced to date. Other worldly in fact. These advanced spiritual soul mates shine a light on us and reflect all our issues back to us in spades. Twin Flame relationships are the ultimate challenge. They inspire great healing within but if you are not ready to shift all of your nonsense, dramas and negative patterns it is very unlikely you will ever be lucky enough to fully connect. The Universe only tends to allow this union when both parties have gone through a whole lot and are ready for a whole lot more. So have you met your Twin Flame yet?

The chances are you have not. These are rare connections and many Twin Flames are in spirit rather than walking the earth plane. Or at least this has been the way of it for eons. Up until the dawning of the Age of Aquarius, it was very common for your Twin Flame to support you in spirit. You see your Twin Flame is a completely independent and autonomous unit. Yes, they are your other half; the other part of you. But equally they are whole in themselves and can get by without you. The chances are you will only connect with your Twin Flame when you have reached such a level of independence within yourself that you can actually manage quite well without them.

This might not sound very romantic. But the Twin Flame connection is so powerful that it is about spirit and soul much more than a mere physical connection; though that is all included if you are lucky enough to hook up in this life time.

Many people connect with their spouse or main Soul Mate during childhood. But it is really not very typical for Twin Flames to connect during childhood. Typically both parties have to have evolved to a certain level of consciousness or vibration before the universe allows the connection. You do not happen upon your Twin Flame in a casual way, nor do you go out of your way to find them. It is quite simple, when the time is right you find each other.

It is very common for a Twin Flame to be in another country or another continent and very unlikely they will be living in your neighborhood. Because this is primarily a spiritual connection, the universe likes to test things by keeping Twin Flames apart for quite some time. This is the union of two mature souls who have probably been to hell and back and who have finally found each other and suddenly it all makes sense.

This union is everything you have wished for and more. It is mutual and reciprocal; not unrequited or one sided; not dysfunctional or co-dependent. There is really no separation from your Twin Flame. They are a part of you, even now. Chances are they are waiting to find you even as we speak. The beauty of this connection is that usually there is a strong telepathic link that dispenses with the need for words. You do not even have to be alone in the silence. Tune into the universe and see what impressions you start to get about your Twin. Do not assume that they are a lot like you. Often times their role is to compliment you, so they may well have had quite a different life path up until the point when you connect.

It is very important that you sit loose to the situation. Stop, look and listen. The universe will start to give you very definite clues in the form of synchronous coincidences. There will be subtle signs which you may well resist at first because you will not quite believe what is happening. There will be magic in the air and yet you may feel some resistance too. Sit loose to it all with a wry smile on your face because of course there really is no panic. You will feel quietly confident and assured deep within. This all makes complete sense as they are your twin. They have been wanting to connect with you just as much as you with them. so why sweat it?

So what are the odds of connecting with your Twin? God only knows: literally. After all they are one soul in a sea of souls. It is possible to put too much emphasis on finding your spiritual Twin. If it is meant to be it will be. This is not really one you can force anyway for the universe will not allow this. The Twin Flame connection flows only when the time is right.

The logic is. If we are meant to connect with our Twin Flame in this life time we will cross paths soon enough and both parties will just *know*. There will be no doubts. Like magnets drawn together in a compelling, unavoidable way the nature of the Twin Flame relationship is undeniable. It leaves no room for analysis and doubt. All the "will he or won't he?" torture is nowhere in sight.

The down side of these dramatic shifts is that serious established relationships that seemed so right will surprisingly fail to enable the Twin Flames to connect. If your Twin Flame is currently single; well then it is only a matter of time before you naturally connect.

Remember that connecting with your Twin Flame may well be challenging. When you initially connect, after the inevitable fireworks, you may feel some resistance and adjustment. This is only natural. Hooking up with your Twin Flame is a major reality check that can be more than a little bit uncomfortable. It is often like dealing with a part of yourself you have chosen not to look at for quite some time.
This all makes sense. Connecting with your Twin is like looking squarely in the mirror, and seeing the naked truth warts and all. No one is pretending that this kind of connection is going to be plain sailing. There is also quite a high chance that your Twin may be coming out of a relationship in which they have had to fulfill certain karmas. There will be adjustments on all sides.

Even if you do connect, your opposite number may not yet be ready or brave enough to leap into the void with you. It all takes time.

People's lives and emotional processes have to be in sync and there is usually a lot at stake. Of course the things in the way of this magical connection ultimately work to confirm its validity. The challenges heighten mutual determination but only if it is the right time for this connection. Bravery is required on both sides.

Connecting with your Twin Flame does not usually follow the same pattern as the straightforward romantic falling in love process. It surpasses the traditional romantic images of strolls on the beach hand in hand, candlelight dinners and gazing at the stars - it is much more of a crazy rollercoaster ride. Enjoy!

THE SOUL ALWAYS KNOWS WHAT TO DO TO HEAL ITSELF. THE CHALLENGE IS TO SILENCE THE MIND.
CAROLINE MYSS

CHAPTER EIGHTEEN
Mermaid Magic

There are a lot of preconceived ideas about the psychic world, and the supposed mystics who haunt its corridors. Is the mystical profession an elaborate con, or are there genuine healers in circulation who can actually make a difference?

Unfortunately a great number of people, usually men, view this phenomenon with a disinterested cynicism. It is as if such flaky ideas appeal immeasurably to their own sense of superiority. Sadly, they are by-passing a myriad of experience with such a restricted outlook. As with anything a bit of careful balance does not go amiss; just as it is possible to give too much importance to a psychic reading, so too it is easy to get stuck in an endless maze of logic. We miss out on the subtle nuances of our lives by focusing relentlessly on the rational. What are the cynics afraid of; that there might be something in it? Perhaps the concept of someone being able to rummage through your psychic drawers is too much to bear.

By definition, a black and white reaction to life's diversity is limiting. The color washes out of existence if we adhere too strongly to what makes sense. We all have male and female alike, the propensity to think in a masculine or a feminine way. It is the feminine part of our psyche that connects with spiritual truth. Unless you are a rational fundamentalist of course.

There are two gender-based reactions to life's realities. The macho dismissive stifles thought with its rigidity and non-compromise; whilst gentle feminine openness is liberating and potentially frees the mind. The truth is there are alternative ways of knowing and experiencing reality, which are equally valid and at times infinitely more enlivening than predictable cynicism. This is not to recommend that we lose the run of ourselves in endless flights of fancy, but spiritual awareness does open our eyes to different dimensions of perception.

Although science may no longer accept it as literally true, the concept of a left and right side to the brain is useful. Psychic ability accesses the creative part of the mind, usually referred to as right-sided brain function. It is this part of the mind that enables singers and authors to write, and journalists to come up with rather spooky headlines. Intuition and instinct play an important role, and it is their ability to listen to the small voice within that gives psychics the edge. We all have the capacity to recognize a gut feeling, and we all have a measure of psychic skill. This is one of the mind's faculties that may be developed.

Intuition is closely related to inspiration, and when the creative juices are flowing, a writer taps into the disconcerting experience of channeling. Comments like "That book just wrote itself," or "That song came to me after five minutes at the piano," are typical of material that comes from nowhere. If you amplify this experience and add the skills of telepathy, and precognition you begin to unravel the mystery of psychic ability. The problem that left-brained thinkers have is no understanding of how secret and private information arrives in the lap of the psychic. Do those that walk the Wryd Way really have inside knowledge? Do they know or research the people they read for? They surely must. How on earth is it possible to comment with authority on people you have never met?

The protestations of the cynics are ethically important. For a psychic working in the media it is a delicate juggling act coming up with predictions about celebrities whilst preserving their right to privacy. I do try to monitor the phrasing of pieces, but it is a losing battle at times. Even certain things that I requested to be off record have gone into papers, so apologies to anyone who has been offended. In general I feel comfortable predicting weddings, babies, and other happy events. However, this leaves me open to journalists who perhaps want more detail.

Sometimes I find myself in a position where I am aware of things that will occur, and yet I don't feel I can mention it. This is quite a pressure, but one that the cynics will love. I can hardly say I knew that something would happen after the event. Perhaps integrity is more important than always having to be right.

The other criticism that really riles me is that predictions are the result of intelligent guesswork. I would personally have no tolerance for communicating the calculations of my own mind. What use would I serve if all the insights I offer in good faith were merely contrivances of my own brain? To me there is no mystery in knowing things; it is a normal and integrated part of my life. Of course I can only speak for myself, but I am as genuine as I know how to be, and the catalogue of clients I have helped bears testament to this. Actually one of the most healing things someone can offer you is a good heart and a listening ear. Combine this with some psychic insight and things happen.

Legitimate psychic information comes from a variety of sources: the Akashic records; the universal unconscious or collective unconscious; angels and guides; and the psychic's own ability to interpret symbols. The Akashic records allegedly hold the details of our lives. They indicate our life's purpose, and the reasons for which we have been incarnated. There is a sense in which we all have an underlying awareness of what will happen to us. The psychic connects with this telepathically, and is thus able to read past, present, and future events.

Clairvoyance, clairaudience, and clairsentience all play a part in psychic interpretation. These faculties relate to the sensory experiences of seeing, hearing, and feeling. It is quite unusual for a psychic to have all these gifts in equal measure. Clairsentience is actually more common than clairvoyance. This would equate to a strong sense of knowing that comes from deep inside, which may be described as a powerful feeling that you do not have to question. Do not make the mistake of thinking that everything a psychic utters has its origin at this level. That would be dangerous indeed. Always retain a healthy skepticism; notice I did not say cynicism.

One of the problems with psychic interpretation is the timing of events. When you take into account that a divine day is supposed to be equivalent to a thousand of our years, you appreciate that the powers that be are not bothered if that job promotion is tomorrow or next year. Thankfully, I tend to get the age of a person at the time of significant events, which by passes the difficulty to an extent. However, it does not shift the reality that sometimes we have to accept that things will unfold in their own sweet time and not before. Knowing that something will happen is not the same thing as being able to influence it or bring it forward.

There is a huge responsibility that accompanies working professionally as a psychic and healer. It is one I do not take lightly. For a start it is quite daunting to go public, not least because of the assumptions people make. I have experienced many forms of expectation directed at the work I do, and it is part of my pledge to work with honesty, integrity, and to the best of my ability.

Someone said I was brave to stick my neck out by working with the media, and in a way that is true. I am one of the most comprehensively recorded psychics. I am also a very private person. I do enjoy the communication that publishing affords, and I believe that an important part of what I do is to re educate the perception that psychics have all the answers. Some do, but you can actually count those on one or two hands, if truth be told.

Finding a highly accurate psychic, who can usefully effect your life and not cause you a whole new set of problems, is quite a rare find. Some of the people I help are vulnerable, and it is important to tread carefully with predictions in particular, because of the hope people invest in outcomes. I have come across some difficult scenarios where skills in counseling are crucial to giving someone the best chance.

It is dangerous to get yourself into a situation where you are perceived as some sort of definitive oracle. This is in fact why I prefer to give my readings a spiritual angle, and place an emphasis on healing, rather than get someone hooked on the idea that their lives will be okay only when such and such happens. People do not always understand that the more they ask when on things, the more they push that moment away. Desperation and the when question acts as an energy block, and in truth it is much better to give yourself over to the power of the moment. Does this mean I cannot see what is going to happen? Not at all. Nor is it a cop out. The reality is, I am more concerned with someone's well being and equilibrium in the moment, than about their distant, or even desired future.

It is important to be spiritually aware working as a psychic. There are mischievous energies that get their kicks out of our confusion. Protection and prayer are fundamental for me. I would not attempt to dabble with all things psychic in an abstract way. Ironically perhaps it is the grounding and centered nature of Christian faith which enables me to do this work. Having researched the subject over many years, it is wonderful for me to see how this knowledge can be applied professionally. Prophesy and healing are after all recognized gifts of the spirit in the bible.

Psychic readings and spiritual healing can certainly make a difference if done responsibly. So, do be informed, and be careful whom you attend. Make sure you are comfortable with that person's ethos and energy. Psychic insights can absolutely add another dimension to our existence. Accessed correctly and responsibly, this knowledge provide a different, often unexpected perspective. My aim is always to empower clients, and I encourage them as they work with me to listen to their gut feelings, and notice especially what happens when they ignore them.

Living psychically is about having the courage to stick your neck out and stand by your convictions without the fear of looking daft. The conventional logical approach to life is not necessarily the most rewarding. If you tune in to the universe the colors of life intensify; there is no turning back. Psychic insights appeal to our innate sense of curiosity, but spiritually there are more important issues at stake than knowing when our lotto numbers are coming up. Having been brought up in a Christian environment, I was tapped into living with a spiritual awareness from an early age. My father, as well as being a trained medical doctor, is also well known in evangelical circles as a counselor and lecturer. With this background, working as a psychic healer was actually the last thing on my mind. In an unexpected way this ministry, if you dare call it that, has found me.

Originally I was on track to be an English teacher, so I initially pursued my academic education on leaving school. I went up to the Scottish Universities, Stirling and Edinburgh, from my home in Bristol. I immediately felt rather abandoned. What had I done to deserve this exile? However, several years down the line the philosophy, religious studies and publishing degrees suddenly made sense. I was being extensively published in the Irish media, and was applying all the philosophy and theological research in very practical ways. There was also the unexpected, bizarre twist of a powerful healing ability thrown in for good measure.

Working as a healer was not contrived or planned, rather it unfolded as I followed my instincts. I had always noticed that people who would not typically give me much attention tended to queue up to confide in me when something was wrong. Boyfriends have commented on my healing touch; but we will not pursue that too far.

I remember when my father lost his sight completely for a stretch of time, the different reactions of his kids were telling. My brother's response was to run to the woodshed in a bid to become Mr DIY; my sister read endless stories; but I at the age of fifteen was stumped. I did not react in a particularly practical way. I could only reach out with the reassurance of touch, and empathy when the understandable questions of "Why God, why?" rang around the room. Sometimes there are no appropriate words. Things happen which seem unfair, and are even downright outrageous.

Growing up, I noticed a profound resonances within for such situations, but I had not expected to become a healer. Although I was aware of the laying-on of hands in church; I had not particularly related this gift to myself. I identify strongly with Eileen Drewery's sentiment *Why Me?* and I would recommend this book by Glen Hoddle's one time side-kick to anyone who is interested in understanding the dynamics of healing further.

Of course, it is crucial for a healer not to get hooked-up on a power trip. Always be wary unless the healer you attend professes and demonstrates tangibly the love of God. It is God who heals through the willing channel of the healer, and fairly frequently through your local doctor too, I might add.

So how did it happen for me? It was only when my own life disintegrated from every angle that I had a profound experience of integration. All the events of my life, traumas, difficulties etc, suddenly made sense. At the time I was doing some healing on my longhaired dachshund Freddie, with another healer called Ger. The dog had been knocked over in a bizarre accident, which psychically felt like a set up. Without boring you with all the details, this proved to be a watershed moment in my life. The presence of Christ was strong, and I felt the somewhat contradictory strands of my life come together. I certainly went through the most brutal apprenticeship a healer could hope for.

So, is there such a thing as a tarot card reading Christian? Well, there certainly was at one point. Although I do not use cards anymore, the path of Tarot helped the initial development of my psychic abilities. But I baulked at the tag fortune teller, and always disliked how the psychic world was presented in the media. I was not comfortable with it. It did not seem like a "me," that I recognized, and yet it was the path I was destined to take, for a reason I did not really understand. I would prefer to call myself a Christian Hermeticist. Before the clergy start praying for me, although I would be grateful if they did, I have done a huge amount of soul searching on this subject. I do not want to turn people on to tarot cards as their source of guidance in life. Quite the opposite, really. They are a useful tool in the right hands. But they also lay themselves open to much misinterpretation and even misleading energy. It really depends upon the integrity and ability of the user. It often is a case of a little knowledge is dangerous, and sometimes it is better not to know what the future holds, nor even to try to work it out.

There is a magic in living in the moment and in engaging in the full creativity of that moment. I am in truth far more interested in helping people to *manifest* the life of their dreams. My concern is to enable them to transcend the path they are on and to access a higher road, both spiritually and emotionally. Anything is possible, alongside the lessons and adventures we have incarnated to experience.

Not many people may be aware, but in The Vatican there are huge stained glass windows of the main trump tarot cards. These are powerful symbols that connect with, and illustrate our unconscious. They are universally accessible, but since the church quite rightly frowns upon idolatry they have a mixed reputation. Should they be used as tools or not?

At the time of the inquisition people like me were slaughtered by the church. The prospect of spiritual power outside the remits of the male hierarchy generally scares people. Some of this is justified as structures are important but most of it derives from ignorance. But, just as a psychic can be operating without an ounce of compassion, leaving a trail of disaster, so can a priest be self-serving and corrupt. Just as a priest can be genuine and concerned, so can a psychic of integrity provide a service that brings peace and reassurance. God moves in mysterious ways. In my research into the world of psychic guidance, and here the clergy can breathe a sigh of relief, I have come to the conclusion that absolutely nothing replaces the value of a moment to moment trust in the Almighty. Whatever our perception of God might be, we are as well to surrender our lives to faith, trusting that there is a reason for everything.

We might contrive many elaborate designs for our lives, but if they do not fit with the will of God we might as well throw in the towel before we even get started. John Drane, one of my lecturers at Stirling University, has written an important book: *What Is The New Age Still Saying To The Church*. Although it is a comprehensive look at aspects of the New Age movement, in my view it does not go far enough.

I justified my own research into this revival of ancient spirituality as a means of getting to the bottom of things. I decided to play devil's advocate, and got directly involved with aspects of the New Age that grabbed my curiosity. I knew the investigation I was undertaking was walking a spiritual tightrope, but I decided to see where it would lead. My intention was to publish this experience, but main result of going undercover is that I can now work with authority from the inside out. This might seem rather perverse, but at least this tactic challenges people to review their spirituality, and think.

There have been so many upheavals within the church that an understanding of the so-called "competition" is needed. There is a melting pot of pseudo-spirituality for sale, and I would be the last person to advise someone to rush out and buy a pack of tarot cards: I have seen the damage that they can do in the wrong hands. Foster an interest in the angelic realm by all means, but it is dangerous to rely on a pack of cards if there is misguided psychic at the wheel. In the Bible there are plenty of warnings against false prophecy. Jeremiah tells us to watch out for people who "speak visions from their own minds," and John commands us to "test" the spirits to see whether they are from God.

There is no doubt that some people are gifted with profound imagination, and the ability to receive messages from what Carl Jung called the collective unconscious. But, how can we be sure what they are tapping into? It is important to take a message on board, but also to reserve judgment. Something claiming to be prophetic may be a lie designed to mislead you. Do not forget there are mischievous spirits that try to have fun at our expense. In Corinthians, Paul names prophecy as one of the most desirable gifts of the spirit. Wholeheartedly I agree. In the right context prophecy can be healing, encouraging, and positive. With wisdom and discernment there is a place for giving people hope. However, it is important to be aware that there can be a huge gap between psychic ability and true spirituality. They do not inevitably travel hand in hand.

Psychics are trained to think symbolically. They understand the impact that society's universally accepted symbols have upon our psyche. Jung called these the archetypes of the collective unconscious. He believed that the process of psychic integration involved the identification and release of these ancient Symbols.

Jung was controversial in his time. He acknowledged the power of the mind, and accepted the existence of psychic ability. As I have already described, his principle of synchronicity demonstrated the phenomenon of simultaneous events and the possibility of what he called "meaningful coincidence." Jung is the reason that academics will entertain the notion of intuition. But extend the argument further to include the realm of other worlds and its accompanying psychic occurrences, and you wander into subversive territory. This is exactly the challenge I had with the PhD I was researching at University College Dublin, in the department of Philosophy. It was another reason for my foray into the psychic world. I *do* believe that it is possible to present this material academically. Carl Jung is my inspiration in much of what I do, and he strongly influences the approach I take.

I think any attempt to discredit such research stems from ignorance, and reflects the limited thinking of those who dismiss what they do not understand. Further into the future our minds will be further evolved, and we will be much more receptive to perceiving the different realms of existence. Yes, therein is a prediction.

The Jewish tradition of the Kabbalah equates true wisdom with the ability to foretell the future. This is a flattering prospect for a psychic, but as I have learned there is no possibility for complacency in this profession. The challenges keep coming. Every consultation is different just as every healing session has a life of its own. This is work where guidance and intuition are strongly in play. It is not possible to pre-plan or contrive the outcome of a consultation; cynics take note. Whatever happens is meant to happen, and I have a strong belief that the right people ask for help.

As a healer, you are not likely to be presented with a situation you cannot handle. But, sometimes there are situations that seem to be set up by the pranksters of the spirit world. This hazard of the trade is the reason I use a lot of prayer work when I am healing or working with a client. I do not mean to be alarmist but prayer is important because the need for protection is high. I strongly believe though, that there is a reason for everything. All the challenges and learning curves we face do have a purpose, and they are an intrinsic part of our development as human beings. It is always important to keep perspective, and to look after yourself, both as a client and as a healer.

When I had my practice, there were days when I had to delay appointments for the sake of the client because my own energies were not right. I even now would refuse to work when overtired or off-color as this is not fair on the client, and it is not fair on me. There are days when someone could offer me a million to do some work I would in all honesty have to decline. The cynics who think the likes of me work just for the money are most mistaken.

To my mind, healing must be performed in the right conditions, and so must psychic readings. It is actually draining to have people pulling at you for attention, especially when you are sensitive at the best of times. So it is in everyone's interest that I do not work when the vibes are not right. I have at times had to be quite disciplined with clients who start to become a bit like vampires in their expectations. My aim is to empower people, not to become a crutch for them to lean on.

A final thought for those still nervous about how working as a psychic connects with faith in God. As I have tried to explain, it is possible to look into the energies that are shaping our future, but it is not always wise to do so. True spirituality reveres simplicity, and it is good to develop contentment with the present moment of our everyday lives. Grace in the here and now, is certainly the most powerful energy we can ally ourselves to.

Life is complex. The spiritual world is a reflection of this. It is endlessly fascinating, possibly at times misleading; but above all it is educational and developmental. When push comes to shove, simple is best. You will find that even your worst dilemmas will have an organic flow to them. Answers will present, and it is not always necessary to run around many psychics trying to retrofit what you *want* to happen into the equation.

I work to empower and educate people. I am also a secret weapon, in discretionary moments. Mermaid Magic has an alchemy to it, and it delivers on a promise. I am working in quite unique ways as a result of all this research and practical experience. I aim to please, but do not expect an easy ride. The magic comes at a price and it requires your commitment. The alchemy of the creative process is mysterious and special. It is a pathway not accessible to many. But many may avail of it. This Mermaid wants to help. I will not tell you *when*, necessarily. But I will definitely show you *how*.

FAITH IS LIKE WI-FI. IT'S INVISIBLE BUT IT HAS THE POWER TO CONNECT YOU TO WHAT YOU NEED.

CHAPTER NINETEEN
Seeing Stars

Despite my daily, weekly and monthly astrology columns, I do not feel it is my mission to turn the world onto star gazing. This is an ancient, established art after all. But, it is worth pointing out that astrology is an invaluable esoteric tool that assists us in reaching some kind of universal understanding. Okay, so we may not all be able to get our head around transits, conjunctions and sesquisquares. And clearly we are not all going to train to a heightened level of competence any time soon. But ask any genuine astrologer if there is such an achievement as ultimate knowledge, using this amazing tool, and I would hope that the answer is a resounding "no."

This life is a voyage of discovery, one which we can tackle on whatever level we choose. Of course, Astrology may be studied and developed to impressive academic standards. But such information is actually quite inaccessible to the layman, or to someone who does not have a mathematical mind and a certain level of genius. Indeed, in its purist form, Astrological writing can be quite tedious to read and difficult to understand, unless you have the mind of a computer, and the patience of a saint. This is not to invalidate the discipline, of course. But it does raise the question as to its usefulness in the detail for the general public.

It begs the question. Are we happy to read our daily stars as a form of entertainment? Or should we take it more seriously? I guess the answer is: it depends on how it is done, and who is presenting the information. Of course I cannot answer for everyone in the esoteric field; but with my own work I try to maintain responsibility and integrity. Especially since I refuse to believe that the input I make amounts to nothing more than pure entertainment. No doubt there will be those who beg to differ.

Within the esoteric disciplines, there are various approaches that assist the unraveling of practical, useful information. Astrologers and psychics come in many shapes and sizes. The scientists and purists, usually men, are careful to steer a wide berth from all things intuitive and psychic. This rational approach to astrology is systematic and precise; but it also has the potential to blind you with an overload of data. Such formulaic elaborate depictions do not leave much room for a creative interpretation of the skies. Nonetheless this tradition definitely has an identifiable validity and pertinence. Then, we have the astrologers who do not have a problem admitting to psychic ability, usually the women.

Admittedly there are psychics who simply use astrology as a tool on which to pin insights or a bundle of clichés; or who use the astrological signs to offer up a break-down of information aimed at the specific day. I am probably one of these. I actually do not know much about the scientific side of astrology. I channel my work for the papers and the book I wrote *Star Scope,* came from a place beyond myself. I do not know where it came from. I just tuned into the energy and information and it flowed. It was psychically written, as are most of my writings.

In its most elaborate form astrology could leave you tangled in confusion. There are many possible interpretations of charts and astrology traditions can get pretty intricate. Karmic astrology for instance is fascinating, and allows for mind blowing theorizing about the patterns of our past lives. Clearly the grounding of the astrologer amidst this time line investigation has to be good. There is also no ultimate proof to back up this branch of the discipline. Having said that, the leap of faith does yield some insightful moments; but this is specialist stuff.

My own approach seeks to fuse these two elements; and although there would be some who dislike or disapprove of this idea, I am not afraid to stand by it. For the simple reason that it really works. Being psychic, with an intuition that seeks to inspire, amuse and enliven those who respond to my work, I believe I bring another dimension to this age old discipline. Intuitive astrology hits the spot every time, and many clients seek me out because the daily astrological writings ring true for them.

A friend of my mother's caught a very respectable business man reading my column on an Irish Ferry one day. She mischievously asked him what he thought. His response? "I wouldn't be without this column. I live my life by it." Of course he may well have been somewhat facetious in what he said. But she did not seem to think so. I do not know, I was not there. However I do get much feedback through letters and clients, that the astrology writings really do hit the spot.

As with most things, this astrology malarkey takes shape when you choose to connect or take an interest. If you treat it flippantly or with a lack of respect, then no doubt you will find ample evidence to reinforce your agenda. Life reflects our world view back to us much of the time. It is one of the unwritten laws of return. Similarly, if you elevate the utterances of new age gurus to divine status, you are falling into an equally dangerous trap. Suspend judgment as opposed to belief, and the stars will begin to reveal their secrets. All esoteric writing, recordings and transmissions are accompanied by the energy of whoever is doing the work. Their energy acts as a filter for the information. There are obvious accompanying risks therefore if the psychic is less than intelligent, either intellectually or emotionally. I strongly believe however, that those who make the link, are specifically guided to their particular healer, psychic, or astrologer. The one that can help them in that moment.

I am continually reminded that the spirit world functions in quite an illogical, unpredictable, and roundabout way. The beauty of it all in retrospect is that the outcomes are in fact beyond human logic. They are divinely perfect. But often the most pertinent message is the complete opposite to the one wished for, expected or desired. This is why it does not work if we accept only what is easy for us to hear. Do have very grave suspicions of those who tell you only what you wish to hear. Life is about enjoyment and fun of course. But it is also about challenges and development. Already we have moved a long way from pure entertainment.

There are people out there who understand this. Yes, perfectly normal well adjusted people. Similarly, there are those who can actually receive healing from listening to the right voice or message, however haphazard its arrival may appear to be. For this reason I take painstaking time with both recordings and writings in order to provide the best service possible in a commercial setting. I place great trust in the guidance that is accessible to all of us if we choose to access it. The Lord moves in mysterious ways after all. Now this is not meant to be some kind of strange blasphemy. I was recently encouraged to hear, considering my evangelical Christian upbringing, that several members of the clergy are developing an interest in stellar constellations. Of course this study is not meant to replace or displace the message of the gospel. But astrology is one of the most ancient mystical arts; so it is worth preserving its integrity and place in our world. These insights carried correctly can enhance our life experience; and most certainly do not detract from the creator who made the stars in the first place. I believe in the flow of synchronicity, and the patterns of the universe, designed by our creator. What is good enough for the three wise men is certainly good enough for me.

I would be the first to point out that life has to retain some mystery; and I run a mile from the formulaic categorizing of humanity. We are truly unique; being made in God's image, how could it be any other way? However, this does not by any means discount the validity of astrology or other esoteric disciplines. My theory is that all these things can work together. But we need both discipline and discernment to ascertain what does link us to the Truth, with a capital T.

Of course we are not all the same. Our egos would never allow us to admit to this. So thankfully our unique birth charts reinforce our independent autonomy. In fact our detailed astrological charts, when interpreted by an expert can be very revealing and enlivening. Even more significantly, the insights can be useful on a practical level.

So does astrology have any relevance in general terms to our daily lives? Surely all people born under the sign of Cancer are not the same; so why do they all have to read the same commentary in the daily papers? Well of course this is a valid comment, on the surface of it. But make allowances for the beauty of synchronicity and the patterns and rhythms of the universe, and you start to appreciate the bigger picture.

Certainly I have found, primarily through feedback from my writings, that even the most general commentaries have relevance. No, this is not the same as reading your fortune cookie or Christmas cracker message; and look at the significance we sometimes place on these. Each person will reach different conclusions. Taurus types, for example, like to see the proof of the pudding; and of course the need for practical evidence is tantamount. We do not wish to get seduced or sucked in by a load of old nonsense. But I will always maintain that astrology, properly understood provides a gateway into aspects of life we like to think are inaccessible. The very mysteries we are so keen to preserve can be described and explained by this Universal language.

Astrology helps us to understand why we are pressured and pushed in circumstances while others sail through the same challenge like a breeze. There is a very significant forewarned is forearmed factor which comes into play when we know what is going on in the heavens above. How many of us have noticed problems with communication when mercury is retrograde and causing merry havoc? There are frequently spates of questioning re all things psychic and astrological in the media. There have been reporters who infiltrate the ranks of prominent live readings companies, and endless discussions on all things esoteric. Rightly so; up to a point. For even amidst all the possible magic and wonder, it is important to keep the checks and balances in place.

Certainly these live lines need to be regulated, and it is always stated that the contents is "for entertainment purposes only." Many psychics have a problem with this. But it is important to honor the correct legalities. To be honest, to dismiss pertinent life changing advice as "entertainment only" is somewhat insulting. It is important not to throw the baby out with the bath water. How much of life do we trash, dismiss or write off, amidst a desire to have all things definitively proven?

Let us learn from our children and keep the magic of life alive. There is much to be said for the what you see is what you get approach to life. But what happens when our vision gets distorted, even while we feel we are being so insightful? But why not reserve judgment even while keeping your antennae for bullshit firmly in place?

Embark on the mystery tour, with both feet planted firmly on terra firma. At the very least, do acknowledge that astrology provides us with a framework which illuminates the trends in our lives; and allows us to ponder the great unknown. There is no doubt that increased receptivity to all things spiritual comes at a price. This is not some magical meal ticket to a golden, rosy future. Quite the opposite usually. This is where the fun and high Jinx can begin. But being open to other dimensions ensures that boredom, cynicism, and that jaded feeling is kept well and truly in check. This is not some kind of excuse or diversion tactic. It is the stuff of life and deserves our attention.

Of course we have free will and as such we can choose how awake we wish to be; or how conscious if you like. Admittedly, there are times when enlightenment feels a long way off, however much we grow and change; and indeed spiritual awareness is burdensome to many. It is not an easy road to take that is for sure. But the clues along the way can be most entertaining, and an endless source of amusement. Enquiring minds need to be stimulated and need to know. Esoteric investigations bring a depth to life. To take everything at face value is often misleading. Such an approach leaves you without the full armory of knowledge and insight. These ancient tools are at the disposal of all of us to enrich and enlighten. Just do not dismiss it all out of hand.

I HATE REALITY SHOWS LIKE BIG BROTHER AND I'M A CELEBRITY. I WOULD RATHER WATCH A GOLDFISH BOWL.
JANET STREET-PORTER

CHAPTER TWENTY
The Circus

I am not quite sure what possessed me to go for *Big Brother* when the auditions first hit Dublin. But go I did. Even though to be incarcerated for a long hot summer is my idea of hell on earth, I did get through a number of the secret stages and lived to tell the tale. To be locked up for entertainment purposes is not exactly my idea of fun. It would in fact be my worst nightmare. My intensely private nature would find it really difficult to be filmed in the rest room, in the shower and God knows where else; and I could just imagine demanding to be let out on day two of the lab-rat experiment with a threat to climb the walls. In fact, that is just what my psychic friend Anke told me I would do, if I got in.

Being a free spirit who likes to go with the flow and let each day unfold and structure itself; to be awoken with a fog horn would really get my heckles up. I remember not going on a summer camp sun rise walk in my teens for similar reasons. We were awoken at six o' clock in like manner, and I was the only one out of a group of thirty teenagers who had the gumption to say I was not going and slept on.

My tendency for rebellion in the face of authority did not really bode well for kowtowing to the *Big Brother* regime. In the big brother house, I probably would have slept through all the alarms. I would probably have had a problem sitting for long hours on those hideous sofas on eviction night. I would have found much of the tasks and surroundings restrictive and claustrophobic. I have no doubt that I would have been on a warning pretty much from day one.

As you can imagine, I would not have been any great shakes in the house for entertainment purposes either. Aside from the occasional psychic insight, I would not have got drunk or climbed into bed with anyone. Nor would I have enjoyed the tasks or food. I may have liked the diary room as a form of self expression. But really I was a non starter for the whole set up. Billy, my Scottish ex, did not want me to go for it. He rightly said that perhaps the public would not like me on it anyway; so why bother?

On reflection I think I really would have found find the *Big Brother* dictatorship too much. But, I do wonder if the regime would have broken me or whether my stoic, rebellious side would have won out? I have a hunch that the show would have been bigger than my resistance to it. But it is the one question I would have about the whole thing. A morbid fascination if you like. Going into The Big Brother House a personal challenge to oneself that I can understand. However, I am not sure I would be bothered to put myself through the torture.

I guess like most people, I have an obtuse, risky side that likes to push the boat out and test myself. So it must have been for this perverse reason, and for the slightly weird challenge of facing one's deepest fears that I put myself forward. My twisted dark side demanded it.

Big Brother had been on my mind for a while as a possibility. For a couple of years I resisted it. But I do not ignore my persistent intuitions forever. So when the impulse happened upon me as the auditions came to Dublin, I thought I had better do something about it.

When the day came, I decided to attend the auditions and give *Big Brother* a whirl. I figured that I might at least be able to hook up with Dermot O'Leary's program *Big Brother's Little Brother* as the resident psychic or something.

Not wanting to be seen to be going for it though, I went discretely to the Royal Dublin Society at the end of the day. I was allowed to jump the queue when I said "don't you know who I am?" to the organizers. I am kidding only slightly here. I actually picked up that this would work. I was not willing to go through the tedium of waiting for hours. There were lots of people still in line for the first round of what was to prove an enlightening but grueling experience.

The first round of the selection procedure saw each contestant pitted against one other in a bid to stand out amongst a group of ten. The lengthy queue was divided up over many arduous hours into two groups of ten. From these groups, two at a time were pulled out to display their wares and impress two rather obnoxious, antagonistic *Big Brother* employees. I was rather put off at their attempts to psyche us up to a level of ravenous competitiveness. It just did not wash with me, and I was left throughout the process with the thought

Sorry Big Brother, but I am just not that desperate to be on your show.

Perhaps the vibe of this reverse psychology worked in my favor, as I then sailed discretely through everything *Big Brother* threw at me over the next two days. Having reassured the in your face head hunters that I was a sane, grounded psychic, *not* in need of therapy, my hand got stamped with the *Big Brother* eye, and I was put through to the next stage. This involved another wait for the privilege of posing for a Polaroid photo, clothes on, before being ushered to a round-table to await application form number one. This I filled out in super-quick time, anxious as I was to get out of the Royal Dublin Society as quickly as possible. This did me no good whatsoever as we had to wait for our group of eight to finish their forms. As I waited, my worst nightmare started to unravel, and a couple of people at the table recognized me as the fortune-teller in the papers.

I discreetly asked another Mr "trying-too-hard" *Big Brother* employee, who kept asking us if we were nervous, how long the whole damned thing took. He briefed me discretely that I might well be there for the duration, and that there was a thirty page "tsunami of an application form" to look forward, which took half a day to complete, (only a slight exaggeration).

The next bit was an excursion upstairs in groups of eight. All those stamped with the sign of the beast, then had to wait a while for the chance to talk to camera for a minute. This again was a form of hard sell, with no hints at all in advance of how to impress the powers that be. Thankfully here, the TV and Radio work I have done paid off and I was able to chat away fairly animatedly for the required minute. I exposed my soul for what seemed like much longer than a minute before that damned *Big Brother* fog horn announced: enough already.

The minute on camera was handled in groups of six, and there were six separate booths where contestants were expected to talk at the same time, and not be distracted by the noises-off. There was no soundproofing and it was indeed quite difficult to concentrate on what you were saying. Then it was out into the corridor again to sit in front of two, more glamorous, *Big Brother* employees, who were continuously assessing what they saw.

It was the feeling throughout the whole experience. That there were eyes on every corner, and that word travelled fast. I had a producer running up to me when I was filling out the first application form as my prediction of someone from Cork doing very well in *Big*

Brother had obviously rung some pretty serious bells. I knew I was hitting a chord throughout the process, which I found kind of fascinating and not a little unnerving. It actually felt like a destiny experience; though I knew I was going to have to face the ultimate decision of saying yes or no if the offer came in.

Only two of us got through the next bit; which meant that my minute long soliloquy to camera had impressed the producers. Then came that "Tsunami of an application form," which stretched over thirty pages and was supposed to take two or three hours to complete.

There were about thirty or forty people still laboring over their applications from earlier in the day. As I sat down, my heart sank with visions of being there until the wee small hours. Luckily my years of exams saw me in good stead, and I whizzed through it in an hour or so. This caused a few quizzical looks; but I felt I had done my best in the circumstances. Besides, the room was so stuffy I was not going to hang around a moment longer than I had to.

I am not sure I got off any more lightly having done the form quickly though. This humdinger of a psycho quiz is obviously carefully designed to put you through the emotional ringer by psychologists, doctors, lawyers, television executives, and little Hitlers. You are expected to draw pictures; write poems; say who you would least like to see in the house when you walk in (that was easy); state in what circumstances you might break the law (I waffled something about parking tickets and a medical emergency); tell a joke (I don't know any); talk about your sex life (or lack of it); declare how many lovers you have had (not as many as you would think); state what books, films and food you like (all fairly obvious); state how you handle anger (fairly constructively); what makes you angry (too many questions); sad (going in the house); happy (not going in the house); which celebrity do your friends say you look like (Stevie Nicks, Nicole Kidman, Joss Stone); who do you admire (My Dad).

~ 280 ~

yadda, yadda....ad infinitum.

The worst question really was "is there anything you would not be willing to talk to Big Brother about?" Of course I said my personal life, and therein shaped the bulk of my interview for the next day.

How predictable.

By the time I got home I was shattered; though I was obviously lucky to have completed the process in record time what with queue-jumping, having come late in the day, and the ability to write fast. But I have to say, I still felt pretty bleak after the experience.

Because of my psychic ability I was able to get a very strong sense of what it would be like to be in the house, and I have to say I did not particularly like what I was picking up. I am more sensitive than most to energies and some of the energies surrounding the whole production process were heavy indeed. I really began to doubt my ability to be protected enough to do the show, and was sure I would find it far too exhausting to be in the glare of all that electrical equipment 24/7.

I have noticed this at times when I have done television in the past. It is quite easy for a psychic to become quickly drained by the equipment in studio and of course psychic energies are known to affect electrics too from time to time; one reason why I will not readily get into a lift. When I did *The Afternoon Show* once, a psychic healing slot for animals, the studio lights cut out in rehearsal. I kept very quiet, hoping it was nothing to do with me.

The *Big Brother* selection process still was not over, and I had to make an interview time at the Royal Dublin Society the next morning, which for me, being number D141, was eleven o' clock in the morning. With *Big Brother*, you become just a number as soon as that all-seeing eye is stamped upon your hand. Even so, I used my own name in the video interviews. I referred to myself as *Psychic Sarah* in the one minute rant; and in the second more intense interview with *Big Brother* himself, I also referred to myself by name. I am someone who can easily buy into that kind of de-personalization. Even though D 141 is a lucky number. I am not a number.

On arrival in the morning there was an unexpected staggered discussion group going on. *Big Brother* seems to enjoy springing surprises and the next stages were no exception. So, I sat down to a discussion with about twenty interchangeable faces, which romped through all the predictable topics: Dublin nightclubs, racism, sexuality and fame.

I was called then to sit centre stage and the subject veered onto all things psychic. I thought it was all going rather well, when the producer then called a halt asking the rest of the group if they were not all annoyed yet that the focus had been on "this woman" for the last twenty minutes? *Oops!*

I shut up then, knowing I had made my mark and waited until I was called for a lengthy interrogation by two big brother producers; one male, one female. Needless to say this interview was predictable in that they went straight to the subjects that I had said I would not be happy to talk about. I had assured them of some kind of answer; but never have I chosen my words so carefully. I did answer the tricky personal questions, after a fashion. But it was slightly scary in parts, as there is indeed stuff that one does not want hauled into the public domain. Yet another big reason *not* to do *Big Brother*.

Thankfully, I did not get picked to partake in the final two stages of the selection process; which I gather involve getting past a doctor and a psychiatrist. Being fairly *au fait* with my foibles, I do not think the shrink would have blocked my progress; though he might not have been best-pleased with someone who can argue the hind leg off a donkey and who is able to analyze until the cows come home. That is a Virgo for you. I guess the worst he would have done is yawn, and admit defeat. Besides, judging on the contestants who were selected, I obviously was not quite mad enough to get into The House anyway. As a professional, the psychiatrist may well have been aware that psy-

~ 282 ~

chic is close to psycho in the dictionary. But, I have learned to run-rings around most of the arguments thrown at me along the way. I have intelligent responses that the media do not always expect of a mere fortune teller, and I can keep up with the best of them in an argument.

Having had several run-ins with psychologists and skeptics about all things psychic, I am really okay at coming across as grounded and matter of fact about it. Also with a father who is a well known counselor and psychotherapist in evangelical circles I really have done a lot of soul searching on the subject. It does not mean that it is not tricky emotionally, and like anyone I do have my moments. But generally I keep my cool, and to be honest after some of the experiences of the past few years, to even have thought about going into The Big Brother House could be considered quite brave. Out of the frying pan into the fire, you might say.

My big motivation for going for the *Big Brother* audition in the first place was to build a profile with a view to publishing. My reasoning was that the *Big Brother* experience could be a launch pad in the United Kingdom. Drastic measures I guess. It could have worked out really well or been a complete disaster. This was the risk I took in going for it. To be honest I am not sure how wise it is to put oneself forward for all that negative attention. Those who brave The House do seem to get quite a pummeling in the media, so I guess it really was not the best idea. I have a good sense of humor; but to what degree I would have managed to stay buoyant in the house I am not really sure.

On balance I think it is pretty safe to say that if I had gone in the house, I would not have been one of those girls who took her top off, jumped on a bottle or hooked up in the Jacuzzi. So in this respect it is probably safe to say I would also have been pretty boring. I am not an exhibitionist and indeed the cameras twenty four seven, would probably have had the effect of making me quite introspective.

I probably would have become quite maternal towards those who were lowering themselves, and no doubt would have mounted a rebellion or two against the dictatorship. Yes, it would have been fun psyching everyone out; that would have been the enjoyable part. But as for staying sane throughout, if the audition process is anything to go by, the whole thing could have been pretty soul destroying. On a good day I could probably have done quite well with the process. But to be realistic over three months, how many good days would there have been. For the most part I would have been worn down and worn out.

Despite the fact I spend much of the time writing about celebrities; fame is actually not something that excites me. What is it anyway? My father says the celebrity world is so ephemeral; and I always remember a comment by Ewan McGregor where he muses that fame is "just so difficult to keep track of." When you are famous, how do you measure exactly *how* famous you are, and more importantly, how on earth do you quantify how long it will all last?

Having worked for many years in The Kitchen nightclub, I rubbed shoulders with a fair share of so-called celebrities. Indeed I probably met most of the main Hollywood mainstays in the company of Bono and co. But so what? At the end of the day they are just people like you and me, and if anything that is what I learned. As for wanting to be seriously famous myself? No thanks.

Yes, like anyone, I would like to be creative and successful. But as for the intense scrutiny of living life in a goldfish bowl, you can keep it. So why did I even consider The Big Brother House; which is of course the closest things that Joe Public can get to the goldfish bowl experience?

Like all women I guess I am a mass of contradictions. My reasons for going for this were in fact quite the opposite of what you might think. Apart from the thought that the exposure may have launched a book or two, I went to the auditions after an intensely lonely time. I was looking for an out, a reset, which would reshape my life, and bring the big shift I needed.

    I am always happy enough in my work. I enjoy writing the regular columns. But in recent years life had become just that; nothing but work. Having had many Christmases alone, I felt it was time to call a halt to so much isolation. I had no active desire to leave Ireland though; so this is one problem I would have had being in The House so far from the beach and sea that I adore. The delights of a small, claustrophobic film-set in Boreham Wood would definitely stifle someone who needs a daily dose of ozone and a walk with the dogs.

    At the auditions I was asked how I would be different from *Big Brother's* Scary Mary who was the first to be evicted the previous year. I could only think to say that I was known for being fairly accurate with all things psychic and that I was not a witch. But of course I am only too aware of the way Mary was portrayed in the papers; and I am not sure I would have coped very well with being portrayed in distorted ways for entertainment's sake.

    Of course, my experience would likely have been totally different to Scary Mary's. I could have had the time of my life after quite a stretch of isolation, and ended up making life-long friends, whilst boosting my writing career. But, who does that ever really happen to once they walk across the *Big Brother* threshold? I think it is safe to say that all things considered, The Big Brother House was not for me.

IT WAS THE QUEST FOR THE WEIRD THAT BROUGHT ME SO FAR.
TERENCE MCKENNA

CHAPTER TWENTY-ONE
You're A Star!

Shortly after the *Big Brother* debacle, I had the privilege of working with the Shinawill team again on *You're A Star*. A couple of years before this invitation, I had predicted the full line-up of the teen group Six for Louis Walsh and Simon Cowell on *Irish Popstars*. Just as we did for *Irish Popstars*, we filmed a few psychic insights on the show, and then I read for the remaining contestants one to one.

I described my first impressions of the candidates and gave clues as to how they might do in the competition and beyond. I wanted to be fair and help everyone equally, so I came up with some psychic clues to give each of them their best chance of winning. Of course I was not allowed to indicate who might win, not to the contestants, nor the film crew, so I phrased it all quite carefully. From a psychic point of view, the winner of this competition was not really a difficult call. Lucia was the star with the biggest voice and stage presence for sure. Once again I did a magic envelope, the contents of which were to be revealed on Brian Ormond's Show after the final result. Although I had my reservations about another envelope scenario, I was quite happy with what I came up with. I wrote a cryptic psychic rhyme, which was ringing in my head when I woke up one morning. I had been asking for guidance on an unusual approach to the whole thing. I thought it was a bit dull to have just a name in there that, rationally speaking could be either right or wrong.

Also, getting a name right out of the last six acts was to my mind not really that impressive when you have already predicted six people out of thirty two for a similar program previously. This time I was aware that something slightly different was required. I was keen not to set myself up for being misunderstood; and was also keen to do something unusual and a little cryptic, without it being a cop out.

Even though I am confident in my ability to be relevant, nothing really can be taken for granted, and one has to be constantly aware of agendas, and whether or not one is beginning to fall foul of ego stuff. The spirit world only assists those who are clear in this way. After all it is not really myself coming up with the information at all. I am merely a receptor for what I am given. So when I get it right, it is not really relevant to give me a pat on the back anyhow. I am only as good as the information I get given, if you like.

This clairsentient feeling ability is tricky to master. But it is also pretty reliable and trustworthy once you do. The energies that you work with also have to be tried and tested. It is obviously crucial that you know what to trust and what to ignore. The skill comes in being able to discern what degree of knowing you have in any given moment.

It is all very well predicting ad infinitum; but it really does become a bit boring when it is always right. After a while it is almost a case of so what? It is for this reason that I try to put across the nuances of the way the psychic stuff works in what I write, so that people grow to understand it more.

Of course many of us do have our own intuitions and insights. We all come up with something as we go about our daily business. But there is a huge difference between a definite psychic knowing and an intelligent guess, with a bit of rational thought thrown in. At the end of the day, the real psychic stuff is not really to be performed. It is a gift, meant to help us on our journey, spiritually, emotionally and physically. So one might ask, do we begin to abuse it when we expect our friendly psychic to come up with the next winner at Aintree? This type of prediction can be done by accurate psychics; but generally it is important not to overdo the use of the gift for material ends.

I can only speak for myself, but when I am working, I do have to wait for that magic moment. It is the point at which I just know something without a shadow of a doubt. To be honest not all psychic information has this intense degree of knowing attached; and sometimes readings can be, as we have all no doubt experienced, totally inaccurate. I often describe psychic knowing as quantifiable in percentages. When I used to do readings I would say to clients, I am eighty percent sure or ninety percent sure of this if I had *any* feeling of doubt whatsoever. But I always make it absolutely clear when I am one-hundred percent.

The knowing when I *know* thing is such a powerful feeling, that there really is no doubt. I know something to be the case, it really is the case. I get that, oh here we go again moment deep inside, where I know that what I am going to say is not necessarily going to come across as the most rational thought or comment in the world; but invariably, it will turn out to be correct. The beauty of this is when it happens way before the event. It was in this spirit that I wrote that envelope back in Portumna for *Irish Popstars*. I was confident in what I had come up with, or more precisely, what I had been given. I like it when I get that special moment, but it does not happen in that way all of the time. Nearly always when I am writing or talking psychically accurate information comes through, as long as I am fully receptive, grounded and really listening. One cannot always guarantee that every question will be answered. Some things we are not meant to ask, let alone know.

Being a psychic is not about being a performing monkey. Spiritual skills are not really meant to be novelty acts. I have made some exceptions in discerned moments. But generally, I will not perform on cue. This is the main reason why I turned down The Irish Skeptic's personal challenge to me. They were fascinated that I was claiming to get lottery numbers regularly, and wanted to set me a challenge. I was stupidly arguing the point on line on their discussion boards, and stated that 9, 11, and 19, were due to hit in the 49's draw. I wrote this clearly on line, and the numbers hit within the hour on the next 49's draw. This annoyed the skeptics intensely; and annoyed me even more, as I did not get to back the numbers being too embroiled in arguing with them. Lesson learned.

The skeptics wanted to prove my psychic ability under their strict testing conditions, which actually showed no intelligence or understanding about the true nature of the Gift. Spirit gives the information to a psychic on a need to know basis. It is not conjured up out of the psychics brain. Spirit will give demonstrations yes; but it will not perform on cue to satisfy a load of scientists who should know better.

I took umbrage at the ignorance. But I am not adverse to being tested if it has a higher purpose. I have put myself on the line many times in the media in observed conditions. This has a purpose, and I intuit when it is okay to agree. I am not afraid of falling flat on my face. I know that I will not. Because it is not me doing all this anyway. I am a channel for God's work, here to help people, again as guided.

People may have heard of Rhandi the magician's *Million Dollar*

Challenge. He was allegedly willing to pay a million to the first psychic who could prove their ability under agreed test conditions. A television company was interested in doing a documentary on the subject, and we started to negotiate terms with Rhandi, who was indeed originally open to the idea. My friend Carrie coordinated the research and enquiries for this project for Vision Independent Productions. Ultimately we found him wriggly and evasive, as we tried to pin down the nature of the testing, and the prerequisite conditions. I was willing to go for it this time, as long as we could establish a test that would genuinely compliment psychic ability, and adequately demonstrate it.

Rhandi became aware through our negotiations of my run in with the Irish Skeptics, and started to hide behind them. He wanted me to first be tested by the skeptics in my own country; knowing that I would not allow myself to be tested by them on principle. His conditions were that a psychic must be provisionally tested in their own country so as not to waste his time. I wanted to be tested by *him*. I noticed there was a flaw in his challenge. I gather no one ever got through the net to the second phase of the challenge. Rhandi never actually tested anybody.

It became obvious to me that the *Million Dollar Challenge* was nothing more than a good bit of public relations for his institute. People bandied the test round as if it was the Holy Grail of revelation, and Rhandi the Golden Fleece. The reality was, he was never ever going to agree to test anyone. He had no intention of risking his reputation or parting with his money; nor even devising a test that could be deemed fair by both sides. The farce was finally discontinued in 2016.

The truth is psychic information must not be forced, nor must it be manipulated for effect. So I refuse to be the psychic who tries too hard to prove it. The one time I did concede to respond when put on the spot by a skeptic, I actually freaked myself out.

I was on Raidio Teilifis Eireann's *Tony Fenton Show* just after I had done *The Irish Popstars* prediction re the six kids. Tony clearly did not have much tolerance of all things psychic, and he thought he would try and catch me out by asking what record was he about to play next.

I was at home in Dalkey on the phone, nowhere near the studio miles away. I just felt Tony was about to play *Beautiful Day* by U2. I was sure, I just knew. So it flew out of my mouth before I had time to second guess it. Of course, it was correct. God gave me the information, and the universe revealed its warped sense of humor at the same time. This is the only time I have bordered on disturbing myself with all this psychic stuff. It was a powerful moment, just as the *Irish Popstars* prediction had been; and the skeptics numbers prediction too. Could I keep rolling out these predictions? Probably. But I was starting to resist the performance side of what I did. When the skeptics set their challenge I said a firm "no." I did not want to be responsible for winning the doubting Thomas brigade a ton of money. They surely would have backed my predictions, and that in itself would have jinxed them. I certainly would not make a habit of such challenges. But on the *Tony Fenton Show* it was clearly it was Bono to my rescue once again. It was comforting to know he was still there for me, and useful for something.

My psychic rhyme for *You're A Star* got lost in translation somewhat. It revealed Lucia Evans as the show's initial winner. But of course she then had endless problems with getting her career off the ground. This made absolute sense of her reading as well as of my magic envelope. Much to my puzzlement there was no contract showing in her destiny. This was very odd, seeing as I could see that she would win the show. It was the Nadine factor playing out again. For just as in *Irish Popstars*, where Nadine lied about her age, all was not as it seemed with Lucia. She was similarly picked out, but for one reason and another, she ended up with no contract on the back of the show. The rhyme in its detail was very important to my prediction for the show, and I made this abundantly clear. Unfortunately in the rush on the night of the final, it got overlooked, and viewers just saw a picture of Marilyn being removed from the envelope by Brian with important writing above it which was not read out.

Oops.

The writing which was not highlighted said, "there is something wrong if it is not Marilyn." Even though I knew that Lucia would win the show. The rhyme says clearly that neither Jeanette nor Marilyn would win. Marilyn was in the envelope not because I was hedging my bets, but because she quite simply was the one who would benefit most from the show at that time. I was making a point with the rhyme. Various agendas on the show, did not want either Marilyn or Jeanette to win. It was going to be Lucia who won, but she was not going to be able to avail of the prize.

ODE TO YOU'RE A STAR

With Venetian harmonies ringing in the heavens
This has been a game of sixes and sevens
Of one thing we are now certain;
Very soon it will be curtains.
From day dot Marilyn and Lucia hit the spot
One a little doleful; the other a whole lot soulful
Not the bane of Brendan's life, Jeanette Cronin shone
Even as the Marilyn Factor grew strong
Our Monroe and Manson cut a groove of this there is no denying
But if I said they were gonna win I really would be lying
As Marilyn Fever took a hold, was there anyone left to break the mould?
As Marilyn Mania got a grip, who was left to let it rip?
I bet you'd give a Nickel and Dime to know to know the winner
Even as you eat your dinner
And now it's time to reveal
Our You're A Star winner by a steal: LUCIA!

Lucia Evans is a Libran, hence the line: *with Venetian harmonies ringing in the heavens.* Libra is ruled by the planet Venus. The line *by a steal* refers to it being a close-run thing with The Sullivan Brothers. It was also a veiled reference to some of the behind-the-scenes agendas at play on the show. There is a big mention of Marilyn in the rhyme because Ms Bane had the potential for a huge international career. Contrary to some of the reporting after the show, I did get the prediction right. But yes, it is a terrible poem, I do concede.

The rhyme clearly states that neither Marilyn Munroe (Jeanette Cronin), nor Marilyn Manson (my nickname for Marilyn Bane) were going to win *You're A Star*. But that Lucia would. I was misrepresented on the show this time. But it was a lesson, not to try to be too smart. Keeping things simple and clear is always the best way when conveying psychic information. Lesson learned.

Anyone who watched the show will know that Lucia was always the big favorite to win. The bookies rarely get it wrong after all. So it really would have been no great shakes if I had simply written Lucia's name on a bit of paper and stuck it in an envelope. With *You're A Star*, I fell into a bit of a trap. The television company did not listen, or rather chose to ignore my psychic rhyme. As I explained, I felt I needed to make things a bit more interesting. I wanted to make the contents of the envelope cryptic; food for thought if you like. Because of the complex agendas at play on the show, this actually proved to be a relevant and accurate notion. None of these points were meant to be detrimental to Lucia who has a spectacular voice and fully deserved to win the show.

Lucia shines bright whatever she does, and she certainly does not need me to fight her corner. Lucia means "light," and this is just what she brings through when she sings. She has the ability to make every song her own. The general message of this *You're A Star* experience is, if truth be told, that it is impossible to manipulate outcomes, whatever our motivation. Destiny is destiny.

SYNCHRONICITY HAPPENS WHEN YOU ALIGN WITH THE FLOW OF THE UNIVERSE RATHER THAN INSISTING THE UNIVERSE FLOW YOUR WAY.
AKEMI G

CHAPTER TWENTY-TWO
Synchronicity

Most people think they have a fair idea of what synchronicity is. We are all agreed that *Synchronicity* is a particularly fine album by The Police for a start. But sit down and try to define the quality of these magical moments and you will likely run into difficulty. We all have examples of intriguing, significant coincidences that have happened along the way, and we undoubtedly all get quite a thrill when a bit of synchronous magic brightens up the day.

Synchronicity is in fact quite an involved and controversial subject academically. At its most sophisticated, this troublesome phenomenon has been running rings around the phenomenology circuit for eons. Carl Jung talked about "meaningful coincidence," whilst the materialist Freud dismissed it all as quackery, giving it the scathing label, "spook complex."

Liable to rile the nearest skeptic, synchronicity as a concept seems to endanger the safe ordered perception of the logical mind. The what you see is what you get factor gets short shrift when the allure of a meaningful coincidence takes centre stage. Suddenly common sense and rational approaches to life have to take a rain check, and the world of the die-hard cynic potentially comes a tumbling down.

On the other hand, we common lore folk love the notion of a bit of magic in our lives. Even if we possess a measure of doubt or cynicism, such notions give us potential meaning and intrigue to our sometimes humdrum existence. Our general western reserve also bestows upon us an innate fear of losing the plot. We do not want to be seen as too off-the-wall, so we far too easily we dismiss our synchronicities as mere coincidence.

The phenomenon of synchronicity in many ways has had a bad press. We are reluctant to give the ramblings of our secret delight, when something cool and coincidental happens, too much airtime. Why? There is of course a danger in reading too much into every little thing, and one can no doubt go too far. But on the other hand, we risk reducing life to a purely material, painfully tedious, level if we ignore synchronicity altogether. I do believe we are in danger of missing out on a whole lot if we do not begin to give synchronicity more airtime.

Of course the universe famously plays tricks on those who profess to understand its mystery. But in my opinion, synchronicity holds the key to decoding much of the riddle-of-life we spend our time trying to understand. We only have to be brave enough to try a different approach. Taking a leap of faith to test it all out can reap dividends and we can get much closer to what is really going on by identifying our natural connections. If we would just open up and pay a little more attention; who knows what could happen?

We are all interconnected by unseen energies and electrical charges; and even the cynical, pragmatic scientists who investigate quantum physics are not far off reaching the same conclusions. There is much current research now claiming that scientists have identified the part of the brain which can predict the future. I can verify from experience that it certainly exits. But it will be a victorious day for the intuitive when science finally catches up with science-fiction.

We do not have to understand meaningful coincidences in order for them to happen. But there is no denying that an awareness of intuition, symbols and archetypes helps us to more readily tune into our weird and wonderful universe. Synchronicity reflects our inner and outer reality and as such offers an apparently objective statement from the universe that our intuitions are correct.

I do believe that we are much more powerful than we appreciate. There is in fact a strong argument to suggest that the more tuned-in to our creative essence we are, the more synchronicity tends to enliven our existence. Our inner-tuition provides us with meaningful signals, which once we learn how to decipher them, can greatly enhance our understanding and experience of life.

Many of those who have researched synchronicity, of which the most famous is Carl Jung, conclude that there is not much to distinguish intuition and synchronicity. When you know who is on the end of the line, is it a form of telepathy, synchronicity, or a bit of both? When you just know something beyond a shadow of a doubt, what is happening deep within? It is when our inner moments are reflected in the outer world, that our realities collide.

As above: so below.

There is, in a moment of synchronicity, nothing much to distinguish between the two. Our inner-tuition is reflected and validated by an external event and we feel vindicated and liberated in one fell swoop. I am not totally convinced that intuition and synchronicity are one and the same; but they are certainly linked. You do not generally get one without the other; though it is undoubtedly possible for even the most hardened cynic to occasionally get a moment of enlightenment without seeking it out.

Intuition comes from somewhere within our psyche and it acts like a strong lead or indicator as to what can happen. If you are clairvoyant to boot, you will also get inexplicable messages about what is actually going to happen, which are impossible to verify until the event. Synchronicity on the other hand seems to be an external reflection of what is going on deep inside. Perhaps you had a profound dream which is then replicated in an event the next day; or perhaps you are powerful and need to monitor your thought processes very carefully lest they reflect in an external event you had not bargained for.

I got a big warning about this one day, and have been very careful ever since; especially as I have seen the phenomenon play-out many times in different ways. Several years ago, I was bored one night in my job as Hostess of U2's Kitchen nightclub and innocently made a slapstick joke to the security guys to "Go give Bono's brand new Mercedes a flat tyre!" I do not know what possessed me, but clearly something did. I was horrified to then arrive the next evening, and find the manager of The Clarence Hotel changing the monstrous wheel of Bono's new pride and joy. *Oops.* Was I picking up the event, or did I in some bizarre way make it happen? Now, that is the question. I am sure one of the security guys did not take me up on the flippant suggestion. Not that I was directly responsible you understand. I probably was simply predicting the event.

There is no doubt that synchronicity and intuition *can* occur simultaneously. Like when you think of someone you have not seen for a long time and they then appear like a vision before you on a crowded street. Often enough, our inner and outer worlds collide with such Synchronicities. But it is worth being aware that we can also receive false intuitions that are never destined to lead to a synchronous event. My client list used to be full of people who had received misleading information from readings, which were in essence a mish-mash of inaccurate nonsense. People do waste a lot of energy waiting for synchronicities that are never going to happen. Just because you have been told something is going to happen, does not mean it is actually going to do so. Be careful out there, and wait for your own synchronicities to kick-in. That is where the real the magic lies.

Other people's predictions can be somewhat disempowering as you sit and wait for events to kick in. Be pro-active in your destiny and synchronicity will assist you. It is guaranteed.

Skeptics would doubtless point out that there are one hundred and one coincidences happening on a daily basis to each of us. These do not register as meaningful to us because they are not on our radar or expectation. Think of all the times we do not get run over when we run for the bus. Our luck is surely in on those days.

There is of course something to be said for caution around the subject. It is only too easy to get caught up in the excitement of our coincidences that we sometimes read too much meaning into them. We may even be inclined to make huge life-changing decisions based on what just happened. Certainly intuitive people are more likely to do this, and personally, I make decisions in this way much of the time. There is no doubt that this approach has led me into some very interesting, illogical, but magical scenarios. But, it is not a straightforward route through life, and there are definitely blind alleys we can all too easily waltz down.

There is a likelihood of chasing too many rainbows if one gives too much credence to coincidences, at the expense of good old-fashioned commonsense. Finding the balance deep within is crucial to our success with this thorny subject; and if we are not willing to be objective, grounded and measured as we feel our way with it, getting hooked up on synchronicity is in all honesty a recipe for disaster.

Psychologists are agreed that intuitive people are the ones more likely to experience synchronicity and take notice of it. They are receptive, sensitive and some might say gullible people, who are inclined to give coincidences a lot more airtime than the pragmatic, logical types who need to see the proof of the pudding.

In my view, both extremes get it wrong. It is all too easy to throw the baby out with the bathwater, and miss out on the subtle nuances and messages of the universe if we close off completely to synchronicity. Equally, it is easy enough to wander down a very colorful garden path which leads us into delusional territory, and from which it is very difficult to return to normality.

An unbalanced perception of such universal phenomenon can make one very withdrawn and vulnerable to all sorts of dubious energies. It is quite easy to begin to read meaning into far too much and as a result become delusional and God forbid psychotic in the eyes of the normal world. That may sound a bit harsh, but it does reflect the extreme of what can happen when one goes too far down roads that are designed to quite literally do our heads in.

The healthy energetic approach to synchronicity kicks in when an individual becomes as Jung defined it: Individuated. This level of maturity and unity with the universe is difficult to achieve, and one may indeed have to go down some of the blind alleys on offer, before one gets to the point where one is empowered and truly oneself. Everyone's personal journey is different. But what one might call being in one's power is when the full force and magic of synchronicity kicks in.

The individuated individual is a formidable force indeed. This person has a sophisticated knowledge of symbols; and usually has the ability to analyze, but not over-interpret, life's synchronous moments. Likely to have heightened psychic and spiritual ability, the Individuated person knows the value of meditation, silence and humor. Usually such a person has reached a sense of oneness within, and is enviably self-contained. The phenomenon of synchronicity is important to this soul, but it is certainly not the be all and end all.

Too often we assume that synchronicity reassures us that our lives have inherent meaning; that there is a pattern outside of ourselves that really does give our lives a magical quality. This is indeed the case. But we do become spiritually off-balance if we give it too much importance. Yes, synchronicity in the right hands can become a highly effective form of guidance. But where do we go during those times when the magic dies down? The answer is always within. For it is there we find our inner-tuition, the power-centre that always knows what to do next.

Spiritually aware and conscious people must be careful. For, the potential power of our thoughts, words and deeds is daunting. Our synchronicity moments underline the fact that we are creative beings who are capable of structuring our lives powerfully from minute to minute. Never mind external events; learn to access what you want, need and desire from within yourself. Then it is possible to be creative, honor your dreams, hopes and visions, and get busy manifesting.

The upshot of the Synchronicity secret is that we must project the good stuff into the ether, whilst remaining open and receptive to what is going to bounce back. Get the boomerang effect right? Your rewards will be bountiful and your Synchronicity moments tangible. Get it wrong? And you could be left unraveling the impact of a tricky karmic web with no get out clause.

ACKNOWLEDGING THE GOOD YOU ALREADY HAVE IN YOUR LIFE IS THE FOUNDATION FOR ALL ABUNDANCE.
ECKHART TOLLE

CHAPTER TWENTY-THREE
Cracking The Code

So what is this cosmic ordering everyone intermittently bangs on about? Can anybody join in? The answer is of course an emphatic "yes!" No, I'm not going to reel off yet another account of how Noel Edmund's came through his personal and professional crisis to land the *Deal or No Deal* gig, a wonderful house in France, and the woman of his dreams. I think we are all aware of this by now, and it is just one man's experience. Good for him.

Positively Happy: cosmic ways to change your life comprehensively tells Noel's tale, and it is an interesting read. But, the beauty of cosmic ordering is that it is available to everybody.

Cosmic ordering is a rather grand name for manifesting good things into our lives and it is a game anybody can play. Of course it would be naïve to say that we will all suddenly win the lotto, get our dream job or land the love of our lives in one fell swoop. But part of me is tempted to say; well why the hell not? After all belief is a huge part of what this cosmic ordering shenanigan is all about; and it is my strong belief that we can all tap into its positive effects. Be careful what you wish for, because you are going to ground stuff if you do this right.

But how is this possible? Is it even possible? Or are we all starting to lose the plot by thinking we can be the master manipulators of God, the universe and everything? Well, no, this criticism reflects a misunderstanding of what cosmic ordering actually is. The populist approach to cosmic ordering would have us believe that it really is as simple as dialing up on a hot line to heaven. We put in our request to the mail-order company in the sky and simply await our delivery. It is as simple as this; but it is also a whole lot more. We have to understand the principles in order to place the order effectively.

Trust in God and the universe is a spiritual approach to cosmic ordering. But it is not essential to whether or not it is going to work for you. You do not have to be religious to take advantage of the cosmic ordering system because it taps into a neutral phenomenon; but I will say it helps. Faith in God and in ourselves is no doubt the best way for us to function in this life and it definitely puts an even bigger spin on the cosmic ordering thing. Used in the right way cosmic ordering is not a blasphemy and I do find it works well in tangent with faith. It is not in fact the same thing as demanding from God everything we wish for and quickly. But it really does hold the key to the magic of life and demonstrates how we can tap into positive vibes and allow good things to happen. Life's abundance is waiting there for us to access.

Some may feel that there is something intrinsically wrong with this idea. Does it not make a mockery of human difficulty and suffering if we believe we are exempt from the bad stuff? Well, yes and no. The true understanding of *The Secret* is not so much about *when* is our order going to arrive, as *how* are we going to be content in the present whatever our circumstances may be? Anything else then is a bonus. Believe me you will get the bonus. But only if you work on being absolutely content with what you actually have.

I do believe that through my own life experience I have stumbled upon a secret that will help you land just about everything you wish for. I have uncovered the principle that allows us to balance our act and gain a measure and hopefully more of what desire. This is the skill of masterful detachment. The key to success with cosmic ordering is that we must not strive to make things happen. We must learn the art of wonderful nonchalance. If we can be the observers of our life, whilst maintaining an intelligent interest in what happens; well then we can have everything we wish for. So put in the requests by all means; but do remain somewhat philosophical about the outcome. Receptive but not obsessive. If you want something just that little bit too much, you will give off an air of desperation and it will never happen. Just go about your business, make your requests and prepare to receive many good things.

Cosmic ordering is not about striving for the unattainable. It is about attaining what is yours by divine right. Believe that you deserve what you are asking for, and ditch all the emotional debris from the past that may be holding back this process. Live in the present and you will get all the presents God is willing to bestow upon you. Ditch regrets, guilt, trauma, and angst. For there is no point living with such negativity however hard your road has been. The key is to be thankful for what you have and then ask for the hunches and intuitions that will lead you forward.

Our life experience is of course about a whole lot more than just arriving at our dream scenario. We have to learn, assimilate and listen along the way. But the key to the good stuff is never to give up, however hard it gets. Cosmic ordering is in fact quite a discipline that does not require concentration. But it does require focus; detached focus. Anybody who chooses to make use of the cosmic ordering principle can do so. It is as simple as a dial-in type request once you understand the way it works. Visualize yourself using a heavenly mobile and have a chat with God or the universe. This need not be a religious thing; but like a prayer it certainly works. You will in time find that your mind becomes more a-tuned to the universe and you get a sense of what to ask for and when. You will also need to be aware of what is okay to ask for and what is most definitely not appropriate. We cannot by pass life's major difficulties with this process. But we can control how we react to things, what we put out for and what we expect.

Remember, that what you expect is often drawn towards you like a magnet. So keep it positive and do not even give the concept of bad luck any thought. You are lucky indeed. By trial and error, if you utilize these principles, you will learn that detached expectation is a magical phenomenon that is guaranteed to maximize your luck. Positive, lucky people get positive lucky results, and crucially, they know how to turn around a crisis.

Anxiety definitely blocks the ordering process. So put in your order and chill. Do not worry or fret about the outcome and most importantly do not keep repeating or checking on the request. Simply know that it is done and wait for the heavenly UPS service to deliver at the right time. If you need, or would like a new job, lover, house or car, put in your order and trust that it will be delivered in a perfect way which will really suit you. The powers that be know what we wish for even before we ask. They also have a better understanding of our needs than we do, so be prepared to appreciate how your wish is granted. It will almost certainly be in unexpected ways. The beauty of this cosmic phenomenon is that all you really have to do is ask. Ask and you shall receive.

This is not some new age phenomenon, or cranky newfangled concept that people are going to make a lot of money from, though that will no doubt happen too. It is in fact as ancient as the hills, and as simple as a, b, c with a modicum of faith thrown in to the mix.

I would not be surprised if cosmic ordering is eventually revealed as a scientific principle, operating by cosmic law and the established boundaries of what is acceptable and what is not. We must not for example request anything that infringes on someone else's free will. Be careful with those love requests, as you put out for someone in particular. It may in fact be smarter to ask for someone who is actually going to be *good* for you this time around.

Nor must we put out negatively to the universe to wish harm on a rival. Such requests will certainly be ignored. Or even worse, you may create negative karma for yourself that will backfire spectacularly on you. The universe is not to be messed with in these matters; nor is God. So what do we need to know to allow these principles to work in our own lives in magical ways? Logically speaking, we all have to start just at the place we find ourselves and begin to test the theory. A lot of success begins to happen with the cosmic ordering principle when you test it out in small ways, and begin to have faith in its effectiveness.

The basic lesson is to start with putting out for a parking space near to where you need to go and expect it to be there when you arrive. Believe me it works. Start with everyday examples and begin to get a feel for how it works. When I used to work at The Kitchen, parking was a nightmare on The Quays, but I would always get a spot even though there were only about four possible places to choose from. For a long time my parking spot in Dalkey was a small gap in the double yellow lines exactly the size of my little KA. Eventually I had a conscience and gave up the spot so they could paint the lines. But for a whole year, that spot was always there for me, and was a source of amusement, possibly annoyance locally. I also used to drive the busy librarians in Dalkey nuts when I would go in to do emails without having booked a slot. There was always a computer sitting waiting, or someone would get up to leave just as I arrived. Similarly, my favorite seat by the clock in Finnegan's pub was there for me whenever I choose to go in, however busy it was. I did not think about it, ask for it, or expect it; it is just the way it happened. I do not fully understand why this kind of happens on a regular basis; it just does.

I think once we get used to working with Cosmic Ordering, the organic flow of our lives increases. So, test it out, begin to work with it and see what happens. Try asking God and your guardian angel for what you need on a daily basis before you put out for big houses and lotto wins. Or if you do not believe in the heavenly realms, simply put it out there that you are going to be looked after in your current circumstances. Do not doubt it; you will be.

None of us have a particularly easy road to travel. Anyone who has knowledge of transits and astrology will vouch for that. We will all go through our Saturn returns for example, and there is not much we can do when some of the big planets are cranking backwards in the heavens and stressing our natal charts. However, even so I do believe there are ways through everything if we exercise enough faith and trust in God and the Universe. I have only got through my own issues in this way, so I can promise you that the best way to stay safe and get your needs met is as simple as believing you are looked after. This is where our guardian angel steps in. All we have to do is ask for divine intervention in our lives, and there it will be, oftentimes in quite miraculous ways.

Cosmic ordering is a bit like flexing an unseen muscle. I have not done the research, but I do suspect that intuitive, creative types will be much better at it than cynics and skeptics. I do not believe either that it depends entirely upon elaborate psychic techniques, or highly evolved spiritual awareness. Really, anyone who cares to try this system is guaranteed to succeed. Cosmic ordering is for anyone: the city boy, the doctor on call, the meals-on-wheels lady, the prisoner and the seller of the *Big Issue*. We all have more control over our destiny than we appreciate. So think lucky and you definitely will be so.

Many people are at this stage somewhat jaded with the principles of The Law of Attraction. It is true that like does attract like; and that energies match each other on a frequency level. Equally it is not as simple as that. These universal laws operate at levels more complex than can be put into words. It helps if we keep things simple and remain receptive. But there is no doubt that bad things still happen.

We can boost our luck factor with the cosmic ordering principles. But we need to remain optimistic grown-ups who do not have temper tantrums when things do not immediately fall into place. Working with cosmic ordering is about focus and keeping faith. It is about knowing the power of intention and the creative charge of our thinking. It is about being mindful of the power of our words and what we verbalize also.

People greatly underestimate their personal ability to create. We get trapped in negative thought patterns and disillusion; not realizing that in so doing we compound our own misery and heap more of the same upon ourselves. There is nothing more effective than being open, receptive of clear intent and sound vision. Working to get results involves self awareness and channeled vision. Not all of us are great at manifesting; and this is where the professionals come in. Much of my work in recent years involves powering up the dreams and visions of clients in magical ways. This is an education for all involved; but the results are spectacular. The journeys my clients go on are not always easy. They can be a learning curve. One which greatly evolves consciousness and understanding.

Mermaid Magic utilizes cosmic ordering as an aspect of its expression. To be *au fait* with these principles is of no harm to anyone, and could indeed be the difference between something amazing happening for you or not.

*JUSTICE WILL NOT BE SERVED UNTIL
THOSE WHO ARE UNAFFECTED ARE AS
OUTRAGED AS THOSE WHO ARE.
BENJAMIN FRANKLIN*

CHAPTER TWENTY-FOUR
Cold Cases

One time I had a call from a trainee Dublin City University journalist. Siobhan, an ardent skeptic who was wondering how I felt about *The Sunday Mail's* attempt to sabotage my reputation. "Fine," I answered confidently. "In fact I found it funny." I lied.

We proceeded to talk for an hour or so, on all things philosophical and skeptical. Siobhan was about to update her daily blog, and she was particularly interested in how psychic matters are handled in the media. She was particularly keen to know if I was ever worried about sticking my neck out and making a mistake, especially in regard to helping the police with missing persons cases? "No, actually."

I explained that in my line of work one had to have integrity and that all I did from minute to minute was to follow my intuition and personal guidance. When I feel burdened by a particular issue or case, then in integrity I have to impart the message I am getting. I would in fact be failing as a psychic and healer if I held back. It is not about self-glorification whatever certain people might think. It is in fact about helping people in the right spirit and with a good heart.

People are often afraid of what they do not understand and they assume that psychics are either for the birds, or else they must be fraudulent and on a money spinning venture. You will hopefully have seen from my story that neither of these accusations is true. I am simply a human-being with what we call the "Gift."

Just like everybody I am trying to make my way in the world. Somewhat clumsily as you have seen. I seem to be able to help others more than myself at points. But that is just the way it should be. I will be the first to admit that I have an unusual profession. I neither contrived it, nor did I see it coming. It has simply unfolded organically. My work has proven to be the consequence of following my intuition from minute to minute.

To answer Siobhan's concerns about dealing with missing persons cases, I explained that such work is actually quite draining, and that I usually seek to stay away from the mediumistic aspect of my ability as much as possible. I am a grounded person, and like to sound matter of fact about even the weirdest aspects of my work. But to remain in integrity, I must never ignore the promptings of my heart. I have always followed my heart and yes it has got me into some strange scenarios both personally and professionally. I would not have it any other way.

I have never been one for the safe option. I have to follow my intuition come hell or high water. I do not think I would be able to live with myself if I had not done this throughout my life. But living in tune with one's heart is a double-edged sword. One gets hurt and indeed not doing the obvious, safe thing has made circumstances very difficult for me along the way. I hope though that such blind faith will ultimately prove to be my saving grace rather than my downfall.

I really do not claim to be a psychic that has a huge link with working with the police, or the Irish *An Garda Síochána*. But the media love this kind of thing, and it is always something which the journalists pick up on. I did feel especially burdened by the Trevor Deely case a while back. Trevor frequented U2's The Kitchen nightclub, where I used to work as a hostess. I have to say when he went missing I definitely felt very compelled to help find him. I got very strong psychic impressions of his last walk along the canal and felt very drawn to direction of The Grand Canal Basin. I felt it was hugely significant and held clues to what happened to Trevor to the point where I was really urging the *Garda* to drain The Basin. I do not now remember all the impressions I got at the time, but the *Garda* did come and see me about this case and shortly afterwards The Basin was searched again. But to no avail.

The Basin is forty foot deep and very murky and it is not possible to see clearly under the water beyond a foot at a time. I still do not know to this day what lies beneath the particular part of The Basin I was drawn to, but I would love to find out, as I feel it is an important clue. The Basin was not drained, and Trevor still has not yet been found. I am not saying that this is where he is to be found. It could be this is where a weapon was discarded. But I was definitely guided to The Basin, and believe it holds the key to what happened to him. Perhaps a tragic accident, some kind of shooting incident. There seems to be a gangland connection with it all.

One thing I do know is that he seemed to be reaching out to me. I do hope he is still alive. Sadly, I do not think he can be. I am greatly aware of the heartache of his family and their hope that one day he will walk back through the door. I just hope and pray that they all get closure on this difficult situation before too long. I believe they will. But I am afraid it will not be good news. Trevor is definitely in spirit, and has passed on. I am sorry, very sorry to confirm this, as I know his family still hold hope of finding him alive.

There have only been another couple of occasions when I have felt I had to get a message through to the police. Once when I was talking to my sister on the phone, she said there had just been a gangland killing outside of her house. I proceeded to get lots of impressions of the black guy who had been shot and the reasons for why. In this instance I felt compelled to confidentially phone the Sheffield Police.

I described the circumstances, the killer and the victim. I even got the name of a road, which was relevant, but which I do not now remember. The woman I spoke to had not heard of this road. But when she looked it up it proved to be in the heart of the Sheffield drug district. This was clearly a drug related gang land case of someone who had not paid his bill. I have no idea if the information I gave helped the police catch the killer. But the main thing is, I was sure they would do so, and I told them so. The police woman was not optimistic on getting anyone for such a crime. But I assured her that they would and a week later my sister confirmed that it was in the papers that they had solved the case. The whole purpose of these messages was to help the deceased, and to engage some healing energy to spark fair justice for his situation.

Some people may also remember the United Kingdom cases of Sarah Payne and Holly and Jessica. I felt compelled to relay a couple of messages that I got in those situations also. But it is important to remember that when such cases hit the public consciousness there are probably many psychics phoning in with their impressions. I do believe that it is important that the police and *Garda* work closely with reputable psychics. They know this anyhow; but choose to keep quite quiet about it most of the time. In America, the cops are more open about who they use and the results they get, and of course in Russia the KGB are big on the use of psychics for all sorts of reasons; all very cloak and dagger, but none the less effective.

With Sarah Payne I phoned to let the police know that Sarah would be found ten or eleven miles away from home within a day or two. The police were about to extend their search for the perpetrator to Scotland and I knew this was a big mistake and totally unnecessary. As I predicted, she was found the next again day close to home. Similarly in the case of Holly and Jessica when all hope was gone I picked up that their bodies would be found within a day or two. Again this proved to be the case. One might question how helpful those two calls were regarding these missing girls. But I felt that it was my responsibility to impart the message regardless.

What I do not know is to what extent the healing impact of such definite predictions affects the outcome. It is a mystery; but there does seem to be a link. Am I picking up on what is going to happen or am I in some way affecting what is going to happen? Now, the skeptics *will* be calling in the white coats. But bear with me, and I will develop the point in more detail as we proceed.

The chicken and egg phenomenon with predictions from a credible psychic and healer is something I am still trying to unravel. I do think there are important links between powerful psychics, and the subsequent events they predict. But I do not think it is simply autosuggestion. I have noticed healing occur with animals when I was absolutely sure that it would; and what do they know? I do wonder at times if it is actually possible to create the desired outcome by simply making the prediction. It has certainly worked for me in some of the healing cases I have worked on.

There is no doubt that the more glamorous aspects of psychic work are mysterious and compelling to people. For some reason, which I do not fully understand, we love to read and hear about it. There is obviously a certain mystique and thrill to the thought that there may be other dimensions out there helping us to catch a killer, find a body or solve a missing person's case. But, personally I do not really like the sensationalism that goes along with such cases.

From the psychic's point of view I think it should be a case of remaining helpful, matter of fact and grounded. The temptation to sell out I am sure leads to disappointment and some kind of comeuppance.

Certain agendas do not like this work and make many and varied attempts to stop it in the name of truth and clarity. I would say that this is good in principle. But the trouble is; the baby gets thrown out with the bath water by such attempts and what starts out as a mercy mission, becomes a massacre of what is also good and true. The terrain on this journey is treacherous and its waters are deep and murky. Put a foot wrong and you are screwed. Do not put a foot wrong and you are also sometimes screwed regardless.

I do believe that if a psychic or healer does not work with integrity, then the universe will sort this out before too long and their impact will be much diminished. Indeed they are likely to be reprimanded with quite severe challenges. Karma holds sway in a very potent way with those of a spiritual bent and there is a need to be all the more careful because of this. Lessons are learned the hard way let us say, when one's integrity gets compromised.

I am not sure I fit into this bracket. I certainly hope not. I have been only too aware that I have been walking a spiritual tightrope at times. My Christian upbringing has, perhaps surprisingly to some people, made me very circumspect and cautious about all things psychic and new age. I can see that these phenomena are a symptom of our searching and that there are many roads one might take on life's journey. But, I think the point is that some roads are safer than others.

There have been many times I can tell you when I wish I had not been led into the quagmire. Aspects of my experience could well be called *The Dark Night of The Soul*. Bono once said that "in the midst of a paradox is the place to be." I am not sure in retrospect that I would agree with him. But the testing I have undergone has enabled me to help a lot of people and raise a lot of valid questions. But I have balanced on a spiritual tightrope, of that there is no doubt.

Throughout my Dublin days, I have been what new agers call a "wounded healer." Perhaps a grand term? But not overall a grand experience.

*MAGIC IS BELIEVING IN YOURSELF.
IF YOU CAN DO THAT
YOU CAN MAKE
ANYTHING HAPPEN.
JOHANN WOLFGANG VON GOETHE*

CHAPTER TWENTY-FIVE
The Twain Shan't Meet

Surprised to find me open and willing to talk, Siobhan proceeded to make it quite clear that she was a definite skeptic and likely to remain so. This attitude I have found is prevalent amongst skeptics. It is as if they are reaching out and saying, "please convince me I am wrong, I don't really like being this way." I secretly believe that skeptics are in fact searching spiritually. They just have not consciously realized it.

The doubting Thomas brigade of the universe, skeptics are quite happy to sit on the fence until convinced otherwise. One mistake they make though is assuming that the likes of me are desperate to convert them. We are not. It is a case of live and let live to my mind. "You're a skeptic: I'm a psychic." #whatever.

How dull would be if none of us walking this earth had any belief outside of what we could prove scientifically? Some of us believe in the things beyond the end of our nose or outside of our field of vision; some do not. Some of us are searching and some of us have perhaps found a measure of what we are looking for.

Of course both these mind-sets, which reflect the different aspects of our brain power, are valid realities and both add to the great diversity of our life experience. Skeptics are full of rational left-brained thinking; whilst psychics are tapping into their creative right-sided brain power. And ne'er the twain shall meet.

With my work I am seeking to find the balance between my academic side and my psychic, spiritual side. I believe I actually have managed to make the two meet somewhere in the middle, and I am anxious to encourage others to do the same. I believe that many skeptics and psychics are functioning with a link missing. Many skeptics have suppressed their oftentimes strong intuition; whilst many psychics are quite defensive about having their skills tested and analyzed. The integration of our skills and faculties is where true enlightenment lies. But it is not an easy journey. In fact it is extremely challenging.

Even though I do understand their view point, the one thing I have found in skeptics is a complete lack of tolerance and empathy for anyone's view but their own. They simply cannot entertain or accept any other approach to life. I have had several run-ins with this delightful crowd along the way. On the back of a rather interesting *Marian Finucane Show* encounter one time, The Irish Skeptics Society attempted to set me up. As well as attacking me on the show for my healing claims and web site presentation, they also set me a personal challenge. Based on my claims about picking lottery numbers, they wanted me to choose three or four numbers out of seven in ten consecutive lottery draws and give the proceeds of their offer to charity if I failed.

I did not take up the challenge on principle. It is not that I cannot accept criticism. I am in fact my own worst critic. But I was set up on that show, and once again it was a deliberate attempt to discredit my integrity. The reality is at that time I was regularly getting three and four numbers out of seven in the lottery draws, at Paddy Power in Dalkey. At only one to three euro a go, I was attempting to win between 30,000 and 125,000 Euro. I was trying to find a magical way of clearing the debt I got into setting up my work in the first place. No crime in that; and believe me I got very close. But what ultimately caused me to stop the quest at that point, was a crisis of faith amidst frustration. I was continually falling one number short of the prize, and I felt I had to step back and work out what that meant. Perhaps there was more work to be done?

Several years later when I returned to Dalkey after a couple of years in Cornwall and Somerset, I finally started to win regularly on the lottery in this way. No longer was I always one number short. I regularly hit on four numbers in the Irish Lottery, and three numbers in the Euro. Paddy Power in that year had to pay me out at least 50, 000 Euros in winnings. People winning substantially on three and four numbers does not happen a lot. The book keepers set the odds so high and out of reach, because they believe it is nigh on impossible to hit on numbers. This is hilarious to a psychic who can come up with numbers accurately. Psychics really do have a loop hole here to beat the bookies, if they play it correctly.

I remember the time of the first payout, Dan in Dalkey nearly fell off his chair when I said four numbers had come up in the Irish Draw, and the payout was nine grand. They asked me to come back in the morning as they did not have that kind of money on the premises. The manageress had to get clearance from Paddy Power HQ, and then organize the cash from the bank across the street.

Dalkey's Paddy Power were used to taking money on horses, and paying out the odd fifty pound note; sometimes more perhaps, on horses, dogs, and football. There were winners on numbers now and again. But I was certainly beating the odds, and annoying Paddy Power with my wins. I was in there waiting to do my numbers, one time, and some tourists were ahead of me wanting to do numbers for that night's draw. It was a Saturday night. I nearly told them to back the 13, 15, and 19, I felt was looming, to speed them up with their decision. But something held me back and I simply backed those myself. They hit, and that was another nice win. Perhaps I should have been kind to the tourists though.

I generally found it was the numbers that I did, "in the moment," which proved to be most accurate. I tuned into the energies of the day, and seemed to be very in sync with the Irish lottery, and the Euro Millions. I did not bother with the 49's draw, that was Anke's gig, which she did with her daughter when they felt the relevant surge of energy. I stuck to doing it in my way, and it worked very well. Oh the joys of being psychic. There was certainly less reluctance in these moments. Clearly I had passed some kind of test, and the learning curve of the journey I had been on was starting to reap some dividends.

It is very true that it is nigh on impossible to step off this path of all things psychic, once the journey has begun. But, I am actually academically trained, so I do very much understand the skeptical view point. I think the issues they raise, though not particularly healthy from a spiritual point of view, are valid. Perhaps we need those with this arid mind-set to police certain aspects of the weird and wonderful world in which we live. Whether we like it or not; police it they do. At the same time, this is a negative energy that sucks the joy and mystery out of life. Although I understand it rationally, it is a bleak and arid place to be. Where is the magic?

Believe it or not in certain moments of my life story I have been tempted to join hands with the skeptics. But however bad things got, I found it impossible to lose faith. Even though at times I have felt neglected, forgotten and overlooked, I could never ditch my core belief in God. In fact the more adverse and challenging the circumstances got, the more determined I became to see things through. I was not going to be defeated. I was a believer, and I knew I would ultimately be guided to a good place. Of course, there is nothing quite like a crisis of faith to get you thinking. Equally, there is nothing quite like a crisis of faith to get things moving. I have learned that in the last while, however desperate or hurt I feel it is always best to hang in there and weather it.

Without sounding too maudlin, much of my time during my young adult life, was spent weathering the storm. My best response to all the emotional upset, financial ruin, and hard work of those years, has been to hang in there and get it right in the end. My story is ultimately one of hope, tenacity and determination. Weird and wonderful: if not a little bleak in parts. This whole drama has been my education in how to help others. My choices may not have always been correct. But they were always authentic, and delivered the lessons I was meant to learn. I would not have the depth and range of experience to help others if I had not taken these roads.

*GOD DOES SOME OF HIS BEST WORK
WHEN OUR HEARTS ARE BROKEN.*

CHAPTER TWENTY-SIX
Mystical Madness

Throughout my journey the love of God, men and dogs, has compelled me to hang on in there. Despite a myriad of Christmases alone, mounting debts, disappointment in love, isolation and psychic attack, I kept going. If not for my faith in God, stable background, love of my family and support of my friends, who incidentally did not know what was going on half the time, I would *not* be here today. But then again I think many of us would say that would we not?

The one thing I found, however difficult the emotional and spiritual journey, was that I could not let go. I very nearly gave up several times, and yet I did not feel I was depressed. I had had that delightful experience already, years ago during my second year at Stirling University, and I know the signs. That emotional journey was what psychologist's call an identity crisis. I am just not so sure that is what it was. I think it was simply caused by being four hundred miles from home and hooked up in a rather grim, volatile relationship with a Northern Irish guy; whose only appeal was that he was intelligent, and looked vaguely like Bono. My studies on Philosophy, Religious Studies and Skepticism were stimulating; not depressing. I did not have a big crisis of faith even though I was researching some pretty spiritually bleak material. I think the depression was an emotional response to being with a guy who quite literally did my head in, and abused me emotionally. The skeptics did not get one up on me; John did.

The prolonged stretch of exile in Dublin charted new territory and proved very different. My Astrological chart indicated that I was grappling with a Uranus in Pisces opposition, testing the veracity of my many planets in Virgo. At least that is what an astrologer friend told me. Whatever the cause, it felt like a fight for survival. I was stuck in a set of mounting mitigating circumstances which added up to a whole lot of trauma. I was at times stressed beyond measure, even as I helped hundreds of people sort out their lives.

I was completely effective at accurately reading and healing others. Just not always myself. The whole journey had put me into a very fraught and tricky situations emotionally, physically, spiritually and financially. I stuck my neck out for this work of "Spirit," and I was at times rewarded harshly. There was a constant need to fight on and choose life, as opposed to opting out. Opting out was a temptation I was not going to succumb to. Though I certainly was put into situations where I can understand people who do choose that route. Sometimes life is indeed too much to bear.

Those that know and love me will probably have been wondering exactly what kind of a life a girl who felt the need to sit tight and be alone at Christmas was having. But, I definitely was not depressed, delusional, or mad. Keeping a low profile was the path of least resistance. Whatever it looked like from the outside, I was simply sitting tight, for safety's sake. Under pressure that is for sure. In need of medication? Definitely not. Besides, I did not feel there was any point dampening down what I was going through. I did make repeated attempts to relocate back home to the United Kingdom. But, I was stopped every time, usually by my father, who felt I should stay out in the world and not run home, or back to the past.

Billy, the guy I had moved over to Ireland with, had already returned to his family in Scotland in the hope that I would join him when work permitted. But, this never seemed possible, and one thing after another barred me from relocating. I did not really want to live in Glasgow; but I did need a resolution to my financial difficulties and thought going back to the United Kingdom might sort things out. At least I would be able to pay off what I owed from a distance. Or in a worst case scenario bankrupt myself. The misguided thought that I might lose all my work, kept me in Ireland. At that point I felt really stuck.

On one hand I had Anke telling me I was going to hit it big in the lottery; and on the other I was drowning in debt, but learning efficiency in handling creditors. I was not hiding from creditors, as many do in fear. When I got a letter, I would pick up the phone and negotiate. I would let them know what, if anything, I could pay, and when. They would then make notes on their system, and not bother me until the next time. I do recommend this approach to anyone in this situation. Seek advice also. There are many repayment schemes available now, and it actually is possible to freeze interest on credit cards, and bring the balance down. You do not have to throw good money after bad. There are things you can do to face into the problem, and come out the other side. I knew I was in this situation because I had followed my guidance. I knew therefore that there must be a reason for it. That something would happen to sort it all out. Even in this difficult situations, we must try to sit loose to outcomes. The guidance will come, if we trust, stay centered, and pray, as opposed to panic.

When I investigated bankruptcy in Ireland, I took legal advice, and I was advised that it is nigh on impossible for an individual to take this route in Southern Ireland. I was told that companies could bankrupt themselves to the tune of millions, and start their business back up again the next day under a different name. But for the struggling individual, there was no reprieve. It was costly to do it, It was a High Court matter, and you then had to live with the stigma for twelve years.

I could totally see why Irish people struggling after the demise of The Celtic Tiger were relocating to the United Kingdom. There, under European Union Law, an individual can do the process as a European citizen, for the princely sum of seven hundred pounds. What is more, the protagonist is then cleared of their misdemeanors after twelve months. The system is thorough but fair. There is obviously a fear and guilt factor, which is why I cried with both relief and disappointment when I sorted my Bankruptcy in Truro on 25th January 2012, case 0033.

The Irish media got wind I had taken this route, and they phoned me for an in depth grilling on the day I was due to travel up to Bristol for my parent's fiftieth wedding anniversary celebrations. I was so upset that they were thinking of splashing my story all of *The Sunday Times*, that I aborted the family gathering to process the shock. I was going to be written about along with Shane from Westlife, and a couple of others. I prayed like mad they would leave me out of it, and thankfully they did. I think my story had moved the journalist. I was open and honest, and explained to the detail why I had had to do what I did. I explained it was a painful but measured decision that I was not taking lightly. There was certainly not an ounce of irresponsibility in my situation. It is so easy to judge people going through horrendous financial challenges. The truth is, individual cases are often much more complex than we realize. The human face of these traumas, is distressing, and we should have compassion.

I struggled on for a long time, in the faith that what Anke was telling me was correct. The breakthrough could be any minute now. What I did not realize was that I needed to do this deed first, in order to clear negative energy and reset my life and my situation. I was approaching things the wrong way around. I had been cornered into a no-win situation; instead of a win-win one.

Throughout a very isolating stretch, I attempted to make ends meet. I lost a couple of jobs, had no live-in partner, and debts were mounting fast, coming out of my ears in fact. I had carried the burden of providing for Billy for many years, paying most of his rent and bills, as well as my own, and technically some of the debts were his also. They were all in my name, and I had set up the business, so I did not make him feel guilty or demand help. I just shouldered the situation and sorted it.

My only light relief during this time, was the company of my little dog Harley. I really had no idea how I was going to get through it all, but I knew I would. I had faith, that it had happened for a reason, and that even in the midst of these horrendous challenges, I would be delivered, and things would work out in the best way possible. Naive I probably was, but it was this thought and approach that kept me sane.

Initially my approach was to knuckle down and stay put in Ireland. I began to see that until I accepted Dalkey as my real home once again, things were not going to shift. I was actually supposed to stick with the trials and tribulations, get through them, and come out the other side intact. Somehow. During this time, I could not actually get a clear definitive answer on what I should do. Strong intuitions eluded me for the first time in my life, and I was at times in fear of my life. The reasons for this are complex and I cannot safely go into them. But suffice to say it was a hairy experience. I could not actually work out what God wanted me to do either. There seemed to be strong arguments to both stay and go. All my family and most of my loved ones were in the United Kingdom. Yet here I was, on my own having to stay put in Ireland, to work and make ends meet. I could not even work out the responsible, logical decision. So I stuck with that old maxim. If in doubt: do nothing.

At the time, there were some peculiar spiritual agendas that seemed to want me out of the picture. But the least said about that the better. There seemed to be some funky energies directed at me from so called colleagues, and others in the esoteric fields. One *Aura Soma* colleague, the same one who had identified my energy link with an era of Bono's music, poached my business idea of setting up a spiritual shop in Dalkey. I had naively verbalized my plan to her during the advanced course, and very promptly she organized her minions to help her set it up. The same girl, also poached the house I had wanted to live in on Sorrento Terrace. I was clearly unwittingly engaged with some kind of cosmic karmic rival. I was advised to heal what was going on with this person, that I needed to visit Glastonbury.

In a particular life time that needed to be dealt with, I was apparently ostracized by this group of cult like addicts clucking around "Madam," as we called her. As always I sat reflectively loose to the past life theories which came my way. These people had allegedly drained my energies in some magic ritual and had left me to die in a Somerset ditch. I really was not sure this past life account resonated. But I did observe that my father gave Glastonbury a wide berth when we were younger. Saturday jaunts were all over the West Country. But Glastonbury was studiously avoided. I think this was more to do with crowds, Christian leanings, and not wanting to corrupt his children with thoughts of wizards and warlocks, than any past life issue. However, when I did finally get to Glastonbury with Brian Hunter, an American colleague, to carry out some healing work for clients, I will say a lot of energy cleared off, up, and away. I found the gardens of The Chalice Well particularly refreshing and healing. I knew then I had to visit in a similar vein at least three times to clear the relevant karma. Three is a charm after all. I managed four.

In the thick of this energy, apparently linked to a Glastonbury life time, the manifestations and issues I was dealing with got very funky indeed. I set off for the Lake District to attend my brother's second wedding to the controversial vicar's ex wife. I did not make it further than the ferry. Once I had driven onto the ferry, I inexplicably panicked. I had a compulsion to abort the journey and stay in Ireland. I absolutely could not go.

The ferry security men allowed me to get off the ferry as long as I left my car on board. It was far too late to unload everyone. Having checked I was not planting a bomb and then scarpering, they allowed me to disembark and return to the safety of shore, with Billy and my little dog. I was advised to come and collect the car later that evening. I watched the ferry leave, with my silver puma and possessions on board, and really wondered what on earth was happening to me.

I had had a full force panic attack. I had experienced minor attacks intermittently through my twenties; but had curbed those by learning correct breathing. I found that if I hid behind sun glasses, I could cope with crowds and travel. Over all I had it mastered and was coping fine. Every now and again at times of emotional stress, I would get curtailed. I actually thought I had conquered the episodes for good, quite some time before this ferry incident. So it was a shock indeed to me that this happened.

This dramatic panic showed how contained and boxed in I had become. What I had been experiencing had no doubt been challenging. I never resorted to medication in these times. I had had one term's worth of the lowest possible dose of anti depressant at Stirling University. I did not want to ever use medication again. Whatever anxiety or depression I was feeling, I resolved to face into it, analyze it and process it. I am not saying this is the correct route for everyone. But for me, and my sensitivities to medication, it certainly was.

Obviously, once again, I had pushed so much down into my unconscious, that suddenly BAM! it surfaced and paralyzed me. I knew from past history that I would feel restricted for a time, as I worked out what was going on, and what I had to do to fix it. I was facing into a time of agoraphobia again, while I processed what I had been shouldering. It was typical, I merrily cope with so much, push myself, and then all of a sudden it overwhelms me. It does not emanate from my conscious mind, which is coping, but from the unconscious mind, which is rebelling and struggling.

In my sensitivity, the energies I had been bombarded with throughout this time, suddenly got a grip of me. My exile in Ireland was well and truly official until such a time as I could sort this out.

Some months later, despite the fact that I had missed his wedding, my brother graciously came to collect me to drive me home to see my parents. I was nervous even about this. I felt that if I got home to Portishead, I would not be inclined to return to Ireland. I warned my brother that I could not leave, but please could he come over as I needed to see him. When he got to me, I explained everything to him over a couple of days. He thought he would be able to persuade me to do the quick visit home. But I really could *not* do the journey.

Sometimes, we can get so stressed and cornered into a situation, where one step in the wrong direction will completely blow us apart. I had to know my boundaries in this dynamic, or I would not have got through it in one piece. From the outside looking in, it must have seemed peculiar indeed. I could only trust that I knew what I was doing. I simply had to follow my intuition to process all that had been going on around me. It was pretty desperate. A form of break down perhaps. All I knew was that I then spent many months and years pretty much confined to the village of Dalkey, with the occasional excursion into Dun Laoghaire.

My brother's wife, and my mother, did not understand my behavior, and festered about it for a very lengthy time. My brother on the other hand understood, at least initially. All I know is, it became an issue of resentment for quite some time, that I had brought my brother over from Scotland to drive me to Bristol, and that I had not done the journey. Understandable I guess, as my brother was certainly a busy guy. But I was in dire, dire straits, and to actually see a member of my family was a blessing indeed.

When he arrived, I noted that my brother was actually exhausted, and I was not willing to subject him to that long return journey. For his sake too, I aborted the plan. I knew we were meant to connect though, and I was so relieved to see him. I also knew all would be well with my father. I *had* to believe this, or I would not have been able to live with it otherwise. Thank God I was correct.

Mum and Dad had been over to see me in the previous couple of years. We had walked around Dalkey, went to the magnificent Kish Fish Restaurant, looking out onto Dalkey Island, and braved the walk to Powerscourt Waterfall. My father was quite physically impaired with heart trouble, but we managed walks in Killiney, and it was a very special catch up time. My parents stayed at the Killiney Hotel situated on the magnificent beach, just down from Bono's house, which I paid for as a treat. I must admit, when I kissed my father good bye at Coliemore Harbour, I did wonder fleetingly if it would be the last time I would see him.

Thankfully this was a fear, not a prediction or a reality. I decided not to feed the thought or give it any energy. It had a different quality to when I just *knew* I had to go into Saint Peter's Church to see my Nan during the Sunday morning service. I had been home for a visit with two dogs and Billy the Scotsman, and was about to start the trek back to Ireland when I felt compelled to go in and see my Nan, even though the service was underway. I was right. This *was* the last time I saw her, even though she lived to the ripe old age of 99. Mary lived for nine more years, but I did not make it home in time for her passing. There was too much stress and chaos to cope with, and I had to stay put in order to process and get through it all. I was not chasing rainbows by then; I was floundering in the deep.

In recent years, following my parent's carefully considered move from Conifers the family home, to the flourishing Marina in Portishead, the Universe conspired to create some valuable integration and healing time for me back home. I had not wanted my parents to leave the wonderful house which had been the family home for so many years. There was such a tangible quality of love in that house, that even the estate agents selling it commented on its special atmosphere. I had nightmares about Conifers no longer being available to the family. My father had put such time, care, and attention into building the beautiful garden. It seemed a shame to leave it all behind. My parents did a big clear out in stages, as they realized they were feeling less pleasure in the house, and more the burden of the work it required. The five bed-roomed split-leveled accommodations, and sizeable garden certainly took some maintaining. They had come to the conclusion it was all a bit much to cope with, and set sail to their new berth in the Marina, with its views of boats, apartments, and swans. They enjoy sitting up in their third level corner apartment with its bird's eye view. Apparently they imagine they are on a cruise ship, and relish watching life go by as the boats come and go, and the locals go about their day. This is a comfortable, practical secure home for them, and everyone, friends and family alike approve that the right thing happened in the end. Conifers went to a lovely young family of similar chemistry and constitution as our own when we first moved in during the 70s. My parents felt fully comfortable with the people who were about to enjoy life in the home they had built together.

After I had to leave Ireland unceremoniously for the second time, I found my own place in Portishead. It was the only option open to me for a number of reasons. The dogs were welcome, which was key after the drama with the Tubbermore landlord. The referencing went through within a couple of days, and there was a momentum dictated by the storage and moving company also. This move was ON. So, against everyone's wishes and advice, I returned to my roots on my own terms.

Even though I had wanted to remain in Ireland, I began to see that it made a lot of sense to have some time back in my home town. It was something I had wanted to do several times over recent years; and it was empowering to arrive back, without even the knowledge or support of my nearest and dearest. I had to spring the surprise. It was my only option, and I could not risk friends or family trying to persuade me against what I needed to do for the moment. They would all have to come to understand my actions or not. Either way, it was the right thing for me to do. It certainly proved to be the best thing I had done in a long while. Healing could now take place, and all would be well, after some integration and deep reflection.

Thankfully my family warmed up to the idea. My sister Rache announced she felt like she had "got her sister back." My brother was suitably non committal and cool as usual. And my parents were initially shocked, and then grew to be fairly delighted in modest measure. This was clearly going to be a good idea for the foreseeable future, while I mapped out the next stages of my plans to move to America.

Brian Hunter, was not best pleased. He had wanted me to stay in Ireland for work, and to ensure his visits were enjoyable on his own terms. He did not like the fact I had relocated to "f*cking Portishead." Being psychic he could tune into the energy through remote viewing, and he was not particularly enthralled by what he met across the ethers. He did not understand my reasons for the move either; nor did my parents. I just had to know myself that I was doing the right thing, and trust that they would all "get" it eventually.

They all did. Some more quickly than others.

The simple reality is that at times during this whole adventure, I got very challenged, and even at points *very* frightened. My process and evolution as a psychic was not easy. The Irish phase was important, indeed I do not think I would have become a professional psychic and healer had I remained in the United Kingdom. It was part of my Irish karma to be feted, accepted and looked to for answers and healing by the Irish nation. I did not plan it. But it is what happened. I am still fascinated by the process to this day. I could not have made it up if I tried to. It certainly could not have been devised and meticulously planned. It had its own organic life, and my destiny was apparently dictated by forces greater than my own will or intentions. This really was a case of "God laughs at our best-laid plans.

I had to cope with most of it on my own. I was not making it up as I went along. I was simply listening and following guidance. The revelations, challenges, and lessons were intense and immense; and probably reflected the extent of my calling. There were some spiritual workers I could relate to. But along the way, the experiences and people I encountered were also quite odd. Esoteric types came out of the woodwork and sought me out. I engaged with them probably much more than I should have done.

There was the woman who made me concerned about my lung health; a supposed healer who had visited me in Dalkey with two gay witches. She affected my energies to the point where I found it hard to breathe. Then there was the angel healer who seemed to think she was Bono's soul mate, and imposed her particular attunement healings upon me without my permission. And then, there was the male energy healer, who was determined to make me agree to his energy work, which I was equally determined to avoid.

"Stand still let your body sway forward for a 'yes,' and backwards for a 'no.'" Clive did not bargain for my ability to resist his will, while responding and demonstrating mine. I can do the same with the pendulum. Even if I had been supposed to sway forward, I was *making* myself fall backwards to defy what he thought I was supposed to do.

One of the biggest lessons in the exploration of all things mystical, is to learn to listen to your own inner voice. There is nothing more important than trusting your own knowing. People will try to impose things upon you as they peddle their truth. It may not be yours. The esoteric world possesses some pretty curious participants.

Such psychic experiences were all a learning curve teaching me how to strengthen and deal with psychic attack. The whole journey taught me a lot about working with energy, and I managed to maintain my integrity throughout. My links with Bono in particular seemed to get up a few people's noses, and I must say he does attract some quite peculiar interest on the ethers. There was a Californian witch in Malibu, who did a *News of The World* interview on her work, in which she quite openly stated she thought Bono was her soul mate. She did a spell for his happiness and to bless his love life. I am sure he would have been deeply grateful to know all these witches were out there attempting to fiddle with his life. #Not.

I thought *Omg*, and made contact with her in a bid to protect him. I lived to regret it. This woman had the very specific intention of *being* with him. I think his wife might have had something to say about that, let alone Bono himself. It was crazy in the extreme. I made contact as his friend, and informed her of some home truths. I was naive and pioneering in the extreme. I should have stayed well away, and not given this woman's reality any air time whatsoever. Lesson learned.

There was another similar woman close to home in Dalkey. She claimed to have told Bono's wife that she was going to lose Bono after their twenty-sixth wedding anniversary if she did not step up her game. I was horrified when she verbalized this. I did not believe for a second that she had told Ali any such thing. I also reassured her that their twenty sixth anniversary had passed, and all was fine between them. Again: *Omg!*

All of a sudden these crazy karmic situations presented to me, and they were frequently linked to Bono. I think he is aware he attracts some pretty "challenged" fans. But I am not sure how aware he is, that he seems to have a coterie of witches all living in the belief that they might be with him eventually. I expect he might be pleased if they all have blonde hair. Kidding. It is laughable really; and then I look back at what happened to me, and I laugh some more. At least my connection with Bono was tangible. This man was actually in my life, through a *work* connection. I remember Gerry, Bono's office security guy bringing some fan mail to work one evening. Odd letters used to arrive at the nightclub also. Many slightly unhinged fans would quote biblical verses at Bono. Silly in itself. Do they not know, this man knows the Bible inside out? Some seemed to take exception at Bono's portrayal of the man with horns, on the Zoo TV Tour; while others take exception to his politics. Many fundamentalist Christians are U2 fans, so this would explain some of the criticism leveled at Bono. There were those who did not understand the irony, subtlety, and pathos of his Mr MacPhisto portrayal.

Bono's security unit have created a comprehensive list of people to monitor, or be aware of. Bono is grounded, sensible, and pretty much unflappable. He feels he can cope with anything directly presented to him; and he surely can. I remember him describing how his intuitive antennae was primed, and that he could read a room, and its contents, pretty much instantly. He explained that his years on the stage had given him this heightened awareness, and ability to read all the layers of a situation.

Bono has a natural instinct for avoidance of danger, even whilst running headlong to meet it. His divine protection is high; which makes sense, seeing as he has had significant work to do. But I do not think Bono is always aware of how much goes on behind the scenes. He sure does attract a lot of mad attention. I certainly could have provided Gerry and John, the Waters brothers, with a further few suspects for their dubious fans lists.

I cannot really explain it all in terms of how it affected me. But suffice to say, my dear friend Bono, nearly caused me to come a cropper in more ways than one. I had my own list of potential problems on the ethers, which I kept quiet about. I did alert Bono's security to a coming accident though, which was not going to be pretty, and may indeed be fatal. But I was not sure how they could prevent this. Clearly I was picking up on Bono's nasty bike accident in Central Park, where he nearly died, and had to undergo serious reconstruction in one arm. As with my father, I knew he was going to be okay. But felt I had to say something just in case anything happened on the watch of the guy's I worked with in Dublin.

In the event the accident was on the other side of The Atlantic, and a few years after I had first picked up the warning. So all in all not a very useful prediction. But you just never know. One thing I *could* help with was the healing process, in absentia. I offered directly, but Bono was working with "Satan," aka his Germanic sports physiotherapist, who clearly had him under quite a torturous regime. I knew I had to help regardless; so I asked his permission on the ethers, and did what I could with various techniques to ease and accelerate his healing. Bono had to be ready for his coming tour in record time. There is no proof that what I did, or what God did through me helped. But ready he was. So we could thank Satan. Or God. Depending on inclination.

Psychic attack is a hideous experience, and for those in my line of work who ever go through it I would say, hang on in there, pray and smudge with your sage sticks regularly. Negativity feeds off fear, so do not even go there. Always remember that perfect love casts out fear. Absolutely nothing we go through is beyond God's reach. End of. I guess for a while, despite my productively on the work front, I was the proverbial lost sheep. But, God definitely came and found me. In fact, he never actually let me go. Quite clearly he was carrying me every step of the way to the point where I could begin to put it all into perspective myself. Despite what various factions of the church might think, I did not deliberately wander off. I was never lost from God by choice, though energies and agendas certainly sought to defeat me. It all sounds a bit dramatic, but it was very much a reality. Even the crazy territory creates a reality that needs to be cleared and cleansed. This was all an education in dealing with some very complex energies. An apprenticeship, or baptism of fire.

I was Daniella in the Lion's Den, and only by the Grace of God did I step out of danger. I strongly suspect I was protected the whole time.

*YOU WERE BORN TO WIN, BUT TO BE A WINNER, YOU MUST PLAN TO WIN, PREPARE TO WIN, AND EXPECT TO WIN.
ZIG ZIGLAR*

CHAPTER TWENTY-SEVEN
Faustian Deal: No Deal

Life's challenges continued to present themselves. But soon enough I strengthened, becoming lighter and brighter from the inside out. I had been through so much bullshit, that really, what else could there be? I began to see problems as hurdles to be overcome with the greatest ease I could muster. I became steely and determined. I had surely been through the worst. If I could remain optimistic and centered, and find the good in everything, I would surely survive. Until I did not.

I found that humor, even a dark somewhat bleak humor, covered most eventualities. I was better able to cope, and fairly resilient if truth be told. I had had so much time in isolation, feeling lonely and bombarded with trials, that I got to like my own company. I became quite the hermit. Quite insular, and withdrawn, keeping the company of dogs, and developing my contacts more over the internet than face to face. This may not have been the healthy option. But it started to expand my horizons worldwide, and I began to see beyond Ireland and that there might be other options out there for me.

There were countless tales still of running out of money. But it did not faze me. During the first Irish phase, I frequently emptied my purse to pay for lunch in Finnegans, and at one point owed them five cents. I officially had a tab. My friend Jane supported me in spirit, and sometimes financially, and we did much soul searching on my best options. Jane had been involved in the Irish Mind, Body, Spirit Festival for many years, enabling Louis the founder, to sort the practicalities of timetables, bookings and advertizing.

Jane had found me in a paper predicting lottery numbers which actually hit in the next draw following publication. I had caught her eye on the *The Irish Popstars* show and she made contact. A lively, intelligent Gemini, with a stroke of genius about her, we sorted the world out between us. We understood each other's spiritual journey. Jane set a precedent and had been through much in her own time. She was able to support me, mentor me, and give me hope that there was light at the end of the tunnel. She mentored me financially also, and paid my rent for a time. We felt it was best to try to ride the storm in Ireland and sort all things financial, emotional and spiritual that way. Turns out that was not really the correct practical method to ultimately sort my finances, but it worked for a time. I did a lot of spiritual development courses at this time, expanding my knowledge of consciousness, and how to help people further.

The irony was, my business had flourished initially. In the midst of the Celtic Tiger, I had been able to set up a healing practice in Dalkey, and had my appointments book filled for weeks and months at a time. My reputation was good, and I was able to repay the loans I had taken out to stay afloat. When the SMS phone texts services hit the papers, I was laughing, as these generated my rent monthly with ease. Everything I had set up was working. I was effectively helping people, and I was not stressed myself for once. What started to put the kibosh on it all was the merger of two companies. I had been paid for my SMS and part of my work through I-Touch, a company linked to *The Irish Independent Newspaper*. I was also paid by Telephonica Ireland, who covered my contributions to *The RTE Guide*. It all when wrong when these two companies merged, and Telephonica took on all my work.

The Celtic Tiger collapse effected the functioning of I-Touch, and the merger was very detrimental to my remuneration. Telephonica then cut my income significantly, and there was also a very awkward uncooperative new accountant, who refused to listen to me and answer my emails. I sensed I was being underpaid and she assured me I was not. When she did get around to a reply, it was only to assure me that I was mistaken. I knew I was not. But I had to pace my enquiries, so as not to harass her. I started to have to deal with some very negative energies, which seemed to be picking everything apart, just at the point when I had got it all working.

It is one of the perks, or perhaps the curses, of being intuitive, that I know when something is not right. I had a sense that money was being withheld from me. Not necessarily deliberately but certainly being short-changed was a reality. You can not fool a psychic. You might try to fob them off; but their prompts will be persistent if they are correct. I questioned this several times over months, and still the same reply from the accountant, who refused to check out what I was saying. I just *knew* I was right, and that money was owed to me. It was only by chance that I saw a more detailed spread sheet from the company, and was able to identify the problem. A huge chunk of my income had not been paid, and I was due a substantial back pay. I pointed this out, and immediately, the accountant tried to halve my ongoing income, and pay only half of what was owed. Thankfully the CEO intervened and I got what was rightfully mine. My income was then unceremoniously reduced from seven to four cent per text anyway. Somewhere, someone was making a lot of money at my expense seeing as each text is approx. sixty cent to purchase. Frustratingly I was paid my dues with one hand, and then denied with the other.

In the end this all got too much, and after much fear, and research, I concluded that I could potentially relocate to the United Kingdom and bankrupt myself. I had got into so much debt, that would have been sorted quickly had the Celtic Tiger economy not crashed. But it did; and so did I as a consequence.

Over the years of upset, I had become expert at dealing with creditors, and negotiating, and sorting things. I was also told repeatedly by Anke that I was going to hit on the lottery, and it would all be sorted that way. I said to her that I increasingly felt I might have to bankrupt myself. She assured me I would not have to. I did start to feel hard done by. I had worked so hard, and had done what I felt was right. I had helped people, correctly set up a business, and got it working effectively. I was into expansion and followed all leads when prompted to do so. To have to take the route of bankruptcy was an incredible disappointment.

The practical difficulties began in 2008 when I had to leave the wonderful apartment in Dalkey, where I had lived for nine years. Harley, the sausage dog, did not want to leave the apartment. All my things had been cleared out and brought across to the moldy, haunted Laragh Mews, set in a cul-de-sac off the long impersonal Ulverton Road, which ran alongside the rail track. The energy in the Mews was uneasy. A previous owner died of cancer in the house, and it had kept the resonance of suffering and unease. I ended up sleeping outside the main building in the glass conservatory when Billy was not around. As soon as night fell, the air felt thick and heavy and "active." It was cold in the conservatory which jutted out into the small split level garden. But at least I could see the stars and hear the wind in the trees, instead of the elements creeping up and down the strange stairs which were spiraled in the shape of DNA strands.

Harley must have sensed what was coming, and sat tight in the middle of the large wooden-floored living space which had been Railway Road. I literally had to drag him out of our home. They say listen to your animals. I probably should have sat tight in the apartment. We had tenant's rights having lived there for nine years. But I played ball, and relinquished these, so that the landlord could do the place up to sell or re-let.

As we crossed the threshold for the final time, I got the inner knowing that I would have to move "three to four times in the next eighteen months." *Great.* I was upset to leave my home, and this was hardly a comforting message to receive. But it was at least a preparation for what was to come. I knew such messages when I got them were accurate. They were from a divine source that I could trust. I was always cautious about receiving messages and intuitions from others, as I knew mine were always spot on and definitely correct.

I had put way too much trust and faith in Anke at this time. It is not her fault. She had become a very good friend, and had a wonderful wicked sense of humor and irreverent turn of phrase. We got on very well indeed. I know she cared about me. Well I thought she did. But there started to be a couple of fall outs, which made me question exactly what the relationship was.

The first was when Anke phoned to tell me that Donncha O' Callaghan was in the papers looking fine in his wedding regalia. This was one Christmas, when once again I was facing the festive season alone. I felt this phone call was quite insensitive considering. Anke knew what I had come to naively hope for regarding Donncha. I had been badly treated by Player, and subsequently, I held onto a fantasy that something might still be possible with Donncha. I sort of knew it was not possible; but a girl can dream.

I had really been hoping that something would happen between us. But it was not based on anything in particular. There was no evidence any reciprocal feeling existed. Much more energy had been generated in previous connections. I guess I was just floating on thin air with it all by then. Obviously, I had gone down all the wrong roads, and did not connect with the correct Mr Rugby, in the first place. "Player" had tried to fob me off with Tommy Bowe, who did not have a girlfriend at that point. He was much younger, and undoubtedly cute. But he never made a move, and I only chatted to him intermittently. He is not unattractive, but there was zero chemistry, and he was not responsive particularly to any Facebook chat. Player was just stirring the pot as usual, and passing the buck, I mean the ball.

The whole Mr Rugby notion, had gone horribly wrong. Part of it had stemmed from Jane seeing a vision of my wedding, and the particular hat she was wearing. I had been fed up at Billy's refusal to commit, despite many years together, and I really was hoping to find a life partner for marriage, babies and family. It was of course just an idea, certainly not based on any reality thus far. Donncha had a long term girlfriend, and here they were getting married, and Anke was going out of her way to point it out to me.

Congrats to them! Happy Christmas to me!

I offended Anke when I challenged her on this untimely phone call, and said I had not really appreciated it. Particularly as she had not replied to other messages I had sent. I left a message explaining my feelings on her phone. I did not mean to be unkind. But I was hurting. Alone for Christmas, and the guy I really liked just got wed. Nothing new there then.

It was impossible to ever get Anke direct. She phoned you back if she felt like it, and ran things on her own terms. Fair enough. Anke was so skilled psychically and kind too, that she would have spent far too long on the phone to people, had she not protected herself in this way. Anyhow, this time she was quick to return my call, and tell me what she thought of me. Her daughter was sick, (I did not know this), and she told me in no uncertain terms that she did not appreciate *my* message. Okay. Stalemate, and that was *that* between us for quite some time.

Anke had told me I would be with Bono ultimately, and that I would hit big on the lottery. Neither of these things had happened in the many years I was going to her for readings. A lot *has* happened that she predicted; but not these two main things. I was okay with this, well sort of. I went through what I went through with it all. I was not about to blame someone else for my failings and life choices. But I am not sure she was always right to say what she did.

During 2005, I really needed funds and put in for yet another loan. I said to Anke "but I cannot afford to do this." Her response was: "you will get it all back anyway, and can you afford *not* to?" She was correct in a way. But it is the kind of comment that would have made the bank manager churn in his sleep. The odd thing is, I still have a deep knowing that she is probably correct on things. *Not* the Bono thing so much. Time has really marched on with that. But I do concede that I could win the lottery. I have shown myself that I have a propensity with numbers, and sometimes I can literally pluck them out of the air, and they hit.

Anke found it fascinating that I believed her about the lottery win, but not about Bono. I in turn find it fascinating that she was fascinated, if she actually believed what she was telling me. This part of the story probably is not over. I believe her, in that I do not think she was deliberately lying to me or misleading me. Anke is an extremely loyal person, who will fight to the death for her loved ones, including good friends. She is also an incredibly gifted psychic. When you are stuck with where to live; what to do in a particular relationship; how to retrieve a complex situation etc, she is right on the money. I know Anke genuinely felt I would win. Not only that, she *sees* it. She repeatedly described a scene of me sitting in a pile of gold coins throwing them up in the air in celebration. It was so "in her face" as a reality, that in every reading she would say "there's your money," when the

Ace of Pentacles Tarot card was turned over.

At points I felt like saying, "well it is there so predominantly on the table, *when* is it going to show up in my bank account?" But I resisted that temptation. As a psychic, I understand something of how spirit relays messages to clients. It is not always easy to pinpoint timing. The irony is, I was not a person particularly bothered about money, nor is there a mercenary bone in my body. The paradox is, listening to the prediction created a *need* for the prediction to be correct. Because it was sold in no uncertain terms, I really believed it, and the truth of it resonated.

Anke has been nothing if not consistent on this point of winning money. Money is her thing, her level of expertise. She knows how to work with it, and sniff it out, and she readily tells clients when she sees finances, pertaining to issues and resolutions in their readings. She told me, she was so captivated by the amount she saw in my reading, that she used to lie awake in the morning wondering how much it was, as it felt so very substantial.

In her crystal ball readings, Anke used to scribble the shape of the Euro sign on the table, before the Euro was even introduced into Ireland. She saw the exact Euro symbol in the crystal ball, and said it was linked to the big win. I wobbled a bit on this symbolism when the Euro Millions draw was introduced. Had she just been predicting it's arrival in Ireland? I asked Anke on what day of the week was I going to win, and she described the evening before the weekend. Of course there was no such draw when she said this. But, the Friday Euro Millions draw was introduced not long after. My active concern was that she had simply been psychically picking up on the introduction of the Euro Millions draw. Was she sure I was going to win it, or was she simply seeing the draw come into existence? I am still not a hundred percent sure on that point. When I asked her about it, she said she was "absolutely sure" I was going to win it. There was no reason for it to have appeared in my reading otherwise.

A couple of years down the road on my return to Ireland, following the Porlock and bankruptcy chapters, I reconnected with Anke. She had been moved to extend the hand of friendship again, after her mother's passing seemed to bring us back together. I had reached out intermittently to leave messages of apology or a friendly greeting on that confounded answer machined; and one random day, she was prompted to pick up the phone. It was me phoning from the barn. I too had been prompted to phone out of the blue. Her mother had passed some months back, and it seemed like the nudges I had been getting were from her mother in spirit wanting me to phone her daughter.

Once I was back in Ireland again, we mainly chatted on the phone, but a couple of times I went back down to Wicklow for a reading. I needed to know a couple of things about work opportunities, and my intention to immigrate to America eventually. I asked when Chance, a new client and work contact, was going to manage a breakthrough moment in his situation. He was potentially an excellent on-going client, and we had some important work planned. He had asked me to get a second opinion from Anke about his business and finances.

Chance was a character. He sometimes dressed like a homeless person, yet traveled the world first class on a whim using wits and air miles. He never seemed to do much structured work, and yet was always apparently busy. Not everyone could figure him out, he was certainly unique and complex, and lived a charmed existence. He intrigued many, yet showed himself to only a handful, and even this inner circle was kept segregated. Chance did not believe in mixing waters, let alone drinks.

Chance is a very skilled casino player, and we had both been sensing a large win for him for quite some time. I wanted Anke to have a look at this. Sure enough a big win was showing for Chance at the Indian Casino resort of Harrahs. On his return to Florida, Chance duly went to Harrahs and won six thousand dollars, on the machine with the "beautiful blue, and the three distinct panels that Anke had seen." I had given Anke the list of relevant casinos, and she told me that "Harrahs was the hot one." She also told him to spin using five dollars, not three, or six, or seven. She was correct.

On subsequent occasions Chance won more. We worked together to utilize prime astrological constellations to focus his efforts on winning larger amounts of money. Lions Gate, a rare gateway event which occurred on the 8th August 2015 saw Chance grounding wins against the odds at two different casinos, Pala and Morongo. All the casinos in the surrounding area were active on this special 888 day (8th of the 8th of an 8 year day). Chance won two lots of five grand on machines that should not have logically delivered. In fact the first win came just as he was giving up, and about to return home.

Chance proceeded to occasionally test the water with measured trips playing poker, which is pretty much damage limitation, when you know how to play. He sensed a bigger win still, and was looking for the correct machine, and the correct opportunity. It was precisely at a time that he needed to make a trip to me for work. Sure enough he hit a progressive machine and twenty grand landed in his lap. This one got the casino buzzing with bells and whistles, and he was ushered into meet the man we jokingly call Mr Pechanga.

As slick and immaculately groomed as you might expect, Mr Pechanga, shook his hand and asked Chance if he "felt better now." I was a bit cynical about this, as it had come after a survey which Chance had returned to the casino, which was doubtless very helpful to them. The twenty thousand dollars sorted a whole lot out, and as soon as Chance got home he did one a spread sheets to account for every penny; making sure it was going to be used constructively. Instead of a bills list, he was able to compile a financial to do list, which contained the distribution of all the money he needed for quite some time. An addicted gambler would have returned to a casino and lost it all. Chance was smart, and played the system.

You think it is not possible for psychics to beat the bookie or the casino? It absolutely *is*. But it has to be done systematically, consciously and psychically. I have been able to pick out casino machines for clients on several occasions. I was able to describe through remote viewing the precise location of a winning machine which was going to deliver a red suited, Queen of Diamonds Royal Flush win in poker, at two thirty in the afternoon on a specific day. It did just that. It is possible for a powerful psychic to remote view, and tune into the energies of such places. Not easy, but certainly possible. Psychic applications are really endless. The skills can be used and applied way beyond the scope of what people normally assume.

I call such wins, "cosmic wins" straight from Spirit; gifts from the heavens. Obviously there is the human temptation to "chase the dragon" at casinos. It takes discipline, judgment and luck to not fall foul of all the usual horror stories. As long as greed is not the motivation, God will deliver through miraculous ways. There is no limit to the channels that can be used. These stories are not an invitation for you all to run out to the nearest casino and play. These trips are carefully chosen for specific clients who pay me for the information. They are meticulously coordinated for damage limitation. Really it takes a skilled psychic to apply the tools of the trade. This is not for the common man.

Chance is not a gambler. He is a client who has skills at picking out machines, and playing poker. Video Poker is a meticulous art which requires precision and very specific learned responses. As with Poker, the card game, good results are not simply down to luck, or chance. The skill of the perpetrator dictates the outcome. So long as the casino is in a good mood that day. If you know what you are doing and aim for an "aces with a kicker" win; well then take it, pay your rent and run. Until the next time. It is not gambling if you win after all. I have lost count of the times I have paid the balance of my rent or some bills with a horse win. And why not if it works? Skills of intuition can be demonstrated in an apparently dubious situation, to ground a healthy amount of money. Cynics that ask "why do psychics not win if they are psychic?" are barking up the wrong tree. Psychics that know how to apply their skills and grounded judgment can, and do, win.

I enjoyed my second chapter in Ireland, and loved living in Tubbermore Avenue, Dalkey. The house was typically Dalkeyesque; somewhat Italian looking with an Irish twist. It was a home from home. I was pleased to return there with my American colleague Brian Hunter. Despite initial resistance, Brian chose to support me and accompany me and four dogs, from Porlock in deepest Somerset, across South Wales to Pembrokeshire, and onto the Wexford ferry. After many hours of travel we hit the N11, and as we approached Killiney Hill, the dogs barked with glee recognizing their old haunts of Killiney Beach and Vico Road. They knew they were home, and would soon meet their brothers Stan and Ralf on the beach again. dogs do not forget. I can vouch for that.

Brian extended his Europe trip to get a feel of Ireland, and he liked what he saw. But once he returned to Los Angeles for God knows how long, I wondered if I had done the right thing. It felt very strange to be back, and I realized I had in fact totally disconnected from Dalkey, the place I originally made my home. I had to go through a whole reintegration process, and re-familiarize myself with the daily routine and the energies of the place.

I had left Ireland under a cloud the first time. I was literally propelled and ejected from the Emerald Isle because I needed to go and bring some order to my financial and emotional situation. The universe knew what needed to be done, so that I could regain my equilibrium and a sense of personal freedom, that I had not felt for a very long time. I enjoyed the short time in Cornwall, and the longer stretch in Porlock, and I wondered how advisable it was to be already back in a place I never thought I would see again. I reality I had been away for the guts of three years, and it now seemed like no time at all. Was I destined to start going around in circles again? I was nervous. It would have been fine with Brian as he represented a future possibility. But with him gone, I was back staring the past in the face again.

Having said that Dalkey is my *home*. It is where I set up my adult life, and I came to love its people, village and environment. I had not wanted to leave the wonderful house on Beacon Hill. But my exit from Ireland, via Carrie's house, Grainne's house, and then onto the Irish Ferry at six o' clock in the morning, was all divinely timed. My Aunt Anne came to rescue me, and we drove down through Wales as dusk fell, landing back at my parents house "Conifers" for the first time in many years. I kissed the Welsh soil once I got out of the car on the first leg of the journey to walk the dogs. I am not Welsh, but I was back in the United Kingdom. A place I frequently felt I may never see again. I loved Ireland, but I had been living with the thought that I was never going to be able to leave. I had made my bed, and it looked like I was going to have to lie in it.

I slept *very* well that first night back in "Conifers." To be back in my underground childhood bedroom, now the guest room, was a treat. I was allowed two nights, because my parents really did not want the dogs in the house. They conceded I could stay a couple of nights on the way down to Cornwall to do the bankruptcy "deed," as I had come to call it. On the second morning, mother gave me the money for the legal fee, gifted by my Uncle Michael; and within a couple of days I was on the road again convoying with Anne and her husband Chris, all the way to the end of the world, Land's End in Cornwall.

The view as we approached Hendra Cottage was spectacular. What greeted us was a huge converted barn, which looked undoubtedly spooky, and huge rolling green cliffs populated with rabbits, and not a tree in sight. Set on a hill, Hendra Cottage sat snug and proud, shielded by the small series of mounds behind it. The view from the yard out the back displayed ploughed fields, stone walls and a couple of dusty tracks, which merged with boggy land at the lowest point between the cottage and the sea. The land dipped severely by the marsh, flattened out for a few hundred squelchy yards, and then elevated sharply the other side, gearing up speed until it reached the knolly terrain of the grassy cliff tops, beyond which shone The Atlantic.

The Atlantic Sea over the crest of the cliff looked elemental and formidable. Cornwall was a world apart, and seemed like a different country. The energy felt disconnected from the rest of the United Kingdom. Here was a land, that had its own flavor, history, and tastes. It literally was the end of the line. There were two similar sized houses to the right of Hendra Cottage. But nothing much by way of accommodation between this spot, and the spectacular sands of Sennen Beach miles away. Only Land's End Airport held the promise of an escape route, should this be required.

The place I had chosen to do "the deed", as Jane and I called it, was so far off the beaten track that when Mollie needed a vet for an adrenaline shot to cope with a bee sting in her mouth, I had to drive to the end of my road, a three mile cul-de-sac, to wait by the stipulated farm gate, for a vet who then administered the drugs on the road side. It was like something out of a movie. The easy friendliness and warmth of Ireland felt a long way away. Had I failed? It did not feel like it. But all this was certainly not predicted or bargained for. The high lights of the week were the sugar frosted buns from the bakery, if they had not sold out by the time I got there; and the church service in Latin at Saint Just parish church, on a Sunday.

In lonely moments, I consoled myself that I had dealt with a huge financial debt and burden in taking this path. That surely in itself should be sufficient justification for now living in the middle of nowhere with five dogs for company. I had literally chosen splendid isolation. The days of smooching Bono in nightclubs were long gone. Perhaps I would meet Poldark on the next cliff walk.

I had to keep some such nice fantastical thought active in my mind; especially in such stark conditions. In retrospect, I do not know how I managed this phase. I would never have chosen this location second time around. But oddly, it worked for a short time. It was certainly rugged and beautiful. I must have been deeply afraid to have put myself so out of reach. Yet I had the inner strength to make it work. As usual, I took the positive from the position I found myself in. One amazingly liberating thing had happened, and it was legitimate and allowed. I was finally free from the burden of debt, and the legacy of all those years of trying to build a business and look after Billy. Whatever Anke had predicted could now happen or not. It did not really matter either way anymore. I was FREE.

*WE ALL WEAR MASKS, AND THE TIME COMES WHEN WE CANNOT REMOVE THEM WITHOUT REMOVING OUR OWN SKIN.
ANDRE BERTHIAUME*

CHAPTER TWENTY-EIGHT
Taking A Chance

By the time I got to Cornwall, my inner landscape was filled with thoughts of Ashton Kutcher, not Poldark. I had made an interesting link with this Hollywood actor on Twitter in March 2009. My blonde dachshund Mollie shares a birthday with Mr Kutcher, and to honor the day I went to collect her, I reached out on the internet to her fellow Aquarian, Ashton. I did not know it at the time of course. It was just one of those coincidences that had tracked my existence for some time. One of the perks, or curses, of being psychic and in tune with the universe.

Over a couple of years, the banter of my on-line link with Mr Kutcher got intermittently interesting. It was a meeting of minds for sure, and we had some public exchanges on important subjects, and fun topics. The Mr Rugby thing had gone so horribly wrong, my dog

Harley had died just before Christmas, and I needed a new diversion. I knew about Twitter, but only in passing. I decided to set up some accounts to experiment a bit more with social media. I had Facebook, Bebo, and MySpace accounts also, but did not really use them. I had always thought Ashton looked fun, and when I saw he was on Twitter I followed him as one of his devotees. I "left the crumb" as they say. How on earth could I assume he would spot me amongst his thousands and thousands of followers? Do not ask me how, but I knew I would catch his eye. Or rather; I knew that my energy would stand out and resonate for him. Perhaps not immediately. But soon enough.

As I suspected, Ashton was amusing, informative, and intelligent. I started to learn from him how to utilize social media to maximum effect. Through observing, and watching how he used the internet to market and connect with people, I learned a lot. He followed me on Twitter, and my own fan base grew as a consequence. Mr Kutcher is not only an underrated talented actor, he is also an Angel Internet Technologies investor. Both he, and Guy Oseary, U2 and Madonna's manager, have quite the portfolio of companies under the umbrella, Sound Ventures. Ashton was very engaged and interactive with his followers. He asked them questions, studied their ethos and approach to life, and got them to actively engage with his latest on-line experiments and projects. He saw his audience as a useful fountain of knowledge, and he tapped this to the max. Ashton often jokingly threw out a question into the ethers for his psychic, aka "me." Of course I never missed the cue. Although I was not a "fan" per se. I had never actually seen any of his movies at that point. But I did enjoy the banter and connection.

I caught his attention even more quickly than I expected, and we seemed to have similar intelligence, way of looking at the world, and humor. As I engaged more with his energy, I started to get quite fond of him, and I just loved those melting brown eyes, and that cheeky grin. He was very American, and sometimes goofy. This was cute, just not usually my style. My tastes had been of the brooding Celtic flavor up until that point. But when I found out that Ashton had Irish Ancestry, and a mother with the family name of Finnegan, suddenly it all made sense. There was the depth of soul and spirituality I liked too. He just played the goof half the time because it was what people expected. Underneath it all there was something very different going on. I could see and feel that. There was a feeling that he was performing in certain areas of his life. Where was he able to actually be real? Playing the goofball was the way he engaged his audience, and fulfilled his typecast obligations. I personally liked his deeper, reflective and well-hidden side. The real Ashton, who is in fact called Christopher.

To give Anke some further credit at this point. Just as the mysterious rugby ball kept appearing months before it was relevant, so did the initials A and K. I had no clue what they meant, except to say I thought they meant Ali, for Bono's wife, and K for The Kitchen nightclub. They clearly did not mean this at all. Just as she did with Euro sign, Anke used to draw a squiggle on the table like this: @. I was not au fait with the social media at this stage, and I am not even sure Twitter was in existence when she was doing this. But of course, she was bang on, and gets a huge recorded "hit" with that one too. Basically the A, the K, and the @, were indicators of the on-line connection to come with Ashton, months, possibly a couple of years, before it was a reality.

Anke also used to see "honeycomb" a lot in the crystal ball. When I got to Cornwall I found that the logo of my local super market was the honeycomb. I wondered if I had been brought to the ends of the earth to buy the winning lottery ticket? It certainly would have made a good story or movie if that had been the case. What seemed to be taking shape through the chapters of my life was an etheric treasure hunt. These amazing crystal ball symbols were the clues and stepping stones along the way. I was disappointed about Cornwall and the bankruptcy, and thought I was way off track from my correct destiny. Apparently I was not. So I took comfort in the "honeycomb," which appeared to be like a "flag" or signal that all was as it should be. I took heart, and wondered what the next stage of the journey would bring.

Sometimes a little faith goes a long way. I did not feel I was clutching at straws; I felt assured. Could it be that The New World was starting to open up for me? Certainly I had reached a peak of achievement in Ireland. I was still writing regularly in most of the major publications, and I had done many high profile gigs on television, and numerous audio appearances on radio. I began to wonder if there might be some transatlantic opportunities building.

The connection and engagement with Ashton felt personal. He was more of an on-line friend. I certainly was not looking on him as a career move. I enjoyed the lively exchange of ideas and humor. The blogs he posted onto the inter-web were inspiring and got my juices flowing. I also loved his social conscience and caring nature. He was an altruistic Aquarian, and he sought creative ways to use his platform for good. Yes he put his foot in it a few times politically, out of naivety, or over exuberance. He had on occasion, the bounding nature of a loveable puppy, and he got misrepresented and vilified at times because of it. But he was feisty, determined, and not too bothered overall what people thought. Especially not when his intentions were to raise consciousness for a good cause.

I was delighted when Ashton followed me on Twitter. He had millions of followers, and at that point was only following about seventy-eight people. He was selective, and I was genuinely pleased when he chose me. I knew already I had his attention, and he certainly had mine. But it was cool to be singled out for a "follow." Celebrity "follows" were like gold dust in those times, and potentially good for business, as well as friendship. I deliberately did not bother him with private messages; except one time as he was travelling to Brazil I sent the David Guetta track *It's All Right.*, with its repeat hypnotic trance lyric "Alright." He confirmed he got it, at least telepathically, when on landing he wrote "Alright Brazil." We had countless diffuse exchanges like this. Some may not have been fully conscious. Even this may well have been a coincidence. But, there were many, many such coincidences. At what point does a coincidence become too much of a coincidence, to be a coincidence?

Ashton is highly in-tune, and he has a strong skills of telepathy. Universal or otherwise, the language of "coincidence" became a sub text in our communication. It was well hidden from public view. Not that there was anything going on. If truth be told, it felt like a fun game. A harmless way of communicating which no one else could see; unless they were really clued-up. It was so clever in fact, that if I were to tell anyone about it, they would have thought me nuts. Yep, he is *that* smart. I actually liked him even more for it. I love a challenge.

A bit further down the road, I had contact with him through his private Facebook, and would occasionally send him messages if I picked up some psychic information that I thought would be useful. I gave him unofficial sound-bite readings, and seemed to be guided to say quite a bit at the time he was parting ways with Demi. I did not want to invade his privacy, but I was prompted to send thoughts and perspectives that would hopefully help. I'm not really sure if they did. But as always, I follow my guidance regardless. You just never know as a psychic, when your words are going to be that *one* thing that makes a difference in a crucial moment.

In their final months together, he and Demi Moore had a lot of fun with DailyBooth, a joint investment they had made to kick start their shared IT portfolio. I could tell seeing their interactions on Twitter, and DailyBooth that they would split up. I did not rub the point home to Ashton. But gently supported him when I thought I could, once things were more public. He was obviously about to go through the wringer, and I was concerned. I considered him a friend by that point. A friend with feelings; not "benefits."

The use of DailyBooth, inspired me to develop posting pictures as a form of on-line blogging. I love Instagram now for the same reason. DailyBooth was the first incarnation of picture blogging. It was the forerunner of SnapChat, Instagram, and Facebook Live. The idea was to post "selfies," not out of vanity, but to tell a story. To blog your life in pictures, as an on-line diary. It is a shame it closed down when Demi and Ashton sorted their divorce settlement, as it was lots of fun. Ashton jokingly asked for a reading of his palm one day, and I came up with a comprehensive interpretation for him. Others were just messing around. I knew he was fishing for information, so I obliged. I read his forehead also, probably a week or so later. He was either bored or interested in what messages he might get; or both.

It is amazing what you can pick up with the Chinese art of Physiognomy when a forehead is not disrupted from its usual pattern and artistry by Botox. I responded to Ashton's prompts both times, and gave him a ton of insight, which he hopefully found useful and accurate. I predicted two children for him, a girl and a boy. I did not feel he would stay with Demi, but I did not spell that out in public. Obviously, I did not want to offend either Demi, or Ashton. But, the prediction about the children, if he believed it, would have given him a clue that changes were in the air.

Ashton seemed to have fake accounts too, where he could have fun, and engage with a bit of anonymous banter. His Twitter accounts for the Blah Girls were an experiment set up by his company, Katalyst Media. Probably the Blah Girls were generally manned by a bunch of interns. But I do believe he and Demi messed around with these accounts when the mood took them. Ashton's Fantasy Football shows on live stream were highly amusing also. He encouraged direct audience participation, and had a well informed panel of experts, which included @toojiggy, a former roommate, and @nathanzegura, the premium Fantasy Football expert. These lads used the platform to research their indications for Fantasy Football polls, and indulge their love of sport with this on line television show. The aim was to produce something in real time to a high standard using live streaming. They did a pretty good job.

Katalyst as a company did fairly well, but it became fragmented in the divorce proceedings, and took the hit in a messy breakup. They had miss-fires with a couple of television projects, and the division of spoils with Demi was painful. Ashton's successful show on Netflix *The Ranch* came quite a bit later once things had settled, and he was firmly ensconced with his ex co-star from *That '70s Show* Mila Kunis. In the mean time, he was destined to further expand his investment portfolio in maverick style with Guy Oseary.

Sound Ventures seeks to make profitable what may not appear to be quite normal or desirable. I mean who wants to go stay in some stranger's house when travelling? On the flip side, who wants to welcome a stranger into their home randomly, for sometimes modest remuneration? Welcome Airbnb. Similarly, Taxis are difficult to catch at the best of times. Who wants to text a taxi through an app on their phone, without speaking to central control, in the hope that it will actually show up? Welcome Uber. And so it goes.

In the throes of his break up with Demi, Ashton channeled his grief and surplus energy into an amazing portrayal of Steve Jobs, the world's first feted IT genius, in a sadly underrated movie *Jobs*. Kutcher's depiction of the Apple Founder was vastly superior to that of Fassbender's. But the 2015 movie *Steve Jobs* did much better commercially, with its bigger budget and superior production.

I sensed frustrations within Ashton about his acting career. Here was a highly intelligent individual with a huge IQ, and a myriad of other skills who was generally typecast in romantic comedy, and seen as a goofball. His movies *The Butterfly Effect* and *Jobs* reveal a depth to his repertoire, not seen in feel-good romantic comedies like *No Strings Attached* or *Just Married*. Having now seen most of his movies, I personally like *The Guardian* and *The Butterfly Effect* the best. These movies have a good story-line, some action and some depth.

It was lots of fun to contribute to the naming of the movie *No Strings Attached*, though I still have not received a check in the post. Just kidding. The working title of this project was *F*ck Buddies*, which Ashton seemed to like a lot. I felt it was too hard core and extreme, and possibly offensive to some. He asked on Twitter for suggestions about the movie, and I responded with "*No Strings*." I did not see anyone else say this. Of course I am flattering myself if I conclude I had any influence on the final title. Perhaps I just predicted it.

In many ways Ashton Kutcher is not "seen" correctly by the vast majority of people. I liked too that as a psychic I "got" this. It made me feel empathy for him. There is nothing worse than being misrepresented and misunderstood. I identify with this. Obviously my issues operated on a much smaller scale than his. But I did understand.

One time, when all the live greetings were coming in at the top of the show, I was feeling cheeky, and typed in a breezy greeting: "love you!" He had name-dropped "Psychic Sarah" (me) at the top of the show, as his own "hello." But he looked mortified and embarrassed at my mischievous tweet. *Oops!* A member of the public noticed, asking Ashton why he was blushing, which made it even more excruciating. Aw. I thought that was cute. It was not until I saw the credits for the show that I clocked Demi was producing it. So double oops, right there.

Once I got started on the internet there was no stopping me. But it was a learning curve. Ashton was my main teacher, through observation not intention, nor by arrangement. The irony is a few months before all this developed, I swore I would never have anything to do with on-line social media. How wrong was I.

I have to be careful when I say "I will never." Because every time I say it, I end up doing it. I have said "I will never" to: computers; sport; dating someone called Brian; dating a psychic; and a few more besides. I am trying to think of my last outstanding "I will never," and it is "I will never live in America;" so expect to see that some time soon.

One of my favourite Twitter accounts was a lively account called The Ponycorn which was hilarious. I loved engaging with the 'Corn. The humor was wicked, irreverent, and right up my street. I have no idea for sure if it was Ashton. But it certainly *could* have been. I had hours of fun bantering with "the pony with the horn" at night in my bed on Beacon Hill in Dalkey. There was many a time the sun rose, and I had not yet had an ounce of sleep because @theponycorn had kept me up with some interchange. Not complaining. It was the stuff of life for me at that point. There was nothing sexual with it. Just verbal sparring, veiled references and jokes. By this time the internet was my main friend, and my life was largely run on line. The Ponycorn used to psychically test me, and his tweets were full of nuances, that seemed relevant to goings on in real time. Idle since March 2014, The 'Corn is still "riding the rainbow flame," of his last tweet, and probably will not be back any time soon. Shame.

I found @theponycorn through Ashton's Twitter. The ponycorn began his account with a few tweets; one of which was aimed at @aplusk, Ashton's account. Ashton himself drew attention to the ponycorn account by tweeting: "I do not know who you are, but your name makes me laugh." So either Ashton was "punking" everyone, and was actually tweeting himself. Or the 'Corn was someone anonymous, that just caught his attention randomly. It is quite possible. I will leave you to work out your own conclusions on that one.

Earlier in 2010, April to be exact, I noticed another strange account on Ashton's Twitter page. One week, just as the interactions between Ashton and I were starting to be noticed by a couple of people, an anonymous account appeared, which really caught my eye. In the early days of Twitter, a group of thumbnails on the right of the page displayed twelve of the most recent accounts the person had followed. They were discrete but still in plain view if you were reading someone's tweets. In the run up to this, I had been enjoying and giving quite deep, profound answers on Ashton's blogs on Posterous, a social media site, now discontinued. His *Happiness* blog in particular inspired me. Not so many people responded on these blogs, which showed his more serious side. He also wrote poetry with his father, and shared that, asking for reviews and feedback.

Posterous was a place Ashton could reveal his other faces, and display facets of his character that people may not have been aware of. These blogs were not prolific, but they were interesting. They were just another way of interacting. The sharing of ideas was at the heart of this. I was one voice in a crowd on Twitter, but oddly it felt intimate. There seemed to be a direct connection like texting someone. The energy was that the message was received more as a text than a tweet. I was feeling the telepathic link. In my head it all may have been, but I doubt it, seeing as I am psychic, and not into deluding myself about such things. If something is not real, I know it, and I do not allow myself to indulge it. I knew he was aware of me and keeping an eye on me, if not actively watching me. I could feel it in every bone.

The new Twitter account I noticed on Ashton's page had the famous retro white drama theater masks on black background for its logo. It was the standard recognizable image, generally used by theaters or stage productions. Sometime later I randomly noticed the reverse, negative version of this image, black silhouettes on a white background on Ashton's Quora page.

Hmm Curious

As soon as I saw the new Twitter account, I was hit with one of my definitive "knowing" moments. My heart leapt.

Yes!

BAM! I got the message.

It seemed like a stroke of genius to open up an anonymous account for the exchange of ideas; and so began an elaborate shared journey which lasted many years.

The sharing level of this Twitter account was deep, wide-ranging and normal without affectation. There was no hint there might have been a Hollywood actor behind it. Indeed @unmaskd repeatedly denied there was not. This was the person's way to be themselves, uncensored, and unimpeded.

Introducing his, or her blog over at WordPress, they wrote: *I like this mask the best of all/ It hides my face but bares my soul./All other masks I've ever tried/Would use my face to hide my mind.*

I would not have hung around interacting on this new "masked" account for long, except for one thing. When it began, I was excited, and fully engaged. I thought it was an excellent game, and I said so in a tweet. The reply "Sarah you *know*, " seemed to be pretty indicative to me, and a confirmation that I was right. But at the same time, there were others engaging with The Mask, who were convinced he was John Mayer the musician. Still others thought it might be actor Steve Martin; or Jim Carey; or perhaps Demi Moore; or even Jesus Christ. We could not all be correct.

Had The Mask not said "Sarah you *know*," with such directed energy, I would not have stayed on board for long with the journey. The identity guessing game was a bit too heavy in the air when the account first opened. It got a bit tedious. But eventually the community honed itself down to a smallish group of authentic participants, who acted like they did not care who The Mask was, even as they remained convinced it was John Mayer.

It was all highly amusing. So much went on behind the Mask's back on this matter that I am sure that he, she, or it, would have been mortified if they knew the extent of the discussion. Another few months on, and it no longer mattered. Everyone eventually stopped trying to work out who was running the account. The common ground of sharing, respect, and mutual support that we all found had become the point. It seemed to work for The Mask too. After a definitive blog denying he was anyone in the public eye, a blog which particularly focused on *not* being John Mayer, people finally understood him. No one was supposed to know. No one was supposed to care. The Mask cleverly explained that even *he* did not know who he was; so how could anyone else be expected to know. He admitted only one thing. He was a man.

Just a man. Standing in front of a girl. Asking her to love him.
I jest.

As for finding out the person's name? No one ever would. And if anyone took it on themselves to try, they would surely get mighty confused. The Mask deliberately left a trail of confusion in his wake. He covered his tracks expertly. One time John Mayer was on stage playing his guitar while The Mask was tweeting his fans. The word behind the scenes was that he had given the twitter account over to a friend for a couple of hours. I found this very amusing as a concept. Anything was possible I guess. Or did it just show the power of wishful thinking, and the fascinating way we as humans are prone to project our beliefs, expectations and interpretations onto innocent bystanders?

Another time Ashton was doing a live video broadcast with a fashion expert while Mask was tweeting. I have to admit I was looking to see if there was a phone on his lap. There did not seem to be. A couple of years later, Ashton was one of several entrepreneurs on a stage in Australia judging a business IT presentation. Again this was broadcast by live stream, even as The Mask stopped by for a chat.

The Mask was apparently neither John nor Ashton. Throwing people off the scent was his forte. Preserving his privacy, and concealed identity, was fundamentally important to him; so that he could effectively assess what was actually going to *be* important to him, going forward. The Mask's skills on the geo-tag apps were second to none. Mask appeared in places where neither John nor Ashton could possibly be. All tracks were expertly covered.

There was one time when I sent a "hello" greeting from the barn in Porlock accidentally showing my location in a geo-tag. Ooops. What I thought at the time was:

Right IF The Mask is Ashton, I bet he now appears in the area in the next couple of weeks having seen that.

Sure enough he *did*.

About ten days later he and Mila, his current partner, came across to the Somerset area to attend The Glastonbury Festival, and to get a haircut in Bridgewater, I believe. Why? Anyhow, they did not come to Porlock, home of my geo-tag, but they apparently went to Dunster a nearby village, and a pub near Minehead.

Word travels fast in such rural areas, and the fact that "Hollywood" had come to town, was kind of compelling for folk who did not usually see beyond the horizon of cows, trees, hay-bales, pheasants, rabbits, horses, moors, deer, and gorse bushes.

I was aware that Mila Kunis, was over in London filming *Jupiter Ascending* with Channing Tatum. I also knew that Ashton had accompanied her. I made no attempt to go and see him, as I was already underway in my partnership with Brian. I do not mix and match, and do not like blurred lines when it comes to relationships. I also completely cut off contact with Billy, even though that had only very spasmodic "hellos", with gaps of months at a time. When I embark on a partnership, I am all-in. Ashton had chosen Mila, and I had connected with Brian Hunter. It was simple enough.

So the barn geo-tag was a definite Oops. Did it confirm that Ashton was The Mask? No of course it did not. I am psychic. I probably was only picking up on Ashton coming to the area, and just joined the dots incorrectly. But hmmm. It was another example of the myriad of coincidences which had characterized the link with Ashton over a number of years. I was especially amused to read that one day, whilst traveling through the Mid-West with Mila Kunis his new love, he had used the name "Sarah," in a gas station to preserve Mila's anonymity. I thought that was hilarious; and it also made me sad. The extent of the irony was not lost on me. That he would chose my name to protect his girlfriend when he was guarding *her* identity. Wow, the universe really does have a warped sense of humor. Or Ashton does.

There was no conclusive way to link Ashton with "The Mask." Indeed Mask denied having anything to do with Ashton. When I asked him about it, he said it was similar to the John Mayer theory. Something and nothing. He flatly denied being Ashton privately to me in that moment. However, he did then set me a very curious task, or test. He asked me how well I knew Mr Kutcher. I felt it was some kind of trick question. But he then asked me if I could let Ashton know about a start-up company which had something to do with efficient grocery shopping. He was "asking for a friend."

I thought this was a strange request if Mask was Ashton, since he is of course the master of start-ups. Was I really supposed to private message him to help The Mask? I figured I might as well play along. I jokingly mentioned @GaryVee, an IT expert, and social media buff, as another possible source of help. I noticed that Mask had liked Gary's business page on facebook, and I thought it was a curious clue. Suddenly Mask seemed to panic a little. "Don't mind that," he instructed. "I know Gary." I obviously was not supposed to push that door any further. I did not. But this of course got my little brain whirling.

Was Ashton asking me to private message himself to test me on what I might say? Was Mask actually Gary Vaynerchuk, and did not want me involving him in a direct communication with Ashton who was his friend? This was all kinds of convoluted, and smacked of the energy of being "Punk'd." Then again, you do not actually manage to punk a psychic. Generally, they are one step ahead of the game. I was starting to feel mighty inadequate though, that I could not conclusively solve this. I like to have my point of "knowing" about things. This scenario was slippery and elusive. But intriguing, and compelling nonetheless. In the end it did not matter. It was just a riddle I would have liked to have solved.

I know that both John Mayer and Ashton know Gary. Obviously Gary also knows Gary. In fact probably more than half of Hollywood know Gary. So again none the wiser really. What made no sense was, why ask ME to pitch to Ashton about a startup company, when Mask was actually followed by him, and could message him all by himself? Perhaps Mask wanted "someone, who knew someone" to kick-start interest in this start-up. I doubt it. It smelled more of fun, games and high Jinx to me. But I guess it could have been a totally genuine request. The psychic was probably just getting overly caught up in second-guessing at this point. To cap it all, Ashton "unfollowed" me on Twitter. shortly after I had messaged him about Mask's startup. I had only been very speculative and noncommittal in my approach to him about it. I was literally playing along. Obviously I should not have done Mask this favor when he could have quite easily texted himself to ask himself if he was interested in said start-up. Just kidding.

I then put my own spin on the game, if such it was, and told Mask that Ashton had unfollowed me because I had asked him about his startup. I told him I was upset as that connection had been very important to me. He did a good job at sounding concerned that he should have caused such a rift. All very funny. But actually yes, if Ashton was not the Mask, I actually was upset he had unfollowed me.

For some reason, my Scorpio moon relishes mystery, drama, riddles, and getting to the bottom of things. I really should have been a detective if truth be told. Combine all these tendencies, a stubborn determined nature, and psychic ability, and I may actually have been quite a good sleuth. The Mask adventures and puzzles appealed to many aspects of my personality. What fascinates me is that I never managed to solve the mystery. After a while I was not really even trying. I was not meant to conclusively know who this was. And actually now, I do not want to. The whole experience had a level of mystique and protection, and was not meant to be "solved."

The diversionary tactic once used by Mask that amused me most, was when he embarked upon an adventure around the British Isles. The previous summer he had apparently been all over Europe at a rate of knots, leaping from country to country. Now he was on a (virtual?) cruise on one of the Princess Cruise boats to Southern Ireland, which then was chartered to circumnavigate The United Kingdom. Was he actually on that damned boat or not? It seemed like he could well be. He posted photos from diverse locations such as The Blarney Castle in Cork County; ancient standing stones in Aberdeenshire; Leith Docks, and The Elephant House in Edinburgh, where J.K. Rowling penned *Harry Potter*; Glasgow University featured; along with Stirling Castle; and later Buckingham Palace; The Tower of London; and Westminster Abbey. Spookily many of his photographs echoed my recent travels around the United Kingdom. The universe really was kicking my ass on this one. Very funny.

I followed that cruise ship's chartered course for the sake of amusement, and giggled my way through it. I loved the treasure hunts The Mask set up, and took them with a healthy pinch of salt. But it got a little unnerving, when I researched the pre-mapped intentions of that boat, and found it was set to visit Dublin. Surely not? It would not make sense from someone who had been always so evasive about physically meeting up. Was he going to spring a surprise and stop by for tea? If The Mask really *was* on that vessel, he was due to dock in Dublin. If he was not, then he had an absolutely wicked sense of humor. Either way, he was going to a lot of trouble to make a point. Was this someone simply enjoying a holiday? Or someone spinning a riddle? I mean if you are going to go on a cruise in the summer, surely pick more exotic waters than the grey chilly waters of The United Kingdom?

The odd thing was, the night the cruise liner was supposed to dock in Dublin, it was prevented from doing so by a huge storm. I found this hysterically funny. Mask was quite possibly anchored offshore, unable to come ashore. Alternatively, the real probability was that he was never on the boat, and that even his metaphorical personage was not allowed onto dry land. The universe is so spectacularly logical I thought. The irony was completely perfect.

All I can say about all this is, that when I first saw the black and white logo of the Twitter thumbnail, and then examined the way the account was presented, I was *sure* it was Ashton. I have probably been proven wrong in all sorts of ways since. But since Mr Kutcher is the master of "punking" people, I thought it highly possible he could pull this whole thing off.

I noticed that the Twitter presentation of the two pages was similar. Perhaps this was deliberately done by an imposter. Ashton had his location on @aplusk written as "here", and Mask's location said "here and now." I directly wrote Ashton via private message to point this out, and he quickly changed his public Twitter whereabouts to "California." He then shortly after he unfollowed me, which was in actual fact a genius master stroke if he was The Mask. If he was not, it was kind of mean.

-Up until that point, The Mask was following Ashton and I; Ashton was following the Mask and I; and I was following the Mask and Ashton. It was a curious loop. Hurtful though it was, Ashton's action was super clever. But how was I to read it? Either I had drastically offended the "real" Ashton, who, if the Mask, would have us believe was the "fake" Ashton. Or "fake" Ashton did not want to encourage a direct link, but "real" Ashton, the Mask did. Or, real, fake Ashton was nothing to do with the Mask, and had simply had enough of me, perhaps because I had been diverted by a Mask. It was spectacularly messed up. Just the sort of scenario a person with a Scorpio moon chews on for breakfast.

In theory, The Mask could have deliberately emulated Ashton's presentation to entice people into thinking this account was set up by a famous celebrity. But Mask has far too much class to be doing anything underhand like that. It is unfair to mention him in such a paragraph, as he is a fine upstanding citizen, with wisdom, concern, and a social conscience.

Being "catfished" on line does go on. The whole sock-puppet thing of having a deceptive identity on line is definitely a reality. A friend had someone contact her as if they were acting on behalf of John Mayer, and asked her if she needed money. Obviously a scary way of trying to get someone's bank details. There is also a creepy guy out there emulating Harry Styles with all sorts of Twitter and Instagram accounts. Harry Styles, and his sister Gemma are aware of this person. But the audacity of the guy is scary. He has the northern English accent, the tattoos, the same photos, and the same laid-back approach to life. Fans have complained about him. He literally tries to lure Harry's fans, and some of them definitely think it is Harry. There ought to be a law against it. Well, there *are* laws against this. Several in fact. One such guy is doing jail time in the USA I gather. Harry Styles attracts such crazy energy for some reason. A legion of devoted fans who bitch about any girl he dates, and a handful of guys who pretend to be him on line to seduce the fans, who are so desperate for it to be him, that it might as well be. No wonder Harry himself keeps a very low profile on-line. His fans need to be very careful indeed.

Regardless of my initial hunch about The Mask, which came from pure instinct, and an impulse of mischievous joy, it ultimately was irrelevant who was behind this account. It was never ever going to be revealed any time soon, and it was totally impossible to work out. It would be spectacularly funny if it was Bono, but I am absolutely *sure* it is not. I guess you either knew or you did not. The trouble is, what people thought they knew varied. The whole thing was totally a master stroke of genius. @unmaskd was a private outlet for someone exploring ideas, they could not publically indulge. It could of course have been a wannabe trying to garner attention, but the energy did not match this. It actually did not matter. The Mask was not doing anything sordid, deceptive, or manipulative. They were simply baring their soul behind a "mask", and allowing their spirit some freedom of expression. Their soul shone through. Mask was bright, wise, funny, engaged, cautious and careful, and supremely annoyed when you tried to suggest he was John Mayer. So, whoever they were; they were pretty cool. *That* is what mattered.

Mask's intention is clearly stated on his Twitter page: "Some call me The Phantom of Twiiter. Others suspect I'm The Riddler. But in reality I'm someone who talks about things that make all of us tick." Compare this with Ashton's former intentions for his own page @aplusk, in which he stated that he "makes stuff.""I make stuff, actually I make stuff up, stories mostly, collaborations of thoughts, dreams, and actions. That's me." To me psychically, these two intentions resonate with the same energy. So if Mask is not Ashton, he is someone very similar in type, energy and presentation. Ashton is "Just me." Mask is "True me."

Currently, now a father and happily married man, Ashton's Twitter page reads differently. He has modified his maverick, game playing side. He is a respectable figure who can be relied on, and he is displaying his Aquarian altruism to the max: "I build things, stories, companies, collaborations of thoughts, dreams, and I believe in a future where we all have a right to pursue happiness. That's me, you, US." Ashton has come of age. He is no longer "punking," or "making things up." He is real, responsible, and authentic all in line with complimenting the common good. No more games, just truth.

In the days when the Mask account was being used, 2010 to 2012, the timings and nature of some of The Mask's tweets seemed to echo Ashton's process of parting ways with Demi Moore. There is a Tumblr blog called *Who the F*ck is unmaskd?* This blog parallels Ashton's Tweets with those of The Mask at around the same time, and makes a very plausible comparison of their tone and content. Who on earth went to the trouble to research this? To write this? The Mask did not have many followers, and those who did keep up with the account tended to be John Mayer fans. I actually wondered if the Mask wrote it himself. I certainly did not.

Perhaps Ashton needed this kind of anonymous outlet and support, which was akin to experiencing the kindness of strangers. Whoever ran this account received good feedback, and a listening ear from a group of people, who clearly thought that it was an anonymous account for John Mayer the musician. If John and Ashton are friends, I guess it is quite possible it *could* be John Mayer, since he disappeared from public view on social media April 2010, the same time this account started up. The Mask directly approached a random John Mayer fan to ask if it was "okay" if he followed her. From this direct approach she reasonably concluded that it was Mayer himself looking for a way to connect with his true fans. John perhaps felt the need to have an anonymous outlet to keep himself sane and connected with his fan base. He had been going through a rough time in the media, and had said a couple of unfortunate things about Jessica Simpson, who was "sexual napalm in bed," apparently. Such comments led to him being incessantly misrepresented by journalists; so he removed himself from public view to go find himself in Montana. Quite easily The Mask could have been his way to stay active on line in a more low key way. Equally, the action of seeking out a Mayer fan could have been a clever smoke screen, or a red herring. It is possible

The Mask decided to hide behind a spoof implied identity to further protect himself. Who knows?

It was actually spooky sometimes, the way the Mask's process emulated and matched the emotional process of both John and Ashton. There must be some past life connection between these two (or three). Maybe it was both of them. I am kidding. But it did get mighty confusing for those girls who were trying to actively work out the identity of the person behind the Mask. The whole point of the Mask Twitter account, and its accompanying blog, was that no one would ever know who this is. What is more, they should not care. The account is no longer active really, except for occasional tweets and one reliable posting a year around 28th September. This date represents an important anniversary for said "Mask," and whoever this is checks in with a "hello," in The Fall.

The Mask is more clever than the sharpest of minds he came up against. So be it. One time in the early days it was particularly intriguing to be told by The Mask, that someone thought it was actually an account run by ME. I thought that was very funny. But then I reflected, and realized why someone might think this. It *could* have been run my me, it was reflective of much of my way of thinking. This was an eye-opener. What was even more curious was that The Mask announced to me that I would *like* this suggestion. He was right, I did. But that comment in itself showed something, seeing as Ashton by this stage knew how I felt about him . It was difficult not to connect the dots and create a monster in my head. No doubt a case of two plus two equals six.

Pretty much all Mask like interactions were done publically. This anonymous person apparently was transparent and had nothing to hide. Any private direct messages between The Mask and myself were quite clipped and "well behaved." Proper, even. The Mask had defined boundaries of privacy and a limit to his level of sharing. This was not about to get intimate any time soon. I came just to enjoy the soulful connection. That was what mattered. In fact The Mask fast became a very good friend. This soul was wise, deep, super cool, and really felt like "home" in some ways. Certainly a soul mate of sorts. But, how odd not to be able to see their face, or know their definitive identity. Then again; not really odd at all. *That* was the point.

I thought it was fascinating how protected and unnoticed the account was. I can say all this now, as it is no longer used. Like @theponycorn, The Mask has left the building and put his feet up. Whoever he was, is back out there, engaged in the real world, and getting on with his life. Whatever purpose the account fulfilled for this person, duly ran its course. It was surprising how long it all went on. But ultimately, it made sense that s good thing would not last forever.

Mask once said it would all make a good movie. He is right. It would. If only it had a happier more definite ending, than a discrete disappearance into the night. I still to this day do not know for sure who was behind this "masked" account. They have denied being John, Ashton, and a myriad of others besides. Interestingly, they have not denied being me.

*STUDY NATURE, LOVE NATURE, STAY CLOSE TO NATURE.
IT WILL NEVER FAIL YOU.
FRANK LLOYD WRIGHT*

CHAPTER TWENTY-NINE
Exmoor Knights

I started to panic as I was trying to sleep in the barn on the final night before our journey to Ireland. I was surprised. Obviously, I had grown comfortable settling back into the land of my roots.

My ancestors were from Somerset and Dorset, and much of my childhood had been spent in the West Country. I loved Ireland as my home, yet there was a deep connection to the place where I had spent summer camps as a child. I enjoyed wandering the moors of Exmoor. It had become by safe haven, and the place I could expand my soul and my vision. I was at one with nature in this place, and my energies and fitness had never been better.

Brian had made it very clear he had come to the end of the road regarding the barn. For someone with OCD, a penchant for hygiene and a need for meticulous order, he had done very well with his visits to the ancient dusty, musty barn covered in ivy and imbued with mildew. He had recently told me he would never be able to live full-time in the barn, and that he needed a place to call home. I took this as an encouraging comment of his future intentions. I definitely wanted a place to call home too after all the years of unsettlement. We wanted the same thing, so that was a start. But location was going to be an issue.

Brian had no inclination to move to Europe; and even though I had been accepted for a National Trust cottage, *Sea View* in Bossington, it fell through. So did the dream of Brian's immigration to the United Kingdom. He had too many commitments back home in America, and was so American that living elsewhere would not work for him Ireland started to feel like a possible alternative. But I never would have been able to face a return there if not for Brian.

We had done so much travelling on our pilgrimages throughout the United Kingdom, that we had in a way exhausted the best of what Britain had to offer. Considering his partial Irish DNA I strongly felt Brian should experience Ireland also. But he never seemed to know when he would be able to visit again. He was starting to get weary of all the to and fro travel. Jet lag was an issue, and a big adjustment for him each time he made a visit. It felt like he was not sure how much longer he could sustain and justify regular transatlantic trips. The notion of moving onto Ireland injected some new energy into the proceedings, and he was enlivened by the thought of experiencing a new environment, and country.

As we were deciding to exit the barn, the eco friendly, non flushable, toilet in the outhouse was literally on the point of exploding. Winter was fast descending in Exmoor, and it looked like it was going to be a long, cold, few months. The barn no longer felt like a fit or safe place to stay. On top of that all the signs and synchronicities were aligned for a smooth return to Dalkey, in Southern Ireland. My friend Grainne had viewed a wonderful property for me, rented by another Grainne, and all seemed fine. It looked like Ireland was welcoming me home with open arms. There had been minimal referencing required, (they knew who I was), and I was allotted number 3, Tubbermore Avenue, Dalkey, as my new place of residence for the foreseeable future. In theory.

Landing back in Ireland for the second time was a time warp experience. It felt like I had never left. I swear there were locals who had not even noticed my absence for a couple of years. My doctor greeted me in the supermarket, as if he had only seen me yesterday. If I had remained in Dalkey in January 2012 that probably would have been true. Dr Lavelle, got me through a whole lot during my times of stress. During the times of stress and psychic attack I experienced I had many odd conditions, and funky events. My blood pressure at points was nudging dangerously into hypertension. I had random histamine reactions, infected bug bites, and the most obscure recurring chest infection. I had to be very alert with what was happening with my body. I swear he saved my life, certainly my equilibrium, several times. Bless him.

Exmoor had been a resting place; a place to recuperate, and wait for whatever was to come next for me. At times it felt like nothing new was looming on the horizon. This was it. Me, wandering the fields or the moors with a bunch of dogs for ever. I had reached my destiny. It felt odd that this might be the case. but logically speaking it certainly could have been the end of the road. Not exactly a fail. People would pay good money to live in such surroundings. They did in fact. I was after all semi-retired, and had all the hours of the day pretty much to myself. My obligations and responsibilities pertained to looking after my beloved sausage dog squad. I only really had a couple of radio shows a month to plan and prepare, for CBS Radio, and The World Puja Network. These shows were broadcast live from my mid fifteenth-century barn in Porlock; sometimes literally from the rest room out the back, with the computer perching on the toilet, thereby avoiding avoid the interruption of a barking dog, who might spy a stray sheep out of the window. I still wrote my string of articles for the Irish Newspapers and magazines who employed my services. My clients were an on-going commitment. But over all I was able to plan and live my day in the flow I chose. I could eat when I liked, sleep when I liked, work when I liked. I was on no one's schedule but my own. Quite possibly I was on the fast track to being that strange old lady aged eighty, living in a barn by herself with a myriad of creatures for company. Was this really what I had signed up for?

I loved the surroundings and natural lifestyle, the sojourn at Doverhay Farm provided. Life had a natural mellow rhythm, my dogs protected me and kept me warm at night, and I was able to finally process all the years of disappointment, stress and heartache. I was not sure if anything came next after this. Perhaps it did not have to. This was more than okay really. A little sedentary and repetitive; but I could not ask for a better backdrop and context. Nature was my healer, and my soul got inspired every time I walked out the door. There are not many places in the world that are capable of that kind of elevation. The microclimate found in the Vale of Honey was one of them.

Porlock was prolific when it came to rain, and mist because of the bleak moors situated upon the hills behind the village. The famous, insurmountable on an icy day, Porlock Hill was legendary. This road leads the motorist up onto the eastern fringes of Exmoor, and is the steepest minor road in the country, climbing over seven-hundred feet in less than a mile. With a gradient of 1in 4, you did not attempt this climb if your vehicle's accelerator and clutch were not up to the task. Nor did you descend into the village down the hill, if your brakes were in any way impaired.

It was easy to lose your bearings in these parts if you were not local. The windy narrow road system across the moors led cars astray easily enough as there were various tracks navigating the barren wilderness. For walkers and drivers alike it was a case of pot luck in finding the quickest way from a to b.

I had many arguments with Siri on the finer points of crossing Exmoor. But more often than not she actually did know what she was talking about.

"Hey Siri!"

#nevermind.

Thankfully there were alternative routes in and out of Porlock. I nearly crashed on one of the other descents into the village above Doverhay. I was trying to get back to the barn in time for a remote healing with the powerful John of God based in Brazil. Returning from Minehead through the back roads bypassing Luccombe and Horner, I smelled that smell of rotten eggs an old car exudes when its catalytic converter is about to implode. I was a mile from home. I stopped the car and asked for a farmer's help, and he suggested freewheeling along the road as much as possible before hitting the windy, steep descent into Porlock.

The approach went to plan, but "Duh me." When I got to top of the hill above the farm, I decided to turn off the engine. Of course the wheel locked, and I nearly lost control of the car; thankfully managing to bump start it just before I needed to turn into the hair-pin bend. I turned the key in the lock, and thankfully the car started up just in time; so averting a sharp descent into the hedge on the corner of the bend. Had it failed to do so, I would have had a nasty accident, as I would not have been able to avoid swerving into the jeep ascending rather too quickly on the other side of the road.

Or should I say the *same* side of the road, since all the roads around Porlock were pretty much only one lane. With the wheel unlocked I was able to pull in and let the jeep pass. Phew. I could have been forgiven that some entity or agenda was trying to prevent me receiving the healing that was due to start within the next five minutes. The car, although a battered go-cart, had given me no mechanical trouble up until that point. Then again it would be paranoid to conclude that I was being in any way energetically targeted. Would it not? Hmm.

The Porlock routine certainly gave the sensation of a Groundhog Day, but it was pleasurable nonetheless. In bleak moments I would wonder how I had ended up in this obscure part of Britain after all my previous opportunities. But I put on a brave face. I would talk to friends on line, or on the phone, and there was always something intriguing going on, in social media land which demanded my attention. Most importantly, I was able to help many people with the clarity and background support afforded by mother nature. There was no better backdrop than the barn which merged with the surrounding landscape as part of its organic manifestation.

The barn was a time warp. A time machine to another dimension. Strange things would happen in this creative space. The phrase "Barn Time" was coined as the barn had its own inner clock and throbbing heart beat. The difference in the passing of time within and without the barn was tangible. I could hear ghosts at night, the wind in the trees, owls hooting, bats flapping, and strange sounds coming up through the floor boards. Anything could happen through the ethers in this place as it was built on one of the powerful lay lines linking the west country energetically with London via Glastonbury, Salisbury Plain, and Stonehenge.

The barn was never locked, and any passing stranger could have walked through the door had they known. But it was secure, in this twilight setting, which had me living off the land, in tune with nature and my own rhythm. I could have stepped back in time, down through the centuries, and life would not have been much different. This lifestyle was organic and wholesome. Lonely but therapeutic, if you could abide the isolation.

It really was lonely, I would be lying if I said I was full of the joys of spring. But I did not feel empty or desolate. I was alone, not lonely if truth be told. I had grown to like my own company at last. I did not really need company. In fact I was becoming positively reclusive, and perhaps even stand offish where my fellow humans were concerned. I had been given such short shrift in many situations, that I sort of gave up on the thought of finding a soul mate, having a family, making my millions. I did not really need any of it. Nature was enough, and the soulful grounded feeling the land gave me was everything.

It would have been nice to have some reassurance that there were some more interesting chapters ahead. But stuck in my routine of wandering the moors or the woods daily, I drew a blank much of the time. I sensed America on the horizon. In what shape or form, I did not know. I was not sure I even wanted this. I had retreated from the world really, and America was a vast energy beckoning which I was not absolutely sure I could handle. If The New World was going to feature in my future, I had to make ready and make the most of this time-out chapter.

Sometimes we just have to "be" to let the dust settle, and allow the new phase to come in organically. It pays to be accepting of a vacuum and a transition time. This stopgap allows the universe to breathe in our favor, and line up those new adventures. Energies ideally have to be allowed to flux and flow; ebb and flow. We would not do very well if life were totally full on with no down time. Indeed often times, the down time is the best gift of all. It is a luxury that many never receive, or get to experience. At this stage of life, I could have been in the midst of a hectic family life, or a high demanding career in the city, or a 9 to 5 in some office, or classroom.

Okay, none of those things were ever going to happen to me. But you get my point. The predictable routes were not for me. As a healer and psychic worker, I actually *needed* this time in nature, to clear, cleanse, shake all the trauma down, and come back fighting; for the sake of my clients as well as for myself.

I did not know what would come next in my life, though I knew America would play a part. I used to look up at the track across the mountainous hill at Hurlstone Point, and *knew* I would walk that walk with a visiting American. I was saving that excursion for whoever this would be. I was determined not to walk it until that person arrived. I had no idea who that American was going to be. At one point, I strongly suspected it might be The Mask showing face at last. But no, turned out it was Brian, a fellow psychic and healer from the USA.

Snake Woods, as Brian called it, was a circular walk which began in Bossington, looped up to Hurlstone Point, across this ridge path I was keeping sacred, and then through the spooky woods which then dipped back down to the tiny village of West Lynch. Snake Woods was a journey in stages. The walk was a meditation in ways, and it allowed for the processing of the latest drama, or for deep thought about a client's situation, or the planning of the next trip or work project. Having broken the duck with Brian on his first visit with the circular trek, I walked Snake Woods pretty much daily with the dogs, whatever the weather. I got super fit, and simply loved the wilderness life. I got very used to my own company. It was just me and the dogs, for many months, interspersed with visits from Brian when he could manage them. I healed and I assimilated my thoughts, finances, and emotions. The whole thing was a process of inner strengthening and catharsis.

When I had first arrived in the area I was overwhelmed with the adjustment facing me. I still had my on line companion The Mask, with whom I shared occasional thoughts and snippets of insight. But he was largely quiet during this time frame. If it is who I suspected it was, he was being pursued by someone rather determined that he had known for a long time.

Most of the girls who followed The Mask maintained their belief it was John Mayer. They may have been right, but at least for a while I held onto my initial theories. Energetically it felt during these months that The Mask was moving on and connecting with someone else, perhaps having come through a majorly public and messy divorce. I still suspected that The Mask's blog and account on Twitter, was this person's outlet to help them integrate and cope with their emotional situation. I identified so much with this. Whoever, it was, they were an intellectual match, and the sharing was spasmodic but worthwhile.

The Mask was a friendly background presence, giving off the sort of feeling you could turn to them in a crisis if you really had to. I liked to think I performed the same function for them in return. This certainly felt like a soul family member. In fact they felt like one of my very best friends. There was an innate understanding, mutual sharing and safe acceptance. The Mask allowed for the person's honest expression from the heart, and I, being psychic, was able to receive that completely.

Once I joined The Psychic Society, Brian and I quickly connected as colleagues and friends with our shared intelligence, and warped sense of humor. Our psychic abilities and understanding of what it mean to work with these in practice was also a huge connecting point. We got on excellently well. I remember writing "help help, I'm drowning" to Brian on Facebook's private messaging in January of 2013. His response was "don't worry, I can swim." Something melted inside me when he said that, and I was sold on exploring this path which was presenting in quite a surprising way. Brian was not an obvious choice for me. I had always sworn I would never date a psychic. Oddly, I had also stated that I could never ever date a guy called "Brian" either. So this was the universe messing with my boundaries as usual. I had to laugh. I had another Psychic Society member proposing to me intermittently, possibly jokingly, and I was feeling a bit overwhelmed. The "help help" was a reaching out from the heart, not with any expectation. I think the resulting chats surprised us both.

We bonded quickly, and before I knew it, I was paying for Brian to come and see me on 9th March.

When I had joined The Psychic Society in mid 2012, Brian had jumped out as someone I would like to consult regarding my situation. I approached him for an email reading, and particularly wanted him to concentrate on my location, and intention to ultimately move to America. I had no clue that we would begin to connect so intensely by the end of the year. We began talking almost daily in the New Year. There was a strong psychic charge between us, and an intensely accurate telepathic support. There was also a fun sharing on line with other friends and colleagues, particularly Andrew Brewer, Jost Van Dyke, Kathy Biehl, Justin Mullins, and Brian Hunter. The banter was fun, and The Psychic Society also brought forward more amazing friends and colleagues. I started to feel very connected up with all things Transatlantic, and the momentum seemed to be building for a relocation to the USA.

Brian Hunter is spooky and gifted indeed. He is one of the very few psychics in the world that I would refer clients to for a second opinion, and trust to give an honest, real reading. Brian does not sugar-coat things, which can be quite a stark experience for some people. But what you will get is an authentic and sensible perspective, plus an effective game plan for your situation. Many professionals in the field that know of him trust him too. He is a psychic's go-to psychic. Brian is a counselor, healer, medium and life coach. He is most accomplished as a medium, and has done some very specific cold case work with Christa McDermont, and Danielle Egnew on *Missing Peace*. Between them, they managed to solve some very significant cases which had been left unresolved by law enforcement. They passed their findings through the correct legal channels, and started to then stumble upon issues with following through and getting justice for the victims. There are clips of some of the filming and content of these episodes on Brian's web site brianhunterhelps.com.

Missing Peace was a show designed to solve cold cases using skilled psychics. There was a full team put together by Stephen Hansen, which included Bobby Brown from *Dog The Bounty Hunter* fame, a detective, three psychics, and a former FBI agent. The show was nearly picked up by the *Discovery Channel* and *The Oprah Winfrey Network*. But the buzz about the work, and the team, came at the tail end of a series of shows featuring psychics being used for investigative purposes, and it just missed the boat. Literally it was a moment too late, which was very annoyingly for all involved. What could have been an amazingly effective project, was shelved. I was accepted on the team of *Missing Peace* for its re-launch attempt a few years later. But still it remains a concept idea, and a show with potential only, until it gets the financial backing enabling it to happen on the scale it fully deserves.

It all moved quickly with Brian. The first time we met was when he walked in the door of Stag Cottage. I think he did not know what had hit him. Five barking dogs, a strange English blonde woman, lots of Exmoor rain, and a freezing cold cottage. I am actually surprised he was not on the next plane out of there. I remember noting that his phone "pinged" as soon as he walked in the door. I vaguely wondered who that was, as the energy felt a bit intense. But I parked the thought, and got on with getting to know my visitor.

In subsequent trips I was certainly going to find out who *that* was, and what is more the energy behind it was going to prove an annoying invasive niggle. A blot on the landscape. A thorn in the side. A spanner in the works. All those analogies which make life somewhat burdensome.

Not only did Brian stay for that jetlagged trip of ten days, He also booked to come back again mid April. We knew it was madness, for him to return only three weeks or so later, but we were on course to explore our connection, and what might come of it. I had not planned this, and neither had he. We were both minding our business in life. But once we connected, and got on so well, I thought it was time to roll with what was actually happening. We both did. We talked, shared, dealt with some professional issues, and started to work together exploring our skills.

I saw evidence of Brian's ability very quickly on spending time with him. On one of our first days together we walked into the huge churchyard at Porlock Saint Dubricius church. I asked him where he felt drawn to. Brian is a medium, and reads energy in churchyards. In fact he *loves* churchyards. So how is that for a first date? Hmm. I was initially concerned about his fixation with death, and wondered if it was a form of depression. Perhaps it was, but it was also his work, and he was certainly very skilled at communicating with the residual energies he found there.

In response to my question, Brian pointed up to the top right of the graveyard. It was a bit of a climb on slippery grass, but we made it. The grave he was drawn to, had obvious relevance. It was the anniversary of that person's passing. What were the chances? In a church yard of hundreds and hundreds of gravestones, Brian had picked out the one whose occupant had passed on the very same date we were there, 14th April. I was blown away.

We walked around some more, following the energies, and seeing what else we could find. But then something even more incredible happened when we went inside the church itself. Saint Dubricius Church was built in honor of Dubricius, a thirteenth century travelling preacher, who made it across to Porlock by boat from Wales. There are not many churches established in his honor. But Porlock, has a very significant stained glass window in the bell ringers pulpit at the back of the church.

Usually what we came to call the "power center" of a church is the altar, or the choir area. In Saint Dubricius' Church, the power center is up at the back tucked away. It would take psychics, or a priest with esoteric knowledge, to be aware of this. As we stood down in the church looking up at the window dedicated to Dubricius, an incredible light filled the church emanating from the Saint's portrait. We both captured it on camera. It was a tangible supernatural visitation, and very moving.

We were curious to hear that not long afterwards the church clock broke for the first time in hundreds of years. The huge pendulum was lying on the floor when I went to take a closer look at the stained glass window after Brian had gone home.

Oops.

We hoped it was nothing to do with the huge energy surge in the bell tower the day of our visit. It could well have been. But say no more. I am not sure two psychics can be charged for something like that. It certainly was not intentional.

We researched Saint Dubricius on return to the barn, and found that his Feast Day is also on the 14th of a month. We jokingly started to call Brian "Dubricius," as he seemed increasingly to feel a connection to him. Whether he was literally his reincarnation, or simply had an energy link with him, we were not sure. The name stuck as a permanent nickname nonetheless.

Brian's interest in the Saints of Ireland and the United Kingdom kicked in from that point. We spend many hours and much money, travelling the length and breadth of England, Scotland and Wales researching our theories and following our guidance. These travels were great for me. I got to leave the isolation of Porlock with a conducive companion, and I also was able to revisit all the haunts of my past one more time.

We got up to Edinburgh, Stirling, London, and Stonehenge. I became Brian's tour guide for Great Britain. It was a fun, intense time, full of tales of The Knights Templar, the court of King Henry, and the spooks at Westminster Abbey. On one of the trips into Westminster Abbey, Brian got incredibly sick by the tomb of Edward The Confessor. There was an energy of the plague, and this shrine had been the site of many healings linked to medieval suffering. Being an empath Brian absorbs energies like a sponge, and it was all he could do to get on the plane and fly home the next day. He made it but the feeling of the plague did not leave him for a couple of weeks or so.

On these travels, Brian became an expert on the ghosts of times gone by, and I took a lot of photographs. Rosslyn Chapel was particularly inspiring because of its link to The Holy Grail, and the tales of its Knights. The Rose of England, symbol of the Grail appeared everywhere we went. The Knights Templar would not leave Brian alone either. Every time he wiped photos of the effigies on the floor of The Round Church near Fleet Street, the pictures of the stone knights reappeared. He only finally purged them from his energy field when he got a new phone. Some kind of ancient virus compromised the electronics of his phone, and every time he turned the phone on the knights appeared. I thought it was funny and lucky. He was not so sure. The knights that would not be deleted tracked his progress. No doubt he had some heavy duty karma to balance and fulfill, before they would leave him alone.

My own plans to exit Europe for a new life in the USA, got diverted, and I instead rediscovered my roots and my past. It was a form of soul retrieval to retrace my steps around Great Britain. and Ireland. I found it very healing to walk around places of previous trauma and drama like Hampton Court and Stirling Castle, with someone as grounded and empathic as Brian.

It was no surprise that it took me off guard to be heading back to Ireland. No surprise that I panicked at the prospect either. I had thought I would leave Ireland, and then make my life in America. Here I was returning to Ireland with an American, who actually liked it very much, and enjoyed the prospect of reconnecting with his Irish roots. I reassured myself, that perhaps the divine plan was the opposite of what I had thought; that Brian would in fact come to live in

Europe and join me in Ireland, so that we could work and develop our work from there. Perhaps I did not need Los Angeles or Hollywood at all for the next phase of my career.

Brian literally lived on Hollywood Boulevard, right by the Chinese theatre in a place we lovingly called "Piss pot." On Oscar Night Brian could not get in and out of his apartment block without his papers. He became used to the banging of construction and helicopters overhead, and enjoyed the diversity of the local residents. In a brainstorming session between the three of us in Dalkey, Brian and I were pumping Jane's depth of spiritual experience. Brian needed answers about some of his life's challenges, and an indication of the way forward that would best serve his interests. Highly astute and wise, Jane was adamant. She felt he should get the hell out of Hollywood, ideally LA itself, as she felt it was not helping his energies. He was marinating in a melting pot, a vortex, and an Illuminati hotbed. This might all sound a bit dramatic, but she had a point.

The energies in Hollywood were certainly heavy duty, and not easy to process. It is a testament to Brian's grounded nature, and inner strength that he held his light steady, right at the heart of this corrupt industry for so long. I had been horrified at some of his stories of abuse in the movie industry, and he explained the whole scene in terms of an underground gay enclave. It sounded like everyone was gay in Hollywood, or else they had to fall into socially accepted patterns of behavior to be accepted, and even to work. Obviously anything goes in Hollywood. Brian was on the front line, and he seemed to know an awful lot about the way it all ticked over. He had done some movies, the most exciting of which was *Star Trek, Into Darkness*. Appropriately he played an alien in this one. On another occasion he played a Ghost on a plane. All typecasting really.

Brian used to call his apartment "Pee hole." As an ironic nod to Jane, he changed the name, to "Piss pot," so hoping to modify the energies he was attracting. Of course because he was being mischievous and facetious it did not work. Jane was probably right, we concluded. But leaving his home was not as straightforward as it might seem. The timing had to be right, as a lot had to be taken into consideration. Piss pot offered familiarity, and a fairly reasonable rent. There was no ready cash flow, inclination or reason to do a move for the sake of it. Brian was near his running routes at Runyon Canyon, and Griffiths Park. He was in the heart of Los Angeles, which he loved, and felt invested in. He could not uproot and leave on a whim. It had to be meticulously planned, simply by virtue of the that person he is.

Nothing was done in a hurry by Brian. Everything had to be considered, analyzed, and structured. Brian was not particularly in the mode of following intuitions without good hard evidence to substantiate those intuitions. Mermaid followed spirit to the max. Brian was understandably more cautious. I am a believer in a positive approach, a correct understanding of the Law of Attraction, and following the guidance of spirit. Whereas Brian thinks the Law of Attraction is a load of nonsense. In some presentations it surely is. But overall I cringe at this negative stance. He would call it realism, I call it pessimism. But, Brian is right in a way, the Law of Attraction is *not* a simple fix. It certainly is not as simplistic as people think. Thinking positively, while useful, is not the answer for much of life's complexity. Maintaining a positive response to life's situations is doubtless beneficial, and I certainly cannot be persuaded that is the wrong approach. I would not have survived all I have experience without it.

Many of our discussions revolved around, who was right about this. When Brian's pragmatism and downright pessimism got too much to bear, we resorted to my merry minklement, and magic. It was hard work, and an uphill battle manifesting things in this environment. But it is a measure of one's power, determination and tenacity, that much was achieved; despite Brian's belief that the universe is pitted against him. I felt under trial to demonstrate how this was not the case, and I managed it much of the time. Sometimes, I got sad, dispirited and worn down; but I am human. Oh wait a minute, no: I'm a Mermaid.

Brian liked his jaunts to Europe, and learned to cope with the jetlag with a mixture of techniques, including running, structured meal times, and structured bed times and naps. His approach usually worked pretty well, and he got through lengthy stays in good shape. His time out from "Piss pot" was important to him, and it enabled him to get distance from the very intense energies of Hollywood and his demanding clients.

Sure enough in Ireland work possibilities started to open up, and I thought that if only he would actually move over, we would be able to make a go of it. Of course, Brian could not move over, He had commitments, and strong preferences attached to America, which kept him bonded, and close to all things American. I did not know this when we first connected. But as I got to know Brian it all made sense. I had to accept and embrace other elements in my relationship with Brian which were not unreasonable or surprising. As time marches on, us humans are bound to meet with people that have complex lives, and obligations beyond the remit of any fledgling relationship we might be wishing for. Adapting to past realities, incarnations, and the history of our friends and partners, can be an enriching, bonding, and important experience.

One element I did not expect to be in the mix however, was a very disruptive Brazilian influence from Sao Paulo. The probable source of that "ping" when Brian walked into my life. This guy gave me the creeps, though I was assured he was nothing to worry about. Energetically, I felt different. I trusted Brian to handle it as he had asked me to do. But sometimes this guy felt like a threat, and he definitely was an active interference. Brian kept up his friendship with him for a while, recognizing that time would separate the wheat from the chaff. Brian has a kind patient hard, and rightly does not believe in excluding people. I accepted this. I am not a nagging wife type, who will monitor or influence who my man's friend's are. But I did not find the energy disruptions easy.

One time in the barn, Brian slept the whole time. He gave into the jet lag completely. I found by the end of the trip that this guy was putting all sorts of emotional pressure on him. He had been totally demanding of his time and energy throughout the trip, and had made up a story that Brazilian locals had kidnapped his dog, cut its penis off, and thrown it at him. I knew immediately he was lying, and playing off Brian's good nature. I told him this, and he did not initially believe me. What deeply worried me was that Brian, a talented psychic, did not realize he was being lied to. That troubled me, as it showed a level of emotional confusion regarding this vampire pest that I did not like. I mean why allow someone that kind of power over you?

I understood that they were friends, and that Brian had visited him four times in a year or so, acquiring plenty of Brazilian stamps on his passport in the process. In a way Brian was a father figure for this young person who had experienced more than his fair share of abuse. But I picked up a very tricky energy. He seemed to have Brian by the "short and curlies." On this same trip, this guy wrote emails to me to try and upset me, and he threatened suicide to try and upset Brian. It really was an invasion of our time together in the early days.

I was aware Brian was remaining in contact with him throughout many of his earlier trips to see me. His line was that he was coming to work in Europe, and although technically true, it felt like an inaccurate presentation. I was obviously initially a bit more invested in terms of hopes and wishes for where it might all lead. The Brazilian thing annoyed me immensely, and was a real spanner in the works for quite some time. It meant that there was not the correct momentum and flow of developments that there might have been. It was definitely a buzz-kill for the first year or so.

There are too many tales of energy disruption to recount. But this guy, seemed to have recourse to some powerful entity attachments. At one point, I wondered if he was actually using voodoo to disrupt my relationship with Brian. I do not think so necessarily, but his intentions were so obsessively focused, that this in itself would produce quite targeted surges of energy. For sure his intentions were not good, or desirable, and he was definitely a disruptive influence.

Voodoo is definitely an innate part of Brazilian culture. But not wanting to go too far down that route, I started to make jokes about this guy, whenever something odd was going on. Humor and laughter are *the* best ways to disperse negativity. When there was a huge bee in the barn, I joked it was "Brazilian." One time there was invasion of huge diving moths, they were of course sent by "Brazil." One of those even dive bombed my pillow, so that extended the metaphor further.

I would be the first to say take all this with a pinch of salt. I had to repeatedly double check my paranoia levels first before jumping to conclusions. But having said that, it pays to be aware and it pays to be careful, particularly in situations where energies are loaded and potent. I had to keep my wits about me that is for sure. When I nearly crashed on the way to receive an important healing for the situation, it would certainly make you wonder. But it is also important to say that we feed negative energy and amplify it if we give it too much air time. It is best to play down these things, and not sensationalize them.

The impact of negative energy, curses and entity interference can be very troubling. It is a real phenomenon, but thankfully one that most people do not have to deal with. Psychics tend to get these kind of deep challenges, and ultimately the upshot is, their experience and skills amplify. There is a gift in most situations if you hunt for it. I certainly make it my challenge to find the blessing, even in the direst scenarios. I had many theories about the whole thing, and I intermittently shared these with Brian. I had to talk about it very sparingly. I understood why. So there were stretches of time, where I had to keep faith, and continue to act on a wing and a prayer. I certainly went through stuff, and did feel at times under some kind of attack.

My second exit from Ireland was a case in point. Brian and I had set up our home together. He was not always there, but we settled in and thought of "Tubbermore" as home. I felt a certain Brazilian was not best pleased. Even though the guy had linked up with other playmates, and was doing better with his work and opportunities, I could sense he was still causing problems whenever Brian was with me. Brian's phone actually physically broke on one visit when the guy got angry on realizing he was with me again. I always had a sixth sense for the background disturbances in the force created by this guy. Things were a lot better overall. But that in itself made it all the more obvious *when* he was causing trouble. It was less prolonged and annoying; but oddly more acute when it happened.

Despite my attempts to keep levity and humor in the situation, regarding the Brazilian, I did not know quite what to do. I know he resented me. Early on, he had sent me an email saying that he understood I would reach out for Brian in the night, seeing as he was in my bed, but that he actually preferred the male of the species. I showed this to Brian, and he tactfully said, "I understand why he would say that."

I left it at that. I did not question him about it. Someone's sexuality is their business. But deep down I needed to know if I was actually being enjoyed as a woman or just being tolerated because I was currently useful. Certainly that is what the Brazilian wanted me to think. I felt I had to just observe, enjoy my relationship with Brian, and let the arrows of interference diminish over time. Not easy.

I became niggled sometimes that Brian got defensive if I tried to point out something detrimental about the Brazilian. He clearly felt he could compartmentalize the energies, and handle the guy. I am sure that he was more than capable of keeping him sweet. What he did not seem to always care about was the effect this all had on me. If I even raised that there might be a problematic energy situation caused by the Brazilian's resentments I got short shrift, and was advised to look to myself. I did, and I did not find too much out of alignment. I was being presented with all sorts of challenges when Brian was with me or about to arrive, and they tended to diffuse whenever he left. This may of course have been nothing to do with the Brazilian. Perhaps Brian was right. It just might have been "spirit with horns," as I called the tricky energies, trying to scupper our work together. It could have been all this and more.

I sensed that there were some powerful entity attachments with the Brazilian, and that "spirit with horns," had a tendency to use him to weaken Brian. This is complex stuff. It is karmic, and some of it could have been annoyance, and slight paranoia. I let myself think that so I could take the blame for the most part, and so deal with it that way. But I have a hunch that overall I was correct. I certainly knew what was coming at me, and a bunch of maggots on the path way, a flock of huge deformed moths in the barn, and crazy, random Irish men verbally abusing me, were not part of normal life. They were energy manifestations of something being not quite right.

I did my best to sit loose to it all, or even to completely ignore it where possible. But at points it was definitely not funny. Shortly after one of Brian's visits to the barn in Exmoor, Penny my beloved little dog became dramatically paralyzed after what appeared to be a bee sting. I had not seen any sign of recent injury. There had been a slight yelp a few days before as she jumped off a low sofa in the back part of the barn, and that could indeed have been the source of the problem.

Dachshunds are very prone to back problems and slipped discs. The thing with Penny was odd though. She was small, and her back was not really much longer than a normal sized dog. Perhaps it is also the ratio of little leg to back that has to be considered. Anyway one day Penny was alive, the next she was struggling to breathe in the vets surgery. We talked about getting her up to Bristol for an emergency operation, but there was no time. She had taken some kind of hit for the team, and I had to put her down there and then.

When I got back to the barn, I found a dead bee on the floor beside where she had been resting. I do not know. I began to wonder if the poison had affected her spinal cord. Was it a back disc issue at all? I will never know for sure.

What I do know is that a Psychic Society colleague Jennifer, a highly recognized medium in Los Angeles, did a reading on the energies for me. She said that Penny was a very special energy spiritually, and that she had had a contract to protect me. She took the hit on some very tricky energies that had been targeted in my direction, and the bee had been the transmission for those energies. If Penny had not done this, the consequences would have been worse for me. I knew she could well be right. Enough said.

This psychic had no knowledge of the details of my situation or relationship, and she said this all about Penny's swift exit into the heavens. It confirmed my hunches and fears about what was going on. But still I did not want dark, negative energies to defeat all I was heavily invested in. I was determined to battle on, and hold steadfast to the route I had committed to. The exit of Penny the dog was really tough, and I was not sure how to perceive it. I obviously could not relay these theories to anyone, for risk of being thought crazy. An independent voice had confirmed my worst fears; then again I knew I was correct, because I know these things. It is my job to know these things after all. So even in the midst of craziness, when you know what you know? There is not much you can do about it.

You might have wondered then why I persisted in seeing Brian. He persisted in dragging the energy of this psycho Brazilian along with him. But I know he had a contract to help the boy. Many times I suggested it might be better for his own challenges if he, "cut the head off" this particular snake. But he did not listen. This guy had been a loyal friend to him throughout his own tribulations in the recent years. Brian did not have many close friends, and this relationship was important to him. I had to suck it up or let it all go. Brian did not say that to me, I simply knew it to be the case.

On his first visit to me, he had told me this friend was due to come to stay with him in Piss Pot the following July. It was dependent on him getting the correct visa. I told Brian that this would not happen. I did not at that point, know quite what I was dealing with. But, when he got home, there was a mumbled comment that if I had a problem with this guy visiting then "we had a problem."

Horrified and hurt, I let it go. I knew the guy was not going to be successful in any of his visa attempts. It was difficult for me, but I knew I had a contract to help Brian through his challenges. I could also tell he was being duped by much that was going on in his life. I felt that circumstances had forced him into some very unfortunate corners. It was my role to support, and help him process, and attempt to guide him towards some kind of energetic clearance. He in return was there to support me, ground me, and bring me some adventures, and hopefully a future.

This Brazilian was a bugbear that had to be tolerated for the moment, if not for good. I cannot say I am pleased about the death of my dog, nor the several minor car accidents I had; never having had one in my life up until this point. But I knew I was stronger than any nonsense, jealousy, or indeed dark energy that might be trying to scupper our connection. I do not want to demonize anyone either. I do not believe in doing that. We are all God's creatures after all. Besides, my own grounding and faith in God meant I had a high level of protection. I would not have assumed this, nor taken it for granted. But I did know that it was true.

Brian had to get himself sorted, free, and on track in his life. He had experienced many difficult things. The breakdown of his highly successful property business in Maine; the dissolution of his main relationship with someone, who went through a personality sea change, over a major family issue; a breakdown or a stroke in which his gifts were amplified; the loss of a precious family member through a relocation; and years of isolation in Piss Pot trying to come to terms with it all. Brian needed his friends, but he did not need to be held to ransom by psychotic vampires of any kind. I was there to help guide him to the light. I did my best. But in the end I had to realize that I am not responsible for someone else's relationship with God, the universe, and everything. I had to be detached, and give loving input as best as I could, as we did the work we had to do together.

The National Trust property I shared with five dogs was beautiful, but also somewhat worn and dilapidated. The barn at Doverhay Farm in Porlock was primitive, charming, and spacious. It was a wonderful creative space with its high beams and whitewashed walls.
I shared the surrounding fields with mice, slowworms, sheep and mosquito. I cooked outside when I had visitors, and basically I was camping with an ancient dusty barn wrapped around me. Glamping, on a not so glamorous scale, I guess you could call it.

My accommodations comprised of the ecologically friendly toilet, which was essentially a bucket with a flap lid; an outside washroom; and no heating except for a wood burner in the middle of the room. I loved it for a time, but if truth be told. But it was cold in the winter, and I was being quite monitored by "Tight Ship" the farmer. Brian had unceremoniously named this old sea captain type, and it was a rather appropriate moniker I have to say.

Tight Ship needed me to "settle my account" on Tuesdays and give him his one hundred and seventy five pounds drinking and grocery money for the week; on week's that his son Harry did not need something that is. For some reason he hated it when I went off on the travels with Brian, and I would receive texts asking when I was going to "settle my account" for that week.

Tight Ship had many daughters, and one beloved son Harry. I think I was another wayward adopted daughter in his head. He had kindly allowed me and the dogs to use the barn, after I had to leave Stag Cottage when it was put on the market. I had run out of time to find a place, and I noticed an ad for the Shepherd's Hut up at the farm. I thought the dogs and I could perhaps camp there until I found somewhere more suitable. Tight ship announced it far too small, and showed me the barn on the other side of the farm house. I loved it immediately and said "yes please."

I thought I would never find anywhere for me and the dogs, but Tight Ship's mother used to breed dachshund sausage dogs, so he knew what to expect. He had told me it would be cheaper for me than Stag Cottage. But in the end he cleverly incorporated his council tax into the weekly bill and it worked out at a hundred more a month, for a less civilized set up. I did not really mind.

I enjoyed the connectedness to nature I felt in the barn. I used to love walking out of my gate into the rear hind quarters of a huge beautiful horse called Louis, who kept company with his very short companion, that Brian named "pointless horse." Pointless horse was not actually pointless at all, since all of Tight Ship's granddaughters enjoyed riding this cute Shetland Pony.

Louis was "Just a Horse." He was huge and handsome, and used to break into my yard to roll on the extra rich grass. Louis' huge horse's ass, was a source of amusement to Brian also. When he arrived in Porlock after a long flight, and eternal taxi ride with "The Minx", Caroline from Heathrow, the last thing he needed was to circumnavigate the mud and that horse's ass in order to get into the barn. There was not much we could do about it except laugh. It was all good clean fun.

We had an ongoing commentary on the farm and it inhabitants, which we built upon in order to stay sane. Everyone had irreverent nicknames, and Rodney the ram was Tight Ship's spy we thought. Rodney used to peer in through the glass door at me sitting at my computer with a very quizzical look on his face. He was particularly curious when Brian was visiting. Rodney was probably sent over to collect the extra rent, that Tight Ship may have assumed was owed.

I stuck to my boundaries on that one. I was surely allowed the occasional guest. The barn was already ridiculously priced. I was paying a rental amount for a bed and breakfast establishment. Technically I could have turned up for my cooked breakfast every morning. A stay at Doverhay Farm is actually highly recommended. Tight Ship cooks an amazing breakfast, probably the best in Exmoor. It would have been amusing to make him do a big cook up every day, but I am not sure my arterial system would have thanked me for it, and he certainly wouldn't have either.

I loved the Exmoor night sky, and the wood fires. A precious part of my routine was to collect wood, and light fires in the humongous wood-burner. It was all very therapeutic. Brian had a running joke that Porlock was full of vampires. The inhabitants certainly are a little strange, well some of them. I have to say I gave him a sideways glance one Sunday when we were down in The Bottom Ship for roast pheasant. On the wall of this pub at Porlock Weir was an old sepia photograph of fishermen mending the nets. Slap bang in the middle of this picture was the farmer of Doverhay Farm looking exactly as he does in *this* century. I could not quite believe it. But there was Tight Ship, same as ever. Logically it could not have been him. But...

I never know quite what to think about some of Brian's utterances, but there is always some kind of otherworldly spookiness to them, so ignore them at your peril, you might say.

I was on a day to day bed and breakfast arrangement at the farm. I stayed quite some time, and at points thought I would probably just stay there permanently. Brian used to joke about finding me a plot in the graveyard, which drove me crazy, and of course it made me want to leave as soon as I could.

When it finally came time to leave, it all happened very quickly indeed. It was not meticulously planned, and the speed of the whole thing took us all by surprise. The ecologically friendly toilet was decidedly unfriendly. It was about to explode as it was blocked with some kind of fatty deposit. God only knows how that happened, but I did eventually have a vague recall of pouring some bacon fat down there at one point.

A place in Ireland had been lined up for me with the greatest of ease, and Brian had extended his stay in order to see something of Ireland. He was okay to travel to Ireland as long as he could fly. He understandably hated long journeys in the car, and was willing to let me and the dogs brave it alone right up until the last minute. I did not pressure him I felt I simply would abort the journey if he did not support us to get there.

Thankfully, the spirit moved, and Brian agreed to do the journey very straightforwardly. It all went smoothly, aside from his loss of the five hundred pounds he had won in the Minehead Arcade the day before on the boat's rigged slot machine. I could have told him not to play that one, but he did not ask.

Tight Ship was completely thrown by our quick exit, as were we. I had no lease and on a very informal arrangement. I was perfectly within my rights to leave with no notice whatsoever. His son Harry had started to ration the wood for the wood burner, and with this precious supply under lock and key, and the nights getting increasingly colder, it seemed like a good time to exit, and quickly.

Tight Ship tried to block my exit as I reversed my car to leave the farm at eight in the morning. We had told him our departure time, and he made sure he was there with bells on, to make his presence felt. He started to be unreasonably demanding about needing my new address, and basically he was starting to make me feel like some kind of criminal. I think he thought the rapid departure was "highly suspicious." Indeed Brian caught him muttering this under his breath before he had a placatory chat with him. In the end they bonded over a mutual complaining about this crazy blonde lady, who had sprung this on the both of them.

Normally I would have had no problem leaving a forwarding address. But Tight Ship's behavior actually started to alarm me; so I said I did not know the full address, and would forward it if necessary when I arrived. I knew it would not be necessary as I had already organized my affairs for the exit of the village of Porlock. Also the name had started to bother me: Poor Lock. It ultimately did not feel too promising.

No more would I have to have a Christmas sitting by the knight with no feet in Dubricius' Church. No longer would Tight Ship have to sleep with his window open to hear what was going on, even in the depths of winter. No longer would I have to hear the dubious night sounds in the barn at night, where I had no lock on the door to defend me from predator, be it man or beast. Oh, perhaps Tight Ship's open window was merely a paternal guardian ship gesture. Yes, I will settle on that slightly less disturbing thought. Anyhow, life could now proceed more normally.

Porlock was history. I returned to Ireland, after a couple of years of living in the barn on Doverhay Farm in Porlock. The bankruptcy had gone really smoothly, and after a year or so of rebuilding I was completely in the clear. I felt like a weight had been lifted from me.

I had not realized that Brian had had such major problems with the open-plan nature of the barn. But on reflection it was a bit of a no-brainer. Brian had been sharing his bed with an (allegedly) snoring psychic, and quite a number of dogs. The nest of pillows he built nightly to separate him from me and the dogs was clearly not sufficient. As soon as we got to Tubbermore, our very posh new accommodations in Dalkey, he retreated straight into his room firmly shutting the door behind him. *Oh! Okay. Hmm.*

I was mortified, if not a little upset. It was an adjustment I had not bargained for. We had slept together, traveled together, and now we had a nice home to live in for the times he could tear himself away from LA to visit me. I had to get quickly used to a very different routine from life in the barn. Suddenly I was in a bed without my dogs, who were in the main part of the house, and without Brian. I had not factored the different sleeping arrangements into my calculations of how Dalkey would be different.

*YOU WILL NEVER KNOW HOW STRONG
YOU ARE UNTIL BEING STRONG IS YOUR
ONLY CHOICE.
BOB MARLEY*

CHAPTER THIRTY
Dalkey Daze

Once back in Ireland for the second time, I was very glad to be talking to my good friend Anke again. We had a lot in common and got on incredibly well in general. I explained to her that I had done the bankruptcy to sort things out and tidy all the debris and stress. She did not flinch. I deliberately did not ask her about the big win she had originally seen. After the bankruptcy I did not want to get hooked up on it all again. I wanted to enjoy my time in Ireland. So much of the last chapter in Dalkey had been under a cloud of debt and stress. I was simply relieved to be back, lighter and brighter.

Of course being highly psychic, Anke sensed this, and she subtly reassured me about the win. She recounted a fairly recent story about the son of a client who had just won seven Million or so. It had shown in his mother's tea leaf reading. The letter "P" with the 7 beside it, and the money symbols. Anke was correct in this prediction, and she has been correct in many more. Another woman was given numbers to do in the bookies, claiming she would share a huge chunk of her winnings if the numbers hit. Of course she did hit, and then did not share a damn cent with Anke. A very sweet older client had also won on numbers, and he trundled all the way to see her on the bus to hand her a couple of grand. What a difference in gratitude.

Anke and I have talked about how clients react differently to information and results, and it is indeed a very complex phenomenon. Some will claim the psychic has not assisted at all. They quickly forget what a state they were in when they first sought out help; and they proceed to take credit when the results start to come in. Their karma will no doubt be interesting. Still others remember the help a genuine psychic gives, and they honor it in gratitude. This is the way it should be. In the olden days psychics would be paid with bread and wine and accommodation if needed. Their material needs were provided for in exchange for information. Nothing much has changed, except perhaps the accusatory aspect is more insidious when the timing of predictions gets a bit funky.

A visionary psychic like Anke will see the event. She may not always get the timing precisely right. I have absolute confidence in her seeing. But not so much her timing, especially not for something as possibly far reaching as a lottery win. But she has a nose for cash, and is able to help her clients in all sorts of situations. She sees politicians, lawyers, many male clients, and even jockeys and gamblers. Nothing is beyond her remit. She regularly wins herself on three numbers on the euro. She has the funds to put down a substantial bet, and one euro bet, will sometimes bring her a return of seventy eight thousand. Not a bad day's work.

Anke is very gifted with psychology, and you certainly do not want her as an enemy. By her own admission, when out on the spot she can be the proverbial cornered rat, and the outcome is probably not pretty. Anke is brilliant in many ways. Even when I was talking about possible bankruptcy rather than winning, she stated that all would be well "something always happens." She is correct. Something always *does*.

Anke was a very effective, and spooky psychic, who gave good advice. But a couple of friends got led astray, like Rosalind who just loved Michael Flatley, and who wanted to get into the film business. She was told she would be with Michael, and obviously that did not go too well for her. To this day, she thinks Anke is a fraud and a con artist. I heard of someone else who had had a misleading reading by coincidence, when I went to view a flat to rent some years later. But I am not sure it *was* a misleading reading at all. As Anke herself says, people hear what they want to hear much of the time. I have noticed this myself as a reader, and there is a huge responsibility to make sure that your client really *does* understand what you are saying. People have very selective hearing, let alone memories, especially when they are clamoring to hear the good stuff.

In recent years I have spent hours on the phone to Anke, sorting out the world, and having a good laugh. It is a sadness for me, that this friendship is no more. After the Donncha offense, I eventually returned to Ireland, and Anke and I gave things another chance. While I was living in Porlock, Anke's mother had sadly passed. I knew this, I presume because her mother presented to me. Anke kept coming to mind, and it crossed my mind that her mother must have passed. I was repeatedly prompted to phone Anke out of the blue, after many months. Eventually I gave in and dialed that number again.

Throughout our estrangement I had intermittently kept in touch and left messages on the phone that she never answered. They were friendly messages sent unconditionally. I was not trying to annoy her. I only left messages spasmodically, when prompted, from the heart. I had apologized long ago, probably several times, for the Donncha *faux pas*. Even though I did not really feel I had to justify myself on that one, for the sake of a good friendship, I did so.

On the repeating promptings of her mother, I dialed up Anke again and left a message for her. I then tried again a couple of days later and she picked up. She had felt she should pick up the call. Anke never picks up the calls from her work phone, so this was exceptionally significant. We reconnected gingerly. I was pleased, and it felt right that her mother had been a bridge for this. I then picked up more about her mother, and left her another message a couple of days later which proved to be spot on accurate, and which brought comfort to the whole family. I found myself describing how her mother was laid out, and there were various messages for family members too. Anke was moved, and I was genuinely delighted to have been the channel for these messages. This is where the skills of a medium *can* be so helpful and healing for people. Not much more than a year later, I was about to find out how and why psychic medium messages may *not* always be helpful and healing for people.

Dalkey proved to be very different second time around. But I settled in eventually after some weeks of doubt and turmoil. I was a little panicked still. The sensation of being back was odd, and unexpected. I liked it in one way. But in another it felt out of time, as well as a step back in time.

Sometimes Brian managed to be there for stretches of time. Sometimes he did not. We enjoyed the connection with Anke for a few months. Brian at one remove though, as he never met or spoke to her directly. Both Aquarians, Anke and Brian probably would have had a lot to say to each other. We knew that they would have either loved or hated each other. Aquarians tend to either get on profoundly well, or else have serious issues. There is not much middle ground. So I think the energy of these two powerful psychics was not mixed as a matter of personal choice. Both Anke and Brian had the measure of each other, and probably decided that some distance might be wise. Sometimes psychics meet their match, or should I say, they choose not to. The meeting never happened. So we never found out how combustible or conducive it might be.

My second fall out with Anke maybe held a clue. Brian indirectly went and put his foot in it. On the anniversary of her mum's passing, Anke was understandably still very upset about her mother. This is of course perfectly understandable, and everyone should be allowed to feel grief and pace themselves in their own way. How we come to terms with the passing of a loved one is totally individual, and there is no formula for coping with grief. We have to ride it as best we can.

What concerned Brian and I about Anke, was that she was drinking every month on the date of her mother's passing. This is fine, and her choice. But it inspired a message which Brian received for her from her mother. The message urged her not to let life pass her by in grieving, and to appreciate once again the joy of life, the grass, the outdoors, the sun on her face. It was a lengthy message which I relayed to Anke on the phone. I had not remembered it was the anniversary of her passing to the day, so this message must have felt quite raw to hear. However, because the first messages had helped her so much, we anticipated, or hoped that this would too.

I spoke the message for Anke onto her answer phone. Clearly I should not have done this, as she very quickly went into evasive action and shut down mode, and never spoke to me again as a friend. I got information messages from Anke through Grainne a mutual contact, another psychic and colleague, who had introduced us in the first place. I was not best pleased Anke was talking about me to someone else. She had always said she never did this. Clearly she actually did. She did not have the guts to phone me and have it all out with me. Finally, after I heard what she was thinking, I phoned her myself and she picked up when she heard my voice. She had been drinking, and had the full intention of letting me have it with both barrels. #charming.

I first had gone to Grainne for a reading after she did a newspaper article with predictions in a Sunday newspaper. She had done some celebrity predictions in her piece, and some commentary on U2 was amongst them. when I first arrived in Ireland the first time, this person read for me, and picked up the connection between Bono and I. A Taurus man was strongly featured in my reading, and she even came up with the name Paul right at the end. She spoiled it by saying Paul Mc Guinness. But that was perfectly forgivable really, as Paul was of course the manager of Paul Hewson, aka Bono. All in all it was rather impressive from someone who previously knew nothing.

Grainne then referred me onto Anke, the White Witch of Wicklow, who latched onto the whole thing and ran with it for many months and years. As with all referrals from this person, Anke got the picture quickly. She told me later that Anke picked up a "seven day wonder" in the newspapers about Bono and I when we officially got it together. She was seeing headlines in the papers about the relationship when they first discussed me. It was not what I wanted to hear, and technically speaking I did not think ethically they should be discussing me without knowing me, and even then not really a cool thing to do. But the information is amusing to me now. Seven day wonder indeed. Seven years, and some, more like. Guess it could still be true right? Kidding.

Both Anke, and Grainne have been my intermittent friends and support for a long time. Sometimes they are talking to me, sometimes they are not. I was eventually told that Anke had not been pleased about the message I had relayed to her from Brian. I was upset about this since the first message from her mother had brought her such comfort. It was a great shame this second message brought her such annoyance and distress. I did not know what to do. Once I had the explanation, I phoned to apologize, and Anke picked up the phone. She had obviously been having a drink, and she laid into me unceremoniously and said she was offended and would speak to me again, except to shout at me at this point. She was mean and nasty. I was horrified, as I would have thought it perfectly obvious I was trying to help her not hurt her with relaying Brian's message.

Perhaps what Brian had said had struck an uncomfortable chord. Brian is edgy, and sometimes this can happen with what he picks up. He is not wrong, but he can produce uncomfortable insights sometimes. Anke if anyone should have understood this, as she is exactly the same. Such insights which touch a nerve, potentially bring a deep healing, if the client is willing to process them. Anke clearly was not able to receive the message quite yet. I wrote her a long letter, and actually wrote the message out for her again. hoping it would read better than it sounded. Our intention was to help her not cause her more distress. I also explained that I was offended at how she had spoken to me. I doubt we will ever speak again. I am not reaching out to her intermittently like I did the first time she ignored me. I am not moved to do so. This is a shame, and not like me. But I warned her that I too had reached my limit. I think it is her turn to reach out to me. She does not have to apologize. But in terms of equality, and friendship I think this would be appropriate. I know she will never do so, and I do not expect it. No doubt she would be offended to hear me say such a thing. So be it.

I have great memories of Anke. She is talented, funny and has a wicked way of putting things. She will say it is my own stupid fault for passing on what Brian had said to me. I should have known better. She told anonymous she thought I was phoning her to try to get a reaction so that she would then return my call. This is absolutely not the case. I was being totally unconditional with her, and sincerely hoping she would get comfort from Brian's message. We genuinely hoped the message would help her, just as the first one had done. She is psychic, so she knows this. I just wonder quite why she has taken this way out from our connection. Part of her is hiding behind it perhaps. But whatever. That is her prerogative. I did express in the letter that she would perhaps come to resonate with Brian's words at a later stage. So hopefully this is the case. I very much doubt it. But we live in hope.

What on earth is to be done with all these temperamental psychics? Anke, Grainne, and I were a bit of a trio at one point. We witches three. Now, clearly times have changed. Life moves on. As Anke said in her mean phone call. "stuff happens in life, and you will just have to accept this." Anke was adamant she would not forgive me, which to my mind is heartless. I would never say that to anyone I do not think, especially not to someone I knew had been trying to help me. Probably I am missing something here, and others will see exactly what she meant. It left me somewhat baffled, and hurt for some time. It actually stacks up to me as a bit of an excuse. I am not sure why. I am a supportive, fun and interesting friend to have. Clearly she did not feel she needed such entertainment any more. Fair enough.

The great shame of course is that when I hit big on the lottery, I will not be able to get her that family holiday I had promised. Knowing me, I will weaken and honor my pledge. Brian advises me to tell her the money has come in and then wait for her to return the call. That would indeed be amusing. But I am beyond such games at this stage. As you can see being a psychic is just as difficult personally as it is professionally. It is not an easy burden to bear. If even those who you would think would understand do not, how are you supposed to reach people who have even less of a clue?

To this day I get phone calls from people down the country in Ireland randomly asking "what's for me?" I encourage them to book an appointment to see. But there is a pushiness and expectation with such client's that is difficult to deal with. They hate it when you tell them what they do not want to hear. But it is always the responsibility of a reader to be excruciatingly honest. The skeptics assumption that psychics are out there lying to people, is just not true. Not in my experience anyway. I certainly would never justify that. I always tell clients the truth and they know this.

Interpretation of messages is sometimes tricky, as is timing of events to come. Really there is a lot to be said for knowing that certain events are stacked up to happen, and then getting on with life in the present. Readings can start to feed fantasy. It is not always beneficial to be told things well in advance of their occurrence. This knowledge can rob you of life in the here and now.

Technically, Anke could be right about the huge lottery win. But when? Does it land when I am eighty years old? I asked her this, and she said absolutely not. But, obviously now, I do wonder. An event is scheduled to happen when it happens. Is it set in stone? Can it be created or manifested? Certain things can be yes. But the big destiny moments are not up for grabs.

Being professional psychic is a huge stress. Not only are you often misrepresented, you can also be maligned and doubted. It is wonderful when you help clients in the privacy of a consultation or your work together. But there are ethical standards as with all professions. It is not possible to broadcast the successes from the roof tops, since clients want to maintain their privacy. I absolutely cannot break confidences and share all the success stories. Some things have to be taken on trust.

I have proved myself in public repeatedly on radio and television, and in the newspapers. So that does set a precedent of reliability. Indeed it is how many of my client's find me. That, and word of mouth referrals. I have various public testimonials on display on my web site www.sarahdelamer.com.

I admit the tag Psychic Sarah took some getting used to. In the early days of me sticking my neck out to do this work, the various shots of me sporting a grin, sheepishly holding a crystal ball, were a bit much. It took me a long time to learn to detach from the image, and realize it was just a media presentation. It was expected, and people got what I was about through the image. Problem was, I did not think that they did. I really was not a fortune teller and I certainly did not want to be presented as one. But really there was no other way to present the psychic stuff on television, radio and in magazines. It was the nature of the beast. It was not really me; and yet it was. I just had to get used to it. The media work was initially a steep learning curve. The lessons continued for quite some time. But stepping out into the limelight as a fortune teller was so far removed from what I had been brought up to be, or envisaged for myself; that at times I freaked out. I have to say it has taken all my powers of integration to make sense of it all. God certainly does move in mysterious ways.

The second Christmas back in Ireland was a miserable time for me. Tree 3 was up, and I could enjoy that at least. Brian and I had begun to number the Christmas trees to mark the duration of our connection. The Christmas trees sure did seem to be clocking up and time ticking by without any fundamental change to the situation. I was still in Europe, and Brian was still largely stateside. Once again I was on my own for Christmas. The Psychic Society were throwing all sorts of legal threats in my direction, for no good reason. They had stopped supporting my work, and had started to turn on me. Even though I was obviously being targeted with some kind of personal vendetta, I was coming under suspicion. It was totally unjustified suspicion. I was always truthful, authentic, and got amazing results, as you can see from the testimonies. I suspected a couple of sources of the cowardly attacks; but one theory was particularly likely and persuasive.

The Psychic Society had been getting weird complaints about me, and some very odd emails. Sound familiar re the emails thing? The CEO described the tone and content of the emails to me, without giving me their direct contents. The emails were obviously from an immature, jealous, angry person. They sent them anonymously through the company web site in an attempt to discredit me, or cast doubts about me. Someone thought it was funny to try to undermine my good name and prestige on the panel. The Psychic Society is a fake name for the purposes of this account. If anyone recognizes themselves in the story, it is entirely accidental. One might ask *why* you are seeing yourself in something that is actually nothing to do with you? Names throughout this account have been changed and identities preserved, unless the protagonist's are obviously public figures. Okay, you get my point.

At this time all of a sudden I had a myriad of problems of a quite extraordinary nature. Many unusual challenges and events were kicking off around me. The dogs became a major issue, and I started to have a contretemps out of the blue with the Tubbermore Avenue landlords. I had understood it was okay for me to have my dogs in the property. Apparently it was not. I am usually protected regarding my accommodation and the dogs. But I met the landlady randomly on Killiney Hill on 23rd December. I did not remember her very well, but I *do* remember catching the energy of an accusatory glance from a female of a certain age, whilst on my walk. In retrospect I realized it was the landlady giving me the "evil eye" for keeping company with my four little dogs. Very quickly I got a formal letter from the landlord asking me to get rid of the dogs so that I could stay there as a tenant. He was not even adverse to me putting them down, so that he could keep his tenant. I was horrified. Especially as I ultimately found out they actually had a dog themselves. I refused, and started to investigate my rights and the legalities. I began an elaborate stalling interaction with the landlord trying to hold onto my home. I explained that many inspections had been done, and that the dogs had caused no identifiable problems whatsoever. He persisted in his view that he thought the house too small for four little dogs. I assured him it was not, and that they were always out with me on the beach or the hill, or else sleeping, and talking quietly amongst themselves.

The landlord was not budging from his position which I found so unreasonable and strange. I am usually quite persuasive, and he was almost being illogical in his demands. I had been there for a couple of years and nothing untoward had happened to the property. I took a rain check and asked myself what was *really* going on with the situation. It started to all look like a device to eject me from Ireland once again, or at least from my home with Brian.

I was given official notice, and that very same afternoon, saw a removal company flattening shipping boxes just up the road. A couple had just moved into one of the large houses on Sorrento Road from London, and they freely allowed me to have the boxes, as long as I gave a donation to their favorite children's charity. Within twenty-four hours I had been given notice, acquired boxes, and had pretty much packed to leave my home. Oddly, these were American shipping boxes, so I began to prepare for what I thought might be a move to America.

The next day, I went to the beach with the dogs, and found a green letter "P" on the beach. It was one of those plastic letters from a child's learning-to-spell set. I knew from this that I was returning home to Portishead, where I was brought up. Do not ask me *how* I knew this, but know this I did. It made some sense to have some time near home before a move to America. I was happy enough with the idea. If I was going to ultimately be stateside for some time, it was actually a good idea to have some family time beforehand.

The irony is, I had literally just settled back into living in Ireland again. The day before I met the landlady on the hill, I had decided that I would be okay in Ireland, and would settle there, even if Brian was not going to move over. I knew he was not going to, and I was not longer sure what to do about getting to America myself. I had hoped we would live and work together, but Brian had a big block on living with so many dogs. He had a running joke that my pack of dogs multiplied by at least four every time he visited. I guess it must have seemed that way.

The truth is, he was amazing with the dogs, and helped me heal them through various health mishaps and struggles. Both Lottie and Mollie are still alive thanks to our mutual healing efforts. The female dogs both had mishaps with their backs and mobility, and Lottie was even paralyzed for a time. The vet had suggested putting her down one weekend. We said a resounding "no." I consulted another vet the following week, and he was supportive of a steroid, rest and healing approach. Thankfully it worked, and Lottie is fine again Patience, healing, and knowing what dose of steroid to give and when, saved her and got her well. Today she is running around causing havoc with the nest of them Thanks to Brian, "creature," aka Lottie, the dogs who suffers, and needs a lot of sympathy and encouragement, still lives.

Brian also seemed to have a big block on getting married, even to facilitate a visa and my immigration. I understood this. I never wanted to be someone who married for any kind of perfunctory reason. It would have been a practical idea, but Brian was not open to helping me in this way. A mutual friend, voice over artist on an extremely popular Disney series, offered to marry me to facilitate my visa, to help us both out. But on researching it, he soon realized he would be committing a felony if he did so, and backed down. I would not have taken him up on that offer anyway for a myriad of reasons. But it was a kind gesture nonetheless. Interestingly, my second marriage proposal with a visa-related flavor, came from an openly gay man, famous for playing a posh zebra, and some hyenas in a Hollywood cartoon. Score. Thank you K. Your kind heart precedes you. Woof!

There was no doubt the universe was unceremoniously ejecting me from Ireland for a second time. Anke had told me she would never speak to me again. A string of things were happening on the back of this. I had a neighbor turning up drunk on my doorstep randomly threatening me about some rubbish in the street. He did not believe my explanation that the refuse company had forgotten to collect that week, and that I had organized them to come the next morning to sort it. I had to email the evidence to him to prove my point. This irate jerk of a neighbor was breathing his fumes into my face, and not budging. I had to call Brian from inside the house to come and see him off.

I then had a man follow me in intimidating fashion because he thought I cut past him at the roundabout in my car, at the other end of the village. I drove around the Dalkey roads, and this old guy with a grey beard and disheveled hair was stalking me in his car the whole way. I contemplated driving straight to the Garda station, but in the end I stopped near my house, and he got out of his car and started screaming at me. Again for no good reason. I just stared at him incredulously.

This energy was absolutely abnormal and crazy. Something was clearly going on. A couple of days later, I then had my car totaled by two little old ladies doing a totally illegal U-turn down by Select Stores in Dalkey. I was driving innocently down the road, and they pulled out sharp from behind a jeep in front of me. Not my fault. They sat in the car and stared at me. I drove off, not wanting to traumatize them further. Of course legally I should not have done so. But I reported the incident as soon as I could; as did they.

There was a horrible week or so, where the Garda in charge of the case was debating if to prosecute both parties for leaving the scene of the accident. But thankfully, he saw sense, and left it to the insurance companies to sort amongst themselves. It took some clever resistance, detailed accounts, photographs, and explanations to counter the old lady's claims that it was my fault. I succeeded, with the help of Brian, who knew what to say and when to say it, and the upshot was

I got a new Silver Puma with undamaged bodywork.

This was a good result, and shows that if you keep your cool, even trauma and drama can turn around as order is restored. The battered black Puma, actually needed to be totaled. It had seen better days, and its couple of years of driving around country roads in Cornwall, and then Porlock had not served it particularly well. Only a few days before all this Bono had generously called it a "sports car", up on Vico Road, even as I joked it was a battered old go-cart. "Look at you in your sports car", was the comment that greeted me, when I pulled in to say "hello" to Bono and his wife.

I had been doing absent healing work for Bono on his injuries, after the nasty bike accident in Central Park, and I wanted to see how he was progressing. As usual he warmly greeted me, and grasped my hand over the heads of several barking dogs.

Crazy lady.

Bono said he still had some numbness in his hand, because of the damaged nerve endings. But overall significant improvements. It was good to see him for the first time in a number of years. I am not sure how much of a buzz there still was. But it is always good to see him, whenever our paths cross. His parting words are frequently "see you on down the road," which of course makes total sense for a rock and roll star who is only intermittently at home. As per his historical pattern, he tends to appear when I need a bit of energetic support or encouragement. I was certainly going through the ringer, so this was a good reconnection, however fleeting. His wife was gracious, beguiling, and quietly smiling, as always.

All of these crazy events were not even the worst of it. One night I opened the door to find a load of maggots wriggling up the garden path, literally trying to get into the house. Things were hardly looking up. You will see why it was tricky not to conclude that a curse or some wealth of ill- feeling towards me might be playing out.

Curses in their various forms are real enough, and their manifestations can be serious. Those suffering evil intentions from some unknown source, may well experience very invasive, odd events like these. There is also the possible indignity of not being taken seriously if one dares to point it all out. Many healers and light-workers will dismiss such concerns, saying "look what you have attracted to yourself to understand why this is all happening." Or, "No human could conjure such things to inflict upon another." But this is a bit of a cop-out. One can be clear energetically, having processed a myriad of issues, and *still* have this happen. In actual fact, this is probably when it *does* happen. It is another example of being tested. The challenge is to balance these more sophisticated karmic manifestations. Standing your ground in the midst of what may, or may not, have been done to you, is a very tricky lesson.

Silence is generally the best way to deal with such things. I had to be very careful with all of this going on. I had to keep a level head, and my feet on the ground. I stayed fairly detached, though would have been deeply upset if I gave it too much attention or importance. It is very crucial not to feed the energy by acknowledging it or giving in to fear. That gives it the upper hand. I was determined to be normal and take it in my stride. I acted like these were all separate events, and not in the least bit connected; though deep down I knew they were. Quite possibly they were manifestations of hideous energy or psychic attack directed at me. I was not even going to give it the dignity of trying to work it all out.

I did not get too freaked out, and deliberately maintained detachment for sake of self preservation. The most unpleasant part was the interminable wait to see if I was going to be prosecuted for driving away from the old ladies. The maggots on the pathway were not much better. But I dealt with them by pouring boiling water right onto their slimy white heads. Immediate stillness. Perhaps I froze further progression of the energy with that action, as things did settle after that.

I did not feed the drama going on at all. But I had no one to talk about it with really. The best medicine was to laugh it off with Brian, even though in truth I felt bombarded and unsupported on all sides. I was on my own with this one. I had to pack up, prepare to leave Ireland again, when I desperately wanted to stay, and deal with all this bullshit from my home base.

Psychic, spiritual, and energy attacks can produce some very tangible phenomenon. Curses if they are done effectively can conjure up negative attachments, spiritual haunting, and psychic oppression. So this is a serious matter, and it pays to know what you may or may not be dealing with. Discernment and wisdom should be key responses.

Hexes, ill-wishes, jinxes and curses are all evil intentions designed to bring someone down. Even hoping that some misadventure will befall someone or that something bad will happen in a general sense can take on the life of a curse. It is important to be aware that our thoughts are powerful, and that we have the creative capacity to cause a whole lot of harm with our bad intentions. Such thoughts, wishes and deeds have serious consequences for the perpetrator. Some may not realize that the power of the curse reflects back three fold, sometimes ten-fold on the person creating it. So unless you really have major super natural powers of self protection, there is no good that can come of harboring such resentments. Even if you actively dislike someone it pays to keep your thoughts and wishes as pure as possible. Bless them rather than curse them, for your own good if nothing else.

The power of the curse lies in the imaginative projection of ill will. You do not have to take out the spell book or do some elaborate ritual to cause yourself a whole lot of harm, even as you wish harm on someone else. Some say that a curse will work only if the target receiver is aware of it. Certainly this helps as the person's fear feeds the energy and the curse can thereby become a self inflicted misery. However, this is not the full picture. An experienced spell caster can cause merry havoc on someone and although they may not actively be aware of what has been done, they still can experience some pretty puzzling and unnatural consequences. An effective curse however makes itself known pretty quickly, and measures can then be taken to avert the tide of destruction. There are specific ways to return this energy to sender. Plus, under universal law the guilty party has already set themselves up for a pay back, unless they are phenomenally well protected.

Many of us acknowledge positive energy as a force we can recognize and measure. But not so many of us are willing to recognize that negative energy is also real and can be pretty damned destructive if we do not have the means to deal with it swiftly.

Everything is energy. If we can focus energy and move it positively for good; then unfortunately the reverse is also true. A curse is an energy attachment planted on someone to harm or hold them in place. As described it has an impact on the caster. But there are ways around this, and expert casters know how to ground the consequences of their actions elsewhere. Usually the consequence will befall the person asking or paying the caster. In the voodoo cultures, witch doctors, and aboriginal cultures this would very much be the case.

What we need to understand is that we are powerful energetic beings and that none of us are exceptions to the rule ultimately. God sees all. Some may believe that cursing is a good way to get rid of our own negative emotions. But the boomerang effect and main law of magic is that whatever we put out there into the universe *will* return to us times three. An act of revenge or malevolence will always return to haunt the perpetrator. Whoever, or whatever was causing all this funky stuff to happen to me, could expect to have quite some return for their efforts. Not least because I am able to stand firm and deal with such things. I will not say I have no fear. But I am stubborn, and no one treats the Mermaid thus, and gets away with it. #shame.

WILL NEVER APOLOGIZE FOR THINKING DIFFERENTLY, FEELING DEEPLY, AND LOVING UNCONDITIONALLY.

CHAPTER THIRTY-ONE
It's a Dog's Life

I am sitting on a few secrets it is true. Secrets which have at times given rise to the temptation to sell my soul for a buck or two. But whatever kiss and tell urge may have flickered across my mind for a fleeting second, I knew in my heart that I could never follow it through. I was just not that sort of girl. Besides in terms of salacious detail, my tale was hardly overtly scandalous. I wonder if I would have discredited myself, or gained a weird kind of respect if I had done so? Neither I suspect; but the answer to that we will never know. The journalist in me was tempted: the compassionate, self-respecting Sarah was not.

In protecting certain people including myself, I have had to keep quiet and suffer in silence much of the time. Perhaps I did put myself under even more pressure than I had to. But, maybe if I had done a tabloid tale or two, *Mermaid in The Kitchen* would never have happened. The tale has to be transparent and honest; but definitely not destructive. I did sound-out a couple of well heeled contacts along the way about a sponsorship, mentoring type deal. But I fully understand why that was not appropriate. We do not live in the day and age of hand-outs. Besides mentoring for the kind of work that I do probably does not give the man of the world any kind of return. Whatever the skeptics might think, the work I have been doing has not brought me anywhere close to being a millionaire. In fact it has kept me on a very tight reign.

I was not willing to trade on my name and good reputation by setting up a fully fledged psychic line business. I did not want to be responsible for what other psychics might tell someone. Having researched the subject so extensively, and experienced so many kinds of readings, I was not happy to sell this on to the public. My own readings? Yes, I trusted those. The readings of others? I could not in all honesty vouch for. So rather than cash in, I kept my integrity.

I obviously have a healthy respect for those in my profession because I am aware of the difficulties involved. But, I could only ever sanction my own work. I certainly did not want to be reprimanded for someone else's. Nor did I wish to cynically cash in on the profile I had built up. So, my situation and choices have very much enforced the need to keep at it.

As with many of us in this profession, what is coming in just about covers what is going out. May be I am in line for that lottery win, who knows? I certainly win regularly on three and four numbers out of seven. But the conclusion thus far is that early retirement does not seem to be an option when you are on a spiritual path of this nature. It may be a puzzle to some people why I stopped reading for people during this time. It actually got to a point where I felt that I would be not acting in integrity if I were doing this work simply for money. So I stopped as soon as I felt I was not able to give my clients one hundred percent commitment. After several years of helping people in very productive ways, it was time to step back and sort myself out. Besides, I wanted to develop my writing career and it had started to become possible to help people through the media. I was reaching a broader wider audience, and it was not always essential to do one on one readings. I have had plenty of feedback that I was also helping people through what they were reading in the papers, or hearing on the radio.

I had felt since the age of seventeen, that I would eventually be published. I just did not anticipate that it would come about in this way. The intuition was strong. The means by which it would happen; I left to fate. In fact the three things I knew for sure at the age of seventeen have all come about in some shape or form since I moved to Dublin. One involves writing; the other involves Bono, not in a scandalous way I hasten to add; and I am still trying to recall the third.

On the back of my well known *Irish Popstars* prediction, the papers embraced my work and I have not looked back since. The media work seemed to be an ideal platform on which to build a writing career, and surely my publisher would surely not baulk at the idea of me having a bit more of a profile? There was a need for money yes. But I did not have the time, energy or inclination to continue what had actually become quite a lucrative healing practice. Even though I had taken the time and trouble to build a business, as soon as the vocational aspect changed I had to put the brakes on. Out of integrity, when my work was at the height of its demand, I stopped. It was yet another illogical, but totally unavoidable decision, guaranteed to give the bank manager, and myself, restless nights.

I have been assured that, because I have not sold out despite the various tests I have been going through, God will not leave me without funds. In fact, according to Anke's persistent prediction I am on course to win that large amount of money. There were times where I would have considered such a win a kind of compensation for all that

I have been through. I honestly would have chosen to bypass that win and not suffer in the ways I have suffered. But if it proves to be some kind of karmic reward for being obedient and listening to my calling, then I will take it. I am not longer in a position where I need it to happen. That in itself is liberating. The reality is, it is very dangerous to be told you are going to win money. It spikes curiosity, and "when" is the obvious next question. Such energies are notoriously difficult to predict. I find that there is an element of pushing something away too, when we incessantly ask "when." It could almost be said to be irresponsible to tell a client they are going to win money. There would be the human temptation to live as if it has already happened, and then any frustration about money would obviously be compounded if the win does not come in quickly.

As Anke has demonstrated, if there is a win in your destiny, there is a win in your destiny. They say it is impossible to win on the lottery. But one thing is for sure, you are definitely not going to win if you do not buy a ticket. Anke used to say to me, " you are going to win, but if you do not, the money from your books will be amazing enough in itself." She was in effect saying, I would be on course for a prolific writing income also. Again, we will see.

Throughout the tests I have endured, I have lost count of the amazing ways money has come to me. I sometimes have to get creative. I know how to work the banking system with the help of spirit. My high end computer was actually paid for by the bank through a clerical error as Halifax Ireland closed down. So instead of paying well over two thousand euro for a computer, I paid only four hundred. I have had checks paid through by banks that should have been declined. I have found money, won money, been given money, and earned money. Money has many ways in which it can flow to us. We just have to be open. I have been in some nerve wracking situations. But have learned to trust. I am always delivered and looked after. Eki used to say my multi colored circular purse in Scotland was magic.

There was always money in it. She was right, there was.

Along the way, if I have wanted particular clothes, I have been able to manifest the means to get them. If I have needed to buy a meal, do a trip, or register for a course, or even buy a dog, there has always been a way to achieve it . Sometimes, often times, I get a deliverance at the last minute. A miracle occurs, and the required item or event I have wanted or needed comes about.

I usually know spirit is engineering a move of house when for some inexplicable reason I suddenly do not have rent. I have lost count of the number of times I have been moved on to the next wonderful place in this way. I end up using my using my deposit for the final month's rent, then look around for the right place. Very quickly I find it, and usually it is the only one I have to look at. I get it, money comes in, and the move is on. I realized that spirit was shifting energy every time I moved, and I grew to see it as a cleansing and clearing process.

That prediction of having to move three or four times in eighteenth months certainly proved to be correct. Every six months, some issue arose, such as a landlord selling, or a rent increase, or a need to make a quick exit. I came to see Dalkey and Killiney as my home, and did not get too hooked up on the bricks and motor. As long as I was in the correct area, it worked for me. What was interesting was that every move I made in that time, progressed me further. I had six months in a mouldy mews after the Railway Road apartment; then came the Bedroom Studio Apartment in Castle Street Dalkey. Harley the dog got sick and died in this one. My Christmas present that year, was a taxi driver bringing my dead dog home from University College Dublin hospital, all wrapped up in his blanket. "Player" was being a jerk just to top it all off nicely. Merry Christmas!

I then headed up to Killiney and was ensconced right next to The Fitzpatrick's Hotel, occasional residency of the rugby team. I could swim at night, and the hotel was an extension of my apartment next door. This situation ended badly. My lovely Black Ford coupe was reacquired by the bank, and I was six weeks without any money for rent. Oddly, this was all coordinated by the universe. It was a testing time though, maintaining my faith that things would work out. I knew they always did, but sometimes the protracted vacuums where I had to await the will of God were beyond spectacular.

Mollie the dog, now had Jake her life's companion, and we all needed a bigger place. Suddenly, I was down to the last week in the Killiney apartment with no more wriggle room. I saw Beacon Hill advertised on the property web site on Daft.ie, and took the plunge. It was more rent still, but all of a sudden I had both rent and deposit, and was able to do the move. The dogs and I loved this place.

Beacon Hill, which runs parallel to the far end of Sorrento Road towards the sea, houses the old customs houses. Situated on the small hill above Coliemore harbor in Dalkey, the grounds of the four or five slate grey houses are set up in commune style. Accessed by a magical, charming, private steep laneway off Nerano Road, this is a hidden oasis. My neighbors were wonderful, friendly Russians, and kind Irish families. I was in heaven. It literally felt very heavenly. I was woken by the most spectacular sunrises, and the bath tub was big enough for about three people. Not that I tried that. But it was Mermaid heaven nonetheless. It was my ultimate place in Ireland. My days spent between number 1, Beacon Hill and Killiney Beach were wonderfully therapeutic.

I spent an idyllic couple of years in my bedroom overlooking the Nerano statue of the sailor looking out to sea. Erected in memory of a son who never came home, it became somewhat symbolic of me never getting home to see my family. I did not know if I would ever see them again. I had to knuckle down and sort my situation. Beacon Hill was my final home in Ireland, before leaving to do the bankruptcy in Cornwall. I absolutely loved this magical setting. Even when it snowed, Beacon Hill was charming. We got stranded up there a few times, and it was pretty treacherous attempting the descent into Dalkey village. It really was the best place I have ever lived I think. I was very sad when it came to a very abrupt untimely end. I was literally propelled out of there with immaculate timing. It was all my choice, all my own doing. As usual when a move was needed, the rent was not there for the last month. The deposit covered that, and I took it as always to the last possible moment. I had never unpacked into Beacon Hill, and my boxes were already in storage, the dogs and the effects I would need for Cornwall were jammed in the car. I left the keys in an envelope on the door, and departed. I gather the landlady showed up twenty minutes later. I just missed her. It was time to go to Cornwall, to the house on the cliff I had been paying for since October. Even though I did not want to leave Ireland, I had Cornwall as my safe house. It was my official home for a few months before I even arrived there. How ironic that someone on the brink of choosing bankruptcy had the use of two beautiful houses by the sea.

As usual, God, spirit and my intuition timed my exit to perfection. My things were put into storage ready to do the move, and I had to put myself and five dogs into the car and get the hell out of there. I was not thrown out. But I needed to get away from what had become a scary situation with the landlord. We had had a misunderstanding about the dogs and my renovations on the house. He had told me I could take the carpet up in the front room. I did this, And proceeded to do it on the stairs too and my bedroom. It was so much more practical with the dogs. He did give his permission for all this; but seemed to conveniently forget this when it was time to carpet the place again. He rightly kept my deposit, but wanted more. Obviously having done bankruptcy, I was not able to help him out there. It was also not my obligation to do so.

I had been living at Beacon Hill with seven little dogs. They loved the house and the communal gardens, and the neighbors all enjoyed the puppies as they were born and grew. Mollie and Jake, had made five puppies. I knew this was on the cards after Jake arrived. As soon as he met Mollie, I then got the name of a third dog Charlie. I had no intention of buying any more dogs, so I then knew it was inevitable that Mollie would have Jake's pups. One thing was very clear, Charlie was going to be important.

Sure enough, nature took its course. Mollie and Jake were both young, and really they were at the youngest they should be to have puppies. It was dangerous enough for Mollie, and she did have a few problems with feeding the dogs afterwards. I had to wean them under the vet's guidance, as Mollie very quickly got a calcium deficiency which threatened her life. She went off to the UCD training hospital for the night, and thankfully did not return wrapped up in a package by taxi as Harley had done. I was able to go and collect my still living, though wobbly and weak, dog.

While pregnant, Mollie was like a football as she was carrying five pups. I loved the experience of looking after her through pregnancy, and then helping her birth the five puppies was just amazing. I am so glad I had this experience with my dogs. It was a real blessing and healing thing. There was an indescribable feeling of joy when all the pups arrived. I actually felt a hole in my heart had been plugged. I received an incredible emotional repair from the whole thing. Not quite sure why, and it might sound a bit odd. But I knew I finally had my own family.

This may all seem a bit strange, obviously dogs are not a human family. But after everything I had been through, and all the disappointments, this unforeseen development was totally beneficial. I loved every minute of the process. I helped Mollie with her birthing plan, and she rested on my belly as I lay on the floor between puppies. She pushed one out every twenty to thirty minutes, so there was quite a gap between them. Out they all came one by one: Ralphie Boy, Charlie, Accrington Stanley, Lottie, and Penny. I saved Penny as she was born. She was tiny and lifeless covered in film. I gently washed that off and rubbed her into life, Jake also helped and licked all the puppies for Mollie. He was every bit as caring as Mollie was. It is not true that the adult male dog gets jealous. Not in my experience anyway. Jake was a loving partner to Mollie, and a caring dad to his pups. He looked just as shell shocked as any new father when all the puppies arrived. It was quite charming to see how the dog family did not behave that differently to us humans.

The journey with the dogs was charming beyond words. But I now had rather a lot of dogs to deal with. Gavin, came to see the puppies, as he and his partner were agreeing on dogs for Christmas. Gavin's father had bred bull dogs, But Gavin saw the dachshunds, and fell in love. I assured him that they were big dogs in little bodies, and he was sold. I knew this was for the best, but I was initially heartbroken too. For six months I had been managing with seven dogs. This was not realistic in the long term; but it sure was fun in the interim. Gavin saved the day, and gave two of the male dogs a wonderful home. Stan and Ralf fell on their little paws, and remain ensconced up on Bono's campus for the duration. When we randomly meet on the beach, they all still know each other as family. That bond is so sweet to see.

On the morning Ralph and Stan were due to go to Gavin's house, I woke with Stan lying on my heart. It was as if he knew he was going. Of course he did. What I did not know was what to do. Did this mean he wanted to stay, or was it his way of saying good bye, and that he would always stay in my heart. Possibly he was just cold, there was thick snow on the ground outside. I felt so bad, letting them go, but knew they would be greatly blessed and loved in their new home. Sometimes, what is right, is not easy. I sure could not manage seven dogs for several years. Even five dogs was going to prove a challenge.

*FOLLOW YOUR BLISS AND THE UNIVERSE WILL OPEN DOORS FOR YOU WHERE THERE WERE ONLY WALLS.
JOSEPH CAMPBELL.*

CHAPTER THIRTY-TWO
All That I Left Behind

It can be a mixed blessing having an idea of what the future will hold. In fact there have been times when I wish that I did not know. Premonitions of dark events like 9/11 are undesirable. Besides, what can you do to top something, which is going to happen anyway? I remember one day months before 9/11, Anke saw a vision in her Crystal Ball of a plane flying into a building in New York City. She could not bear to look further, but see it she did. With such predictions a psychic is actually powerless. Would the authorities had listened to us if we contacted and told them what we just saw? No, of course they would not have.

In reality, unless expressly asked by government or police, I have learned it is best to stay quiet. It is wise not to dwell on such negativity. Keeping it positive is imperative to good results with this work and constructive outcomes, especially when the stress has been intense. As for world events, what can you do but pray?

I have learned that the only true protection in the midst of a huge test is a pure and open heart. If somehow you can nurture this, then nothing can touch you. If you can maintain innocence whilst being discerning, then you help yourself immeasurably. God's Grace is of course indestructible; but it pays to be "As wise as a serpent, and as innocent as a dove."

I have become very aware that what one expects and projects out to the universe will come about. We underestimate the power of our creativity all too often. It is therefore imperative that we keep our thoughts, words and actions as *pure* as possible. We will see whether or not Anke's prediction comes about. So, watch this space. I mean regarding the win; not the Bono bit. Sorry to disappoint you Bono, just in case you were interested. Just kidding.

Since the days of hankering after Bono, life has been eventful. I was swept off my feet by one of the best boys from Ulster Rugby. A "Player" who blindsided me and dashed my hopes unceremoniously. I was then textually pursued by John, a Welsh footballer who wanted to "take me places" because I am his type He magnanimously considered that he could "have lots of fun with me," without consulting me first. I also had my ex Billy wanting me to have his baby, even though we were not in a relationship. Billy had started to have huge remorse that he had not had a child with me. But as with all things pertaining to Billy, the suggestions and offers came too late.

I had had to look after John, a famous Celtic striker footballer, and his girlfriend Sarah one afternoon in Dalkey for our mutual friend Donald McLeod. They were over in Dublin from sunny Glasgow, and wanted to see something of the Irish culture. We had lunch in Finnegans, therefore and John settled in to watch a football game on the big screen. He was a gambler at that point and had a serious stake on the wrong team. He had backed Tottenham Hotspurs, and as I watched the game I told him that actually Fulham were going to win. He had money on the wrong team. He quickly phoned his bookie to reverse the bet; and thanks to me made thousands. He bought me lunch.

John then persistently texted me for some time trying to get me to meet up with him. I was not attracted to him in *that* way. Or perhaps he wanted some more betting tips. But not long after, I was horrified to hear about his battle with cancer. John's brush with death changed him. I returned his texts at that point, and did what I could with distance healing to help him. Thank God he pulled through, and is now happy and married to Sarah with a brood of kids. Some things do work out in the end.

My life as a tipster flourished. I seemed to have a ministry to sportsmen in particular. I tipped the Rugby lads handsomely one lunch time up at Fitzpatrick's Hotel, just before they headed off to win the 2009 Championship. I briefed Ronan O'Gara that the result was going to be down to him. It was. Ronan's drop goal, right at the close of the match, left Ireland the winners 17 to 15 against Wales in Cardiff. If Ronan's steely nerve had failed in the dying seconds of that match, Ireland would have floundered and not won the championship. I knew they were going to do it, and through the posts that ball did go. Ronan did not like to think it was all down to him, because of course any match is a team effort. But I knew it was important to prime him specifically this time. It literally was going to be *him* who had to clinch the result, and I knew it. I knew I was meant to tell him this too. And as usual when I know something like this, the relevant person crosses my path.

Literally the Irish Team were about to get on the coach to go begin the journey to Cardiff for the final show down against Wales. A few of us were in the computer room talking horses; not a word to the IRFU. I tipped them a fourteen-to-one horse for the race at four thirty. Mick O' Driscoll wanted a demonstration and set me a challenge. He did not believe it possible to psychically pick out horses or winning teams etc. I had already relayed the most important message of the day to Ronan, that he was going to clinch The Championship for the team. But Ronan was at that point primed to back the horse too it seemed. He scuttled down the corridor on his phone, possibly to catch the tip. Equally he may of course been chatting to his lovely wife Jessica. Ronan by his own admission loves the horses, and even owns a couple at this stage I believe. Of course the tipped horse ran in a winner right on cue. But I did not get so much as lunch that time by way of thanks. Any guy who had overheard that tip could have made thousands from the information. At least it all showed I was becoming quite a useful tipster, and gave me something to keep up my sleeve for a rainy day.

I was pretty jaded with men by this point. All the men I was stumbling across, seemed to be sexually interested for a time, but long-term commitment phobic. Time was indeed running out for me to have a child. I had spent my life avoiding the scourge of single parenthood, and I was not going to fall into that trap now. I did not want a child enough to subject them to life without a stable father figure. I also wanted a loving partner for myself. Indeed I wanted this more than I wanted a child. So I was not going to compromise on these points any time soon. It looked like I was going to end up single and lonely.

Once again it was Bono who brought a bit of levity back into my life. His timing was good throughout the years, and our paths tended to cross when I really needed a lift and a soul connection. I had not had much contact with Bono throughout the rugby shenanigans. It had been my way to try to forget him. It failed miserably.

I bumped into Bono and Simon randomly in Dalkey car park, no doubt on their way into Finnegans for a pint. As usual Bono was charming and sweet, and being spontaneously serenaded by him cheered me up immensely. I am not sure the little ditty will hit the top ten any time soon though. Anyone in the environs of Dalkey station car park could have watched with wry amusement, as Bono gallantly swept me off my feet, dancing me around and singing:

"*Her name is Sarah and she drives a blue car/ You'd like to get to know her 'cos she is a Star!*"

Thank you Bono, I needed that.

Throughout my two phases in Ireland, I had lots of fun on the phone with Anke. We liked to push the boat out and test our psychic skills, as well as catch up with all the gossip. One time, when I was back in Ireland for the second time, she phoned me, and we discussed horses. We decided to see if we could pick out some winners. I had funds, but needed some more to buy a ticket for Brian's next visit. It was never totally clear if I was going to be able to bring Brian over for the next assigned trip. Every time it looked doubtful and blocked, yet every time it did somehow come about. We had important work to do together, and the funds seemed to always arrive in time to get the correct ticket. When it was right, and meant to happen, it happened. Spirit and the universe kept us on tenterhooks about it. But it usually came together in some miraculous way or another. It felt a bit like something good was about to happen. Certainly it had to, so that the trip could actually take place.

Anke intuited that we should look at the four thirty race in the place beginning with the letter P. It could only be Pontefract. Anke could not see the horses on the computer, but she did have her paper in front of her. I looked at the race, and it was quite a line up. About twenty horses or so. Anke suggested a horse called Dubai Dynamo. I liked that horse, and I did get a bit of an energy charge from it. But while I was looking at the race, and the shirt colors of the jockeys, the yellow of Arrowhead kept jumping at me. I kept scanning the line and squinting slightly, and my eye kept deflecting back to Arrowhead.

Something had changed within me. Usually I would have backed Anke's horse to the hilt. I felt something different this time, and I honored that. It was nearly like a test. It was also a nice affirmation. I did put a smaller bet on Anke's just in case. But I went with my heart and did a few hundred euro bets on Arrowhead. I did not feel too bad or guilty. It is not gambling if you are winning after all. I also did not have any other means to buy this ticket for Brian to come and see me, all the way from America.

I knew psychically Brian was going to make the trip over, and I knew logically I had to manifest the money for this. So I trusted that Anke's phone call was timely, and that this was going to be the way the money would ground this time. I stuck my neck out and put a few handsome bets on Arrowhead to win each way. With good odds of fourteen to one, I would hit nicely if he won. He did.

Being guided by spirit to bring in money in such ways, can be very nerve wracking. It is not easy. You might think it is easy money. But in actually fact it is a very stressful way to live. I have learned to work with it though. There are very definite tests along the way. I must not force lines of numbers for example. I must wait to be shown what numbers to play and in what draw. At any one time I have a line or two that I know is going to hit. I have done it for long enough now to know for sure that it will. But not a moment before it is meant to.

What I have learned is, winning in this way is most definitely not a random event. It is actually possible for a psychic to utilize their skills to bring in the wins. I cannot encourage others to work with this, as it is so specialist, and the pitfalls are real. It seems to be a unique skill, that Anke, Brian Hunter and I have worked out how to implement.

Brian has recognized that numbers have an energy and appear in waves. They act a bit like the ebb and flow of the tides. So it is very possible that the same numbers will hit a few days in a row in the Irish Daily draws for example. Brian is expert at assigning lucky numbers to clients. He reads their energy, and then gives them a combo of four numbers to work with, or to have for life as their lucky numbers. We have had clients win on the numbers using this method. But it can take patience and application, and above all needs an understanding of the principles at play.

Anke has seen this large win for me for many years. She may well be correct. But I am no longer invested in it. I do not need it to happen. But I will be delighted when it does. I do know she will be right about this, as I have often sensed it for myself to. Problems arose when I got ahead of myself regarding this prediction. Ann fed into this, saying "phone me when you win tonight," as I left her house to drive back up to Dalkey. I know she used to lie awake trying to work out how much it was. I know she was seeing it and not lying. But it was over sold in the excitement, and the information got me into a lot of trouble as it was clearly given prematurely.

Some years previous to all this I had ended up writing to explain the whole thing to Bono. I told him that Anke had said I would eventually be with him, and that I would win the lottery. He must have thought we had both lost our marbles. But when I met him on the beach shortly after, he was genuinely concerned for me. That was kind of him. I really had got into a pickle and needed to sort myself out. I guess it was an example of a little knowledge is dangerous, at that stage. Clearly that large win was not any time soon when it was first told to me. I should have not acted as if it was landing any minute. Also I should not have relied on that to deliver me from the plight I was in when the Celtic Tiger collapsed. In the end I chose to do what Anke had said I would not have to. I took myself off to the end of the world and made myself bankrupt. Perhaps I did not have to do this. But it sure made sense in terms of stress levels.

I rented the cottage near Lands End in Cornwall. I was lonely and scared. All I had was my dogs for company. I lived at the end of a three mile cul-de-sac, and only had the seagulls and the ghosts in my house for entertainment and distraction purposes. It was such a relief to have all the debts written off though. I figured God, Spirit and

The Universe, could and would look after me.

I had embarked on all the work in Ireland in good faith, and I had helped a lot of people. It was now time to help myself. I buried the Tarot cards that had helped so many Irish people sort out their lives in a secret spot up at Beacon Hill; and I prepared to cross the Irish Sea, possibly never to return. It sure was a come down to be taking this way forward. After being told I would win for so long, it really did not seem fair to have to sort the finances in this way. I was not judging myself too heavily. I knew I had done all in my power to sort the situation. I was taking the right action in the circumstances. It was certainly a lesson in humility. Truly I knew then, I was willing to do anything if I was guided to do it. I could at least be proud of my obedience levels in the face of adversity.

I did not want to take the shame of bankruptcy anywhere near my family, so I chose the remotest spot in the United Kingdom to do the deed. So remote was I, that the man in charge of my case did not require me to visit him in Plymouth. He resolved all the issues for me on the phone. He allowed me to keep my modest car too, which is just as well as there were dogs to be walked, and groceries to be bought.

As I had learned, I made the best of it. I was sleeping in a haunted, converted, huge, damp old barn. I camped in the kitchen as it was unfurnished. I could not get my own stuff down from my parents garage to fully move in. I was at the end of a long inaccessible road, and it would not have been logistically possible to get a truck down there. I slept on a double Lilo camping bed, which deflated during the night, and I had to drive miles any time I wanted to get bread or milk. I was afraid. This was all unknown to me. In retrospect, I am proud of my bravery. Knowing what I now know about the process, I would not have taken this route. I need not have been as nervous. It really is a very straightforward thing to do; and a wonderful release for those who truly have tried everything they can to sort their situation. Some things just cannot be sorted without intervention. There is actually no shame in it.

I enjoyed Cornwall, and treated the whole experience like an extended holiday. I walked the rugged cliffs, and hoped to stumble upon Poldark or something. I had read Poldark in my youth, and enjoyed the first TV series very much too. The irony is, if I had stayed put, I would have likely met Poldark, aka Aidan Turner, seeing as much of the most recent TV production was filmed in Botallack, where I walked the dogs. It was evocative to see all the spots I had read about as a teen; and I did find it therapeutic to be a long way from everything that had happened to me in recent years. Objectively speaking it was all a big fail. Here I was alone on a cliff, bankrupt with five dogs. I had dealt with the huge cloud hanging over my head at last.

I really did not know how to move forward after this. Notions of Bono and rugby players were long gone. I had my masked companion on line. I had a hunch who he was but no conclusive proof. But he became my confident and best friend in my isolation. So if I thought things could not get any stranger, they were clearly about to. There was quite an irony in not knowing conclusively the identity of the person closest to me in that moment.

There were no easy ways to look at all this. This Cornish interlude was a fail. Well, it was not going to work long term. My brother in law Graham visited on Saint Valentine's Day with a friend to play golf in Saint Just. They wanted to whisk me away from Hendra Cottage immediately. Graham's friend was a policeman, and I think he was even concerned for the safety of a female living on an isolated cliff miles from the nearest town. I was blissfully isolated, and it served a purpose. As soon as I could though I organized a move a bit further north to Porlock, where at least there was a damp haunted cottage available to me with a village wrapped around it.

I do believe I have come very close to winning big on several occasions. As I have been describing I regularly win small amounts, and a couple of times I have just missed the jackpot. Once, around the same time as I predicted the line up of the *Irish Popstars,* I was running to meet up with Billy my wayward ex. I omitted to do the numbers that subsequently hit that night. I had dreamt the numbers ten days or so before that, and had been doing them for the previous draws. Of course they came up on the one night I did not buy the ticket, and I missed out on one and a half million. *Oops!*

I asked Anke if this had been the win she had seen, and I missed it somehow. She said, "clearly not, since you do not have the money." I felt it was a sign that it was indeed doable for me to win. But clearly there were many lessons to happen along first. Despite the myriad of near-misses, Anke's prediction was a double edged sword. As described it landed me in the midst of a huge quandary. In combination with the prediction that I am destined to waltz off into the sunset with Bono, it also got me into financial difficulty, and then did not present the solution. To be fair Anke did make her "something always happens" comment. And she is absolutely right. Something *does* always deliver me when it has to. This could be a reflection of my obedience and willingness to do as guided. But the costs of this approach to life, have been immense. You start to get a longing for some stability and peace, if I am being quite honest.

If it is in my destiny to win, it will happen. At least I am not emotionally invested in it any more. It will also feel very normal when it does happen. I will very likely tell no one, and continue to live as normal. In fact Anke has predicted that is just what I will do. Makes you wonder if such a win is even necessary. But that is not the point. It is clearly a destiny moment Anke has seen. It will happen when it happens.

EXCHANGE THE MASK YOU WEAR FOR THE OPPORTUNITY FOR YOUR STORY TO BE INCLUDED IN HIS STORY.
FOR YOUR STRUGGLE TO BE USED AS A BEACON OF HOPE IN THE LIVES OF HURTING PEOPLE AROUND YOU.
TRACEY METZGER

CHAPTER THIRTY-THREE
Groundhog Day

I tried to stay as positive and productive as possible throughout the duration of my personal challenges. Interestingly, the lessons began when I moved out to Dalkey the first time. I can only conclude that in some way it was all a big test, reflecting the fact I was about to bring some quite controversial thoughts and experiences into the media. I certainly was about to stick my neck out and perhaps my personal circumstances began to reflect this. I am not saying I consciously brought it on myself. But it did seem to be something I signed up for, karmic or otherwise.

Warren, a *Sunday Mail* journalist who penned a detrimental article about my work, in fact did me a great favor. The powers that be probably had no idea how badly timed the piece was from a personal point of view. Nor that it nearly caused me to give up totally. It brought me to a point where things suddenly seemed insurmountable and on top of recent emotional challenges it was nearly the straw that broke the camel's back. Not wanting to be headlines for all the wrong reasons I pulled myself together and got on with life.

Warren's piece got the ball rolling, so I guess I can be eternally grateful for the negativity of the attempt to discredit and undermine me on this occasion. Hopefully my pen and spirit were mightier than the Sword's. There certainly was a very dark unjustified agenda with this attempt to expose me. Warren's line was that my daily column in *The Independent* was repetitious, and the implication was that I was some kind of fraud. Any of my regular readers will know what nonsense this is. Compared to many other astrology columns in papers, my writings are actually quite detailed and sophisticated. I actually get regular appreciation letter commending my astrology files. Warren's concept amused me though. The thought of being stuck in some kind of spiritual groundhog day, with my thoughts and ideas endlessly repeating, was an interesting concept. I could think of worse fates. For it was not such a bad thing if the material is worthy of repetition. Many of us are quite bad at hearing spiritual messages and sometimes need to hear something several times albeit in different ways before we actually take notice.

Ironically one of the repetitions I was apparently guilty of was an over enthusiastic use of the phrase "smile amidst adversity." So, there you go. An instance of synchronicity, prediction and repetition all rolled into one. How appropriate. Of course an article like this always serves as a kick up the bum. But what really got to me was that it was based on a really unfair and inaccurate premise. It was doubtless an overt attempt to discredit my work. To my mind it looked like just what it was; a rather weak attempt to bring me down. Why?

At the time Warren's piece went to press the election was looming, Galway's water was gammy, and Bono had just been to an important breakfast awards ceremony. Why bother picking on Psychic

Sarah?

Oh well. Sorry Warren; it did not dispirit me. Not for long anyhow.

My main response to Warren when he phoned me was that my work was not designed to be picked apart. It was done with a good heart, and it was for those of a spiritual bent rather than for the cynics.

Of course there can be an element of simple entertainment and amusement in reading your daily astrology column. But generally my aim is to make people think and create an edifying, positive thought for the day. Equally it is important to remember that is only one aspect of the work I have been doing. Warren and I had a laugh, but I could tell the piece was still going to go in, and despite what he said in the first line, I did see it coming. Just because a psychic can see or anticipate and event does not mean it can always be stopped.

My daily columns are largely spiritual and philosophical musings, which perhaps would not look out of place in a spiritual or inspirational diary. They are designed to inspire and give a synchronous sound bite for the day. There is also a healing energy behind them, which hopefully lifts the mood and puts a spring in one's step.

I try to keep the columns generally positive, though of course because of tricky planetary movements at times they sometimes do contain a warning. One thing is for sure; my work is definitely not a cynical attempt to pull the wool over anyone's eyes. Nor is it some kind of dubious fraudulent behavior. As I explained to Warren, with the amount of writing that I do, you would expect there to be a lot more repetition than there actually is.

Obviously, there are only so many ways that the ideas can be put across and one does have a specific way of phrasing things. But most importantly I do believe that the thoughts for the day work with the phenomenon of Synchronicity. Certainly I have found that personally they seem to hit the spot in various ways, applying equally to different people and situations. Same words: different meanings. Of course, the paragraphs are designed to relate to the specific star signs on the specific days. But it all works within the bounds of synchronicity; which I believe is the way the universe works with us if we are willing to watch, look and listen.

Those of a spiritual, or curious bent seem to get what I do. I get a lot of good feedback from those who get inspired when they read a point which reaches to the heart of what they are dealing with. My work is not designed to be trashed; it is designed to inspire and encourage people in the daily grind.

In actual fact the error Warren had detected was an *editorial* one. He was being anal about something that was actually nothing to do with me. As with all forms of the printed word, errors can sometimes happen in translation. Astrology columns are no exception. It actually amuses me if a column is accidentally repeated. So what? It must be synchronous and mean that the message is relevant today also. No. Big. Deal. I mean, *really*. Does a journalist not have something better to do than pick apart what is essentially an entertainment column?

The *Sunday Mail* also wrote cynically of my connection with Bono. I "worked closely with him."

Yeah? What of it?

They also cited the fact that I have "rather disturbingly" been used by the Garde to help find missing persons.

Why disturbingly Warren?

Rather wittily Warren did write that he hoped that I was not finding the same body over and over again. But he totally overlooked the spirit in which I do my work, which is that I seek to *help* people with a good heart. Idiot.

I would be the first to admit that the road to hell is paved with good intentions. But I actually think that the only difficulty or stress I have inflicted in following this unusual calling is on myself. I have certainly never had any complaints, nor negative feedback from those I have helped. Quite the opposite. My work by the grace of God has created spectacular breakthroughs against the odds in the lives of my clients. With healing, manifestations, and guidance, I have been able to help steer people through situations, that would have been overwhelming for them otherwise. I can not reveal client information, so you will have to take my word on that. But when I engage my energy to help people, "things happen." That is a given.

Much of my public work relies on the phenomenon of synchronicity. This includes the SMS messages and the daily columns in particular. I find that when I am in a bit of a corner myself and check the Sarah Virgo thought for the day. It always hits the spot.

So do all the Virgos in the world have the same things going on in their lives as the same time? No of course not. But the same words will have a relevant application to every single Virgo. The reason this works is somewhat mysterious. It is entirely down to synchronicity, a powerful phenomenon, which has certainly rendered my own life very colorful.

Of course one could go crazy with the over interpretation of meanings and symbols and too much Jungian input. But synchronicity in its purest form is simpler than that. As I have explained, it taps into universal truth. It is I believe the primary means by which the heavenly realms connect with us. When something miraculous and meaningful happens, we often dismiss it and question it too much. But, what if we actually paid it more attention? Would we not have a more curious, varied life less dependent on routine and predictability?

Well, that one thing *is* for sure.

I AM OPEN TO THE GUIDANCE OF SYNCHRONICITY, AND DO NOT LET EXPECTATIONS HINDER MY PATH.
DALAI LAMA

CHAPTER THIRTY-FOUR
Coincidentally Yours

Never mind Warren, Siobhan, the fledgling journalist, and the gaggle of skeptics who have haunted my existence since I stepped into the public eye. If you want to understand more of what it is like to be psychic, and want to find a way to develop your own intuitive skills, then there is one thing you really should know more about and its synchronicity.

Working with synchronicity is about learning to spot those moments which shine a light on your existence. The clues offered up by the universe can be intense and magical when you are on the right road. Have you ever been thinking about someone you have not seen for months only to bump into them in a busy shopping centre? Or have their name flash up on your mobile moments before you key in their number? Then tried to analyze what those coincidences in life big and small really mean? This is the tantalizing nature of synchronicity, and it holds the key to many exciting possibilities if you care to acknowledge it.

We all have examples of intriguing, significant coincidences that have happened along the way. But sit down and try to define the quality of these magical moments and it is likely you will come unstuck. It does not help that we tend to be ruled by our logical minds, which tell us to put everything into a safe, ordered box, and dismiss apparently random events. But these synchronicities are happening everywhere in our daily lives, whether we choose to notice them or not. If we close our minds to this phenomenon we run the risk of reducing life to a purely material, painfully tedious, humdrum level. A dead pan existence which the skeptics seem to think is eminently more desirable than a life full of magic and possibility. I know which I would aspire to, or most prefer.

Synchronicity is a magical phenomenon that has the power to transform and enhance our lives if we decide to give it airtime. It is my belief that a greater understanding of synchronicity unlocks our innate creativity and oomph, as well as our ability to manifest good things and choose the life path that is right for us.

We are all interconnected by an energetic world wide web. Understanding synchronicity greatly enhances our life experience by helping us tune into our weird and wonderful universe. These moments have an energizing significant quality that connects us to each other and to the hub of life itself. Synchronicity reassures us that our lives really do have an inherent meaning. It is comforting to think that there is a pattern and destiny within the chaos, emphasizing life's magical quality.

Synchronicity really is not the reflection or projection of a mad psyche, or an imagining designed to make us feel better. Psychic really is not the same as psycho, whatever the skeptics may think. Synchronicity is a real event, providing food for thought, if not nourishment for the soul. It directly reflects our inner and outer reality. For, it is when our inner moments are reflected in the outside world that our realities collide. When this happens, our inner-tuition is validated by a wonderful external event. We feel vindicated and liberated in one fell swoop. Magick!

There definitely seems to be a link between heightened intuition and synchronicity. My life as a psychic has been full of events too numerous to mention, that continually reassure me that synchronicity is a phenomenon which hits the spot time and time again.

There is no doubt that synchronicity makes us aware of the powerful forces at work in the universe and encourages us to increasingly trust our hunches. It is when we pay attention to what is really going on, that our intuition kicks in and begins to help us in practical ways. As we trust it, we then begin to access the power centre within that always knows what to do next. Intuition is a significant part of our psyche, which *can* be opened up and developed, making us even more prone to the synchronicity moments that reveal so much. It acts as a strong indicator and yields profound clues about what can happen next.

Although my upbringing was traditional and academic (my father is a doctor, psychotherapist, Anglican lay-reader and author), I was also taught to be empathetic and open to life's magic and mystery. My Scorpio Nan was well known for her intuition. Towards the end of her life, even at the ripe old age of ninety nine, she remained in tune and connected with something beyond herself. Her memory became severely impaired, but she still possessed a strong measure of The Gift, which I obviously inherited from her.

Even though Nan's mental faculties dwindled, she remained sharp in her connection with me merrily singing *In Dublin's Fair City*, whenever I was on the end of the phone. Nan was always able to predict the arrival of an unplanned guest and would have inevitably made their favorite food the day before on an intuitive whim. She had an amazing warmth and empathy, and like her son, my father, just knew how to read people.

Jung famously coined the phrase meaningful coincidence, when he researched the phenomenon of synchronicity; and he identified three different types of this magical moment. The ability to predict events is the first of these. Some of you may remember that I blew the socks off Louis Walsh and Simon Cowell when I predicted the full line up of The Irish Popstars, six months before the judges had themselves decided. I put names in an envelope in October, and the protégés were unveiled in February, minus Nadine Coyle who had famously lied about her age. My sixth choice was her replacement: Sarah Keating.

Coincidence is the second type of Synchronicity, which you may experience when a book falls open at the right page, or drops off the shelf in the library. Or you get that phone call just as you are dialing the person calling you. I was amazed to see Bono's drawing of *Mermaid in The Temple Bar* for the I cross charity released in November 2002. We had bumped into each other on the beach in October, when I had just written the first chapter of my book Mermaid in The Kitchen; which turned out to be the first draft of this book. Anyway, I subsequently opened up the paper to find his Mermaid sketch staring back at me, dated October 2002. Even though we know each other, neither of us was conscious of the similar title and theme of our work at that point.

The third example of Synchronicity is telepathy, which may come in the form of a dream, vision, or sensing what someone is experiencing a distance away. When I lived in Edinburgh, I would regularly turn up on my pregnant friend's doorstep with the relevant craving of the day. Even quite obscure things like kumquats, black-eyed beans and melons from the corner shop found their way into my bag, (paid for of course) as I arrived for our daily chat. By opening our minds to synchronicity we are able to amplify our intuition. Rather like flexing a psychic muscle, it is a case of use it or lose it.

The observation of synchronicity offers us a practical way to develop intuitive awareness. The more tuned in to the universe we are, the more able we are to recognize the right way forward. Our intuition, when it is truly jumping, enables us to access our best options. And by being more psychic and intuitive we allow destiny to take a hand in a profound way. As we grow, and become increasingly aware, synchronicity can also be a highly effective form of guidance, revealing clues from our guardian angel, higher-self, or innate psychology.

When I needed guidance about what to do with my beloved dachshund Freddie, who had been making improvements after a nasty road accident, I looked out of the window, and there against a clear blue sky were three images which answered the question. The first cloud was in the shape of a dachshund lying down, the second was of a dachshund running; then there was a gap and finally there was an image of a dachshund leaping heavenwards. The answer was clear; it was time to let him go.

Synchronicity gets us into the groove most effectively when we are as Jung described it: Individuated. This level of maturity and unity with the universe is difficult to achieve. We can but try. The individuated individual is a formidable force indeed. This person has a sophisticated knowledge of symbols and is usually able to analyze, but not over interpret, life's synchronicities. Likely to have heightened psychic ability and spiritual awareness the individuated person knows the value of meditation, silence and humor. Let's just call them Little-Miss-Perfect, or Mr Right-On-Cue. Of course, everyone's personal journey is different. But with synchronicity offering to put the wind in our sails, we can certainly look forward to feeling empowered and free.

A word of warning. There is a definite danger in reading too much into every little thing, and one can no doubt go too far. But I do believe we are more powerful than we realize, and synchronicity definitely underlines that fact. We are indeed so creative that we can manifest quite effectively our hopes and fears simply by focusing. It goes without saying then, that it is best to keep it positive.

A negative spiral of thinking helps no one and you may in fact be blocking your synchronicity moments if you give your insecurities too much air time. Remember we are creative beings who structure our lives from minute to minute. So learn to access what you want, need and desire, as opposed to what you dread and fear. Project the good stuff into the ether by ditching negative thought patterns. It is better not to think at all than to think negatively. Empty your mind of emotional debris and clutter, then relax and begin to visualize every good thing. It really is as simple as that.

Remain open and receptive to your destiny. But at all times use your skills of discernment and wisdom too. Your synchronicity moments will then naturally increase and you will have ample confirmation from the universe that you are well and truly on track.

THE INTUITIVE MIND IS A SACRED GIFT
AND THE RATIONAL MIND IS A FAITHFUL
SERVANT. WE HAVE CREATED A SOCIETY
THAT HONORS THE SERVANT AND HAS
FORGOTTEN THE GIFT.
ALBERT EINSTEIN

CHAPTER THIRTY-FIVE
Inner-Tuition

One really invaluable tool when you are accessing the everything is energy ethos is a healthy intuition. The irony is, science agrees with the psychic principle that everything is energy. Energy can be read, affected, transformed and transmuted. We all have a sixth sense, and it makes perfect sense to develop and grow this muscle.

Having a healthy intuition gives you a short cut to answers. You get to that place where do not know how you know, you just know. The more you flex this skill, the more it will serve you. The main hurdle is starting to trust those small whispers within. For how do you know they are not just figments of your imagination? How do you distinguish between sound hunches and flaky ideas? Is it really possible to just know that you are right about things, and how is it possible to build this kind of confidence in your talents?

It is true that some people are more intuitive and psychic than others. But it is my firm belief that we can all learn to develop this skill. Whether we are inclined to do so is another matter entirely. Some people just prefer to chew the cud, mull things over and go around in circles. Personally, I am up for quick dynamic answers and sound decisions based on just knowing you are right about something. Sounds cool does it not?

Learning to trust yourself and your inner-tuition is a very empowering process. The key is starting to recognize the difference between your normal train of thought and an intuitive impulse. The main immediate distinction is that your intuition will keep coming at you if you ignore it. The subtle repetitive hunches that will not go away are your inner-tuition urging you to sit up and take notice.

Where your normal thought process will naturally float on through your consciousness, your intuition has a different quality. It is easy enough to notice it as it is apparently random. The beauty of it is, is that it is anything but random. You just have to get over the hurdle of trusting it, and it will start to work for you in really magical ways.

Beginning to listen to your intuition is an exercise of trust. But how silly it would be to let pride or too much questioning get in the way of this very magical quality? To begin to act confidently on your hunches, it is crucial that you develop an antennae for the apparently left of field thoughts that fly in from nowhere. Sit up and take notice of a prompt to phone home when it happens, or a hunch to take a different route home that ends up avoiding all the traffic. Your intuition is a practical tool, it is not random really, it just appears to be so. The truth is, your inner guide, knows more than your logical mind at any given moment.

When you notice that your normal train of thought is randomly interrupted by an out of the blue insight or hunch, that is for sure your intuition. It appears with no announcement. It does not come as a result of your seeking it out. So do not chase it around the room. Simply relax and recognize that you get the best promptings when you go about your day.

The key to making the most of it, is acting on it when it occurs, and learning to be in a state of constant listening. When you can do this, you can expect to be guided in quite spectacular and amazing ways. Accessing your intuition and learning to make it work for you, is really an easy enough habit to get into. All you have to do is act on the hunches, learn to listen to them and they will amplify very quickly for you. The problem is that we tend to ignore those out of the blue insights, unless they are real jolts which you just have to listen to. Yes these unquestionable intuitions can happen to us all at times. But the best way to really develop these moments is to get used to using your skills on a daily basis.

A practical way of assessing how far along you are is to keep a daily notebook. Log your routine, thoughts and experiences, and observe how many of these are feeling and intuition based. Are you relying on logic to get you through the day. Or are you staying in tune with the universe and keeping your ear to the ground? If you are working in receptivity with the universe, your hunches and synchronicities become much more frequent, powerful and reliable.

The first brave step is to make the decision that you are going to honor your left of field apparently random hunches wherever they may lead. Test them out, do not second guess the game. You will soon see that the universe knows many short cuts to the places you wish to get to. Apart from this, you will develop a new found freedom. It is very liberating and confidence boosting to have this level of trust in yourself and in the flow of life.

Yes, you will have to be brave at times and stick your neck out. Yes you will get challenges and you may well have to live with the fear of looking stupid to others. I have lost count of the many times my family thought my decisions were nuts, and yet I turned out to be absolutely right. You just have to get used to working with the clues, and be receptive to what you are being shown. The key is not to take other's opinions and reactions personally. Just remember, they do not actually know: *you* do

When you step into the universal flow, you will find that every step you take becomes like a magical mystical treasure hunt. I personally would not live in any other way. I have always lived this way, and it certainly beats boxing yourself in with judgments and restrictions. Anything is possible, if you only trust and believe.

Test your receptivity and listening skills. This is not about coming across as a know it all. You actually need to be very flexible and humble to live like this. It is not so much that you know, it is that you know you will be shown the steps to take. You have to be willing to respond quickly and to think on the hop. Your intuition amplifies when you really listen, so practice really hearing others. what are they really saying when they speak. Remember, it is not so much what you say, as what you do not say that reveals your inner truth. Learn to read other peoples' energy in this way. It will really help you to grow and will stretch your skills of knowing.

Be aware that sometimes your intuition may tell you stuff you do not want to hear. This is of course difficult and will be a test of your ability to really listen and accept the flow. Remember too though, you are the creator of your reality, so there may well be steps you can take to circumnavigate such hurdles. Your intuition will lead you the way, if you put out the intention to be receptive and responsive.

Most importantly, do stop that automatic negative mind chat. it is so easy to fall into this when we are in stressful situations. All the old ghosts and fears come out of the closet. It is better not to think, thank think the undermining thoughts which sabotage your process and damage your self esteem.

Using your intuition is a confidence booster, so negative thought patterns can have no place in your world. If you give into them, you will surely squash your intuition and it will become unusable. Ditch the self saboteur and give your undermining voices no air time. They will affect your ability to listen and hear the clues.

Your intuition is supportive and gentle. But it works best for you when you follow it quickly. do not wait too long for those repetitive urges, for if you do, you may miss out on some important moments and information. Intuition responds best to quick action. This you will soon see once you get confident in identifying it and acting on it. If you are really concerned about the intuition you are getting, you can acknowledge it and notice it. You are not obliged to act on it right away. But I do suggest that you do not ignore it for long. If it is important it will recur repeatedly until you listen.

Intuition responds to the laws of gratitude too. As with everything, the more it is used and appreciated by you, the more it will work for you. Walk around with a consciousness of being grateful and you will find that your intuition produces some really magical moments in your daily life.

As you gain in confidence, your self esteem will grow. This may be difficult for some people to take on board. But do not let them undermine your belief in your inner knowing. Do not listen to too many voices. When you need an answer, tune into to *you*. No one else knows your life as well as you do after all. There is no point in giving your power away to others who may not have your best interests at heart, or who may not really see things in the right way. Your intuition is your inner teacher, you do not need another one.

A main feature of intuition is that it excites you and engages you with your passions. It is the best ever guide to lead you on the road to fulfilling your dreams. Your intuition knows that anything is possible. It will not undermine you with doubts. It is the part of you which can access miracles, and it is the part of you which always knows what to do.

Honor your intuition with no hesitation and allow it to help you connect with your destiny. There is no point in going around in circles in life. Who wants to live in a dead end job, situation or location? Ask and you will receive all the knowledge you need to get you from A to B in grand style.

The key is to allow it all. This way of living is not for control freaks who like everything planned to the maximum. To make the most of your intuition, you need to suspend judgment. Do not have a plan. Have a goal and a dream yes, but not a plan as to how to implement it all. Allow your intuition to unfold it all for you. Sometimes you will not be able to see the way ahead, but it is in those tricky times, that your intuition comes into its own. Live like this for a time, and you will soon see that it is the only way to live. Once you start on this road, there is no turning back. So think about it carefully, then be open and embrace it all. Embrace the magic. Everything is energy.

Your willingness to trust your intuition is everything. You have to be willing to make a mistake, and yet you will not do so, if you only trust what you are being shown. Be mindful that the best things in life, come along when you stray from the tried and tested path. Access this magic. Access *you*.

EVERYTHING IS ENERGY AND THAT IS ALL THERE IS TO IT. MATCH THE FREQUENCY OF THE REALITY YOU WANT AND YOU CANNOT HELP BUT GET THAT REALITY. IT CAN BE NO OTHER WAY. THIS IS NOT PHILOSOPHY. IT IS PHYSICS.
ALBERT EINSTEIN

CHAPTER THIRTY-SIX
The Law Of Neutrality

I think nothing quite matches the Law of Neutrality as an ethos and survival tip. I am sure by now you have your own theories on the Law of Attraction. Most people recognize that exercising gratitude is a good core exercise for our lives. But does it *really* amplify our blessings? There is certainly something to be said for the appreciation of every little thing in our lives, from the morning cup of tea, to the luxuriant evening bath. There is every reason to believe that the Law of Attraction works, at least in part, when we name and count our blessings. I think we all understand the power of our thoughts, and most of us are very aware of our patterns and behaviors that perhaps need to be modified or changed.

In this life, it is easy enough to get demoralized. Sometimes there is a feeling in the air, that however much work we do on ourselves, however many good intentions we express, life still trundles on in much the same way. Life has the same ebb and flow and balance whatever we do and of course we are still human; still susceptible to mood swings and disappointments.

Even so we know that there is always a benefit in self development, even if it is just to increase our understanding of our lives and to facilitate important shifts for ourselves and our loved ones. It is well recognized that the more work you do on yourself, the quicker you can process things, and the quicker you are able to embrace the next lesson, the better you cope with life.

It is part of the maturing process. We are all on a quest for happiness and authenticity; even those of us who cannot see the value in being too self analytical. We are all essentially in the same boat. We all essentially want the same things, and we all want to blast away anything which may be getting in the way of the lives we really wish for. Does it really matter how conscious and switched on we are? Yes, I am sure it does. It is notably true that those who do a lot of self development and conscientiously work to elevate their vibe and their consciousness, do indeed help the people around them. Such consciousness work has a ripple effect, which is undoubtedly powerful if not immeasurable.

If we are all honest, we are aware that our actions affect those around us. We are obliged to be responsible for ourselves, for our families and for the planet. Some of us may do this in fancy and elaborate ways, others may do this in practical and imperceptible ways. We are all experiencing aspects of the same journey, and we are all here to embrace the changes going on around us. It very much starts within us, whoever we are, whatever our status.

But in considering again these recognized laws of attraction and allowing, I am keen to come up with an even simpler concept, which could in fact lie at the heart of everything. What if in actual fact, the true key, the true secret were even more simple?

The reality is, we are all human. Whatever shifts of consciousness we embrace, whether negligible or immense, there will always be more challenges ahead. I think if we thought about it properly and deeply we would not have it any other way. Life's light and shade is what makes the journey exciting.

There is no doubt that huge planetary shifts have taken place in the last few months. And for every one of us who increases our vibration there is certainly an incredible knock on effect on those around us, and on this wonderful planet we all share. It is quite simply the 'Butterfly Effect', the ripple effect; and it is most powerful.

There really is no point giving up on it all with a dismissive thought such as we are human and life remains the same whatever we may do. Yes life ebbs and flows, and the good and the bad co exist in equal measure to maintain the balance of things. We cannot shine the light except in the darkness it is designed to illuminate, and the darkness cannot totally extinguish the light either. The yin and yang of the universe is held at all times in perfect balance.

Let us just say that we all sense and know that something has been happening to our planet in recent times. The acceleration of time for example has at points been quite tangible. There is an awakening of consciousness happening all around us. The days are whizzing by, and the weeks and months are accelerating us through the calendar at break neck speed.

We all remember what the Doomsday mongers were saying about the 21st December 2012. But the truth is we got through that and we now have an on-going opportunity as a people and a planet to move things up a notch. We have the opportunity to take our lives forward in a wonderful way, so that we may all step into a new dimension and enjoy life more fully, without fear, judgment and angst.

It is already observable that the old world structures rooted in fear and control are failing and falling away. This may not be the safest of times. Indeed we can see the world over that our banking systems, governments, and natural environment are crying out to be heard.

The sum total of events, dramatic and disturbing is urging us to finally wake up, and take appropriate action.

There is no doubt that we do all need to work on ourselves as individuals to help heal the planet in this transition time. To help each other, and to raise the vibration of the planet so that the impact of any chaos or turmoil is lessened. We all need a chance to assimilate events and adjust to the energetic changes taking place.

Whatever we do, conscious or not, we all seem to have a linked destiny in the future. well this makes sense on a practical level anyway. But, my view would be we might as well take the high road and access our best selves in order to embrace the events which are to come. At least then we stand some kind of a chance.

I would always err on the side of positivity and optimism, and this route strikes me as more authentic and honest than the road we could choose to take as the self saboteurs and destroyers of our best destiny path, both as individuals and as a planet. I do not think that kind of skeptical resignation really helps anyone and it is certainly a vibration crasher.

My strong belief is that despite the ever present reminders of our humanity, we are intrinsically divine beings. That is the Truth of it all. This is not I believe, some fantastical made up illusion designed to make us all feel better in the midst of potential destruction. The real illusion is I believe that we are all destined to decay and die. This is the lie. Yes, life goes on, we may pass on, we may ascend, and even if we all willingly jump off the planet or are forced off the planet during these powerful energetic transitions, the true reality is still, that our souls will never die.

I am loving this idea of neutrality as we face into the unknown. I know many of us are familiar with the laws of allowing, the Law of Attraction, as popularized in the book *The Secret*, and of course the law of probability. The later of course, being well favored by the skeptics, scientists and mathematicians among us.

I think the law of attraction may be quite alien to the average skeptic. But oddly not to the physicist. This is where science and all this "who-hoo" stuff finally connects. No one is going to argue with the everything is energy concept at this late stage in our evolution. Even the men of science recognize that everything is energy. This is the best starting point when we discuss the laws of the universe, and this is the point at which we all connect. Everything is energy. We know this to be true. Einstein said so, and it is pretty much an indisputable fact. I have always thought that the simpler the thought the easier it is to grasp. Simple really.

The Law of Neutrality originates in the Law of Allowing The Law of Allowing, which is the free flow of ideas and events, allowing everything to just be. If the good stuff, the challenging stuff, the blessings and the upset are all equal, well then we know what we are dealing with in life. The question is, is it possible for us as human beings to get to this magical point of could care less, even as we actually care and love with all our hearts? Well yes, Zen masters down the eons have achieved it. But can we as mere mortals achieve this? It is my belief that if we simplify our expectations and resign ourselves to life as it IS without giving up, well then, yes we really can.

The real question is whether we can become detached enough to let all things good and bad wash over us or through us without sticking, without holding on. Are we in some way becoming less than human if we achieve this apparently cool way of being? To live like this is certainly a Zen kind of art form. But I do not think this attempt makes us less than human, nor is it some kind of denial of our humanity.

The Law of Detachment works in a similar way. Detachment is known to be one of the best ways to manifest something into your life, in combination with the Law of Attraction. We put out the request to the universe, detach, step back and allow the universe to deliver as it sees fit. Our detachment must be exercised in the full awareness that the universe probably knows better than we do, so may well deliver what we ask for in a completely different yet perfect form. The process of effective manifestation sure does require our detachment. It requires us to completely get out of the way, out of our own way if you like.

We are most of us, quite aware of this process of manifesting. Put in simpler terms it is a kind of sods law. If you do not care too much, you may well get what you thought you wanted. In lay man's terms it is Murphy's Law in operation. If you are not working too consciously with your manifesting skills, then what you do not wish for or what you fear tends to manifest. It is the Law of Attraction working in reverse. You see it works. It works powerfully in reverse also.

The key to good manifesting is therefore this neutrality, which acts to counteract the fear or negative expectation we may be carrying, possibly in our unconscious, if not in our conscious minds.

I think we are all quite experienced in these matters. Most of us know how important it is to stop our negative head chat. It is for sure, better not to think at all, than to fret, to worry or to carry fear. Yet, our success rate at manifesting probably varies. Then again this is not a competition in manifesting. It is more about finding where you fit now into this manifesting of abundance loop. I mean what if the power simply lies within you regardless of any teaching or advice you might listen to along the way? What if the power simply lay within you to achieve all these great things, even without any help?

As with all things if we give our power away, we tend to get diminished. What counts is our authenticity, our own expression of life. This is in essence is our life challenge going forward.

The best answers are always simple. The best answers have always been dangling right under our noses for quite some time. Finding our authenticity and true self is also more simple that we thought.

We all tend to fixate on finding our mission, our role or our place in life, when in actual fact, our true mission is to simply be. Obviously there is nothing wrong in trying to discern your correct life path. But do remember, as you continue this journey, everything is equal under the heavens. It is my simple belief that our mission in life is to live in the way that most suits you. Whatever makes you happy.

We are all special in the expression of our authentic self, whatever that may be, and that is the truth. Whether we are a mum, a baker, a butcher, a candle stick maker or the president, this truth remains the same. It is only the simplicity with which we find our transparency and walk the talk that counts.

I think the most important thing we can do for ourselves and for the planet now is to ditch judgment. If we are aware that we tend to judge others? It is more than likely we are judging ourselves even more harshly. The reality is judgment helps no one. It is the one negative spin which leads to destruction, criticism, and giving up. What is the point in that? We have to go on in life. So to lighten our load of judgment is the best possible gift we can give ourselves and the planet too.

This is at the heart of the neutrality ethos. Non judgment is a sweetness which allows for the fact that anything goes. Everything is equal under the sun. Everything is okay in the eyes of God, in the eyes of the Divine. All are equal under the heavens. Even the dark came originally from source, and aspects of the dark just need a bit of assistance to return or at least get to a point of transmutation. This point of neutrality is the key to releasing us from fear.

At the moment, we are somewhat caught up in a fix it, which in actual fact may not be as important as we think. It may in fact be a bit misleading to think we are in anyway doomed. What if it were actually okay to be sad, mixed up, angry? To really feel these moments and to let them all wash on through, instead of suppressing or denying it all?

This Law of Allowing applies even to these apparently negative experiences too. It certainly accelerates the point of healing if you can simply embrace where you are. Allow it all. This allowing is probably the most important shift we can make at this time. Try to be neutral about things as they happen. Simply allow them and move through it all. It is much better to be authentic to your feelings than to live in denial. This is true authenticity, where nothing is taboo.

Suppress the shadow and you will never access your path of abundance. Embrace your shadow and what is, and you just might.

The reality is, abundance is all around us. It is very misleading to think of abundance in terms of the money we have, or the material comforts we possess. I can remember, making a pledge to myself at a very young age, that I would always feel rich and abundant whatever material items or monies I had, or did not have. After all, you can get rich guys who are anything but abundant in their souls, and you can get guys on the street who have it all. Strange but true.

What counts is authenticity, grace and soul. If you can maintain these qualities with a truck load of cash, well then you will surely do great things in the world. The point is, it is also possible to do them regardless of what you have in the bank. The sooner we realize this and see things are they are. The sooner we can all make those shifts we so longingly wish for. The key to great manifesting is to allow the "vacuum" to work for you. For it will surely deliver when you are at the point of neutral surrender.

*JUST REMAIN IN THE PRESENT MOMENT
AND THE WHOLE PAST IS YOURS
AND THE WHOLE FUTURE IS YOURS.
FORGET THE PAST, FORGET THE FUTURE,
THIS MOMENT IS ALL.
THIS MOMENT HAS TO BECOME
YOUR PRAYER, YOUR LOVE, YOUR LIFE,
YOUR EVERYTHING.
THIS IS IT.
OSHO*

CHAPTER THIRTY-SEVEN
The X-Factor

Because of the tricky events we have all been dealing with, a disconcerting pragmatic cynicism has been creeping into our consciousness. Our dreams get compromised and visions turn to dust. It is as if everything we had hoped for is not in fact a reality which is able to happen. This may sound rather bleak, but I assure you, it is only how things appear. It is not the truth of it. The true reality is there is an ever present possibility of magic and wonderment. Great things can still happen and your miracles are ever present and ever possible.

Why not give yourself a boost and turn things around? Opt for a consciousness life style change which will empower you, despite what may have demoralized you in the past. Access this approach using the attraction factor for the time ahead and find out what is really possible. Face reality and expect miracles.

The X-factor is something indefinable which we all recognize when we see it. It is a magical principle, person, event which contains a compelling quality that draws us in. When the X-factor is in full operation we experience something that inspires us, fascinates us, and possibly makes us a little envious. Star quality is intangible, yet so recognizable. The good news is, there are many wonderful ways you can boost the magical happenings in your own life. Want to know how to work with the universe to boost your own X-Factor? It is now no secret that it is possible to create the life of your dreams by focusing your intentions.

As above, so below is a phrase which holds much truth and power. If we tap into this cosmic truth and work with it effectively, it is literally possible to ground many good people, places, and things into our lives. Is it really possible to live the life of your dreams by focusing your intentions? The answer is absolutely *yes!* The whole universe is made up of different frequencies of atoms which manifest as both solid matter and etheric energy. It is the energy we align ourselves to that dictates what will unfold in our lives.

The energy frequency we choose to vibrate with is really what makes up our destiny. This may be challenging to accept sometimes. But we do have personal power, responsibility and creativity within. We are not just victims of fate, unless of course we are oblivious to these truths, or make no effort. Armed with our potential, this knowledge and a huge dose of faith, there is not much beyond our reach. We simply have to embrace a willingness to experiment with the laws of nature.

The Law of Attraction is a well known concept at this stage. But not everyone knows how to implement it. It is crucial to commit yourself fully to your goals and intentions for this to work. If you harbor any doubts or wobbles, well then you might as well sit back and observe the failure. The success of this attracting principle is that it requires your faith first and foremost.

It is fundamentally important to be very specific in what you are putting out for. The universe does not like uncertainty or dithering. Life responds to our definite action and focused intention. There are times when we must remain detached and not too invested in the outcome. So it is a fine line of intention and detachment that works best. A vision board is a great idea when you first start to work with the law of attraction. Collect images which match what you wish to achieve. Have what you want on a collage for your screen saver, or carry it on your phone as a wallpaper. Tune into this vision board regularly, and work with it in fun ways. This does not all have to be serious and laborious. It really should be light and fun for great results.

Be very careful what you wish for. You can see the hot water I got into at times, learning the ropes here. The best way to work out what you really want is to ask yourself *why* you want it. Be very honest with yourself. It will not work if you fudge issues, and do not understand why you want what you want. If you want a new partner, because you do not want to be alone. Well then you can expect the results to be less than ideal. The best way to attract the right partner is to be totally comfortable with yourself home alone. I went out looking, and you saw the results. You need to also have a very clear picture of the qualities you would like to see in your other half.

Before you finalize what you are really working towards be absolutely sure you will enjoy the results. Use your imagination. How do you feel when you are experiencing this new situation. Are you stressed you will lose it all, or are you relaxing and enjoying the results of your manifestation? This clue is often the difference between success and failure. You know that expression, be careful what you wish for? Well, it is absolutely true.

When you are manifesting it is important to phrase your requests carefully, both in your mind's eye and with your words. The most effective intention you can hold is to put out for "this or something better." This gives the universe a chance to deliver on something that could prove to be ten times better than what you had originally wished for. Always remember, the universe sees around corners. Unless we you are a well developed psychic, you generally do not. Even an effective psychic is not shown everything. Remember, information is revealed by the universe on a need to know basis much of the time. We cannot assume what is going to happen; nor must we behave as if we are entitled. Humility, openness, and receptivity to guidance is absolutely key; as is an innate trust in God to deliver.

When you are manifesting it is very important to feel as if you already have what you are intending to bring into your life. This is along the lines of fake it, 'til you make it. When you work with your intentions, have the faith and belief that all this is already yours. Visualize it, experience it in your imagination and really work with the details. Consider the consequences, the effect on the lives of those around you. Really, it pays to be responsible and mindful of all that your request entails. Be careful what you wish for.

Above all act "as if" all you wish for is already yours. This does not mean you are walking around with your head in the clouds. You are holding energy, and giving it a chance to take root on the ethers. So not share your manifestations too readily, if at all. Others, even the well meaning, have a habit of casting major what if doubts on the proceedings.

I have got to quite an advanced stage with manifesting now. So I do not let what others think bother me or affect me anymore. I fact I use another technique identified by Brian Hunter called a "push-pull' technique which amuses me greatly. Where I know others are doubting, deriding, or belittling my ambitions, even in their heads, I put out the energy of watch this space. Those that know me, are aware I will pull it off when I say this. It is part of their fascination with me I think.

Over all it is best to hold the energy of what you are doing so that others cannot cast a shadow on your best intentions. Keep the creative energy to yourself and do not share it. When we are manifesting it is important to hold the energy so that it may amplify. When you talk about it and share it you are potentially dissipating all your efforts, especially if someone ends up calling you nuts.

Live in faith on this and trust that what you want and desire is a match for all that is. 'This, or something better will meet with you in the right time and place. There is no panic about this. It is all on trust. Signaling to the universe that you believe in magic and endless possibilities is fundamentally important. This shows that you are open and willing to receive in abundance. If you close up and second guess everything, and over think everything, this will block your flow. The universe only requires your receptivity.

If you want to be happy, smile more. Act as if you are happy. If you want to shed excess pounds, eat with the belief that you are already your ideal body weight. This will align you with this truth and what you eat will serve you not sabotage you. It is all about intention and the consciousness with which you do things.

Be warned. This process is not for control freaks or the overly anxious. It helps if you are a fluid and adaptable type of personality. You have to be willing to modify your behaviors and responses in order to effectively manifest. So adopt this openness and allow the process to unfold. Surrender to the flow. Allow the events to happen which align you to your intentions however odd they seem. This is the *key* to success with manifesting. The universe sometimes delivers very strange experiences as the magic unfolds. It is all part of the fun. But it is so important not to panic and revert to logical thinking. Trust that the universe knows the short cut is absolutely key. De-stress yourself, and do not worry about how long it will all take, or what you have to do next.

Do not over question things. The universe responds well to our detachment and receptivity. A beautiful paradox which can sort out just about anything you are facing. Let go of your resistance and doubt. The universe likes a vacuum, so if you find you are full of questions, mad ideas and too much pent up energy, take a breath. Keep requests straightforward and simple. They can be ambitious, but they must not be confusing. Try not to worry about the timing of events. Divine timing is everything in this situation. Again trust that the universe knows what is best for you. Your delivery is on the way, but it may get diverted or delayed at points. The main thing is to trust that the delivery time is going to be absolutely perfect for you.

This is not all about sitting back and waiting. A mistake we can make with manifesting is to do all of the above, and then sit back and wait, wait, wait. Once that frustration sets in it is game over. So as with all things, this is about balance. You do have to be responsive and take action when it presents. The balance is fine between receptivity and responding when required.

Know how powerful you are. But also be aware how your thought processes can undermine and disrupt your energy field and results. Action is really crucial in the right moments. Spotting those moments is the main trick. When we are aligned with the correct receptivity, we must actually respond when the opportunities come along. This will not all land in your lap. You also have to engage with constructive right action at the correct times. If you want a new job, you obviously have to send off applications. Or do you. I say this, but sometimes you actually do not. The intention is sometimes enough if you are powerful enough.

Overall what helps is showing the universe that you are willing to participate. So even if the job comes in another unusual way, it is important to say "yes" instead of picking it all apart as not quite right. The reality is, the universe is much more intelligent than we are. So be accepting of what happens as the right thing. I mean look at me. I left an M.Phil course early to come and work in a nightclub in Dublin. I was supposed to be in line for the management job, but ended up in the cloak room. Imagine how I felt? But deep down I knew it was right, and it was my destiny to stay put.

So apply for the jobs, join the dating web site, plan that dream holiday and put a deposit down. Show willing. The universe responds to your inspired action. This is not action for the sake of it. Take actions that compliment your intention initially and then get out of your own way. Before too long the magic will kick in and you will experience the synchronicities and the miracles.

SMALL MINDS CAN'T COMPREHEND BIG SPIRITS. TO BE GREAT YOU HAVE TO BE WILLING TO BE MOCKED, HATED, AND MISUNDERSTOOD. STAY STRONG.
UNKNOWN

CHAPTER THIRTY-EIGHT
It's A Gift

Whenever I am asked about my work, I think people expect me to rave about it. They seem a bit thrown when I err on the side of caution with how I express myself. Truth is, this is not an easy path to have taken. Yes, I can now help people and advise with authority. But at what cost along the way to myself? It has been immense on a personal level, I assure you.

I cannot bring myself to sound the trumpet about my work, as I have mixed feelings about it. This work is quite vocational, and it is certainly not as glamorous as it might appear on the surface. There can be interesting challenges daily, as I have demonstrated. I have to remain mindful and responsible to others, and make sure that I always deliver the best of myself in integrity. This is a big ask. It carries a personal cost.

Processing energy and helping clients sometimes leaves no room for my own issues and challenges. The beauty is, because I am doing God's work, I am then looked after. But it is often in some very weird and wonderful ways. Ways which defy logic. I have so many stories of deliverance, miracles and manifestations. But to be honest it would be a treat not to have to live at such a pitch sometimes.

Obviously it is wonderful to be able to help people, especially in situations where all their other options have failed them. It is exciting to be able to turn over some magic in their lives, and deliver healing and results. But there can also be a pressure, as there is no one to answer to but God and the client. I have to have absolute faith that the person who has asked for help will be helped towards their best outcome. It just goes to show that spiritual workers are delivered the clients they can truly help. I have not been let down yet. I would not even entertain that as an option as I do have total faith in how God uses this work. The more sophisticated my skills and talents have become, the more challenging the clients have become. This makes total sense.

To do this work effectively, you need to be quite self monitoring. Wisdom, integrity and discernment are key words which I have to embody to bring my clients through their process. It is fundamentally important never to work for the money. Ironically, you will not last long in this business if you have the wrong impulses and motivations. Spiritual law has a habit of tripping you up if you get too big for your boots.

I have to charge for my services however; sometimes quite a considerable amount. There has to be an energy exchange, and the client has to commit to the process and the intentions we have set. It is not an easy path to take for anyone. Sometimes clients get spectacular results really quickly, which blow my mind. Other times, their process is arduous and challenging. Karma has a part to play here; as does the client's ability to self sabotage. Sometimes work has to be modified where clients have known better and not followed advice. I have to redefine the relationship, reminding them that they employed me to do a job, so please let me do it. They soon get the point, when they realize their action just set them back.

In priming and preparing to work at this level, I have been put through the wringer on more than one occasion. There should in fact be danger money some times. The energies one deals with are not always marvelously pretty. It is definitely not a career I would recommend to anyone. Simply because it is not a career. Nor is it a business really. Yes, I am a professional doing a job. But I challenge any one to find the rule book for this. It cannot be learned, it is in fact divinely ordained.

Initially, getting started on this road, was more exciting than I had expected. It was a case of following the daily leads and there seemed to be a universal flow and momentum to the way things were unfolding. I would get a call for a radio slot one minute, an email requesting an article the next, and the next again a sports reporter wanting a match prediction for the sports pages. By the end of the day I might have two desperate parents on the phone needing healing and advice about their special needs child.

Every day had its organic flow. There was no office to attend nine to five, which is a blessing, because I was convinced I could no longer hold down a normal job. After years burning the midnight oil in the night club, I needed to be my own boss, and let my own work take shape. Throughout a day, freedom of movement is fundamentally important. I have to respond in the moment and think on my feet; especially if backing some horses. In truth doing this work requires bucket loads of faith and huge trust, even down to the details of daily life.

One time, whilst living in the wilderness of Exmoor in the barn, I had run out of money. I was walking my five sausage dogs around the circuit we called Snake Woods, and I found an I-phone by a remote bench. Thankfully it was still charged up, and on return to the barn I was able to phone a number in Switzerland to sort out its ownership.

The owner had been wondering where it was naturally, and they were still in the area, so I met them for dinner, arranged remotely by this swizz relative. We shared some interesting psychic spiritually based tales, and to thank me they insisted on giving me twenty pounds, which then fed me for the next couple of days. I thought this was cool at the time. But in retrospect, surely there are easier ways to get fed. I have numerous tales like this, way too many to recount. You would seriously fall asleep. But they are all pretty amazing, coincidental and fabulous.

Cash flow issues are often challenging as spirit likes to keep me on my toes. I bring in good money, but sometimes I can be without penny in the bank. I may have hundreds or thousands one day, the next day, next to nothing. This is not because of a gambling problem I hasten to add. It is because in recent years I have worked with my American business partner Brian Hunter. We pooled our talents and resources, and sometimes when bills or rents needed to be paid, there was a huge outlay. Based in Los Angeles, Brian is the "man who listens." He has incredible skills as a counselor; and is phenomenally magical and wise. We met on the panel of a psychic society; a panel I should never have joined, since I am too maverick and independent to kowtow to the dictates of a CEO approach to healing. On the upside, my time on this panel, expanded my horizons and contacts in the States; even as I got increasingly frustrated and became victimized.

At one point in an attempt to discredit me, The Psychic Society seemed to be going around all my contacts trying to undermine my reputation. I say seemed advisedly, and for legal reasons. But it was blatantly obvious what was going on. Either that or coincidences just got even more "coincidental" than usual. For some reason, and by their own admission, they could not cope with the developing direction of my work. It was no longer a "fit" in the words of The Psychic Society's CEO. Fair enough. I was upset though as I valued the connection and all the friends I had made through the panel. Initially I tried to appease the situation and argue the point. But I came to quickly see, this was in actuality correct. They were definitely not a fit for me. Not in the way I had hoped they would be. There was a complete impasse in the negotiations, and they were not willing to discuss or resolve things as they had done previously, on a couple of minor occasions. Instead of gracefully letting me go, they commissioned a survey of my work and web site. Apparently, based on the appearance of my web site, fifty people were asked "would you trust this psychic?" Forty two of them said "no," seven said "don't know," and one said "definitely not." Contrast this bullshit to this testimony someone wrote on visiting my web site, and I think you will see the dichotomy:

"Hi Sarah, I just went onto your web site and focused my attention on connecting with some of your positive energy and I felt what I can only describe as a chunk of "dark matter" fall off me. Nothing sinister or anything like that just a lightening, and a sense of something soothing like a balm being laid on my heart chakra. I hope this doesn't sound too weird. It was a genuinely lovely experience. Thank you for sharing your energy."

Whatever happened to the fair assessment and testing this company prided itself on? I could have read for those (supposed) fifty people, and blown their minds. I was not given the chance to do so. This was quite literally a witch hunt; petty and ridiculous. I had been extensively tested to join the panel in the first place. I was known throughout Europe, and parts of the USA for my accuracy, reliability and good character. This attempt to assassinate my work and my business was inexcusable. They must have viewed me as a threat I guess.

In response I quickly set up an impressive panel of spiritual workers called One World Psychics. I was indignant and wanted to keep the camaraderie with colleagues that had become important to me. They then managed to get this shut down too. For no good reason they seemed to be after blood, and not going away any time soon.

I had unwittingly signed a contract with them *not* to set up in competition with them for up to two years after leaving the panel. I remember this contract landing in my in box, and I did not want to sign it. Even though I did not thoroughly read it, it felt energetically problematic. In the end I signed it with my nick name and not my legal name, a ploy which unfortunately did not work. I am wary of all such documents which claim ownership of your career and product, especially when you are *not* actually employed by the protagonist. The company's request was obviously carefully researched to protect their interests. But it was in essence a very unusual ask.

All members of such panels are seen as self-employed, and they have their own autonomy. This was an attempt to control how someone was able to move on, after parting ways, for whatever reason. I did not like the conditions of this divorce. It was too much of a liberty. I should never have signed it. The document had been created in response to another member of The Psychic Society leaving, and setting up a rival panel. Obviously it is understandable to want to protect your product as a commercial venture. I actually had no intention of setting up such a panel ironically. It was their actions towards me that gave me the idea. How is that for a paradox? Their fear created the very thing they were afraid of.

All I knew was that I did not like the apparent underhand measures I was experiencing. The lack of support and understanding, I did not like one bit. It was bordering on mean and bullying. I was advised by someone who then left themselves, when they saw how I was being treated, that the CEO had even written a post about me on his business pages, detailing everything I had written to him on the matter. Just as he did not give me permission to start a panel, I did not give him permission to publish a private email. I did not say anything in it that I am not saying here. But he presented me as being some kind of liability, and the comments from ex colleagues beneath it were very telling. Some were silent, those who knew and liked me, and who knew this was all bullshit. Others, laid into me unceremoniously, and took the opportunity to pitch themselves in a wonderful light supporting their hard done by CEO. A select few sat on the fence, and remained diplomatic and sensitive to both sides of the situation. Some very prominent important members left over this treatment of me. I was known to them as an honest, authentic and accurate psychic. They had their own reasons for leaving also, which they had observed over time. It came to light that I was not the first ex member to have received such treatment. This incident was particularly nasty, but there were some previous incidences I heard about, that explained the actions taken more clearly.

This was a highly revealing human affair, that shocked me and blind-sided me somewhat. It also showed me who my friends are. It demonstrated very clearly that it was right to leave the panel at this point. Spirit had other ideas for me. I was being extricated for my own good ultimately. I was sad and had to accept this, disappointing though it was. It sure was not a fit any more. It probably never had been.

All of a sudden my panel, One World Psychics had accusations of spam, plagiarism and copyright issues flying at it. My web site hosts had no choice but to suspend the account, while they investigated. I heard from the CEO's lawyer, who proved elusive and impossible to respond to. I managed to track down his email address through internet research, and presented my evidences. I took legal advice, but basically decided to suck it up.

Brian Hunter my colleague was very supportive, explaining my case and my work to the CEO. He then advised me how to legally and energetically distance and proceed. Brian was rather freaked out at the treatment I was receiving. He said he had seen nothing quite like it before. To his credit he did everything he could to try and smooth things out. But it was not to be. My rivals were nothing if not clever. Brian, who remained neutral throughout stayed on the panel, in spite of their treatment of me. It is an Aquarian thing to remain detached in complex situations. I felt a bit complicated that my two Aquarian friends stayed put on the panel, considering how I was being treated. But it was an exercise in detachment for me also. I had no right to request or dictate what was right for someone else, just because of the way I was being treated. I got support and affirmation from many quarters over the whole affair, so I did come to understand the full picture.

Brian kept saying throughout, "never underestimate your enemy." He was trying to make a point and said it ad infinitum. It drove me crazy. But he was correct, as usual. I really did not want to give these people the time of day any more. I just wanted to exit gracefully and get on with my life. I had not really needed to join them in the first place. Being on the panel of The Psychic Society had initially been a beneficial thing. But this was fast becoming horrible and worrisome. It felt like all the good work I had done in previous years was under threat. They really had no right to do this. I answer to no one, only God. Certainly not to The Psychic Society. Why could they not just leave me alone? I was hardly a threat, nor did I ever intend to be.

I am someone who prefers to quickly move on rather than engage in petty nonsense, if something is beyond repair. I always give things a fair chance, and I reached out to the CEO to see if we could find any common ground. He had formerly been very supportive and understanding, and the shift was baffling me. He had given me the benefit of the doubt in a couple of situations which seemed to have a personal vendetta element. He had received anonymous emails about me saying all sorts of unmentionable things. I did not for a minute think this was a client. I had never had complaints about my work or my readings. There were some complex clients and issues it is true. But I was able to explain those in full. Psychics attract all sorts of people as you can imagine, and there has to be an element of protection in place, particularly from someone who has set up such a panel.

I am fairly confident that some, or all, of the anonymous complaints could have been coordinated by a certain Brazilian who was totally fixated on Brian. This guy had already caused many problems. Quite a number of odd things kept happening. Unusual Facebook accounts requesting friendship, weird emails, direct emails, and pointed postings on his own social media. Some of these things may have been nothing to do with him. But I am sure some of them were.

One time he deliberately put up a shot of a video chat between himself and Brian, which had happened in the run up to Christmas. It was effective. I was in the wrong for having found it. But my guides prompted me to look at his instagram page. I sometimes get inner promptings, and I usually do not ignore them. This video was clearly put up for my benefit. I was horrified and upset, not knowing what to do. Brian and I do not even video chat, and so my conclusion was that they kept in touch with video chat rather than just emails or messages. Apparently it was just a seasonal Christmas thing, and a tradition of their friendship. Even so, I felt it was bordering on inappropriate and certainly was invasive of our relationship. Perhaps I was wrong to have been upset by it, so I parked it, and decided not to react. Brian was typically Aquarian and all-inclusive. He rightly kept this guy as a valued friend, despite the difficulties and upset he was causing me. This, I had to understand. To cut a long story short, I think the South American was very angry I had displaced him in closeness to the person he looked on as a soul mate. This guy was deluded in many ways, and purposely persisted in keeping his "in a relationship" status up on Facebook. Wherever he could, he posted less than subtle references about Brian being a special friend. One time after Brian had just left me, He wrote a Facebook post about his "heart being up in the air and on his way home." There were also comments addressed to his mother, where he was saying he was excited that he would soon see Brian. *Oh really? News to me?*

The guy was entitled to think and feel what he wanted. There was not much I could do. I largely kept my cool, but was intermittently hurt and annoyed by it. What I did know was that if these two ever met up, I was done with it all. That was my own internal boundary. I know better than to issue ultimatums. I have never done so, and never will. I do not believe in trying to control people. One can only say how is one feeling, and then trust that the person close to us will take our feelings and best interests into account. It is always important to monitor if you feel you are being respected of course. Not recommending being a door mat anytime soon. Life is complex, relationships add much joy if we can take the stress bits in our stride.

Obviously everyone prioritizes their own agendas, including myself. We, as humans have no right to dictate who our friends and partners connect with. But we can expect a certain amount of respect. Throughout my journey I have had to monitor if I was being disrespected or not.

When I had Brian visiting me, and woke up to find him sitting at the computer at two in the morning probably chatting to this Brazilian, it did not fill me with joy. The time I got an email from the Brazilian about how excited he was that Brian and I were visiting Stonehenge was extremely irritating. One time someone asked me on Facebook if I had a boyfriend, and I said "Yes Dubricius," I was not pleased at all to hear that the Brazilian knew about this private nickname, and that he had kicked up about me using it. Brian called me and gently reprimanded me on writing such a thing publically. While, I was horrified at the level of sharing there still was between them. "Dubricius" was *our* thing. It was nothing to do with an annoying

Brazilian boy.

I suspected that they called me a "witch" too, which I guess I could laugh at. But in truth deep down, I felt it was somewhat disrespectful. The stories are many, and varied. I tried not to react, and decided not to wallow about any of it. I moved on from all the attempts at interference, taking the approach that I did not want to dictate how someone should be in relationship with me or others. But the one thing they all had in common was the irritant factor.

Thankfully after a couple of years the incidences started to subside. I never really referred to this guy, and trusted it was all in a better place after a while. The Brazilian had actually found a boyfriend at last, and was getting on with his life. I was very relieved when I heard that. I had predicted it in fact. His level of interest in Brian had been very unhealthy, and over invested, and was not good for anyone. He saw Brian as a ticket to America, and was very pushy about getting to help him with visas so he could get out of Brazil. He needed to let go, and move on with his life, or I certainly would. Being tolerant and understanding, I always gave the benefit of the doubt. I trusted Brian, so I rode out the situation, and focused on the good bits. I figured, time would tell.

Sometimes we are inclined to rush our fences as humans. People have a life before we meet them, and it is wrong to expect complete exclusivity. Love is freedom after all. I do think it is important to watch for signs you are being disrespected. But the question is, what exactly does that mean? We have to remain reasonable and supportive to all our friends. Life is a learning curve.

I had met Brian through The Psychic Society and it made lots of sense, that the Brazilian, along with his other invasive actions, would make an attempt to discredit me. I may be wrong that he anonymously emailed The Psychic Society through their comments box. But it sure did feel suspicious to me. It could also have been one particular problematic client who was known to pull stunts on occasion. But if I had to put good money on it, I know who I think it was.

The CEO told me they had had quite a few immature, angry ranting emails, calling me a "witch." I got similar comments sent through my private web site emails also. Thankfully, The Psychic Society did not give such complaints too much attention. But they certainly did not help my cause, once the other dark energies had kicked in.

There had been a very complex situation with the phone in for readings set up also. I had been accused of soliciting for clients through the readings I was giving. They said I was commandeering their clients. Actually it was the other way around. I had had client's contact me through my own web site, and I referred them to this phone line service for readings, if they only wanted a shorted consultation. I work quickly on these phone in lines. I can provide a lot of information in super quick time. So I used to tell clients about the line, and indeed was given my *own* line for my web site. I was not just working for The Psychic Society anyway through this service provider. I had my own lines through my own web site.

Suddenly as part of this witch hunt, I was being accused of all sorts of things I was not guilty of. On the phone and chat forum client's are able to take advantage of the psychic reader if they are so inclined. They can request refunds for readings they have had, and they can make reports if they are less than satisfied with what they are told. They can also make things up in attempts to get refunds. The whole system is wide open to abuse on all levels. These panels and services are a minefield for a professional psychic.

In readings, I am not about to tell someone something I do not see, just to make them feel better. I always advise them to get a second, even a third opinion. But I have to in integrity say what I see. *Any* authentic psychic will say the same thing. I needed clients for sure. This was my work, and it helped me keep things afloat on a practical level during this phase and chapter. There was a certain level of desperation because of my situation with Brian. But I did not actually break any rules. We had two lots of rent to pay, two lots of bills and travel tickets so that we could meet and do our work.

Brian's situation was beyond complex, and I had been called in to show him another way. I was under a lot of pressure to keep everything afloat. Not only did I have my stuff to oversee, I also had to make sure Brian was okay. This was before we started to develop more comprehensive ways of working together. I also had an important soul contract, to help pull Brian out of the level of despair he was feeling. I felt obligated to prove and demonstrate that he was still loved and cared for by God. At times I wondered if my emotions were being played. But over all I do not think they were. We had a genuine connection and got on well. I did not like the manipulation and drama which sometimes occurred. But I treated it as symptomatic of the trauma Brian had been through.

Brian had a similar contract to help me in return. To provide companionship, humor, support and hope. I had been lonely for many years, the whole Irish debacle was challenging to say the least, I had had to bankrupt myself, and to top that I had not had sex for *years*! I seriously began to wonder if everything was still working.

I threw myself one hundred percent into the relationship with Brian. The Mask was not interested in meeting up, ever. Clearly he or she or it, liked the connection as an on-line friendship *only*. I needed more, and because I got on so well with Brian, and the attraction was there when we actually met, I went for it. We had met at a time in our lives, where we were a stronger force together than apart. Brian brought blessings of enhancing my ability to travel around once again. I did not like leaving the dogs in a kennel. But it was a home from home family concern and they seemed to do okay there. I only left for up to six days at a time really, so it was probably good for my familiars to have a change of scene also. I am not sure. I did it on trust anyway.

Regarding The Psychic Society I did not do anything out of desperation. I was under extreme stress and duress to make sure there was a handsome income. I had to pay two lots of bills, provide bank rolls for casino trips, and make sure two lots of rent were covered. Brian did well at casino, but sometimes played on when he should not have done so. Easy for me to say. Obviously he wanted his own money and more independence, and this was part of his way to find this. Sometimes it worked, sometimes it did not. What I did not like was the hideous pit of despair the failures put him into. I began to get very concerned. At points it seemed that casino was more important than coming to see me. He would declare he could not possibly travel to see me unless he had a good winning trip first. I came to understand the complexity of his mind and situation in no uncertain terms. No one knew the pitch of stress I was under. I had to stay calm, and keep everything on track. My contract and intentions required it. I was heavily invested at this stage, literally.

As always I trusted spirit to guide and deliver me. So even in midst of these difficulties with The Psychic Society I sensed there must be an important change happening. I tried to sit loose to it all for this reason. But I did become alarmed at points as it all seemed so unnecessarily vindictive. Having said, that the gift in the situation, was that it led to further career developments and greater independence.

I obviously was not cut out to follow rules. Rules which became ever more ridiculous apparently. Last I heard The Psychic Society were proposing finger printing and criminal checks of all prospective new members. No. comment.

I really had to fight my corner on this one. Brian used the analogy of a ring fight, and he was not far wrong. All of a sudden I was getting emails from the offices of Simon Cowell, and Ashton Kutcher. I was laughing to myself. "Good luck with Bono.".Surely whoever was doing this, was planning to approach his people also.

Basically all my back stories were under threat, true and honest, though they were. I advised Simon Cowell's offices that I had indeed been on a show with Simon and Louis Walsh, and suggested that they double check their details.

I reminded Ashton's offices, that Ashton had mentioned me on *The Jimmy Kimmel Show* as his twitter psychic. Unasked for, he had opened his interview using me as an example of one of the interesting people he had met on twitter. Ashton was following me on Twitter at this point, and we had a fun social media connection. I advised the San Francisco office that I would sort this out personally with Ashton. They were questioning my web site presentation, saying that Mr Kutcher was mentioned there without permission. The particular testimony under scrutiny was actually written by a client.

Just as the whole back story was not made up, the testimony was also authentic: "Good Morning Ms Sarah. Ashton Kutcher is right. You are certainly on point with everything. I haven't had a reading with you in years but you were so truthful." I pointed out that Ashton had not asked me if he could mention me on a public show, and indeed at one point it looked like I was about to be derided by Kimmel, so I was nervous that it might actually be detrimental to my standing potentially. "Is she mad?" said Kimmel. It was a predictable comment from someone who clearly knows nothing at all about psychics. Ashton realized what was happening, and because I had supported and helped him a lot in different ways, he jumped to my defense, calling me "on point". He kindly made it clear that I was impressive as a psychic not crazy. The next day when I joked about it with him on Twitter, he said: "That was for U" in a tweet. I responded: "why thank you - I think!" What could have been a bit of a disaster for me was turned around nicely by Ashton's generous comment.

The actions taken allegedly by The Psychic Society, started to get decidedly unfair, if not downright dirty. I had done *nothing* to warrant such treatment. It was as if someone was trying to totally squash my spirit as well as my business. In response to the freeze someone put on my carefully built web site, a colleague took over the operation, and set up an even better panel. She was able to have select members of The Psychic Society who had wanted to be on One World Psychics on this new panel One World Metaphysicians. Eventually the freeze was also lifted on One World Psychics on condition that no members of The Psychic Society be on it. In the piece about me on his Facebook business page, the CEO of The Psychic Society had magnanimously said that *anyone* could be on my panel if they wanted to be. He was clearly trying to sound reasonable, and fair to the people he did not actually employ. This was hilarious to me with all that was going on behind the scenes, that was apparently not being declared.

All the emails to Simon Cowell and Ashton Kutcher came at a highly coincidental time if it they were not connected to The Psychic Society's attempts to undermine me. Why would Ashton and Simon after so many years suddenly take exception to my work, and how it was being presented, precisely in the week I was being attacked by these people? It is fairly obvious that the office workers of both men were contacted who knew no better. The validity of my back story was kosher. I had every right to present myself and my endorsements as I wished to. Everything I mentioned had taken place in full public view, and I was not betraying any confidences.

My friend and I agreed that she would run One World Metaphysicians for two years, while I was under "observation." We would then review it all, and see if I wanted to take over once the two year time frame had expired. One World Metaphysicians stayed live throughout the requisite two years, as it was all done in someone else's name with their backing. I was never in competition with The Psychic Society anyway.

The intention of the One World Metaphysicians was that it was to operate without agenda. It was spirit guided, pure and simple. This panel of wonderful teachers and healings was compiled to hold light for the world. There was no payment to join beyond a discretionary, donation to assist with running costs. There was no obligation to pay even this, nor was there any obligation to display the web site logo. Members of the panel are there because they *get* it. I was originally guided to set up One World Psychics after the Paris bombings, and massacre at the Bataclan Theater. The panel was intentionally non-profit, so it could not be said to be in competition with any commercial enterprise. I was so sick of all the pettiness I had encountered, that I felt the world needed something not run by human agendas of profit and status.

One World Metaphysicians is a place for expert spiritual workers to be found. I had Psychic Society panel members approaching *me* to be on this panel, and I also asked a few of them to join. I was not head hunting to usurp them away from The Psychic Society. Indeed many of them were also on Bob Proctor's psychics panel anyway; which incidentally *is* a commercial enterprise in direct competition with other such panels. The Psychic Society were okay with Bob Proctor hosting their members on his site. But they felt me to be some kind of incredible threat. I found this whole episode to be a completely unnecessary petty expression of rivalry. Quite ridiculous. I was hurt and offended in equal measure. At one point The Psychic Society had been my saving grace. But *whatever*. It is all water under the bridge at this stage.

In Porlock I was largely isolated and lonely, keeping company with my five dogs, who were my familiars, and passed as my family. The friends I made through The Psychic Society were amazing. I thought I was going to be protected, nurtured and understood in this environment; and for a while it felt as if I *was*. I was able to set up my own radio show *Soul to Soul* on CBS Radio, through the contacts The Psychic Society had with CBS. I then expanded my reach to the exclusive *World Puja Network* and got my own show *Heart to Heart* on that too. The *World Puja Network* was *nothing* to do with The Psychic Society. I got that position on my own merits, through a timely connection with founder Maureen Moss. She got me set up for the new season, then announced she was abandoning ship for the moment. I loved the interviewing process, and interviewed some major names in the metaphysical world. Many of the people I interviewed are now on the panel of One World Metaphysicians.

Mysterious emails also went around panel members of One World Psychics in an attempt to discredit me. A couple of Psychic Society members who had *asked* to join the panel then asked to leave. I explained to them what was going on. They still left and remained on the Psychic Society panel. A couple of people told me what they had received, and I explained the situation. They then stayed. Someone who had worked with the CEO on his retreat, asked to be taken off the panel because of their business association; so this in itself revealed the source of all these emails defaming me. In the post on his business page, the Psychic Society CEO denied that his company were doing these emails. I have this direct evidence that they were behind it all. Certainly the indicates were strong indeed. The true light workers with no agenda remained on One World Psychics, which then became One World Metaphysicians.

I loved interviewing people, for CBS, and *The World Puja Network*. I certainly preferred it to being interviewed myself. I did not want to make a lasting career out of broadcasting. But I did find it very fulfilling and interesting. At one point it looked like every psychic in America had their own blog talk show, so I bowed out of the whole thing once the experience had gone as far as it could for me. I never want to look like part of a crowd. I am really a bit of a hedge witch. I work alone, and do not thrive on being part of a team. I can do it for a time, but more often than not it has a specific shelf life. The whole Psychic Society debacle shows that I am not designed to answer to people. I need to honor my own authenticity and autonomy.

The main upshot of the whole saga is, that Brian Hunter and I became partners who worked effectively to help some very complex cases. God really upped the ante with the clients needing assistance, and by his grace we get incredible out of this world results.

IT'S THE LITTLE DETAILS THAT ARE VITAL. LITTLE THINGS MAKE BIG THINGS HAPPEN.
JOHN WOODEN

CHAPTER THIRTY-NINE

Nuts and Bolts

The upside of The Gift is that it greatly helps people, if not always the person who possesses it. I do love the rewarding aspects of what I do. It is great to see someone dealing with a really difficult situation, walk out of the door with a spring in their step. These days when I work with a client I work largely on line. I do readings, healing and life-coaching remotely. This works because? Everything is Energy.

Sometimes I get asked "how on earth can you do it this way? Don't you need to see me face to face?" My response? "Be wary of the psychic who *has* to see you!" My regular clients know this, and trust me implicitly. The people who find me generally do too. I do not work for people who want readings on the spot or instant answers on the phone to "prove what you can do." Such people are typically energy vampires, who do the round of all the psychics out there, and are essentially looking for free information. It might seem harsh, but doing this work, the psychic has to have very clear boundaries, for self protection, and also for the protection of the client. It has to be done correctly and professionally or the results are less than satisfactory.

Any work that I do is designed to be right for the client, and is solely done to benefit them. I do not suggest services for the sake of it. I follow my guidance and present the correct offers, deals and recommendations based on the client's needs. I do not encourage a dependency on my work. In fact I am actually happy if they never feel the need to work with me again, as long as they got their result. So long as we have effectively shifted the issue oppressing them, it is a job well done.

My work has become increasingly more akin to spiritual life coaching, in this bid to empower people. It is important to me that I make sure the person is functioning as fully and effectively as possible in all areas of their life. I take time to go over every aspect in which they feel thwarted or stuck. I then assess if we need Brian's input for the case or not.

Balance is the key to our happiness and equilibrium. My work is much less about predicting what is going to happen next, and much more about what can we *make* happen here? I can do the usual predictive reading yes. But I inform clients that is much more powerful to get creative and change the possibilities in front of them using manifestation and intention.

My work is not so much about information as about empowerment and getting specific decided results. This is much more dynamic and exciting than the "what is for me?" thing; which assumes your destiny is set in stone and that is that.

I would probably be a bit snobby about the term fortune teller if truth be told. I am a bit wary of the image and expectations which people attach to the head scarf, loopy ear rings and crystal ball. I do not relate to that at all. I do not really aspire to working on the end of Brighton Pier. But I guess there is a first time for everything. I have nothing against Mystic Meg and her ilk. Indeed I am fully aware that is how some members of the Irish public in particular perceive me. There is not much I can do about that, except explain how I work when people make contact. I will not see you face to face. This is for my protection, and your best results. I work very connectedly reading your energy down the line or across the ethers and I do not need to see you. This also protects me from some of the stalkers who have nodded in my direction. It makes perfect sense to shield myself from any nonsense, energetic or otherwise. It allows me to do a better job.

Many people assume that psychics take advantage of vulnerable people. This is nonsense. Certainly in my case it is nonsense. Sometimes, us mystics are the last port of call for people who have tried everything to get sorted. Sometimes as a healer, I work for someone who has tried everything else under the sun. I make no false promises; but I do remain committed to clients until they get a more than satisfactory result. In short I deliver. Or God delivers through me.

I know many people also assume that it is just women interested in seeking out this kind of help. Nothing could be further from the truth. Men are human and need help to. They may not always admit it so readily is all. Men are certainly more pragmatic creatures than most women. So they may have to suspend judgment somewhat to avail of help. But the beauty of this work is that it meets you where you are. I explain things to you in your language. You only hear what you can understand and handle. This is the discernment part. I do not deliberately withhold information. But I do have to be very careful and responsible in how I work and in how I present things to the client.

Sometimes yes, the people looking for help are vulnerable. But more often than not, they need wise, grounded accurate guidance. I have dealt with people experiencing a whole spectrum of issues. Of course I can not divulge these in the detail because of client confidentiality. In general terms you could say I have had to get a handle on anything you care to mention.

High Court shenanigans, divorce settlements, conception issues, and the sex of children, illness, depression, work, relationships, money, serious business dealings. You name it. I have probably had a brush with it in some shape or form. I tend to steer clear of party bookings and entertainment events. I have done some such appearances for charity. But I generally avoid places where people assume you will come along and deliver some cheery inoffensive predictions, and light hearted banter. It does not really work like that. The reality is, this is *not* entertainment; nor is it for entertainment purposes only. This is serious stuff, and people take it seriously. I am not personally capable of doing flippant or superfluous readings. I prefer to dig deep and really help someone with whatever it is they are facing. Sex, gender, creed and race are irrelevant. If someone needs help and I can help I will do my best for them.

When I begin to work for someone I have to put aside my agenda and expectations. Every healing and reading and work process has its organic flow. I have to *really* be present and listen to what this is *in the moment*. There is absolutely no point in trying to second guess what is happening, nor what is going to happen. Also it is completely necessary that I switch off from my own life, and give myself over 100% to the person I am working with. I actually stop readings intermittently for this reason. Whenever I need to recharge, reflect and sort things, I make myself unavailable to clients unless it is absolutely urgent. I will not read for a client if I am not in the right space to help them, as I do not think it is fair on them.

A reading builds in layers. Someone can sit there in silence and say nothing at all throughout. Or they can chip in intermittently and ask questions as we proceed. It can be as interactive or as hands free as the client likes. I think the end result is generally the same though. I do not need prompts or cues from the client to read them. All the information is there present in their energy field. In fact sometimes it really is better they say nothing at all.

I like to make sure people get what they are paying for, so I do urge them to think about the work in advance, and make sure they are clear in their intentions, goals and the information they need. It is important they take responsibility for themselves in this. I will make sure all their issues are covered. But it is best they exit the reading having had everything answered.

Sometimes in a session the energetic interaction is much more important than the information. Some clients are truly stuck in a primordial soup, which is keeping them paralyzed and ineffective. Such sessions are primarily healings. An energy shift is needed, and the magic happens when this occurs. Often when someone books with me, they start to see results in the lead up to the appointment. This is because when you engage with my energy, God is already working on it all for you. Of course he does not *need* me in the mix. But if you have called me in, then generally you will notice that miracles happen and that you start to get answers once we make contact.

There is more than a bit of a mystery attached to this work. I am always interested to hear what has happened to a client who has booked with me in the run up to the work; and also then what happens in the couple of weeks after it is complete. More often than not amazing shifts occur which free the person to get on with things much more efficiently.

The nuts and bolts of a reading begin with setting the scene with some astrology relevant to the client's star sign. I do not need this to do a reading. But it provides some added interest and a context as I begin to connect. It also helps to explain current astrological trends to the client and put what is going on in some organic framework also. This all helps set the scene, and the detailed picture then falls in on top of that building brick by brick.

Once I start a reading, the information flows thick and fast. Specific names, timings and places pop into my head. These are usually a signal to steer us to talk about the next subject of import. The names and places are always accurate without exception. I am not one of those psychics who says I have an 'A' name. I will say "who is Annabel?" and Annabel it is. Not Anne. nor Bella. *Annabel.* Likewise Margaret will always be Margaret, not Mary or Matilda.

As for literally hearing and seeing things? I choose not to develop those aspects too much; though audio and visual messages do present the odd time. I choose not to major on clairaudience or clairvoyance as I would find too much hearing and seeing uncomfortable to deal with. The odd flash is fine. I am primarily clairsentient, which means I get the feeling, from the heart. I use intuition and tune into what I feel the person needs to hear. This is most certainly not the same thing as what they want to hear; though thankfully sometimes it is.

In the past I have done readings with other psychics in the name of research. I try to down play looking too much into the future these days, for all sorts of reasons. I do have a couple of supportive friends I exchange questions with, when I or they feel stuck in a moment. This kind of support from a psychic friend is a wonderful gift. But again it must not be overdone. Anything over cooked in the psychic work starts to turn sour pretty quickly. It really is best not to over ask the same question. Also it is crucial not to second guess the spirit world. There can be some very funky events and reads if we fall foul of this curiosity. Less is definitely more. Even better is nothing at all.

Throughout my crisis times I relied heavily on Anke, and the sound spiritual wisdom and guidance from June. Both Anke and Jane got me out of some corners. They also got me into some, whenever I over asked or over listened. It is so important to keep one's own perspective, even as we seek advice from others. Anything can lead you astray. Even the best intentions.

I sometimes wish there was another me out there who could read me in a definitive way. My friends Kathy and Brian come close much of the time. In fact along with Anke, they form a powerful trio of "professional Aquarians," all born on 27th of January. So if you want sound wisdom and vision, *do* seek out an Aquarian. I am a wannabe Aquarian, as I have Uranus conjunct the Sun. This gives me some very Aquarian qualities, and must be part of the reason I have so many wonderful Aquarians in my life. What makes me *super* psychic is my Pisces ascendant, and Scorpio moon. My Virgo sun then grounds the whole thing and ensures you get your results. The Mermaid has a fishy tale and shares risky insights, but she is also quite practical.

I have used psychics myself as you can see. For many reasons, observational information being the main one. This hands-on learning curve was important. It showed me what not to do, and helped me to see the variety of ways messages come through. Observing the different energies and approaches has enabled me to hone interpretation. Anke was not always brilliant at interpreting the symbolism and meaning of what she saw. I was able to apply what she picked up and make it relevant. I seemed to be *au fait* with symbols, their meaning, and intention, when the spirit world used them to communicate.

I pride myself on the grounded nature of my presentation in both readings and esoteric writings. Too much in this field is inaccessible, and comes over as most odd to those not inclined to understand it. I seem to have been able to build a bridge between skeptics and psychics, so that the one is more inclined to understand the other. Because I am academically trained, with a modicum of intelligence, I am able to bring other skills to the table. It is this mix, which enables more people, across a broader spectrum of inclination to understand and receive messages.

In the name of research, and in crisis times, I have looked at what a select few psychics pick up. I have my team of "go-tos," which helps me immensely when I need objective input. But I tend to rely on myself as much as possible in recent years. In the past, I was floundering with some very tricky circumstances, and I needed support where I could find it. In retrospect I wondered if listening to others had actually created some of my issues. But I would not dream of not accepting my personal responsibility in the scenarios I faced.

Which came first the chicken or the egg? Did I need the support because I had gone off track listening to other people? Sometimes, yes I think so. Other times, definitely not.

All of this demonstrates how careful you must be when you pass your power over to someone else. What works best is if you stay as objective as possible about your life. It is a balance though, and there is no shame in seeking help f you really need it. Of course you must trust the person you are working with. If you do not, you will hold yourself up immensely. Sometimes, that surrender to the help provided is in your best interests. Other times, it most definitely is not.

I assess this balance all the time with clients. Where are they at with their relationship and interaction regarding what they are being shown and told? A time comes, when I have done everything I can, and they must be cut loose to roll with the energies. This is a crucial point in the proceedings. The work generally comes together in this moment. An empowered client is thus pushed from the nest. They may feel worried, concerned, cut loose. But I only ever do this at the right time. Using my own experience as a guideline, plus my innate instincts about the client, I make judgment calls. This work requires discernment, wisdom. bravery, and huge leaps of faith. I get results for clients. For myself, I have been through the karmic wringer. The upshot is, it enables me to be effective now for others.

Many years ago now I was given some very loaded information about my love life and my financial situation. I have to say these two predictions put me through a lot of suffering. They were sold to me in no uncertain terms. I am not stupid and I really trusted the information. It resonated as true. Indeed it may all yet be true. Was it a creative set of predictions, which would align with the events happening. Or was my destiny set in stone? Equally, I may well have blown that path in so many ways with certain actions that I took.

These are amazingly important questions to consider when manifesting for your own life. Do you want or need to trust someone's guidance? Or are you going to tap what is innately powerful about yourself and roll with it? There may be times when you need to do a bit of both. As with all things, balance is key. But it just goes to show, it is not a good idea to take anything for granted regarding your fate.

To be fair, nothing has happened really to contradict what was predicted. But it has proved to be a much more circuitous route than anticipated. Dealing with the reality as it stands, much of it looks all kinds of wrong. But I have seen enough of life now, to not dismiss anything. Anything can happen, and when you are aligned with a spirit of adventure, it probably will.

One thing though, it is so, so important not to get hooked up on issues of timing. This will literally rob you of your life. Issues of timing have been way off in my case. Even if the events eventually happen, so much has now gone before, that really it would have been better not to have been told. This is where a little knowledge is dangerous. There is such a huge responsibility in presenting information correctly. There is also a huge responsibility in receiving it. Sometimes it is not beneficial to have an accurate prediction. But for something like a lottery win, you do have to buy a ticket. So IS the win there, or are you creating it. Perhaps I could have gone many years, buying no tickets at all, and then suddenly be gifted one for Christmas which hits the big one. Again anything is possible. What I do know is that *how* the timing was presented was irresponsible. The "any minute now" energy certainly does apply to a random win falling from the skies. But when the years roll by, how immediate is that really? In terms of eternity the concept is immediate. In terms of human life, it starts to feel more like a lesson than a reality.

I personally get the client's age at the timing of key events. This is definitely more practical and useful than being told something is going to happen "in the blink of an eye." Going for readings those few years back put my world into a spin, and it has been very difficult to come back from the brink. I loved the entertainment aspect of the readings, and there was a high level of accuracy to them also. But when push comes to shove, those two main events did not happen. I would always urge people who go for readings to be very careful who they see. And even then remain a little detached and observe the reading and its outcome.

There is definitely a mixed blessing in being able to read the future. But I am less and less sure it is a good idea for people to know the future. I am less and less convinced that it is a blessing at all. I would not now go for a far reaching reading unless I was really cornered by something. Even then I would think twice. I prefer to trust my own intuition and the advice of my team, and the Aquarians in my life. Destiny can work in the strangest way.

What happened to me, enables me now to help people. Destiny and spirit, God and the universe can be quite cute leading us down paths we have not intended for ourselves. We are here to learn. There is a divine economy in operation also. Where many things can be sorted through one person, entity, outlet, that is the route the divine intelligence of the universe will take. I have tried to step of this wheel believe me. But to no avail . It seems my destiny is to help people. This is obviously what I am meant to be doing. Living through some major traumas in order to advise and help others get some perspective. I would have no authority to assist others if not for these experiences. Because of them, I can speak with assurance and certainty and absolutely know what I am talking about.

There is no doubt that what is a Gift, can sometimes feel like a curse. There is no doubt I make some people very nervous and uncomfortable. Who am I to have set myself up like this. By what authority do I even do this work? I hope on reading this, those who are interested now have more understanding. Equally, I may be causing much more confusion by being this transparent. It is the risk I now advisedly take. Certainly it is a risk I have deferred for a very long time. So many questions arise when thinking of putting pen to paper about one's life experience. "Who on earth would want to read it," being the main one. I am well aware as I write Mermaid in The Kitchen that some will annihilate my world view internally as they read it; even if they can even be bothered to read it. I will be judged for sure; I may even be vilified. I doubt I will be praised for putting pen to paper; though hopefully it will be at least a fairly good read. People will be interested in varying degrees of engagement. Some will not read it at all; some will dip into it for the juicy bits; while others will bravely wade through it; Some may be curious, even relish it, probably a small minority. While some will nervously wonder what on earth I have said about them. I hope I have managed to be kind, fair and balanced throughout. Writing any kind of revenge book, despite all the trauma I have experienced is *not* my intention. I trying to be fair, honest and transparent in the hope of helping people, as well as explaining myself, and a bit more about the work I do. At the end of the day, sometimes we have to do something for ourselves. I have not needed to write this as a purging cathartic experience. Much of it was written privately years ago, and it played that role then. I parked it all several times, because of the huge dilemma which presents when you choose to write about your life. How can this be done without hurting other people? Well the answer is I do not really know. I have tried to be as respectful as I can be, without compromising the honesty of what I went through. Apologies in advance to those who are in any way offended. If you recognize yourself it is completely accidental, as all names from the more "awkward" incidences have been changed to preserve privacy.

I THINK THAT ALL WOMEN ARE WITCHES, IN THE SENSE THAT A WITCH IS A MAGICAL BEING. DON'T BE SCARED OF WITCHES, BECAUSE WE ARE GOOD WITCHES, AND YOU SHOULD APPRECIATE OUR MAGICAL POWER.
YOKO ONO

CHAPTER FORTY

Am I A Witch?

The Witchery, situated on Castle Hill is appropriately named. Built on the sight of the burnings and persecution of hundreds of female witches centuries ago, The Witchery is not surprisingly haunted. The active atmosphere hits you as soon as you walk down the ancient Boswell's Close to reception. It is like stepping back in time. At once charming and creepy. The reception staff check you in from a church pulpit, and the style is informal but decadent. Classed as a five star hotel, this is where celebrities such as Michael Douglas and Catherine Zeta Jones stay when they come to savor the Old Town delights of Auld Reekie aka Edinburgh. Dannie Minogue has called it a "lust den," and Andrew Lloyd Webber believed The Witchery Restaurant to be the prettiest restaurant he has ever seen: "Is this the prettiest restaurant ever? I think so!"

The Observer newspaper highlights The Witchery as "A place for those who like their beds four poster and baths designed for two." *Harpers and Queen* magazine describe the Witchery as being "almost as famous as Edinburgh Castle itself."

The popular Old Rectory suite, which can be booked up as much as nine months in advance, is described by The Times as the most romantic love nest in Britain; "A pure unmitigated pleasure palace." The Witchery has nine specially designed and renovated suites called various appropriate names, such as The Armoury, The Old Rectory, Sempill, The Turret, The Vestry, and The Library. The names, the setting and the general atmosphere feel like a live enacted game of Cluedo. During our stay it began to feel like it might end up being Ms Sarah in the Inner sanctum hit over the head with a mallet by a statue of Queen Victoria witnessed by super sleuth Brian Hunter.

On arrival Brian Hunter and I were met by a Scottish leprechaun, the camp, delightfully hospitable Roxy. He was full of enthusiasm and stories and informed us that we had booked a "cracker" of a suite. He was right, on stepping across the threshold of the Sempill suite, on the opposite side of the cobbled street, I have to say we were both blown away. Basically we had booked a five star type apartment for the price of a good hotel room. So either it is much cheaper comparatively to do the penthouse thing in Scotland. Or The Witchery is an acquired taste and does not suit everyone.

I have to say I am not sure I would recommend it to God-loving church-goers. I am one of these of course, but I have an armory of weapons with which to test and battle spirits, and experience of coping with all kinds of challenges delivered on the esoteric plane. Plus my companion was Brian, who is fearless and even more able to cope with nonsense than I am. Put it this way, I would not have stayed there alone. But with Brian it was more than okay. I felt safe, though wary, and on guard. I could tell the energy of the place was less than savory. And in truth I am not sure how advisable it was for me to stay there. I am rather sensitive.

Judging by the guest books in the suites, The Witchery does a roaring trade for romantic couples on honeymoons and anniversaries. Plus those quizzically looking to get spooked if at all possible. We did not inform The Witchery staff that we were two known reputable psychics, as we wanted to enter into the proceedings without prejudice and expectation. I am sure Roxy had a lot more ghost stories to share, if only we had asked. But we wanted to stay open-minded and receptive to what our own experience was going to be.

Travelling up from London on the train after meeting Brian from Heathrow, all seemed well. We were all set for a catch up time and I was greatly looking forward to a couple of nights in the famous Witchery Hotel Suites. I used to live in Edinburgh, and the Witchery was all part of the gothic mystique of this aptly called *City of Ghosts*.

I was not a Goth I hasten to add, but I have always loved the dark and ancient magical feeling this city conjures up. The Witchery Restaurant founded in 1979 by entrepreneur James Thomson, has a great reputation for service and high class food. But it was the haunted suites, upstairs and across the cobbled street, we were here to investigate.

Upon entering the Sempill suite, which to be fair sounded like something straight from the pages of a Harry Potter book, we were amazed at the coloring and tastefully chosen antique furniture. Plus the four poster bed was probably the best bed I have ever seen, and (theoretically) slept in. We had an early check in, so simply enjoyed the suite and the surrounding streets of The Royal Mile, George IVth Bridge, and The Grassmarket. As an added bonus we came out of Saint Giles Cathedral just in time to see The Queen of England making her return car ride from the Castle to Holyrood Palace after meeting with various dignitaries.

It was a historical time in Scotland, as the nation prepared to vote for independence from England. So Elizabeth II was there with bells on, playing her PR opportunity to the max, in a bid to assist David Cameron. Brian snapped a picture of her Majesty as she passed by in her cavalcade. What was incredible to see was that Brian had caught in the photo, a witch in her pointy black hat peering through the window at The Queen from the other side of the street. The contrast button on Instagram made the image even clearer. It was more evidence this area of Edinburgh was haunted; as if we needed that after what was about to happen.

We returned to Sempill at night fall, which comes late in Scotland. The land of the midnight sun does not feel far away in this country where night descends reluctantly at eleven o'clock at night, and dawn brightens the sky just after four in the morning. We had already put out our breakfast request on the little witch door knocker. We were fully looking forward to that wonderful bed and the sumptuous bathroom with roll top bath and power shower. As we ate the chicken kebab takeout in the small sitting room, I could see energy flickering in the long corridor.

The hallway of the suite is clearly haunted, and I began to feel a little uneasy. The room we were eating in had a presence of an old woman, and I was sure I needed to keep the light on in that room throughout the night. It was not a very uncomfortable haunting. But it was very real, and I did feel more uneasy as bed time approached. I had a bath and looked up at the ceiling. I could see what looked like spots of blood spilling through the ceiling. I also heard a lot of rattling, which thankfully turned out to be the air conditioning servicing the main bedroom. As I got into the bath I heard Brian call my name very clearly. I jumped out the bath thinking he had seen something interesting. But no, he was organizing his clothes and assured me he had not called my name. Hmm...

I finished up my bath and told Brian about the apparent old dried blood spots. He shared that he had sensed a murder upstairs many hundreds of years ago, and that the blood had leaked through the ceiling into this Sempill apartment. I was continually aware of the spirit in the hallway throughout our stay in this suite. And Brian woke up giggling because he heard a drunk Scottish ghost singing the psalms to him on his side of the bed "even though I walk through the valley of death, yet will I fear no ill" was what this drunk was singing. Again Hmm...

These hauntings all made some kind of sense, and even though spooky, they are sort of within a norm of acceptability. They were whisperings on the ethers, faint echoes of distant times. In such a loaded location, it was really nothing surprising. I had fully expected to feel uneasy in the suite. It probably was not the best place for a light worker such as myself. As for Brian, he is fearless, so at least I kept good company.

The Witchery and The Royal Mile are built over an ancient street which housed many businesses and was a refuge for the poor during the plague. Edinburgh has many layers and many spooky presences. Even the main street holds secrets below. Tours are regularly available of the underground caverns and vaults; and of course Edinburgh has more than its fair share of ghost tours. Our night in Sempill was comfortable enough, although it clearly is haunted. But it was nothing compared to what we experienced in The Inner Sanctum Suite a couple of nights later.

We enjoyed a trip through to Stirling Castle in the interim, and I was able to stir up the memories from my time at university there. I could clearly see I had not imagined it. This was one beautifully depressing place. As I stood in the same spot, where I had stood with my Nan, I heard the echo of her words "don't spend your life chasing rainbows." I realized, I had failed miserably at following her advice. I had quite obviously spent my whole life "chasing rainbows," with varying degrees of success, but ultimate failure. Or so it seemed.

Here I was, back at Stirling, in some kind of soul retrieval moment, and I am not sure how good it felt. Admittedly, it was healing to be there with the grounded presence of Brian. But suddenly I felt quite lonely. Life had turned out so differently than I had hoped or expected. Indeed it had not really turned out at all. I was in flux, I had no surety for the future whatsoever. What had I achieved really? I could help people if they trusted me to do so. That was as good as it got. In terms of my personal life, I had not found peace, calm and a settled home. But I guess that was just as it was meant to be for the moment.

On Sunday, after the melancholy stirrings of Stirling we were excited to return to The Witchery and our booking in the first original Witchery Suite. The Inner Sanctum was in the main part of the hotel. It was one of the original rooms, available above the restaurant for anyone who did not feel inclined to return home that night. It became so popular and was so much in demand, that the proprietor slowly expanded the property, buying as much real estate surrounding the restaurant as possible. Currently, there are nine incredible rooms to stay in, and we planned to investigate them one by one, gathering together all possible ghost stories to assist the marketing and intrigue of the place. Well that was the intention, which was modified somewhat, when we realized The Witchery wants to be seen as more of a romantic place than a spooky one. Okay. Good luck.

Before our stay, the staff were aware of three hauntings in the various Witchery buildings. In *The Secret Garden* restaurant, Derek Acorah, the famous medium, who worked on *Most Haunted*, verified the existence of a little girl ghost. *The Secret Garden* is built on the site of an old school play ground. Apparently this little girl ghost did not die painfully and is quite happy as she goes about her day (night). But she does leave a trail of little wet feet sometimes across the restaurant floor.

In The Inner Sanctum suite, a monk has been seen, and the temperature in the room is known to drop around three o' clock in the morning. I sensed from the guest book, that the majority of people who have stayed in The Inner Sanctum are not totally sure if it is haunted or not. We can absolutely assure them that it *is*. In the night ahead, we both experienced one of the most spooky and unsettling events that has ever happened to either of us. Brian is not easily impressed and I am not easily spooked. But what happened next left us both someone bemused and reflective.

On entering The Inner Sanctum I immediately sensed the male ghost in the first seating area. I am not sure I would have said it was a monk. But I definitely saw energy and sensed a male presence as soon as I stepped into the suite. I sensed quite a tall head master or rector type of energy, which makes sense as at one point this building was once the rectory to a nearby church and it hosted many important meetings for The Church Of Scotland. On reflection it was probably the monk.

I was not too bothered by this male energy right at the door of the suite. I just assumed the night would be much the same as the night we spent in The Sempill Suite the couple of nights previous. I could not have been more wrong.

In The Inner Sanctum the first thing you notice is the bust of Queen Victoria. It is a larger version of the figurine you will see on the set of *Eastenders* and it totally dominates the suite. I was puzzled by the presence of Queen Vic. at first. But on researching how much Queen Victoria loved Scotland after her beloved Albert died it made sense. Even though Queen Victoria wore mourning clothes for the rest of her time on earth, she found comfort in Scotland, and in her close relationship with her man servant John Brown (played by Billy Connolly in the movie *Mrs Brown*).

Something about the statue troubled me as we settled into the suite and I stupidly used a crystal, herbal cleansing liquid called *Serapis Bey*, by Aura Soma around the statue. I felt the energy around it was heavy and not quite right. I perhaps should not have done anything. But in a way I felt justified with what then happened during the night.

Both Brian and I awoke at four o'clock in the morning, and even though it was light outside, we began to experience a major haunting. Looking at the Statue sideways on from the bed, Brian noticed there were hairs growing out of the Queen's chest.

We both saw this clearly, and were somewhat repelled and fascinated at the same time. Interestingly neither of us got up out of bed to check it out. But the chest hair was very visible, and I think it was important we *both* saw it.

I had already noted that her crown looked like horns in the night time light. So the mark of the beastly hairs was a rather troubling in addition. In retrospect I am surprised how cool we both were. Not much phases Brian. But I can tell you if he had not been there I would have vacated that room fairly quickly.

Incredibly, we just fell back to sleep, and a couple of hours later Brian woke me up again. I immediately noticed that the statue had turned a ninety degree angle and was now positioned looking straight into our bed.

Omg?!

Even more disconcertingly, Queen Victoria with her chest hair and horns, seemed to be looking straight at me with disapproval. On photographs I took, there is a marked difference in the energy of the statue. On our arrival in the room, she was very much Queen Victoria and the lace around her head was apparent. She was looking as feminine as possible you might say. But by the end of the night, the statue had become something else entirely. It was much more male, intense, brooding, and I am reluctant to say it, demonic.

I think we reassured ourselves at the time by saying it was probably a trick played by the hotel on their guests. But in reality it was not this at all. It was something much more sinister. There was no sign of any remote control device upon waking. At check out I told the hotel receptionist manager about it and he said "that's a new one." He looked puzzled and there was no reference to a similar event in the guest book. I am sure Brian did not move the statue and I certainly did not. It actually took two of us to move it back around to its correct position in the morning. It was very heavy.

I am not overly dramatic as a psychic and I take it all in my stride. But there was definitely something off whack with the energy of the room after this event. I am left wondering, did I stir the beast with my clearing gesture? Or was I in fact correct to attempt to shift this energy out of the place? I felt a strong connection between the statue of the devil which dominates the restaurant below, and the Statue of Queen Victoria in our bedroom.

This was very much an alarming event. It seems we were for some reason singled out for this experience. I have to say it affected me quite deeply and is sobering too. The force it must have taken to move the statue was incredible. It indicates a dark and powerful energy, Not one that you would want to mess with.

Am I a witch? Queen Victoria might indeed have thought so. Some energy was stirred by my actions. I had not intended it. Indeed, I intended to protect and cleanse the space. Looks like I did the opposite. Brian taught me a lesson. He leaves things alone. Lets things be. Clearly I should have done the same. Equally, had I not done this, perhaps the statue might have started walking across the room or something. Maybe I performed some kind of damage limitation? NO. Didn't think so.

But, the "witch" question is an interesting one. I sometimes joke that I am a witch; but I certainly do not set out to be one. I do not perform spells or rituals, and I would never join a coven. You would find me sitting in a church before you ever saw that. I do not like the term "witch" really, except as a joke, because of the connotations it evokes. I am a Christian, does that even mean it is possible for me to also be a witch? I guess not, and yet both tendencies and ingredients are right there in the mix in my psyche. I like to think of myself as a Christian wiccan. Right there in the midst of a paradox is the place to be after all.

The very word "witch" intrigues and horrifies people. It is a loaded label. Just look at the history behind it. There have been witch hunts, persecutions, murders, and distrust of those who walk the magical ways through the ages. The powers that be who dictate to the sheep, hate the idea that there may be witches out there who are living contrary to their laws, demands, and stipulations. For those who look to external authority to tell them what to believe, watch, and follow, witches present a problem. The existence of magical unusual people who live on their own terms sparks interest, but also outrage. These people set themselves up to be persecuted and judged, simply by being who they are. I have certainly experienced my fair share of bullying over this issue. Ironically so; seeing as I am *not* a witch, despite what people might think or say. I am a magical, mermaid mystic. I get results for people, and my work creates change only because God and the universe use me as a vessel to channel good things for my clients. No matter how much I try to go under the radar, and be as anonymous as possible, I still attract attention as someone "unusual." It is something people see in me when they look me in the eye. Something about how I am in the world. As my school friend Jan recently said: "different worlds."

Jan is an immensely talented, intelligent and hands on lawyer. She would have also made an excellent teacher, and probably many other things besides. We recently reunited after many years of no contact. I returned to Portishead for a while to be near family, to catch up with everyone and everything after so many years in the wilderness. This was an amazing integrating and healing experience. Much needed for everyone. A time which increased my family's understanding of me, and the paths I have trodden; and it was very healing for me to be closer to those I love for a time.

Another huge up side of being back to my roots, was that several old school friends re- emerged. It was great to catch up and reconnect and share our life experiences. Jan, open to understanding, even though not really open to all things psychic listened to my journey with interest. She shared that just before her father had passed, they had agreed on a signal word. She would not share the signal word, and I actually asked her not to, as I knew it would be shown to me at the right time. The spirit world was clearly setting up something of a demonstration for her.

One Sunday while strolling along Clevedon Pier, with Ginny and her wonderful autistic boy Arron, I told Jan to watch for what happened that evening. She still had not told me the trigger word. But what I picked up was that she needed to watch for the context in which it appeared. She had told me she had heard it many times since his passing, as it was a relatively common word. I immediately recognized that she needed help unraveling how to receive her father's message. I explained that she should observe the context in which she next hears the word, and to particularly watch for what happened that evening.

I do not think she could quite believe what happened next. She did not tell me right away, but when we next met, she explained what occurred that evening. She was in a friend's house, looking out into the garden at the statue of a snail. The friend randomly said "Why, I do believe that snail is winking at you!" The friend had no idea of the agreed trigger word either, and Jan in her pragmatism was still not getting it. She was there staring at a snail; which indeed was the trigger word, and still not connecting the dots. The friend's comment sealed the deal, and left her in no doubt. She literally pointed out that the snail was winking at her!

Jan became a reticent believer, becoming increasingly full on, as she kept finding snails in strange places after that: on her car window, on the doorstep, in conversation. The Snail synchronicity has its resonance now, and it is clearly her father's way of saying "hello" to her whenever he can. They had agreed this word as evidence of the afterlife, which neither of them believed in. It took a psychic friend to tell her how to watch and apply the message. So we mystics do have a use sometimes, even for skeptics.

Some things in the psychic world are a stretch too far for people. I understand this, because I feel the same way. I am a big skeptic myself regarding other's work. You can see why. There are very few I even consult, let alone trust, and these are good friends, not random professionals. I think a random professional psychic would have a great problem reading me accurately now. I know Anke, Brian and Jane all feel the same way, and they all long for someone able to read and help them. Well they have me. Jane had a very difficult level of healing needed a year or so ago, and she did not think there was any one who could hit the spot for her. Thankfully my guides delivered as they always do. I will not take credit for such things. Though, I am relieved and grateful when miracles, and energy shifts occur through my "contacts," to benefit someone.

The more evolved and complex you become, and the more awake, the more tricky you are to read. Many spiritual consciousness workers will relate to this also. You really get to a point, where it is not advisable to be read. Share with friends who understand you, absolutely. But put your life in the hands of a stranger? No thanks. Not unless they come highly recommended, or come to you as a referral. Having said that I do not want to squash the fact that spirit can lead some wonderful people your way. Be open, despite my words of caution about who you connect with on these deep levels. When you work with someone energetically, you are opening to their energy, as well as their Gift. So if they are not fully evolved, or have issues themselves, there may always be a potential "funk" in their information. This is where your own wisdom and detachment is required. Take the pieces that speak to you, while remaining open. You never know, they may yet blow your mind. So hear the message, and do not discount it. Equally, do not go out and put yourself on the line because of it. This depends on the nature of what you have heard of course. It may be that you are supposed to completely trust the message in its context. Be wise and responsible and remain aware that generally the truth resonates. People know when they are being told the truth, and they know when they are being conned, whether intentionally, or by some rogue spirit that might be attached to that psychic.

Spiritually, this whole area is a minefield. There are entities out there that attach to people, and feed off their situation. If a psychic does not keep themselves clear, they are potentially dangerous to you. Again we are back to that Biblical recommendation: "test the Spirits." You cannot beat the insights of a highly honed psychic having said that. I can look at someone's energy field and see what programs they are running. I can see how they are blocking themselves, and I can see all the ways in which they are open, and all the ways in which they are closed.

I have to respect these boundaries. Sometimes, you have to hold your breath, and just let a dear friend, or family member be. They will come to things in their own time, there is not much you can do about it really. It is generally best not to interfere. Much damage can be done if you push out of time. Wisdom, consideration and love are key. Never mind your own ego which wants to help, sometimes it is not meant to. People find the energy of a magical person disturbing because it unsettles them. We all love a bit of magic, and the idea of it. It reaches back into childhood, to those times when we were innocent, when we felt anything is possible. As we mature, and grow into adults, we fall foul of fear, constriction and having to behave in socially acceptable ways, less we get judged.

This is where people like me *are* different. Yes as a human being, I care about what you think. But if you push me and challenge me too much I will start to not care. I will defend myself in order to preserve my energy and my boundaries. Not because I have to, but because I will not allow you to invade my energy field with your negativity. I will leave you to function and continue in your set ways. There is nothing I can do, if you are not receptive. It is not my job to create believers in the world. I do not go out of my way to do this. I simply follow my inner guidance, and act accordingly. Those who are meant to receive it, will do so.

I am not God, nor do I claim to be. I am not garnering for attention. I am a very private person, and the prospect of putting this material out there, while vaguely exciting in moments, is also completely daunting. I prefer to hide under a rock if truth be told. I am sure that is just what I will be doing, once this information is out there for human consumption.

What I pray though, is that the story reaches you in *some* way. I do not want pity, I do not want admiration, I do not want to be vilified. I just want you to receive some of what I am saying at the level you can hear it. Some of those who read this, may be "Muggles" in the process of applying to "Hogwarts." Others may be contenders for "Slytherin or Gryffindor." You do not have to be a Harry Potter fan to be open to the idea of magic, but it helps. J. K. Rowling has done much to open people's eyes to the fantastical world of magic. She encapsulates the battle within and without of light and dark; good and evil. Some people try to dismiss the presence of darkness in our world. God knows how they manage to do that, when it is all around us. Some factions of the "love and light" brigade get hooked on keeping things fluffy, light and as pretty as possible. I agree, who wants to feed or give energy to the dark? We can all channel our angels, unicorns, rainbows, and pixie dust. But, the reality is some things, are out to get us. We need to monitor our energy, be aware of how to protect ourselves, and primed to take action when required.

A spiritual battle rages, and this has *always* been the case. Do not forget the most deceptive of all angels, can appear as a being of light. We need to be alert, and careful what we open up to. The fight is real. Sorry. My story if anything will show that it is.

Having written this book over a couple of months with 4 pence in my bank account for the duration, I was pushed into the classic "struggling writer's" corner. The universe created this vacuum of pressure, so that I would feel the urgency of the task in hand. I knew that the 4 pence thing was a cosmic joke to take in my stride, since something happened most days to provide for me, as I aimed for the deadline of Thanksgiving.

Admittedly, the food bank on a particular weekend was a low point. I will always remember that moment. The response of those around me was telling. I will not elaborate; but I am eternally grateful to the food bank lady who made sure I was okay, and organized supplies outside of office hours, because for the first time I literally had no other way. It just goes to show that when responding to universal nudges and guidance, I have to be totally willing to do *anything*, even if it be humiliating and stressful. I trust in the witness of acting in this way. Faith can move mountains.

On the upside, as I conclude this fishy tale, I just scored on a six horse accumulator. I set myself this challenge a while back, and it is spectacularly difficult. Getting a mixture of placed and winning horses is very doable for a psychic. But to get *all* winners? Nigh on impossible! There is a reason why book keepers pay out so highly on accumulators. Even a one euro bet can net you thousands and thousands on an each way bet of five, six, or seven horses.

The horse which clinched this for me, only yesterday, was one called "True Self." I backed Willie Boy at 10 to 1, running at Newbury. Then Daly Tiger 5/2; Brahma Bull 1/6; Like An Open Book 3/1, The King's Baby 6/1, and True Self 4/9, all running at Thurles in Ireland. My Irish winning karma continues; and as I write a chapter about identity, there is nothing more fitting than concluding as my True Self.

The Mask would approve.

*YOUR HEART IS WHERE YOUR TREASURE
IS, AND YOU MUST FIND YOUR TREASURE
IN ORDER TO MAKE SENSE
OF EVERYTHING
PAUL COELHO, THE ALCHEMIST*

Optional Soap Box

I agree, the concept of a spiritual battle raging is not a very satisfactory way to conclude these creative memoirs. There is another way. A place to be found in the eye of the storm. A way of exercising productive detachment, combined with intense engagement.. The way of the heart.

There is an innate protection in being heart-centered, and in following the leanings, nudges and intuitions of the heart. Prayer is our conversation with God, God's reply whispers to us, through the veil, into the heart. The heart is the way forward. I have always, always followed mine. To the nth degree, even when it defies logic. It has led to some fascinating places, and has instigated some encounters with some amazing people. There is no fear in following your heart. Or there should not be. The heart holds an intelligence the brain does not possess. It holds an energy that is expansive, all inclusive, and brave. Anything is possible when it is done form the heart.

Remember too, neuroscience agrees. You are energy. *Everything is energy*. The issues, problems, dramas and karmas you face on a daily basis are the result of your belief systems, and the programs you consciously, or unconsciously, run. Such patterns can be dispensed with when you fully settle into your energy field, and become aligned with the universe.

Who we *think* we are, and who we *actually* are, can be worlds apart. Unless there is not much distance between your personality and your higher self, the way you present yourself to the world can be misleading. It is at the point of integration with God or Source, that we become ourselves, and realize our full potential as creative beings.

I am puzzled at many aspects of my life experience and do not really understand them fully. The early phases of my route to enlightenment were certainly a puzzle. I can recall events, and tell you about them. But it is if much of it has happened to someone else. It is like a journey I went through at one remove. You see, the real me, is the me YOU see. It is my SOUL, my essence. This is the me that GOD sees. My True Self.

You would think that an intelligent, fairly attractive, warm person would have been married and settled with family by now, instead of contending with numerous adverse tests and challenges. Some of it has been decidedly unreal, and most of it has been spectacularly surreal. Much of the stuff that has occurred has been done *to* me. But I am not a victim. I have also put myself through things I need not have gone through. But I am not a self-saboteur. I have followed my heart and my inclinations. I did not have to. But I chose to live it all out that way. Through various trials and tribulations, I have been reminded of who I am, and what I know. What I have always known. What I incarnated knowing. I am not defined by the more difficult things that have happened. I remain untarnished. In the thick of the most severe challenges I may well have been annoyed, upset, pissed off and angry. I was fully engaged at the time, and got hurt like anyone else. But has it destroyed my spirit? No.

When we find ourselves through our connection with God, infinite source, our anxiety levels naturally diminish. The chatter in our heads disperses, and we get into the flow of being. The well spring of life is ours to access. You can see what happens, when you are shut down and anxious. Your sensitivities, unharnessed by your heart, can produce a myriad of things to contend with. Depression, anxiety, agoraphobia, drama, tension, fear, to name but a few. When you seek outside of the framework of divine law and divine timing all kinds of chaos ensues. For whatever reason as humans we reel in adventures, impasses, and traumas. It is called living life. As if we did not have enough to fill our days already.

So what are you choosing? I am not sure any part of my story will help you decide your way forward. Some may be inspired to follow their intuition more freely. Others may be even more terrified to step outside the structures of pragmatism and control. Whoever you are, despite the belief systems and programs coursing through your veins, I hope you will see some light at the end of the tunnel. We are powerful beings, creative and full of potential. Surely it is worth giving your soul a shot. The monkey in your head has fed enough off the chatter for the moment perhaps? Consider dropping that boundless energy into your heart space. The light of truth, and the love of God and yourself, are the keys to turning things around. You are way more than the sum total of your stories.

I am really not much to do with the events I have recounted here. I hope you have had fun reading all the intrigue and drama. But this is not me. These things happened to me, and I take responsibility for my part in them. But I do not really relate to them very much at all anymore. It has been an odd experience going through it all again. Not something I especially wanted to do. To write this, I had to tune back into those energies, some of which were very uncomfortable. So in a way I have relived the events which have brought me to this place. I can recount them in my memory. They are my stories, the events of my life, the things I have lived through. But they are not me. In one way, they are nothing to do with me. The liberation is in the detachment. When we release and heal, we have a clean slate. And the factor which brings us this opportunity? Forgiveness. The beauty of truth, whether it be good or bad, is liberating. If we can forgive ourselves and others, then we are set free. Even better, if we can come to love ourselves, as well as those onto whom we project our desires, passions and expectations, our options are limitless.

It is such a difficult thing to love oneself. We are taught that self-love is narcissistic, indulgent, and selfish. This is not the kind of self love I mean. Imagine that all your stories, dramas and upsets happened to your best friend, or a beloved family member rather than you. Would you not be gentle, kind and concerned, rather than critical and judgmental? Perhaps you would be more unkind to them than to yourself. That is also possible, and raises a different set of questions. But generally, I think we give others more compassion than we tend to give ourselves.

So ask yourself. What do you identify with? What are you defined by? Are you free to be whatever, whoever you want to be, or are you restricted in some way. If so. What is restricting you? Analyze it. Is it your belief system, all the things you feel you should be doing, the obligations you should be fulfilling. Or is the way you have cornered yourself by circumstances. Whatever it is. Set yourself FREE. Know yourself, free of victimization, fear or shame: True You!

Let go, and let God...

DON'T GIVE INTO YOUR FEARS.
IF YOU DO YOU WON'T BE ABLE TO
TALK TO YOUR HEART.
PS:- HERE'S TO HAPPY ENDINGS!

The Meaning Of Life

42

DID I SEE IT ALL COMING?
PRETTY MUCH.
LIFE IS FOR LIVING,
AND
CHASING RAINBOWS...

ABOUT THE AUTHOR

SARAH DELAMERE HURDING IS ONE OF IRELAND'S AND AMERICA'S BEST KNOWN MYSTICS. A SEER, HEALER, LIFE COACH, WRITER, AUTHOR, ACADEMIC, FORMER CBS RADIO HOST AND WORLD PUJA NETWORK PRESENTER, OM TIMES FEATURED WRITER AND CONSCIOUSNESS FACILITATOR, SARAH BRINGS A FULL RANGE OF TALENTS TO THE TABLE.

Sarah is known for her accuracy, healing and manifesting abilities. Louis Walsh and Simon Cowell were stunned into silence when Sarah predicted the full line up of Irish Popstars SIX. She read for 32 talented kids and accurately named the final six. Sarah has also have been publically recognised as an effective healer. She can lift pain with her hands pretty much instantly, and has helped clients with all kinds of issues and conditions. Her specialities are lifting pain and depression, as well as energy boosts, major clearings and resets using distance healing techniques. Once you sign up with Sarah, her commitment to you is relentless and strong. She works with you 24/7 with advice, guidance, energy, prayer and mutually agreed intentions for days, weeks and months depending on your needs. Find Sarah at www.sarahdelamer.com

#mermaidmagic

Acknowledgments

Endless gratitude to my wonderful parents Joy & Rog & siblings Simon & Rache, Brian for encouraging me to be brave enough to write & publish this, Bono for soulful inspiration, June for pertinent pointers, Miriam for magical energy shifts, Kathy for mutual sharing, Ann for destiny insights, Jessica Killingley for marketing tips, Unmaskd for unmasking, Dad for helpful edits, Jan & Ginny for braving the first drafts. My doggies for love & life fun.

Printed in Great Britain
by Amazon